War In Peace

Volume 6

War In Peace

The Marshall Cavendish Illustrated Encyclopedia of Postwar Conflict.

Editor-in-Chief
Ashley Brown

Editorial Board
Brig-Gen. James Collins Jr (USA Retd.)
Vice-Admiral Sir Louis Le Bailly KBE CB
Ian V Hogg; David Floyd
Professor Laurence Martin
Air-Vice Marshal SWB Menaul CB CBE DFC AFC

MARSHALL CAVENDISH
NEW YORK, LONDON, TORONTO

Reference Edition Published 1985

Published by Marshall Cavendish Corporation
147 West Merrick Road
Freeport, Long Island
N.Y. 11520

Printed and Bound in Italy by L.E.G.O. S.p.a. Vicenza.

British Library Cataloguing in Publication Data

Brown, Ashley
  War in peace : the Marshall Cavendish
  illustrated encyclopaedia of post-war conflict.
  1. History, Modern—1945- 2. War—History
  —20th century
  I. Title II. Dartford, Mark
  909.82 D842

  ISBN 0-86307-293-3
      0 86307 299 2   vol. 6

Library of Congress Cataloging in Publication Data

Main entry under title:

War in peace.

  Includes bibliographies and index.
  1. Military history, Modern—20th century. 2. Military
art and science—History—20th century. 3. World politics—1945-
I. Marshall Cavendish Corporation.
U42.W373 1984 355'.009'04 84-19386
ISBN 0-86307-293-3
      0 86307 299 2   vol. 6

Editorial Staff

Editor	Ashley Brown
Editorial Director	Brian Innes
Editorial Manager	Clare Byatt
Editorial Editors	Sam Elder
	Adrian Gilbert
Sub Editors	Sue Leonard
	Simon Innes
Artwork Editor	Jonathan Reed
Artwork Buyer	Jean Morley
Picture Editor	Carina Dvorak
Picture Consultant	Robert Hunt
Design	EDC

Reference Edition Staff

Editor	Mark Dartford
Designer	Graham Beehag
Consultant	Robert Paulley
Indexers	F & K Gill
Creation	DPM Services

Editorial Board

Contributors

David Blue served with the CIA in various countries of Southeast Asia, including Laos, and is a writer on and a student of small wars.

Gordon Brook-Shepherd spent 15 years in Vienna, first as lieutenant-colonel on the staff of the British High Commission and then as a foreign correspondent for the *Daily Telegraph*. A graduate in history from Cambridge, he is currently Chief Assistant Editor of the *Sunday Telegraph*.

Jeffrey J. Clarke is an expert on recent military history, particularly the Vietnam War, and has written for the American Center of Military History.

Major-General Richard Clutterbuck OBE has been Senior Lecturer in politics at Exeter University since his retirement from the army in 1972. His works include *Protest and the Urban Guerrilla*, *Guerrillas and Terrorists* and *Kidnap and Ransom*.

Alexander S. Cochran Jr is a historian whose area of research is modern Indochinese affairs with particular reference to the war in Vietnam since 1945. He is at present working in the Southeast Asia Branch of the Center of Military History, Department of the Army.

Colonel Peter M. Dunn is a serving officer in the USAF. His doctoral thesis is on the history of Indochina during the mid-1940s.

John B. Dwyer served both with the infantry and with armoured units in Vietnam. He was editor and publisher of the Vietnam veteran's newsletter *Perimeter* and has been a writer and correspondent for *National Vietnam Veteran's Review* for the past few years. His particular interest are Special Forces and Special Operations.

Brenda Ralph Lewis has specialised in political and military history since 1964. She s a regular contributor to military and historical magazines in both Britain and the United States.

Hugh Lunghi served in Moscow in the British Military Mission and the British Embassy for six years during and after World War II. He was interpreter for the British Chiefs of Staff at the Teheran, Yalta and Potsdam conferences, and also interpreted for Churchill and Anthony Eden. He subsequently worked in the BBC External Services and is a former editor of *Index on Censorship*.

Charles Messenger retired from the army in 1980 to become a fulltime military writer after 21 years service in the Royal Tank Regiment. Over the past 10 years he has written several books on 20th century warfare, as well as contributing articles to a number of defence and historical journals. He is currently a Research Associate at the Royal United Services Institute for Defence Studies in London.

Billy C. Mossman is a well-known American writer and historian. He is currently working on a volume on the Korean War for the US Army Center of Military History.

Bryan Perrett served in the Royal Armoured Corps from 1952 to 1971. He contributes regularly to a number of established military journals and acted as Defence Correspondent to the *Liverpool Echo* during the Falklands War. His recent books include *Weapons of the Falklands Conflict* and *A History of Blitzkrieg*.

Chapman Pincher is one of England's leading authorities on international espionage and counter-intelligence. He is the author of political novels and books on spying, the most recent of which is *Their Trade is Treachery*, which deals with the penetration of Britain's secret services by the Russian secret police.

Yehoshua Porath is a noted scholar at the Hebrew University in Jerusalem. He has made a special study of the Palestinian problem and is the author of two books on the subject, the most recent of which is *The Palestinian Arab National Movement 1929−39*, which was published in Britain in 1977.

Contributors

Antony Preston is Naval Editor of the military magazine *Defence* and author of numerous publications including *Battleships, Aircraft Carriers* and *Submarines*.

Brigadier-General Edwin H. Simmons, US Marine Corps, Retired, is the Director of Marine Corps History and Museums. At the time of the Inchon operation and the Chosin Reservoir campaign, he, as a major, commanded Weapons Company, 3rd Battalion, 1st Marines. Widely published, he is the author of *The United States Marines*.

Ronald Spector is an expert on Vietnam and has recently completed a book on that subject for the Center of Military History in the United States.

Andres Suarez served in the Cuban ministry of education from 1948–1951, took part in the Cuban revolution, and served in the ministry of housing from 1959. From 1965, he has been Professor of Latin American Studies at the University of Florida. Other publications include *Cuba and the Sino—Soviet Rift*.

Sir Robert Thompson KBE, CMG, DSO, MC is a world authority on guerrilla warfare, on which he has written extensively. He was directly involved in the Emergency in Malaya in the 1950s and rose to become permanent Secretary for Defence. From 1961 to 1965 he headed the British Advisory Mission to Vietnam and since then he has advised several governments, including the United States, on counter-insurgency operations Sir Robert Thompson is a Council member of the Institute for the Study of Conflict, London. His books include *Defeating Communist Insurgency and Revolutionary War in World Strategy, 1945—69*.

Patrick Turnbull commanded 'D' Force, Burma during World War II. His 29 published works include a history of the Foreign Legion.

Contents of Volume

Assuring destruction

The connection between nuclear theory and technology

During the 1950s the main elements of a nuclear balance were first established, as the Soviet Union broke the nuclear monopoly of the United States. By the end of the decade the strategic scene had taken on an appearance that was still generally recognisable in the 1980s. Atomic (fission) free-falling bombs for delivery by aircraft, the original means of carrying out a nuclear attack, had been supplemented by stand-off missiles for the bombers and by newly-developed ballistic missiles. Some ballistic missiles were designed to be launched from submarines and others from sites on land; a few of the latter were already housed in underground silos. Development of effective missiles had been facilitated by the emergence of thermonuclear (fusion or 'hydrogen') explosive devices which not only multiplied the weapons' destructive power but also permitted the construction of much more compact re-entry vehicles.

At the start of the 1960s, Western policy towards nuclear strategy was in a state of great uncertainty as the criticism of American policy – the only one open to detailed scrutiny – that had been mounted by academics and other analysts in the late 1950s began to erode official doctrine. While the weapons bequeathed to the 1960s by the preceding decade were to remain in service for many years, adapting to changing strategic needs, the strategies of the earlier decade proved less durable.

US nuclear strategy since 1954 had been based on the policy of massive retaliation: that the threat of an overwhelmingly destructive nuclear response would provide a deterrent to aggression wherever and in whatever form it might occur. Nuclear retaliation was not to be confined to answering an attack on the United States. Rather, in Secretary of State John Foster Dulles's words, the capacity to retaliate 'by means and at places of our own choosing' would hopefully deter the kind of aggression that had proved so expensive to repel by conventional means in Korea and would allay the fear of a conventional Soviet assault on western Europe which was imposing heavy military burdens on Nato. It was never officially stated that retaliation had to be targeted on Soviet cities or that it needed to be 'all-out'. But although the USAF did have a list of military and industrial targets, the plan was not flexible enough to meet various contingencies and there was considerable justifica-

tion for the popular belief that nuclear deterrence meant the threat to destroy cities on a large scale.

It was only to be expected that the Soviet Union, on the other hand, starting from a position of inferiority, would minimise the importance of nuclear weapons early in the 1950s. It did, however, move much more directly than the US towards a missile force, largely bypassing the strategic bomber stage. By 1960, the Soviet Union had established a substantial force of intermediate range ballistic missiles (IRBMs) capable of hitting western Europe, and had pressed ahead with developing large liquid-fuelled intercontinental ballistic missiles (ICBMs). Soviet progress in this field was dramatically displayed by the launching of the first satellite in 1957. However, the Soviet Union did not proceed to deploy a large ICBM force, either because of known defects in the weapons, or more probably because Soviet Premier Nikita Khrushchev believed a small force was sufficient to provide security and political leverage while reducing military expenditure.

Bridging the 'missile gap'

Nevertheless Khrushchev's boasts about Soviet nuclear power, coupled with demonstrations of Soviet missile technology, succeeded in alarming the Americans into believing that they were at the wrong end of a 'missile gap'. This became a major issue in the 1960 presidential election campaign and provoked President Dwight D. Eisenhower into an acceleration and expansion of the programme to deploy the solid-fuelled Polaris and Minuteman missile systems. Once in office, President John F. Kennedy further expanded these programmes. The completion of the Distant Early Warning Line (DEWLINE) of radars in Canada and of the Ballistic Missile Early Warning System (BMEWS) in Britain, Greenland and the US itself, linked to the North American Air Defense (NORAD) centre in Colorado, guaranteed the US time to launch a retaliatory response to any Soviet first strike, and made it possible to stand down the politically sensitive airborne alerts. The US Navy's aircraft carriers were released from a part in the strategic targeting plan.

The receipt at the end of 1961 of the first high-quality photography from reconnaissance satellites made the US realise that it was they and not the Soviet

Union who were far ahead in the missile race, whether measured by quality or quantity. Indeed, during the revived Berlin crisis of 1961 it was possible for an American defence official to declare that the retaliation the US could launch after absorbing a Soviet first strike would be more powerful than the original attack. It was presumably concern at this state of affairs, coupled with the failure of Soviet pressure on Berlin, that prompted Khrushchev to his abortive effort to redress the balance by installing some of his plentiful shorter-range missiles in Cuba (October 1962). At the same time, we now know, the Soviet Union began a much more determined effort to build up its intercontinental and submarine-based missile forces, an effort further intensified after the Cuban humiliation, the fall of Khrushchev and the ascent of Leonid Brezhnev.

While these developments were taking place in deployment and diplomacy early in the 1960s, an important though by no means always clearly defined strategic debate was taking place in the US. President Kennedy and his Secretary of Defense, Robert McNamara, had been convinced by the critique mounted against massive retaliation as being incredible, inadequate as a deterrent and likely to lead, in Kennedy's words, to 'humiliation or holocaust'. But as guarantors of an alliance network widely believed to be incapable of mounting an effective conventional defence against possible Soviet or Soviet-inspired aggression in many parts of the world and particularly in Europe, they could not wholly disavow the 'first use' of nuclear weapons. Consequently, while undertaking a vigorous programme of conventional rearmament and preparation for counter-insurgency operations, in which they demanded the support of their allies, they also set about revising nuclear doctrine.

'City-sparing' options

McNamara's first effort, outlined in June 1962, was to make recourse to nuclear weapons a more manageable and therefore more credible 'option', to use one of his favourite words. Essentially, he sought a plan for a limited, and therefore 'winnable', nuclear exchange. To do this he advocated a strategy of 'damage limitation', by which he meant a capability to use nuclear weapons in ways that would leave the enemy ample motive to restrain his own nuclear strikes. Increasing accuracy of long-range nuclear weapons and improved capabilities for command and control opened the possibility of 'city-sparing' attacks on enemy military forces. A 'city-sparing' strike would not necessarily attack the enemy's nuclear forces; the danger of attacks on those would be of provoking a pre-emptive attack by an enemy fearing that if he did not use his nuclear weapons he would be disarmed. McNamara therefore revised American strike plans to be more selective, avoiding cities and the enemy's command and control, separating for the first time nuclear war plans against China and the Soviet Union, and retaining reserves as the ultimate deterrent against Soviet attacks on American cities. McNamara also vainly urged Congress to support far-reaching programmes of civil defence to curb the indirect effects a damage-limiting strike might have by way of fall-out.

There were, however, graver difficulties. The scale of the envisaged nuclear strikes remained large and it was far from clear that the effects of nuclear war

would be very noticeably moderated. Moreover, the qualities needed in a city-sparing nuclear arsenal looked rather similar to those suited to a disarming first strike and the Soviet Union, at least in its public pronouncements, chose to depict the new American strategy as just such a threat. Moreover, while Soviet forces were weak, there was no doubt that a counter-force first strike might indeed be the best damage-limiting strategy for the United States, and this certainly appealed to elements in the US Strategic Air Command which saw the new strategy as a basis for greatly increased force levels, now that the targets were much more numerous than a limited set of vulnerable urban areas.

By the mid 1960s the demands for these increased force levels probably did more than anything else to disenchant McNamara with damage limitation. It was also clear that the strategy was having a questionable effect on Soviet-American relations. There were signs that the Soviet Union was responding by adopting a strategy of pre-emptive strike or 'fire on warning' to offset its weakness, while also – though McNamara was slow to see this – accelerating its efforts to eliminate its inferiority and overtake the United States in strategic weapons, a goal it had attained through various routes when the decade ended.

Without abandoning the concept of controlled use of nuclear weapons or of maintaining several strategic

Centre right: The first salvo launch of the Minuteman ICBM at Vandenberg air force base, California in February 1966. The Minuteman was the USAF's first solid-propellant ICBM and replaced the liquid-propellant Atlas and Titan I. Minuteman has a range of 11,000km (6900 miles).
Right: A Polaris nuclear submarine lies at anchor with its missile tube covers open. The Polaris was the West's first submarine-launched ballistic missile. Each ballistic-missile submarine carried 16 missiles in vertical launch tubes aft of the sail (conning tower).

Previous page: A US Army SM-78 Jupiter IRBM missile is launched during trials in 1958. The Jupiter was the army's first and only strategic ballistic missile and was the first such missile to have a re-entry vehicle which used ablative cooling.

options, from 1963 McNamara began to emphasise the idea of assured destruction: that is, the unquestioned capacity to destroy the Soviet Union 'as a 20th-century society' if the Soviet Union attacked the United States. By quantifying the necessary level of damage – on one occasion as 400 delivered megatons to kill 74 million Russians or 30 per cent of the population and to destroy 76 per cent of Soviet industrial capacity – McNamara may have been trying to prove to his military lobbies that American forces were adequate, but he gave a macabre emphasis to the exact opposite of damage limitation. McNamara also curbed and ran down American nuclear forces, stabilising them at a level adequate to ensure the required quantity of destruction. Under assured destruction theory, any further nuclear capacity beyond that level was redundant. The missile force needed was calculated at 1000 Minutemen, 54 Titans and 656 Polaris, and while more than 400 B-52 bombers were kept, the huge force of over 1300 B-47 medium bombers was phased out. Other weaponry abandoned included the Thor and Jupiter missiles stationed in Europe, now thought a dangerous,

vulnerable temptation to a Soviet first strike. By the late 1960s, the costly war in Vietnam provided added budgetary reasons to restrain nuclear forces.

In theory, to build strategic stability on assured destruction required the acceptance of vulnerability – assured destruction needed to be mutual. Though this doctrine of mutually assured destruction (MAD) was not easy to sell explicitly to one's own people, the atmosphere of detente bred after the settlement of the Cuban crisis and symbolised by the Nuclear Test Ban Treaty of 1963 – more a much-needed public health measure than a piece of effective arms control – lessened critical scrutiny. The same political climate blurred the recognition by the United States' allies that the problem of the nuclear guarantee, addressed by the doctrine of damage limitation, was unanswered by assured destruction. Within Nato, the American promise of nuclear action if conventional defence failed was never repudiated and the exact role of the large number of tactical and theatre nuclear weapons deployed in Europe during the period remained obscure.

Even before McNamara departed in 1968, the

Top: The huge Soviet SS-9 Scarp missile, some 36m (118ft) long, trundles through Moscow during the May Day parade of 1968. This missile has a range of over 12,000km (7456 miles), though it has since been replaced by the even bigger SS-18. Above: Inside the silo of a Minuteman ICBM. Silos are at least 7km (5 miles) apart and are some 24m (80ft) deep. They are constructed of concrete with a steel lining and are surrounded by a two-level room containing launch-control equipment, though they are in fact fired from remote underground launch facilities manned by an SAC crew of two, some distance from the silo.

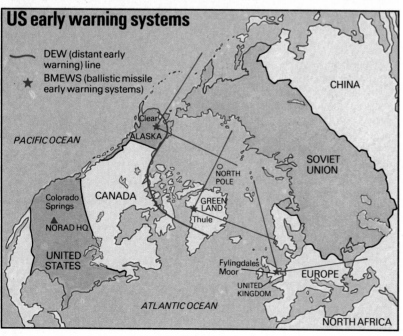

US early warning systems

— DEW (distant early warning) line

★ BMEWS (ballistic missile early warning systems)

CHINA

Clear
ALASKA

PACIFIC OCEAN

NORTH POLE

SOVIET UNION

Colorado Springs

CANADA

GREEN LAND
Thule

NORAD HQ

UNITED STATES

Fylingdales Moor

UNITED KINGDOM

EUROPE

ATLANTIC OCEAN

NORTH AFRICA

success of assured destruction as a basis for stability in Soviet-American strategic relations or in the so-called arms race had become highly questionable. In the first place, the Soviet Union showed no signs of levelling off its own strategic nuclear effort at 'parity' with the US, still less at the level of inferiority that McNamara once expected it to accept. The Soviet Strategic Rocket Forces, founded as a separate command in May 1960, had acquired a powerful range of weapons: the liquid-fuelled SS-7 and SS-8 in 1962 and 1963, some of which were first silo-based in 1964, followed by the huge SS-9, some equipped with a 25-megaton warhead, and the SS-11 and SS-13, the latter, appearing in 1969, being the first Soviet solid-fuelled ICBM. Early rather crude efforts to put missiles to sea in submarines were followed in 1968 by the deployment of the first Yankee-class ballistic missile launching submarine, a noisy answer to the Polaris boats. By 1970 10 Yankees were in service.

Assured destruction

Technology also dealt a dangerous blow to assured destruction by improving the chances, at least in theory, of a more effective strategy of damage limitation. On the one hand the increasing accuracy of missiles made counterforce strikes against even hardened silos seem possible, beginning years of anxiety about the long-term 'survivability' of land-based ICBMs. This problem was exacerbated by the emergence of the multiple independently-targeted re-entry vehicle (MIRV), which made it possible for a single missile to launch several threats against enemy missile silos, thus enhancing the probability, given appropriate targeting, of an effective kill.

MIRV technology, originally deriving from the effort to maximise the effectiveness of weapons against soft targets, by spreading the explosive more evenly, then adapted to counterforce work, also became relevant to offsetting another major technical development of the 1960s, the first plausible systems for intercepting ballistic missiles.

Ballistic missile defence (BMD) had been experimented with in the 1950s but rejected as ineffective. In the 1960s new accuracy of guidance, improved acceleration of interceptor missiles, better radars and computers, and new thinking about the effect of radiation in space all made BMD seem more practicable. By 1964 the Soviet Union was at work on a small system for the defence of Moscow and Leningrad, and in 1967, after long resistance to something so destructive (at least in theory) to the doctrine of mutually assured destruction, McNamara agreed to deploy an American system called Sentinel, based upon a long-range interceptor, Spartan, and a close-in interceptor, Sprint. Ostensibly this was to defend American cities only against the weak attacks a small nuclear power like China could launch. Later the system was adapted to defend missile fields against a Soviet attack, and later still was abandoned altogether.

The flaw in these early BMD systems was their vulnerability to 'saturation' by massed attacks, made more threatening by the new MIRVs. Especially for soft targets like cities, the balance of costs always seemed to go against the defender. But at least defence no longer seemed so inconceivable as in the early days of the ICBM. Maintaining a deterrent was clearly going to be a dynamic, costly business in

which both superpowers felt compelled to compete. Moreover, by the end of the 1960s there were three other nuclear forces, the British, French and Chinese.

It therefore seemed worth trying to see if the balance could be stabilised by agreement and in 1967 President Lyndon B. Johnson proposed negotiations for some form of nuclear freeze; acceptance of the invitation to negotiate by the Soviet Union in 1968 set in motion the Strategic Arms Limitation Talks (SALT). Not resulting in an agreement until 1972, the course of these talks saw a curious reversal of roles engendered by technological progress and the changing state of the Soviet-American balance.

Negotiating a nuclear freeze

At the outset, the US was particularly concerned to stop the Soviet experiments with BMD, so subversive of the McNamara notion of deterrence by mutual vulnerability. The Soviet Union, on the other hand, showed alarm at American development of MIRVs and the general quality of American offensive weapons. By the time the negotiations concluded, the Soviet Union was alarmed at the rapid evolution of American BMD technology and disillusioned with its own. The US in turn, though somewhat reassured by the progress of the BMD competition, was viewing with concern the pace of Soviet deployment of ICBMs and particularly the threat posed by the SS-9

Above: Brezhnev and Nixon sign the SALT 1 agreement in May 1972. This document included three separate agreements: the Treaty on Limitation of ABMs; an interim agreement with a protocol on 'Certain Measures with respect to the Limitation of Strategic Offensive Arms'; and a 'Statement on Basic Principles of Mutual Relations'. Below: Part of the BMEWS is this DYE III site in Greenland.

and its successor the SS-18 to the Minuteman force, an anxiety from which the much-vexed debate over the MX basing mode directly descended. Technology, however, also came to the rescue, for it was the refinement of satellite reconnaissance that by-passed the Soviet objections to 'on-site' inspection.

The nuclear history of the 1960s thus ended on a mixed note of hope and menace. Unprecedented levels of destructive military power were being addressed by equally novel concepts and instruments of arms control. Prospects for the new initiatives were shadowed, however, by deteriorating political relations between the superpowers and, as detente eroded, the 1970s, like the 1960s before them, opened in an atmosphere of diplomatic confrontation which could not fail to be reflected in the nuclear balance.

Laurence Martin

Far left: An RAF Vulcan, once a mainstay of Britain's nuclear capability, flies over the BMEW station at Fylingdales, Yorkshire.

Chronology 1961-65

EUROPE & NORTH AMERICA

1961
April
15–20 **United States** Anti-Castro Cubans with support of CIA attempt invasion of Cuba at Bay of Pigs, but are defeated.
June
3–4 **United States and Soviet Union** President Kennedy and Prime Minister Khrushchev meet in Vienna.
July
8 **Soviet Union** Nikita Khrushchev demands withdrawal of Western troops from Berlin.
August
13 **Germany** East German government closes frontier between East and West Berlin and builds 'Berlin Wall' to divide city and halt all traffic.
20 **Germany** United States reinforces its garrison in West Berlin.
December
19 **Albania** Government breaks off diplomatic relations with Soviet Union but not with China.

1962
March
14 **United Nations** Seventeen-nation disarmament conference opens in Geneva.
18 **France** Signs Evian agreements to establish independent Algeria.
June
United States Secretary of Defense McNamara outlines new US strategy of 'graduated deterrence'
October
16 **United States** President Kennedy informed of Soviet missile sites at San Cristobal in Cuba.
22 **United States** President Kennedy announces on TV that he has ordered a naval and air quarantine of Cuba.
25 **United States** US destroyer searches Soviet-chartered freighter *en route* to Cuba.
29 **United States** Secret US-Soviet talks result in Russian agreement to dismantle and withdraw missiles and American undertaking not to invade Cuba.
November
2 **United States** President Kennedy announces lifting of quarantine round Cuba and removal of missiles.
30 **United Nations** U Thant becomes Secretary-General.
December
21 **United States** Britain and US sign Nassau agreement to provide Britain with Polaris missiles.

1963
April
17 **United Kingdom** Royal Navy commissions first nuclear-powered submarine HMS *Dreadnought*.
June
20 **United States and Soviet Union** sign 'hot-line' agreement.
August
5 **United States and Soviet Union** sign nuclear test ban treaty prohibiting all nuclear testing in atmosphere.
November
22 **United States** President Kennedy assassinated.
December
21 **Cyprus** Greeks and Turks clash.
26 **Cyprus** Battalion of British troops separates two communities and establishes 'Green Line'.

1964
27 **Cyprus** UN peacekeeping force becomes operational.
April
20 **Soviet Union, United Kingdom and United States** agree on reduction of production of fissionable material for military use.

August
9 **Cyprus** Extensive bombing of Greek targets by Turkish Air Force.
7–9 **Cyprus** United Nations peacekeeping force brings about ceasefire.
September
21 **Malta** Britain grants independence.
October
14–15 **Soviet Union** Khrushchev is dismissed from all positions and replaced as First Secretary of the Communist Party by Leonid Brezhnev.

CENTRAL AMERICA

1961
January
3 **United States** breaks off diplomatic relations with Cuba.
25 **El Salvador** Military coup.
April
17 **Cuba** Invasion at Bay of Pigs by anti-Castro Cubans backed by United States is defeated.
May
1 **Cuba** Castro declares Cuba a socialist state.
30 **Dominican Republic** Dictator Leonidas Trujillo assassinated.

1962
Dominican Republic Juan Bosch elected premier.
August
31 **Trinidad** Gains independence.
October
Cuba Crisis over Soviet introduction of missiles to Cuba.

1963
March
30 **Guatemala** Colonel Enrique Peralta Azurdia seizes power in coup d'etat.
August
5–7 **Haiti** Invasion by Haitian exiles from Dominican Republic is defeated.
September
25 **Dominican Republic** Government of President Juan Bosch overthrown.
October
3 **Honduras** Colonel Osvaldo Lopez Arellano seizes power as president.

1964
July
26 **Cuba** Organisation of American States imposes sanctions.
November
Bolivia Military coup overthrows Paz Estenssor.

1965
April
24–25 **Dominican Republic** Junta overthrown in pro-Bosch military coup.
28 **Dominican Republic** US Marines intervene.
30 **Dominican Republic** ceasefire agreed by OAS.
May
6 **Dominican Republic** OAS agrees to set up peace force.
13–19 **Dominican Republic** Further fighting ends in truce.
August
31 **Dominican Republic** Provisional government formed under Hector García-Godoy.

SOUTH AMERICA

1961
November
7–9 **Ecuador** Military coup; Carlos Monroy becomes president.

1962
March
Argentina Military coup overthrows President Arturo Frondizi.
July
18 **Peru** General Ricardo Godoy seizes power.
August
8–11 **Argentina** Army mutiny.
December
11–12 **Argentina** Military revolt put down by loyalist troops.

1963
March
3 **Peru** General Nicholas Lopez seizes power.
April
2–5 **Argentina** Armed rebellion defeated.
July
11 **Ecuador** Military junta seizes power.

1964
March
31 **Brazil** President João Goulart deposed and replaced by military government.
November
3–4 **Bolivia** General Rene Barrientos seizes power.

MIDDLE EAST

1961
June
Iraq Kurds begin revolt at Sulaymaniyah.
July
1 **Kuwait** British troops committed to forestall Iraqi attack.
September
28-30 **Syria** Opponents of union with Egypt seize power and dissolve UAR.

1962
September
Yemen Imam Ahmed dies and is succeeded by Mohammed al-Badr.
27 **Yemen** 'Free Yemen Republic' proclaimed by General Sallal recognised by Egypt and communist governments.
March
28 **Syria** Coup d'etat.

1963
January
18 **Aden** joins Federation of South Arabia.
February
8 **Iraq** General Kassim deposed and executed. General Abdul Salam Arif becomes president.
March
8 **Syria** Coup d'etat.
June
Iraq Renewed government offensives against Kurds.
November
18 **Iraq** President Arif pledges support for Egypt.
December
10 **Aden** Attempted assassination of British High Commissioner.

1964
January
4 **South Arabia** Radfan occupied by Federal Regular Army with British aid.
April
13–15 **Syria** Unsuccessful revolt against government.
June
South Arabia British troops clear Radfan of rebels.

1965
August
24 **Yemen** President Nasser and King Faisal agree to end support for republicans and royalists in civil war.
September
17 **Iraq** President Arif replaced by his brother General Abdel Rahman Arif.

SOUTH ASIA
1961
December
18 **India** seizes Portuguese enclaves of Goa, Damão and Diu with little resistance offered.

1962
October
10 **India** Operation Leghorn, an attempt to enforce Indian border claims against the Chinese, begins.
20 **India** Chinese troops overrun all Indian resistance north of Brahmaputra valley.
November
21 **India** Chinese declare unilateral ceasefire.

1965
April
India Frontier dispute with Pakistan in Rann of Kutch.
August
5-23 **India** Border clashes in Kashmir and Punjab.
September
1-25 **India and Pakistan** Serious fighting in Punjab and Kashmir.
27 **India and Pakistan** accept United Nations demand for end to hostilities.

SOUTHEAST ASIA
1961
January
Laos US begins reconnaissance flights.
4 **Laos** Prince Boun Oum organises pro-Western government; Soviet Union and North Vietnam step up aid to Pathet Lao.
April
3 **Laos** Government and Pathet Lao agree to ceasefire.
September
1-4 **Vietnam** Viet Cong attacks in Kontum province.
November
16 **Vietnam** United States promises to support government of South Vietnam against Viet Cong.
December
11 **Vietnam** First direct military support for South Vietnam arrives in Saigon on US aircraft carrier. First US troops killed.

1962
February
3 **Vietnam** 'Strategic hamlets' programme begins.
8 **Vietnam** US military assistance command (MACV) established.
March
2 **Burma** Military coup
May
Thailand 5000 US Marines sent in.
July
Laos Neutralist coalition comes to power.
August
Vietnam First Australian forces arrive in South.
October
5 **Laos** US military advisers withdrawn under Geneva agreement.
December
8 **Brunei** revolt by TNKU against the Sultan; British troops committed.

1963
April
12 **Borneo** confrontation with Indonesia begins.
May

1 **Indonesia** Netherlands hands over West Irian.
16-24 **Laos** Pathet Lao seize Plain of Jars.
18 **Brunei** revolt ends.
September
16 **Malaysia** established. Sarawak and North Borneo join after being granted independence.
November
1-2 **Vietnam** President Diem killed in coup d'etat. Power passes to General Duong Van Minh.

1964
January
Vietnam First US U-2 spy planes arrive.
30 **Vietnam** General Nguyen Khanh seizes power.
February
4-6 **Vietnam** Viet Cong launch offensives in Tay Ninh province and Mekong Delta.
March
6 **Borneo** First clash between British and Indonesian regular troops.
June
20 **Vietnam** General W.C. Westmoreland appointed commander MACV.
August
2-4 **Vietnam** Clashes between North Vietnamese and US ships in Gulf of Tonkin.
5 **Vietnam** US carrier-based planes attack North Vietnamese naval bases.
7 **United States** Congress gives President Johnson authority to take 'all necessary measures to repel any armed attack' against US armed forces (Gulf of Tonkin resolution).
17 **Malaysia** Indonesian landing on south coast of Singapore crushed.
November
4 **Vietnam** General Khanh replaced by civilian premier Tran Van Huong.
December
31 **Vietnam** Total US strength in South 23,000.

1965
January
8 **Vietnam** South Korean troops arrive in South.
27 **Vietnam** Armed forces depose premier Huong and restore General Khanh to power.
February
7 **Vietnam** Viet Cong attack US installations near Pleiku airbase. President Johnson orders retaliation.
8 **Vietnam** US Air Force attacks selected military targets in North in Operation Flaming Dart.
March
2 **Vietnam** 'Rolling Thunder' bombing campaign begins against North.
8 **Vietnam** First US ground combat force, 9th Marine Expeditionary Brigade, lands at Danang.
June
12-19 **Vietnam** Air Vice Marshal Nguyen Cao Ky becomes premier.
18 **Vietnam** B-52 bombers used for first time in Arc Light bombing raids.
28 **Vietnam** First major US operation, in Bien Hoa province. US strength now over 50,000.
October
1 **Indonesia** Attempted coup is defeated by Indonesian Army and followed by massacre of hundreds of thousands of Indonesian communists.
November
20 **Vietnam** Month-long battle of Ia Drang Valley ends in defeat of North Vietnamese forces.
December
31 **Vietnam** US strength in South now 181,000.

EAST ASIA
1961
May
16 **South Korea** General Chung Hee Park seizes power and is later proclaimed president.
October
20 **China** defeats India in border war.

1964
October
16 **China** explodes its first atomic bomb.

AFRICA
1961
February
4 **Angola** MPLA attacks in Luanda.
9 **Congo** Patrice Lumumba murdered.
March
Angola UPA massacre several hundred whites.
April
22-26 **Algeria** French military revolt.
27 **Sierra Leone** Britain grants independence.
May
31 **South Africa** becomes a republic and withdraws from Commonwealth.
July
19-22 **Tunisia** Attacks on French military bases bring retaliation in the Bizerta incident.
August
Congo New government formed under Adoula.
September
17 **Congo** UN Secretary-General Dag Hammarskjöld killed in air crash.
9 **Tanganyika** Britain grants independence.

1962
March
7-18 **Algeria** Ceasefire between FLN and French Army. Ahmed Ben Bella becomes prime minister.
June
30 **Tunisia** French evacuation of bases completed.
July
1 **Burundi** becomes independent monarchy.
1 **Rwanda** becomes independent republic.
October
9 **Uganda** Britain grants independence.

1963
January
Portuguese Guinea PAIGC attacks begin.
1-15 **Congo** United Nations offensive in Katanga.
13 **Togo** Military coup.
August
15 **Congo Republic** successful military coup.
October
13-30 **Algeria** Hostilities on border with Morocco.
28 **Benin** Military coup.
December
10 **Zanzibar** Britain grants independence.
12 **Kenya** Britain grants independence.

1964
January
12 **Zanzibar** Nationalist rebels overthrow government.
20-23 **Tanganyika, Uganda and Kenya** Mutinies suppressed by British forces.
February
17-18 **Gabon** French troops intervene to prevent a military coup.
April
26 **Tanzania** is created out of a merger of Tanganyika and Zanzibar.
July
6 **Malawi** Britain grants independence.
9 **Congo** Moise Tshombe becomes premier.
September
25 **Mozambique** Guerrilla attacks begin.
November
25-27 **Congo** Belgian paratroops brought in by US planes seize Stanleyville and rescue white hostages.

1965
June
19 **Algeria** Ben Bella overthrown by Colonel Houari Boumedienne.
October
13 **Congo** Tshombe ousted by President Kasavubu.
November
25 **Congo** Kasavubu ousted by General Mobutu.
11 **Rhodesia** White-run government declares independence from Great Britain (UDI).
December
22 **Benin** Military coup.

Left. Charles de Gaulle pursued an independent policy within Nato from the time he became President of France in 1958, asking the USA to remove its nuclear bomber bases in 1959, and in 1966 withdrawing France from the integrated military structure. He even threatened to leave Nato altogether, but fell from power before he could put this policy into effect. Below: In contrast to France, the British commitment to Nato was unequivocal. Here Centurion tanks take part in exercises at Hohne in West Germany.

The uneasy alliance

New problems
for Nato

The 1960s were not comfortable years for the Nato alliance. The decade saw deep divisions open up between allied powers, and a prolonged strategic debate which led to fundamental changes in the planned military response to possible aggression. At the heart of Nato's problems lay two permanent grounds for disagreement: the relationship between the United States, as the preponderant power, and its European allies; and the place of strategic nuclear weapons in the defence of Europe.

Looked at from one side, Nato was a means of tying the United States to the defence of western Europe; from a different angle, it was the mechanism by which the US extended its power and influence over the allied states. The European Nato members experienced a corresponding conflict of feeling: they feared desertion by the US in a future war, but some resented US domination.

The essence of the US commitment to Nato was nuclear. The US provided only between 10 and 25 per cent of the various conventional forces of the alliance – in stark contrast to the overwhelming preponderance of Soviet forces in the Warsaw Pact – but Nato was dependent on the Americans for its 'nuclear umbrella'. The strategic thinking prevalent in 1960 assigned Nato conventional forces in Europe the role of 'tripwire'. They were not believed capable of resisting a Soviet conventional assault; their function was to trigger off massive nuclear retaliation. In this scenario, the US forces stationed in West Germany figured as 'hostages on the Rhine'. Since US troops would be casualties at the very start of a Soviet attack, the US government would have the motivation to carry through the nuclear response.

But as the era of massive retaliation gave way to the new balance of mutually assured destruction (MAD), the changed logic of the nuclear situation made the Nato European powers nervous. Would the Americans really carry out an attack on the Soviet Union that would inevitably bring down massive destruction upon the United States itself, in order to defend western Europe? As France's strategists succinctly put it, would one country ever be prepared to die for another? President de Gaulle certainly believed the answer to this question was no, and set about creating an independent French nuclear deterrent. Britain, of course, already possessed a supposedly independent deterrent, but no British government ever considered this an alternative to the alliance with the US; British nuclear weapons were always viewed simply as a contribution to the combined Nato effort.

Nato and nuclear force

Nato strategists worked furiously on solutions. The move towards a damage-limiting nuclear strategy, designed to make the use of nuclear weapons more feasible, left the problem unanswered, since it still did nothing to guarantee that the US would embark on such a risky course on behalf of its European allies. To address this crucial issue of credibility, between 1960 and 1964 the US sponsored the idea of a Nato 'multilateral' nuclear force – a jointly-manned ballistic missile force which would theoretically give the European powers the ability to initiate a nuclear response in their own defence. However, the multilateral force idea was never adopted.

Finally, in 1966 European objections to the US monopoly of nuclear decision-making were met by new organisational developments in the alliance. In

December 1966 two new committees were established, the Nuclear Planning Group (NPG) and the Nuclear Defence Affairs Committee (NDAC). These gave the European states fuller participation in Nato's nuclear affairs and stilled many fears.

In 1967 the alliance finally agreed a revised strategy. The 'tripwire' doctrine was abandoned and replaced by the principle of 'flexible response' which had dominated US strategic thinking since the Kennedy era. Basic to this rethink was a changed perception of the conventional balance in Europe. It had always been the most fundamental assumption of Nato strategy that the USSR enjoyed total conventional superiority in Europe; nothing could stop a mass Soviet tank drive through Germany to the Channel. But a fresh analysis of Warsaw Pact and Nato strengths and weaknesses, carried out in the 1960s using more sophisticated techniques than just the counting of numbers of divisions deployed, suggested that a conventional defence of western Europe was feasible. Indeed, it appeared that Warsaw Pact and Nato forces were very evenly matched.

The new policy assumed that US strategic nuclear power would hold the ring, keeping nuclear weapons out of play. Tactical nuclear weapons were if possible

Above: A 175mm M113 SP gun, barely recognisable in heavy camouflage, is deployed in its woodland firebase during Exercise Rob Roy in 1967. The considerable length of the barrel (10.49m – 34ft) means that great internal pressures are reached, and the barrel has a life of only 1200 rounds.
Below: Royal Irish Fusiliers dismount at speed from an FV432 armoured personnel carrier during simulated battle conditions. Such exercises have helped to strengthen Nato forces in Europe and maintain close cooperation within the alliance. Postwar military tactical doctrine has been based upon the role of mechanised infantry – emphasising the need for protecting ground troops while deploying them into the battle zone.

Nato/Warsaw Pact balance of forces 1965-66

Nato forces

UNITED STATES
Total armed forces: 2,659,000 personnel
Land forces
963,000 army personnel organised into 16 operational divisions, 38 surface-to-surface missile battalions, 7 Special Forces Groups, several independent brigades; approximately 7000 aircraft. Forces (including 3 Marine Corps divisions) deployed as follows: *United States:* strategic reserve – 1 infantry division, 1 marine division, 1 mechanised division, half an airborne division; reinforcements for Europe – 2 armoured divisions *Dominican Republic:* half an airborne division *Korea:* 2 infantry divisions *Hawaii/Okinawa:* 1 infantry division, 1 marine division, 1 airborne brigade *South Vietnam:* 1 infantry division, 1 marine division, 1 airborne division, 1 air cavalry division *Germany:* 2 armoured divisions, 3 infantry divisions, 3 armoured cavalry regiments, 1 infantry brigade (West Berlin)
Army reserves
700,000 Army Reserve and Army National Guard personnel
Naval forces
674,000 personnel organised into the 1st Fleet (Eastern Pacific), 2nd Fleet (Atlantic), 6th Fleet (Mediterranean), 7th Fleet (Western Pacific) *submarines (excluding missile-firing vessels):* 80 conventionally-powered, 23 nuclear-powered *surface ships:* 15 attack carriers (1 nuclear-powered), 9 anti-submarine carriers, 263 multi-purpose anti-submarine and fleet defence vessels, 23 destroyer escorts, 135 amphibious assault ships, 160 logistic and support ships, 200 minesweepers, 400 escorts and 15 cruisers in reserve, over 1000 patrol and other craft *naval airforces:* an estimated 8250 aircraft
Air forces
829,000 personnel, an estimated 14,400 aircraft organised into the *Tactical Air Command:* 130 squadrons based in the USA, Europe and the Pacific *Military Air Lift Command:* 37 squadrons *Air National Guard General Purpose Forces:* 102 squadrons *Air Force Reserve:* 50 squadrons
Marine Corps
193,000 personnel organised into 3 divisions and 3 air wings with approximately 1130 combat and support aircraft

BELGIUM
Total armed forces: 107,000 personnel
Land forces: 83,500 personnel (2 divisions Nato-assigned, reserve divisions Nato-earmarked) *Naval forces:* 4500 personnel, 50 vessels (5 Nato-earmarked) *Air forces:* 19,000 personnel, 7 squadrons of aircraft, 2 surface-to-air missile (SAM) wings (all Nato-earmarked)

CANADA
Total armed forces: 120,300 personnel
Land forces: 49,000 personnel deployed in Canada, Europe (6500 men), Middle East and Cyprus (UN forces) *Naval forces:* 20,700 personnel, 52 vessels *Air forces:* 50,600 personnel, 22 squadrons of aircraft (8 in Europe)

DENMARK
Total armed forces: 51,000 personnel (all Nato-assigned)
Land forces: 33,000 personnel *Naval forces:* 8000 personnel, 115 vessels *Air forces:* 10,000 personnel, 10 squadrons of aircraft, 8 SAM batteries

FRANCE
Total armed forces: 557,000 personnel
Land forces: 350,000 personnel. 5 divisions stationed in Europe (2 Nato-assigned), 4000 men in Algeria, 7000 on other bases in Africa *Naval forces:* 72,500 personnel, 424 vessels *Naval air forces:* 12,000 personnel, 275 aircraft *Air forces:* 122,500 personnel, 54 squadrons of aircraft (450 combat aircraft assigned to the 4th Allied Tactical Air Force), 2 SAM brigades

GERMANY
Total armed forces: 438,000 personnel (all except 28,000 Nato-assigned)
Land forces: 278,000 personnel plus 28,000 in the Territorial Force *Naval forces:* 35,000 personnel, 170 vessels, 2 naval air wings *Air forces:* 97,000 personnel, 650 combat aircraft, 15 SAM battalions

GREECE
Total armed forces: 160,000 personnel
Land forces: 119,000 personnel organised into 12 divisions (8 divisions Nato-assigned), SAM batteries *Naval forces:* 17,500 personnel, 114 vessels *Air forces:* 23,500 personnel, 11 squadrons of aircraft (all assigned to the 6th Allied Tactical Air Force)

ITALY
Total armed forces: 390,000 personnel
Land forces: 292,000 personnel organised into 11 divisions, 11 brigades and 1 SAM battalion (7 divisions, 5 brigades and 1 SAM battalion Nato-assigned) *Naval forces:* 38,000 personnel, 308 vessels *Air forces:* 60,000 personnel, 29 squadrons of aircraft (22 Nato-assigned) *Paramilitary forces:* 80,000 personnel in the Carabinieri Corps

LUXEMBOURG
Total armed forces: 5500 personnel (1 brigade Nato-earmarked)

NETHERLANDS
Total armed forces: 135,000 personnel
Land forces: 92,000 personnel (2 divisions Nato-assigned) *Naval forces:* 22,000 personnel, 151 vessels, Fleet Air Arm of 7 squadrons of aircraft *Air forces:* 21,000 personnel, 19 squadrons of aircraft, 12 SAM squadrons (all forces Nato-assigned)

NORWAY
Total armed forces: 32,200 personnel
Land forces: 16,000 personnel *Naval forces:* 5400 personnel plus 2000 coastal artillery personnel, 71 vessels *Air forces:* 8800 personnel, 8 squadrons of aircraft, 4 SAM batteries

PORTUGAL
Total armed forces: 148,000 personnel plus 14,000 African troops
Land forces: 120,000 personnel plus 14,000 African troops (18,000 men Nato-earmarked, remaining forces in Portuguese overseas territories) *Naval forces:* 14,500 personnel, 96 vessels *Air forces:* 13,500 personnel, 250 aircraft (1 squadron Nato-assigned) *Paramilitary forces:* 10,000 personnel in the National Republican Guard

TURKEY
Total armed forces: 442,000 personnel
Land forces: 360,000 personnel organised into 16 divisions (14 Nato-assigned), 4 brigades, 6 regiments *Naval forces:* 37,000 personnel, 105 vessels *Air forces:* 45,000 personnel, 16 squadrons of aircraft, 8 SAM batteries (all forces Nato-assigned)

UNITED KINGDOM
Total armed forces: 440,000 personnel
Land forces: 208,000 personnel. Approximately 20 battalions stationed in the UK, 51,000 personnel in Germany, remaining forces in overseas garrisons *Naval forces:* 100,000 personnel, 407 vessels, Fleet Air Arm largely carrier-based *Air forces:* 132,000 personnel (Bomber and Fighter Command Nato-assigned, 8700 personnel stationed in Germany), SAM squadrons

not to be used, to avoid escalation. The Nato forces stationed in Europe would hope to hold a Soviet advance until massive reinforcements of troops from the US could be brought to the battlefield.

Concurrent with this revision of strategy, cracks were opening up within the alliance. The major fissure was with France. Ever since coming to power in 1958, General de Gaulle had pursued a thoroughgoing nationalist policy. In 1959 he compelled the US to remove its nuclear bombers from bases in France, and set about the creation of an independent nuclear force. De Gaulle deeply resented what he saw as 'an American protectorate in Europe' under the cover of

Nato'. He determined that 'the subordination that is described as integration, which is provided for by Nato and which hands over our destiny to foreign authorities, will end as far as we are concerned'. In 1966 France withdrew from the integrated military structure of Nato – controlled by an American general and an American admiral for land and sea forces – and all allied military forces and military headquarters were forced to leave France.

De Gaulle further threatened that France would withdraw completely from Nato by 1969, but by that time the General had fallen from power. France remained a member of Nato and still participated in

Warsaw Pact forces

SOVIET UNION
Total regular forces (including Strategic Rocket Forces) estimated at 3,150,000 personnel
Land forces
2,000,000 army personnel organised into an estimated 140 divisions comprising 50 tank, 90 motor-rifle divisions. Forces deployed as follows: *Soviet Union:* 114 divisions *East Germany:* 20 divisions *Poland:* 2 divisions *Hungary:* 4 divisions; 60,000 airborne personnel organised into 7 divisions
Naval forces
450,000 personnel organised into the Baltic, Arctic, Black Sea and Pacific Fleets *submarines:* 370 conventionally-powered, 40 nuclear-powered *surface ships:* 20 cruisers, 80 destroyers, 140 other ocean-going escorts, 170 coastal escorts, 400 fast patrol boats, 500 minesweepers, 1200 other vessels; 3000 Marines in the Baltic, Black Sea and Pacific Fleets *naval air forces (land-based):* 400 bombers, 400 other aircraft
Air forces
510,000 personnel organised into the *Long Range Air Force:* 1100 strategic bombers *Tactical Air Force:* 4000 light bombers, ground-attack and interceptor fighters, helicopters, transport and reconnaissance aircraft *Air Defence Command:* 6000 interceptors, SAM batteries *Air Transport*
Paramilitary forces
230,000 security and border troops

BULGARIA
Total regular forces: 152,000 personnel
Land forces: 125,000 personnel, over 2000 tanks *Naval forces:* 7000 personnel, 85 vessels *Air forces:* 20,000 personnel, 400 aircraft, SAM batteries *Paramilitary forces:* 15,000 personnel

CZECHOSLOVAKIA
Total regular forces: 235,000 personnel
Land forces: 200,000 personnel organised into 14 divisions, 3000 tanks *Air forces:* 35,000 personnel, 700 front-line aircraft, SAM batteries *Paramilitary forces:* 35,000 personnel

EAST GERMANY
Total regular forces: 112,000 personnel
Land forces: 80,000 personnel *Naval forces:* 17,000 personnel, 156 vessels *Air forces:* 15,000 personnel, 400 aircraft, SAM batteries *Paramilitary forces:* 70,000 security and border troops

HUNGARY
Total regular forces: 109,000 personnel
Land forces: 100,000 personnel, 1000 tanks *Air forces:* 9000 personnel, 150 aircraft, SAM batteries *Paramilitary forces:* 35,000 personnel

POLAND
Total regular forces: 277,000 personnel
Land forces: 215,000 personnel organised into 14 divisions, 3000 tanks *Naval forces:* 17,000 personnel, 121 vessels, 70 naval aircraft *Air forces:* 45,000 personnel, 1000 aircraft. SAM batteries *Paramilitary forces:* 45,000 security and border troops

ROMANIA
Total regular forces: 198,000 personnel
Land forces: 175,000 personnel *Naval forces:* 8000 personnel, 63 vessels *Air forces:* 15,000 personnel, 300 aircraft, SAM batteries *Paramilitary forces:* 60,000 personnel

military matters through 'liaison' officials, although without rejoining the integrated military structure.

Further trouble was brewing on Nato's southern flank. Greece and Turkey were two members of the alliance who enjoyed neither the stable internal politics nor the good mutual relations which were a strong point of the rest of Nato. Conflict between the two countries over Cyprus smouldered in the mid 1960s, and US support for the Turkish position led to Greek threats to leave the alliance. In 1967 a military coup in Athens overthrew the democratic government in Greece. This was an embarrassment to Nato, but it had long accepted right-wing authoritarian Portugal as a member of an alliance explicitly dedicated to the defence of freedom, and military rule in Greece similarly did not prove too much to swallow.

After 1967, the pursuit of detente with the East became official Nato policy. West Germany was especially keen on defusing hostilities, since this offered the only practical route to a future reunification of the German people. The Soviet invasion of Czechoslovakia in 1968 only caused a hiccup in a process of continuing contacts and negotiations which went on into the 1970s. None of Nato's internal problems had been fully resolved, but the alliance had weathered a troublesome decade. **Graham Brewer**

The year 1967 saw great strains on the southeastern flank of Nato. First of all there was a military coup in Greece, (above, student protests against the coup at the University of Salonika) and secondly, disputes over Cyprus brought two Nato members, Greece and Turkey, to the brink of war (top, Turkish troops ready to invade Cyprus in November 1967).

Manoeuvres and modernisation

The Warsaw Pact in the 1960s

Above: The Pact summit of January 1965. Seated front from left are the Soviet ambassador to Poland; Marshal Malinovsky; and Kremlin strongmen, Alexei Kosygin and Leonid Brezhnev.

Above: Nicolae Ceausescu, who took over the leadership of Romania in 1965. His efforts to keep his country as independent as possible were the cause of considerable strains within the Warsaw Pact, as Ceausescu reduced the size of Romania's armed forces and established friendly relations with Yugoslavia, West Germany and China.

For several years after the signing of the Warsaw Pact in 1955 the organisation had a largely notional role. It disguised the reality of Soviet control of its satellites in Eastern Europe, Albania, Bulgaria, Czechoslovakia, East Germany, Hungary, Poland and Romania. The political institutions of the Pact met only occasionally and usually merely to rubber-stamp some Soviet foreign policy initiative. The military side was moribund; the equipment of the East European armed forces was obsolescent and joint training was almost unheard of. Then in the period from 1964 to 1968 the Pact, under a whole series of military and political pressures, took on a new lease of life. This period came to an end in August 1968 when one member of the Pact, Czechoslovakia, was invaded by the majority of its allies, an event which effectively put a stop to a wide range of possible developments.

One Soviet objective in founding the Warsaw Pact was to formalise East European support for the Soviet Union as leader of the communist bloc. This position was increasingly challenged in the late 1950s by China. Albania, the least important of the Warsaw Pact nations, sided with China in this argument and from 1961 took no part in the alliance's activities. After the invasion of Czechoslovakia in 1968 the Albanians denounced the Pact altogether. The loss of Albania was not significant in itself but the Russians were determined not to allow more valuable allies to follow that example. The Warsaw Treaty Organization became more active both militarily and politically as the Russians increased the pressure for uniformity.

The chief obstacle to this Russian effort was Romania, under the leadership of Gheorghe Gheorghiu-Dej

and, from March 1965, Nicolae Ceausescu. Because of its oilfields Romania was less dependent economically on the Soviet Union than the rest of the Warsaw Pact. The Romanians also exploited the Sino-Soviet split with some very skilful diplomacy, even acting as honest broker between the two sides at one stage. The Romanian attitude was that the Warsaw Pact served only Soviet defence interests and that the individual countries of eastern Europe should be able to develop defence policies which met their own needs. At the same time the Romanians objected to Soviet attempts to introduce greater economic integration in the Eastern bloc.

The Romanians asserted their national sovereignty within the Warsaw Pact. In 1964 they signalled their independence by cutting the length of compulsory military service by a third and in 1965 they reduced their armed forces from 240,000 to 200,000 men. This was at a time when the Russians were urging their allies to increase their forces and defence spending. Romanian troops no longer took an active part in Warsaw Pact exercises. The Romanians also developed their own military doctrine, rejecting the Soviet model which was imposed elsewhere in the Pact. Romanian doctrine stressed national self-defence and preparation for a guerrilla war on the Yugoslav model, whereas official Warsaw Pact doctrine anticipated offensive operations using tactical nuclear weapons. Geographically, of course, Romania is not threatened with invasion by any Nato country; the threat comes rather from her own Warsaw Pact allies. Other Romanian gestures of independence included establishing friendly relations with Yugoslavia, China and West Germany. The

Romanians established their own defence industry, collaborating with the Yugoslavs on several projects, and eventually even bought weapons from the West.

In 1966 Ceausescu called for the abolition of all military blocs and condemned the stationing of military garrisons in other countries. Within the Warsaw Pact the Romanians called for consultation before the use of nuclear weapons and for the post of commander-in-chief to be rotated among the member nations, rather than confined to Soviet officers. The Russians could block all these Romanian schemes but the problem was that Romanian intransigence had the passive support of other members of the Pact. In 1968 the Czechs went even further and expressed public support for some Romanian proposals. The Soviets tried to contain the problem by agreeing to some reforms in the Warsaw Pact structure after 1968. They also encouraged a series of bilateral treaties among their allies. Eight were signed in 1967 and three more in 1968. Significantly, however, Romania did not join in this process until 1970. Besides these overt measures there are indications that the Soviets began to develop new institutions within the Warsaw Pact to bypass Romanian obstructionism. These have not been made public but it seems that a number of Warsaw Pact bodies now exclude Romania from their membership. In this way Pact discipline has been maintained.

Soviet military control

The structure of the Warsaw Pact contained a number of oddities during this period, which emphasised the way in which the Pact was little more than a cloak for Soviet control of the East European armies. Thus the commander-in-chief of the Joint Armed Forces of the Warsaw Pact was a Russian officer, who was also, ex-officio, a First Deputy Minister of Defence of the Soviet Union. The commander-in-chief in turn had a number of deputies, who were all the Defence Ministers of the Pact nations, including of course the Soviet Defence Minister. This ludicrous situation, in which the commander-in-chief had a deputy who was in reality his boss, was ended in 1969, when the Defence Ministers' Committee was formed.

Other indications of Soviet dominance in the Pact included the role of the chief of staff. He was always a Soviet officer, and a deputy chief of the General Staff. Most of his staff were Soviet officers and even the non-Soviet representatives were trained in Soviet academies. Throughout this period the chief of staff

was also head of the Warsaw Pact secretariat. Each non-Soviet Ministry of Defence had, and still has, a Soviet Mission attached to it, headed by a general with a staff of 15-20 officers. The Missions have full diplomatic immunity, but are completely separate from the system of defence attaches within the Pact. The role of the Missions is to oversee training and ensure the combat preparedness of the Warsaw Pact nations. The Missions also select reliable (in other words pro-Soviet) officers for training in the Soviet Union and promotion to key positions (General Jaruzelski of Poland is a product of this system). One last indicator of Soviet control is the Warsaw Pact air defence system. This was totally organised as part of the Soviet PVO Strany (Air Defence of the Homeland), and controlled from Moscow. One consequ-

Standardisation of equipment was always seen as a great strength of the Warsaw Pact, but while a smallarm such as the AK-47 (top, carried by Bulgarian troops) was used throughout the Pact, the more modern equipment (such as the T62 tanks above) was reserved for Soviet forces, and the air forces of the satellites (below, Czech pilots) were mainly defensive.

ence was that until the late 1960s, non-Soviet air forces were almost entirely fighter-interceptor forces.

In assessing the military worth of the Warsaw Pact in this period it is as well to start with the figures. During the 1960s the Soviet Union reduced the size of its armed forces. This was partly because of demographic problems – World War II had dramatically reduced the birth-rate in Russia, and therefore there were less young men available for conscription – but it was also partly because of changes in Soviet military doctrine, which now stressed nuclear weapons rather than the mass armies of the past. To compensate for these reductions the East European armies, with the exception of Romania, grew in size. Thus in 1962 the Soviet armed forces totalled about 3,600,000 men, and the rest of the Warsaw Pact, excluding Albania and Romania, numbered 727,500 regular troops. In 1968, the Soviet armed forces numbered 3,220,000 men and the others 956,000.

In theory the non-Soviet armies could field just over 60 divisions but only half of these were at anything approaching full strength. It was estimated at the time that 16 to 18 East European divisions would have been immediately available at the start of a war. These would probably have included all six East German divisions and certain elite formations from elsewhere. These formations were possibly allocated to the Warsaw Pact in peacetime, but it was generally believed that in wartime the East European armies would have been directly incorporated into the Soviet command system. Thus during the Czech crisis in 1968, the Warsaw Pact staff handled the mobilisation and training of the invasion force but it was commanded by the commander-in-chief of the Soviet Ground Forces, not a Warsaw Pact officer.

Groups of Forces

There was no doubt that the real striking power of the Warsaw Pact, whether for an intervention within the Pact or a war with Nato, lay in the Soviet forces garrisoned in eastern Europe. They were organised into three Groups of Forces: the Southern Group, with

Corruption and inefficiency

Despite the air of remorseless might that has long accompanied stories of the Soviet war machine, on closer inspection the Red Army seems much weaker, riddled with corruption and inefficiency, as this statement from a former serving soldier illustrates.

'In the unit where I served, for example, I had a radar. According to regulations I should have had two of them. But only one of them actually worked, and then only half the time. Why? Because the officers in my unit liked to drink, and to get extra money, and how are they going to get it? They would immediately think of selling spare parts. What kind of parts? Cables, various generators for the radar, various kinds of radio equipment which is in short supply in civilian stores, but which is available in the army. As a result the station would work only for a short time and then die out... my equipment was on its last legs. The second radar would not work because there was no generator – the officers sold it, and drank away the money.'

four divisions in Hungary, the Northern Group, with two divisions in Poland and, most importantly, the 20 divisions of the Group of Soviet Forces in Germany. Each of these Groups was kept at full strength, possessed modern equipment and was supported by a tactical air force. (A fourth, the Central Group of Forces, of five divisions, was stationed in Czechoslovakia after 1968).

The military efficiency of the non-Soviet armies increased considerably during the 1960s. Their weapons, mostly left over from World War II, were replaced by more recent Soviet models, such as the T-55 tank. It is, however, noticeable that the Soviet Union has rarely supplied its very latest weapons to its allies in bulk. Nuclear-capable weapons, such as aircraft and tactical missiles, were supplied but the Soviets undoubtedly kept the warheads firmly under their own control. The 1960s also saw a programme of joint exercises which helped to improve standards within the Pact. Such exercises generally followed a standard pattern, with an attack from the 'West', followed by a counter-attack and deep offensive by the 'Eastern' forces. The exercises usually had a nuclear scenario, and Exercise Vltava held in Czechoslovakia in 1966, included 300 simulated nuclear strikes.

These were impressive displays of force and, together with the successful invasion of Czechoslovakia, must be seen as proof of an adequate standard of military competence within the Pact. However, it was still doubtful that any Soviet officer would have been totally confident of his allies' performance in a war with the West. The Soviet military would undoubtedly have liked to see greater integration within the Pact, but Romanian awkwardness and the passive resistance of other Pact members limited their success in this field. Finally, in assessing the worth of the Warsaw Pact to the Soviet Union, its negative value should not be forgotten. Even an imperfect alliance was highly preferable to the lack of any kind of buffer zone between Soviet territory and the West

Michael Orr

Below: A T55 comes ashore during an amphibious exercise on the Black Sea coast in 1967, in which Bulgarian and Soviet forces participated. Warfare along the coasts of the two great 'inland seas' – the Baltic and the Black Sea – was one of the major tasks for which the Pact forces prepared during the 1960s.

Key Weapons

STEN/
STERLING SMGs

In 1940 the British Army's requirement for a new, cheap, simple-to-operate and reliable sub-machine gun was met by a weapon that by the end of World War II had seen action on practically every battlefront in every theatre of the war. The Sten sub-machine gun set new standards of cheapness and mass production for smallarms and at one stage of the war Stens were being turned out for the equivalent of £3.50 apiece, with one special factory alone producing over 20,000 models a week in 1942.

The first Sten to appear in June 1941 was the Mark I which, despite attempts to keep its design as unrefined as possible, was soon replaced by an even simpler version, the Mark II. The only machined parts on the second model were the barrel and the bolt, while the body was a simple steel tube, the magazine housing a pressing, the pistol grip a steel stamping and the stock a simple piece of tubular steel. The design of its successor, the Mark III, reduced the manufacturing process even further, providing for a fixed barrel and one-piece body and barrel casing. A further variant on the Mark IV version, intended for parachute use with a folding stock and cut-down body, was tried but due to operational problems was never introduced into service. A 1943 silenced version of the Mark II proved highly successful, however, and equipped Resistance fighters all over Europe.

The final version of the Sten, the Mark V, was introduced in 1944; it was better finished, had a wooden stock and handguard and mounted a bayonet, although no attempt had been made to rectify the Sten's main weakness, its habit of jamming at critical moments. Jamming could result from only slight damage to the long magazine which affected the feed.

In spite of this weakness, provided the weapon was looked after and the magazine in particular treated with care, the Sten worked and kept on working when many more expensive and elaborate weapons failed due to the effects of dirt, cold and mud.

The Sten provides a cyclical rate of fire of 540 rounds of 9mm ammunition per minute and operates on a simple blowback method. The loaded magazine is inserted into the magazine housing assembly and the weapon is prepared for firing by pulling back the cocking handle, thus compressing the return spring. When the trigger is pressed the breech block is released and shoots forward due to the pressure from the spring, driving a cartridge into the chamber (by means of feed ribs on the block); the cartridge is then detonated by the firing pin. Inertia and pressure from the spring keep the breech block closed until the bullet has left the barrel when the remaining pressure drives the spent cartridge case and breech block assembly back. The cartridge case is ejected, a new round pushed in line for feeding, and the firing process repeated.

An estimated three-and-a-half million Stens have been produced and the weapon has seen action all over the world since 1945 with a number of armies. Apart from its use with the British Army in Palestine in 1948 and in Malaya in the 1950s, it has been copied in Germany, China, Belgium, Argentina and Indonesia and was also used by the Viet Minh against the French in Indochina (1946-54).

Despite the Sten's success and massive production levels, not everyone had been happy with it and several attempts were made to put forward an improved sub-machine gun. One of the first to be

Previous page: A British soldier prepares to cock his Sterling sub-machine gun during an incident in the fighting for Aden in the 1960s. Above: An early experiment in fitting infra-red equipment to smallarms, here a Sten with silencer.

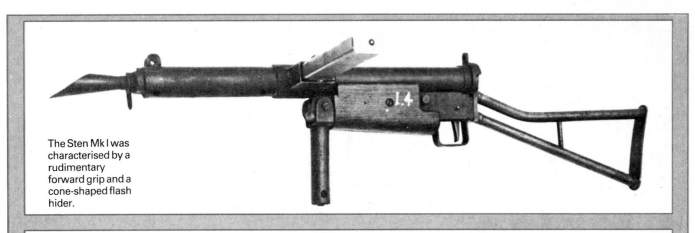

The Sten Mk I was characterised by a rudimentary forward grip and a cone-shaped flash hider.

A modified version of the Mk II was the Mk IIS, fitted with a silencer it was particularly suitable for undercover work.

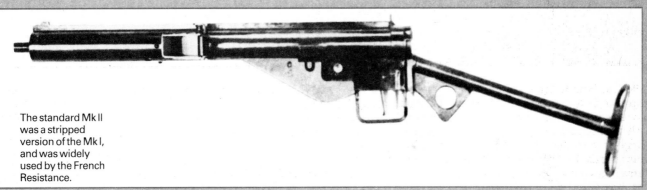

The standard Mk II was a stripped version of the Mk I, and was widely used by the French Resistance.

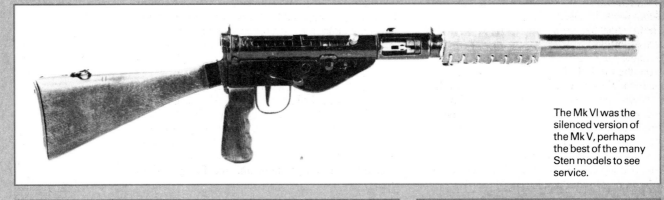

The Mk VI was the silenced version of the Mk V, perhaps the best of the many Sten models to see service.

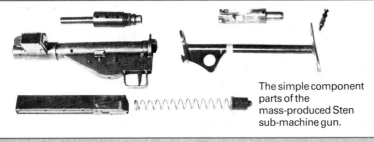

The simple component parts of the mass-produced Sten sub-machine gun.

Sten Gun Mk II

Calibre 9mm
Length (overall) 76.2cm (30in)
Weight (loaded) 3kg (6.62lb)
Rate of fire Cyclical 540rpm
Maximum effective range 90m (100 yds)
Magazine 32-round box
Muzzle velocity 390mps (1280fps)

considered was the Veseley, designed by a Czech engineer who had come to Britain in 1939 to help with production of the Besa machine gun. Unable to return to Czechoslovakia, he stayed in Britain and in 1940 submitted designs for a new sub-machine gun. These were rejected since the Sten had just been approved, but he persevered, building a gun at his own expense which was tested in November 1942. It was a simple blowback weapon, but well finished, and the magazine was of particular interest; it featured two 30-round columns, one in front of the other. Feed was initially from the front column, and when this was exhausted it fed from the rear half. The Royal Navy showed interest and Veseley made various minor changes, continuing tests until 1945, but although the gun was not unsatisfactory there were, by then, other promising designs and the Veseley was quietly abandoned.

Leaving aside several projects which were obviously hopeless, the next one to show promise appeared in September 1942 when George Patchett demonstrated a new design to a military panel. Like the Veseley, it was a simple blowback gun, but since Patchett intended it solely for firing from the hip it had no butt or sights. Trigger and pistol grip were situated at the point of balance and it featured an ingenious trigger mechanism with a simple thumb-operated change lever to provide single shot or automatic fire. The panel recommended that Patchett fit it with a butt and sights, whereupon it would be tested against the Sten and the Welgun, a sub-machine gun developed by the Special Operations Executive (SOE). The trial duly took place in February 1943 and the Patchett was reported to be inaccurate over 150 yards and prone to stoppages from mud and dirt.

After further modification another test was run in September 1943, this time with more contestants including the Australian Owen gun, a modified design based on the Sten, an Australian Austen, and the Welgun. This time the Patchett came second to the Owen, which, considering the Owen was probably one of the most reliable sub-machine guns of World War II, was very satisfactory. Despite Patchett's success it was announced that production limitations made it unlikely that any new design of sub-machine gun would be needed, but if one were, then the Patchett looked closest to meeting the requirement.

In January 1944, however, the War Office issued a set of specifications for future weapons, one of which was for a sub-machine gun; in brief, it had to weigh 2.7kg (6lb), be in 9mm calibre, be capable of putting

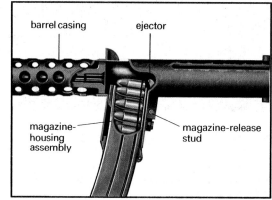

Above: A radio operator advances armed with a Sterling SMG. The 9mm Sterling replaced the Sten as the British Army's sub-machine gun in the 1950s. Although not a radical advance on the Sten the Sterling has proved highly effective as its successful export record has shown.

Sterling L2A3 SMG

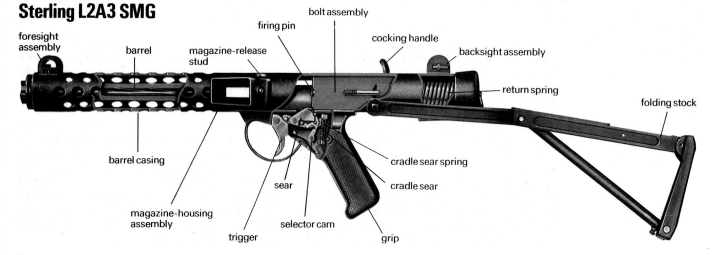

foresight assembly
barrel
magazine-release stud
firing pin
bolt assembly
cocking handle
backsight assembly
return spring
folding stock
barrel casing
sear
cradle sear spring
cradle sear
magazine-housing assembly
selector cam
grip
trigger

barrel casing
ejector
magazine-housing assembly
magazine-release stud

Top: A member of the Royal Ulster Constabulary surveys the damage of an IRA bomb-blast, armed with the Police Carbine version of the Sterling. Above: A sergeant of the Royal Marine Commandos carries a Sterling while on patrol during the fighting in Brunei in 1962.

five single shots into a 30cm (one-foot) square target at 90m (100 yards) range, and have a rate of fire not exceeding 500 rounds per minute. The Patchett seemed a likely candidate to meet this requirement and a new model, with helical ribs on the bolt to scour out dirt and dust, was tested. As a result, on 12 January 1944 20 Patchett guns were ordered from the Sterling Armament Company, followed by another order for 100 for 'special troop trials'. Full trials were carried out in September 1944 and the Ordnance Board announced that 'with regard to functioning, accuracy, endurance and penetration, it is considered that the Patchett machine carbine is suitable for service.' The 100 for 'special troop trials' were actually issued to the Parachute Regiment and saw action in the battle for Arnhem in September 1944.

After 1945 the pressure for a new weapon waned and more applicants came forward with designs. Among the best of these was a design from BSA Ltd, which featured an unusual method of cocking by pushing the foregrip forward and a magazine which could be hinged forward for stowage or to clear stoppages. Unfortunately it proved expensive, which

reduced the number the War Office was prepared to buy for trials, and when a demand for a bayonet was added to the specification, the peculiar cocking arrangement made this addition difficult.

In 1951 further trials were held with the BSA, a new Patchett (with some slight changes to the firing mechanism), and a design from the Royal Small Arms Factory at Enfield. The Patchett demonstrated its superiority over the others in every respect; it provided the desired slow rate of fire, could be stripped without tools, and continued to work in spite of dust and mud. The Ordnance Board recommended that the Patchett should be adopted if the forthcoming EM2 7mm rifle proved unsuitable in the sub-machine gun role. In the event the EM2 rifle was not adopted. The new FN FAL rifle could not function in the sub-machine gun role, and the Patchett became the official British sub-machine gun on 18 September 1953.

Although referred to as the Patchett in the Army Estimates for 1954-55, it is popularly known as the Sterling, since it has always been manufactured by the Sterling Armament Company of Dagenham. In addition, however, over 160,000 were manufactured by the Royal Ordnance Factory Fazackerly; indeed, the Ministry of Defence used Patchett's patents in these guns and, after much argument, Patchett was forced to issue a writ against the Crown to obtain recompense. After a long drawn out struggle he won his case and was awarded £116,975 in June 1966.

The standard production model L2A1 as used by the British and other armies is a blowback weapon feeding from a side-mounted curved box magazine. The Sten's principal disability lay in its magazine, and the Sterling magazine has been carefully designed to avoid stoppages. The cartridge follower carries roller bearings to reduce friction, and the entry is angled so that the cartridge cannot align with the firing pin until it has entered the gun chamber. A folding metal butt is provided, and a pistol grip at the point of balance. The barrel is surrounded by a perforated jacket which acts as a forward grip.

A later version of the Sterling, the L2A2, appeared with several modifications to the original design. The L2A1 featured a number of parts which could be used as stripping tools while the L2A2 dispensed with this facility but included a forward finger guard, a modified chamber and rear sight, and a strengthened butt. The current standard service model, the Sterling Mark 4 (L2A3) includes further modifications including a redesigned wooden butt and a chamber modified to the Nato standard. Further variants include the special Police Carbine and the L34A1 silenced model.

The latest Sterling design is the Mark 7 Para Pistol, a specially shortened version for use in confined spaces. It can be supplied either firing semi-automatic or fully automatic, and there is the option of firing from an open or closed bolt, the latter giving improved accuracy.

The current version of the Sterling has proved a reliable, well-made and effective weapon in a wide range of conditions and has been sold to over 70 armed forces and defence units throughout the world. Its accuracy has proved far superior to that of the Sten and although a more expensive weapon, it retains the Sten's simplicity of operation and ruggedness while achieving a far higher level of reliability – a tribute to the soundness of its basic design.

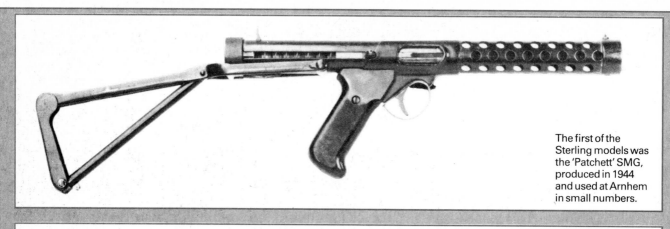

The first of the Sterling models was the 'Patchett' SMG, produced in 1944 and used at Arnhem in small numbers.

The Sterling without its folding stock and with a 10-round magazine instead of the standard box.

The Sterling is sometimes fitted with a wooden rather than the more usual collapsible metal stock.

The silenced version of the Sterling, the equivalent of the silenced Sten model of World War II fame.

The Mk 7 Para Pistol, a cut-down version of the standard Sterling, used by airborne troops and commandos.

Sterling L2A3 SMG

Calibre 9mm
Length (stock extended) 69cm (27in)
Weight (loaded) 3.5kg (7.7lb)
Rate of fire Cyclical 550rpm; practical 102 rpm
Maximum effective range 200m (220 yds)
Magazine 34-round box
Muzzle velocity 390mps (1280fps)

Vietnam: the air war
The deployment of US air power, 1961-68

Above: The dense jungle canopy of the Vietnamese countryside caused many difficulties for the US aerial reconnaissance teams which were attempting to locate enemy positions and movements. It was with this in mind that Operation Ranch Hand was launched in 1961. The operation was aimed at defoliating huge tracts of jungle in order to prevent the free movement of Viet Cong units over large areas of countryside. Here a C-123 releases its load of Agent Orange as it flies low over the jungle. Although at the time Agent Orange was stated to be a 'safe' chemical, since the war many cases have been recorded of deformities in children born of parents exposed to the chemical.

The Vietnam War, particularly between 1964 and 1968, was a war of images and symbols. Extensive media coverage of the fighting provided those who were not there with a host of pictures and sounds which stuck in the mind and still have the power to impress or shock: the little girl, naked and afraid, running away from a napalmed village; the waves of low-flying helicopters, sweeping into battle with their distinctive and evocative rotor-noise; the heat-haze of a runway on Guam, through which emerges the whale-like shape of a B-52, lumbering into the air with its awesome bomb-load; the moonscape of a jungle area forever laid bare by defoliants or carpet bombing. The list is enormous, yet it is remarkable how many of the images are closely connected to aircraft. For there can be no doubt that the Vietnam War symbolised a new era of aerial technology, searing its way into public consciousness through the clatter of a helicopter or the bright yellow flame of a bomb explosion.

But beyond the symbolism of the media images, the persistent presence of air power was at the very heart of American involvement in Vietnam. At a politico-strategic level, even the most cursory review of the rise and subsequent decline of US military commitment quickly reveals that many of the important decisions were directly related to the deployment of air strength. To any major power such as America, aircraft offer the opportunity to intervene at long range and, because they can be withdrawn from a conflict with comparative ease, give political leaders a flexibility which ground forces, with their elaborate and complex lines of supply, often fail to provide. Furthermore, aircraft present a wide range of capability, from reconnaissance and transport to tactical strike support and city bombing, which may be geared to match the political demands of a particular campaign. In the nuclear age the forces involved need to be closely controlled, for there is always the danger of inadvertently escalating the conflict, but air power remains a potent and politically-attractive option in circumstances short of all-out war.

Air power in the nuclear age

American recognition of this fact may be seen throughout the Vietnam commitment. When the French first called for aid in their war against Vietnamese communists in 1950, President Harry Truman and his successor Dwight D. Eisenhower used air power to symbolise their support. By 1954, on the eve of the French collapse, several hundred United States Air Force (USAF) personnel were in Vietnam, helping to maintain a fleet of American-supplied C-47 transports. Nor did they depart with the French, for American backing for the new state of South Vietnam took the form of deliveries of aircraft – F-8F fighters, C-47 transports, L-19 Bird Dog tactical reconnaissance aircraft and even H-19 helicopters – and the provision of mechanics, training staff and advisers to the South Vietnamese Air Force.

Such an early commitment made it inevitable that American air power should constitute something more than mere advisory support once the communist threat to the South Vietnamese regime emerged after 1959. By 1961 a special crew-training squadron (code-named 'Farm Gate') had been deployed to the South, together with a number of T-28 trainer aircraft capable of conversion to counter-insurgency strike support, and President John F. Kennedy was already authorising the use of USAF-manned C-123s in defoliant experiments close to the battle areas (Operation Ranch Hand). American pilots were seconded to train the VNAF and the beginnings of a more permanent presence were indicated by the construction of airfields, radar stations and command facilities.

Americans at the controls

Even before the first American casualties had been suffered (on 2 February 1962 a Ranch Hand C-123 crashed, killing its three-man crew), it was apparent that South Vietnam could look to Washington for a new level of support. This was reinforced by reports of American pilots flying combat missions, often in circumstances of desperation when their VNAF pupils could not cope, and by a steady build-up of air strength in the region. By early 1964, despite repeated assurances by President Lyndon B. Johnson that American personnel would be withdrawn as soon as the VNAF was fully trained and equipped, the South Vietnamese had become dangerously dependent upon American air power for their survival. A more overt and aggressive commitment of force was clearly only a matter of time.

When it occurred, it once again took the form of air power. The immediate American reaction to the Gulf of Tonkin incident in early August 1964 was to carry out retaliatory strikes against North Vietnamese coastal targets, using carrier aircraft from the US Seventh Fleet, and these raids were followed by the deployment of B-57s, F-100s and F-102s of the USAF to bases in South Vietnam and Thailand. But this, inevitably, led to further escalation, for bases such as Bien Hoa and Pleiku invited Viet Cong attacks which were answered in turn by increased air activity. In February 1965 selected air raids were mounted against North Vietnam under the code-name 'Flaming Dart' and in the following month the USAF began

a sustained bombing campaign – 'Rolling Thunder'. As USAF and Navy aircraft inflicted increasing damage upon North Vietnam, bombing targets closer and closer to Hanoi in an effort to force the ruling politburo to moderate its policies towards the South, Rolling Thunder acted as a backcloth against which the simultaneous commitment of American troops to the ground war took place.

But the bombing of the North, together with the tactical 'Arc Light' attacks carried out by B-52s in South Vietnam and against the Ho Chi Minh Trail, comprised a very crude instrument of political persuasion – a bludgeon trying to do the work of a scalpel. The damage inflicted was, if anything, too considerable, suggesting an over-reaction to the problems posed by North Vietnam and leaving the American leadership extremely vulnerable to both domestic and international criticism. North Vietnamese propaganda soon learnt to exploit the paradox, painting a picture of the great American bully using its superior strength to impose pressure upon a poor emergent state, and although there was undoubtedly another side to the story (represented in part by the success of North Vietnamese air defence systems), it was a picture which won a significant amount of sympathy world-wide. Images of the terrible effects of bombing and napalm on civilians were the most powerful single influence in turning opinion against the Americans.

Johnson soon found his policies opposed at an international level and, more importantly, from within America itself. The use of bombers over the North became the symbol of a foreign policy which disturbed and alienated many Americans by its dependence upon brute force. When the air attacks were seen to be failing to achieve their objectives, the opposition grew. It was nurtured by reports of significant American air losses – 938 aircraft by November 1968, each representing a number of dead or captured aircrew – and fuelled by fears that continued escalation would lead to direct confrontation with the Soviet Union or China. As a political instrument the bombing clearly failed, with Johnson being forced in the end to cancel it in exchange for an unsatisfactory North Vietnamese promise to 'talk about talks' at Paris in November 1968. In this respect, air power symbolised the bankruptcy of an American strategy which proved to be

Above: 55-gallon drums of napalm are loaded into the rear of a CH-47A helicopter to be dropped onto Viet Cong positions prior to an assault by troops. Above right: An A-4 Skyhawk, single seat attack bomber. Right: A Vietnamese civilian sits in the wreckage of a destroyed US aircraft. Below: A flight of Skyraiders on a Central Highlands airstrip.

impossible to sustain without at least a degree of popular consensus.

At a lower level of air operations, the heavy dependence upon air strength in the ground war represented a peculiarly American approach to the conflict which proved to be inapt. For most of the period 1965-68 American ground forces faced either a communist-inspired insurgency or a sporadic level of conflict with the North Vietnamese Army (NVA), and the temptation to turn to air power to solve tactical problems was enormous. For there was no doubt that aircraft had much to offer. If NVA or Viet Cong troops would not come out into the open, air reconnaissance or electronically-assisted air surveillance could help to locate them; if they were found, helicopters could be used to move men quickly to the spot, there to be supported by gunships, strike aircraft and even B-52s; if sustained ground operations developed, aircraft and helicopters could provide resupply, medical evacuation and forward observation. But this was taken to extremes and, as American units searched for greater mobility through the helicopter and increased firepower through the strike-support jet, many neglected the low-level tactical responses – patrolling, hearts and minds, detailed local knowledge – which might have produced more long-term results. In addition, as with the bombing of the North, the prevailing state of aircraft and weapons technology meant air power was often a blunt instrument, destroying vast areas of the battlefield by means of carpet bombing, napalm and defoliants for little real gain. What began as a symbol of power rapidly became a symbol of tactical desperation.

Changes in the air

Thus, in three crucial areas – commitment, escalation and tactical response – air power exemplified the scale and problems of American involvement in Vietnam between 1961 and 1968. The conflict in Vietnam was a limited one, closely controlled to avoid escalation, and despite its undoubted impact, air power was still too crude a weapon to satisfy the subtleties of American policy. It was to take the advent of laser-guided weapons and the ruthlessness of President Richard M. Nixon in 1972 to create the sharp cutting edge so clearly absent before 1968. It was only then that air power began to symbolise success. **J.L. Pimlott**

Rolling Thunder
The bombing of North Vietnam

American air attacks upon targets in North Vietnam began on 5 August 1964, after the Gulf of Tonkin incident, when President Lyndon B. Johnson authorised navy carrier aircraft to hit four North Vietnamese torpedo-boat bases and an oil storage facility. At the time this was seen as legitimate retaliation for attacks on the destroyer USS *Maddox*. No further offensives were launched until early February 1965.

By then, with South Vietnamese politics in chaos, a marked increase in the level of North Vietnamese military commitment to the war in the South and the development of a deliberate Viet Cong terror-campaign against US advisers in South Vietnam, Johnson was convinced that a show of force, designed to demonstrate continued American support for an embattled ally, was essential. Consequently on 7/8 February 1965, mixed formations of South Vietnamese and American aircraft attacked barracks at Chap Le and Dong Hoi, north of the demilitarised zone (DMZ), in an operation code-named 'Flaming

Dart'. A second series of similar raids – 'Flaming Dart II' – took place three days later, in direct response to a Viet Cong bomb attack on Qui Nhon in which 23 American servicemen were killed. A 19-day pause ensued, partly to see if the North Vietnamese were ready to cease their attacks (which they were not) and partly to regularise the bombing campaign. When the raids began again on 2 March 1965, with F-105s and B-57s hitting supply dumps at Xom Bong, 50km (35 miles) north of the DMZ, they did so under the new code-name 'Rolling Thunder'. It was the beginning of a sustained bombing offensive which was to last until 1 November 1968, when Johnson halted all air attacks in exchange for North Vietnamese agreement to start peace negotiations in Paris, and was not one which was to enjoy a large measure of success.

Rolling Thunder is usually referred to as *strategic* bombing, but in many respects this is a misnomer. The theory of strategic bombing relied upon effective air strikes deep into enemy territory which would

Ba Lam army barracks in North Vietnam – inset, moments before the attack and above left during the strike – was one of the objectives of Operation Flaming Dart, the air attacks ordered in February 1965 as retaliation for Viet Cong attacks on US servicemen.

Below: Two Vietnamese civilians carry their belongings through the rubble of the Thai Binh hospital which had been bombed three times already. Much unfavourable publicity resulted from the destruction of establishments such as hospitals and schools.

destroy the entire military and civilian infrastructure responsible for maintaining an army in the field; targets such as factories, depots, generating stations, supply routes and so on were of paramount importance. But, unsophisticated and under-industrialised, North Vietnam offered few appropriate strategic targets. In addition, the North was supporting an insurgency in the South which was not dependent upon technology for success and, as a Spartan totalitarian society, was not particularly susceptible to civilian demoralisation. At the same time, with the memory of Chinese military intervention in Korea in 1950, American leaders were acutely aware of the dangers of escalation and needed to avoid any actions which might draw the Soviet Union or China into the conflict.

Searching for a strategy

Problems such as these meant that any use of air power over the North had to be carefully controlled, undermining the impact of traditional strategic bombing, and this was reflected in the strictly limited aims of Rolling Thunder. Initially, it was hoped that attacks against the North would help to boost South Vietnamese morale. Thus, using a campaign of aerial interdiction, it was intended to impede the flow of North Vietnamese soldiers and logistics into the South through the destruction of bridges, roads, transport 'choke-points' and supply dumps. It was believed that a steady deluge of aerial bombardment would impose an unacceptable penalty upon the politburo in Hanoi for its continued support of aggression in the South, leading eventually to a decision either to withdraw or to start serious peace negotiations. The latter was the closest the Americans came to a truly strategic aim, but it was made subject to so many limitations and restrictions that it was unlikely to be achieved through air power alone. Rolling Thunder, in the final analysis, was an unsatisfactory and unworkable compromise.

This was shown right from the start of the campaign, when President Johnson refused to authorise a 'short, sharp attack', intended to destroy all worthwhile targets in the North in a manner guaranteed to shock and demoralise the politburo. Aware that this could cause substantial loss of civilian life, an international outcry and possible Soviet or Chinese intervention, he preferred a more gradual approach, slowly increasing the weight of air attacks to match political needs and the level of North Vietnamese aggression.

The president imposed a series of close political controls which nullified much of the initial impact of the offensive. Pilots were ordered to avoid attacks which might lead to civilian deaths, even if this meant aborting their missions; the choice of targets was carefully monitored, often by the president himself; key areas of North Vietnam, notably the Hanoi/ Haiphong urban complex and a buffer zone close to the Chinese border, were officially termed 'sanctuaries' into which no raids could be mounted without the approval of the White House; and selected portions of the enemy's war economy, including ports (in which Soviet and East European ships were constantly off-loading supplies) and, initially, air defence systems, were not allowed to be touched. Finally, as a consequence of such restrictions, the raids against the North were carried out by what were obviously tactical strike aircraft – F-100s, F-4s, F-104s, F-105s and (in early 1968) F-111s, from bases in South

Rolling Thunder Mission 9-Alpha

Shortly after noon on 3 April 1965, a large mixed force of 79 US aircraft climbed into the skies over South Vietnam and Thailand en route for the 'Dragon's Jaw', the bridge over the Song Ma River, three miles north of Thanh Hoa. This bridge formed the main rail and road supply link from Hanoi to the Ho Chi Minh Trail and the battlefields of South Vietnam and was to become one of the most famous and challenging targets for US air power in the whole Vietnam War. The main strike force consisted of 46 F-105 Thunderchiefs of the 'Fighting Cocks' (67th Tactical Fighter Squadron based at Korat in Thailand), while flak suppression and air combat patrol were assigned to a group of 21 South-Vietnam-based F-100 Super Sabres.

Cruising at 5000m (17,000 feet), the Thunderchiefs rendezvoused as planned with the F-100s five kilometers (three miles) south of the target. Visibility was good and seven of the F-100s went straight into the attack against the bridge's anti-aircraft defences, saturating the area with 2.75in rockets and bombs. As the F-100s pulled out, the first flight of Thunderchiefs rolled into position for the main strike. The size and structure of the target called for extreme precision in the attack and the strike aircraft were armed with Bullpup air-to-surface guided missiles and 340kg (750lb) free-falling general purpose bombs. One after another the Thunderchiefs loosed off their Bullpups at the bridge, but as the smoke cleared over the river it soon became obvious that the Bullpups' 113kg (250lb) warheads had little more than charred the superstructure and massive concrete abutments of the bridge. A second wave of 15 Thunderchiefs, armed with eight 340kg (750lb) bombs apiece, now took up the challenge; string after string of bombs crashed around the target, many exploding impotently on the far bank of the river, deflected by a strong southwesterly wind.

In this, the first of many attacks on the Thanh Hoa bridge, 120 bombs and 32 missiles were launched, inflicting only minor damage to the road and railway, for the loss of one F-100 and one RF-101 reconnaissance aircraft.

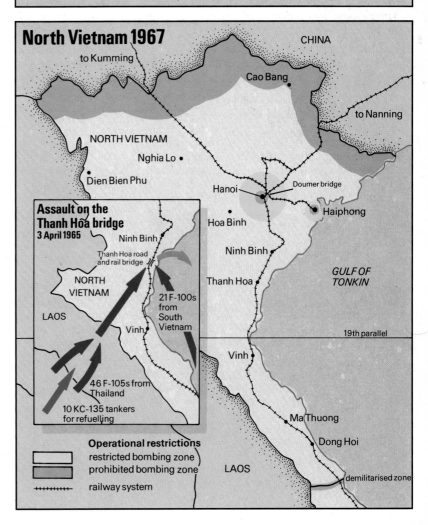

North Vietnam 1967

CHINA

to Kumming

Cao Bang

to Nanning

NORTH VIETNAM

Nghia Lo

Dien Bien Phu

Hanoi

Doumer bridge

Hoa Binh

Haiphong

Ninh Binh

Thanh Hoa

GULF OF TONKIN

Assault on the Thanh Hoa bridge
3 April 1965

Ninh Binh

Thanh Hoa road and rail bridge

NORTH VIETNAM

21 F-100s from South Vietnam

LAOS

Vinh

46 F-105s from Thailand

10 KC-135 tankers for refuelling

19th parallel

Vinh

Ma Thuong

Dong Hoi

Operational restrictions
restricted bombing zone
prohibited bombing zone
railway system

LAOS

demilitarised zone

Left: Watched by a Vietnamese peasant, a US F-105 bursts into flames after being hit by ground fire. The fully-opened canopy of the pilots' parachute is clearly visible in the background; the pilot landed safely but was later captured by North Vietnamese ground troops. Between the initiation of Operation Rolling Thunder on 2 March 1965 and the cessation of bombing in November 1968, 938 US aircraft were lost over the North.

Below: A Soviet-supplied surface-to-air missile, the SA-2 Guideline, which has a maximum range of 50km (31 miles) and can reach a speed of Mach 3.5. This weapon was widely deployed by the North Vietnamese although lack of adequately trained personnel led to a lower kill rate than had been hoped.

Vietnam and Thailand, plus carrier aircraft from the Seventh Fleet in the Gulf of Tonkin – leaving the true strategic bombers, the B-52s, to mount separate 'Arc Light' attacks which rarely extended far beyond the DMZ.

Nor were these the only restrictions, for, despite a steady rise in sortie rates during the early months of Rolling Thunder, it quickly became apparent that practical problems abounded. Some of these were geographical – the heavy forests and jungle terrain made target location difficult, while the annual monsoon (October to March) disrupted flying – but others were operational. Pre-strike reconnaissance tended to warn of impending attacks, so was not widely used; post-strike assessment was difficult because of the terrain. Many of the targets chosen were easily camouflaged or dispersed, while North Vietnamese defensive measures steadily increased in size and effectiveness. During 1965 the number of anti-aircraft guns north of the DMZ doubled to well over 2000 and in April the first Soviet-supplied surface-to-air missiles (SAMs) were located. By the end of the year, 56 SAM sites had been reported, although in August, after the first American planes had been lost to SA-2s, a special 'Iron Hand' mission directive permitted retaliatory strikes. In addition, the North Vietnamese Air Force, safely stationed in the sanctuary areas around Hanoi and equipped with Soviet MiG-15s, MiG-17s and (from December 1965) MiG-21s, posed a constant threat.

By the end of 1965 some 50 USAF and Navy aircraft had gone down over the North and the objectives of Rolling Thunder had not been achieved. The situation was not helped by a political decision to impose bombing 'pauses' – the longest was over New Year 1966 – to test Hanoi's reaction, for this invariably took the form of a rapid build-up of strength and increased infiltration of the South.

Bombing the bridges

Presented with such poor results, Johnson permitted a series of heavier air strikes in late spring 1966. In addition to the interdiction targets already authorised, petroleum, oil, lubricant (POL) storage facilities and power plants at Haiphong and Hanoi were now listed in the mission directives, together with road, rail and river communications with China. The first strike against POL facilities near Hanoi took place on 29 June 1966 and thereafter all the new targets were hit, the sortie rate culminating in September, just before the monsoon, when a total of 12,000 were flown. By then the Americans were beginning to announce a degree of success, citing the destruction of thousands of enemy trucks and watercraft, hundreds of bridges and supply dumps and up to two-thirds of North Vietnam's POL storage tanks, but this was an optimistic picture. The North Vietnamese, although undoubtedly hurt by the attacks, fought back with increasing ferocity. By the end of 1966 the MiGs had been committed to the air-defence battle and, together with the anti-aircraft systems, had managed to destroy a staggering total of 455 American aircraft since the beginning of the campaign.

Johnson's answer was yet more changes to the mission directives, pushing the bombing closer and closer to Hanoi in an effort to force the North Vietnamese to the conference table on American terms. On 20 July 1967 attacks were permitted against road, rail and waterway segments inside the Hanoi/

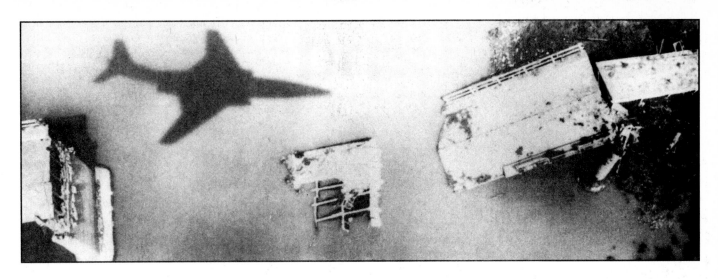

Above: A low-flying RF-101 casts a shadow over the remains of the My Duc bridge, north of the DMZ, after a successful airstrike by US fighter-bombers. Below: NVA troops open fire against US aircraft, using a Soviet-supplied 7.62mm Goryunov heavy machine gun.

Haiphong sanctuary, with the intention of halting all movement between and out of the two cities. Some of the targets had to be visited time after time because of North Vietnamese rebuilding efforts. By the end of this, the third full year of bombing, the politburo seemed no closer to discussing a peace settlement than it had been in 1964. Political leaders in Washington, approaching a presidential election and aware of mounting domestic and international opprobrium, were only too anxious to seek an honourable way out of the bombing campaign.

This was provided by the Tet offensive of early 1968, for as soon as the communist attacks had been contained in late March, Johnson felt confident enough to offer an end to all bombing north of the 19th parallel on the understanding that peace talks would begin. On 3 April Hanoi signified agreement, although Rolling Thunder as such did not end. From April until late October the bombing was concentrated in the area of North Vietnam between the DMZ and the 19th parallel, reaching new levels of intensity which were designed to pressure the politburo into serious negotiations. Once the promise had been made that these would begin, Johnson halted all air attacks on the North, with effect from 0800 hours on 1 November.

By that date, American pilots had flown over 300,000 Rolling Thunder sorties, dropping an estimated 860,000 tonnes of bombs onto North Vietnam – a greater tonnage than was dropped on either Japan during World War II or Korea between 1950 and 1953. The damage inflicted was considerable. By 22 October 1968 US planes had destroyed an estimated 77 per cent of the North's ammunition depots, 65 per cent of POL storage facilities, 59 per cent of power plants, 55 per cent of major bridges and 39 per cent of railway repair shops, killing about 52,000 civilians in the process. The North had, in addition, been forced to divert approximately 600,000 workers to repair and air defence duties. But the objectives of the offensive had not been fully realised. South Vietnamese morale may have improved since 1964, but this resulted more from American ground-force aid and success in countering Tet than it did from the bombing. More importantly, at no time between 1964 and 1968 did the North cease to pass men and supplies into the South; indeed, it has been calculated that the communist main force strength south of the DMZ increased by 75 per cent during this period, with corresponding rises in levels of aggression. At the same time, although the bombing was undoubtedly useful as a bargaining chip in the process of peace negotiations, it was the cancellation rather than the results of the campaign which finally brought the North Vietnamese to the conference table. All in all, the bombing cost the Americans a total of 938 aircraft and contributed immensely to the loss of domestic support for the war. It was a high price to pay for a campaign which produced so few long-term results.

J.L. Pimlott

Sensors and surveillance

New techniques and new machines for aerial reconnaissance

At the height of America's military involvement in Vietnam, there were more than 530,000 of her servicemen deployed in Southeast Asia. Of this number, a considerable percentage was involved in reconnaissance and intelligence work. On the ground, US Army Special Forces probed the enemy's sanctuaries, sometimes on their own, sometimes using native forces whom they had trained. More openly, the army fielded 11 Military Intelligence Companies and 20 Security Agency Companies in the quest for information about the Viet Cong and North Vietnamese regular forces operating in and against South Vietnam. Supporting these agencies were US Navy inshore patrol units which monitored enemy coastal

traffic and the shadowy but ever-present elements of America's non-military intelligence community, the CIA and the National Security Agency. Large as all this presence was, however, far greater effort went into aerial reconnaissance, both in terms of operational scope and technological expertise.

The nature of the war itself dictated that aerial surveillance would be the main information source available to the Americans. The geography of Vietnam and its neighbours Laos, Cambodia and Thailand favoured the enemy, so that airborne platforms were often the only means of effectively reconnoitring the more remote and difficult areas. Furthermore, the restraints placed upon American ground forces, which were not permitted to operate in Laos and Cambodia, meant that only aircraft could monitor enemy activity in those countries.

American aerial reconnaissance broke down into four distinct categories: strategic reconnaissance of the supply lines into North Vietnam from China and the identification of the vulnerable elements in North Vietnam's industry and transport system; surveillance of the Ho Chi Minh Trail as it wound down through Laos and Cambodia bringing supplies to the Viet Cong units in the South; day-to-day tactical intelligence for the ground forces and the direction of air operations in their support; and lastly, reconnaissance in support of the bombing offensives against the North in terms of providing target information, the location and plotting of the various elements of the enemy's air defence system and the provision of evidence of the success or failure of a particular raid.

All four branches of the American military maintained airborne reconnaissance units, although by far the largest force was fielded by the USAF. As with most aspects of US involvement in Vietnam, air force reconnaissance missions started modestly, with a single camera-equipped C-47 transport photographing communist activity in Laos during the early months of 1961. At this stage, American troops were acting in an advisory capacity only, although few doubted that eventually they would become actively involved in the escalating conflict.

During the latter part of 1961, incursions into South Vietnam had reached a level where a much greater reconnaissance effort was needed to keep track of events. To this end, a squadron of McDonnell RF-101C Voodoo aircraft moved into Tan Son Nhut airbase outside Saigon and began reconnaissance

Beechcraft QU-22B
Length 8.03m (26ft 4in)
Span 10.05m (32ft 10in)
Pave Eagle Beechcraft QU-22Bs were used by the

553rd Reconnaissance Wing to relay information gleaned from the Igloo White sensor network.

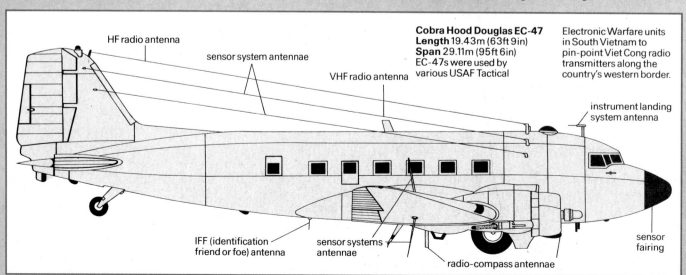

HF radio antenna

sensor system antennae

VHF radio antenna

Cobra Hood Douglas EC-47
Length 19.43m (63ft 9in)
Span 29.11m (95ft 6in)
EC-47s were used by various USAF Tactical

Electronic Warfare units in South Vietnam to pin-point Viet Cong radio transmitters along the country's western border.

instrument landing system antenna

IFF (identification friend or foe) antenna

sensor systems antennae

radio-compass antennae

sensor fairing

Above: The naval Grumman A-6A strike aircraft was fitted with a highly sophisticated all weather day/night target acquisition system known as DIANE (digital integrated attack and navigation equipment). In spite of the effectiveness of such systems, carried by the more advanced US strike aircraft, it was still necessary to supplement them with aircraft specifically designed for reconnaissance and surveillance missions.

flights over Laos in October. The arrival of the RF-101 marked a great advance. The F-101 was originally designed as a long-range escort fighter, and the first reconnaissance (RF) model entered service in 1957. The RF-101C was equipped with either two KA-1 and four KA-2 cameras for daylight operations or two KA-1, one KA-2 and three K-46 units for night work, and was capable of supersonic speeds.

The 460th Tactical Reconnaissance Wing's Voodoos were to bear the brunt of USAF photo-reconnaissance sorties for the next six years. During the period 1962-64, the RF-101s charted the growth of the so-called Ho Chi Minh Trail, the communist supply route into South Vietnam. Operating from Don Muang in Thailand as well as Tan Son Nhut, the Voodoos were in the forefront of operations when the

shooting war began in earnest during 1964 and an aircraft of this type acted as a pathfinder for the first 'Flaming Dart' raid on North Vietnam on 7/8 February 1965.

With the escalation of the war, additional reconnaissance aircraft began to arrive in Vietnam. Whilst the RF-101s bore the brunt of the day-to-day work, May 1963 saw the arrival of two RB-57E aircraft at Tan Son Nhut. These machines formed the sharp end of the highly secret Patricia Lynn programme which set out to test new reconnaissance equipment under operational conditions. Modified by General Dynamics (from B-57E light bomber airframes), the RB-57s initially carried one infra-red and four optical cameras. The infra-red camera was of the greatest value as the enemy used the hours of darkness to

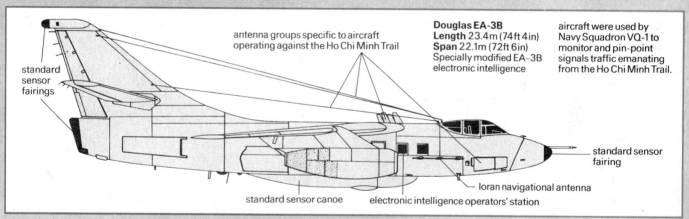

Douglas EA-3B
Length 23.4m (74ft 4in)
Span 22.1m (72ft 6in)
Specially modified EA-3B electronic intelligence aircraft were used by Navy Squadron VQ-1 to monitor and pin-point signals traffic emanating from the Ho Chi Minh Trail.

antenna groups specific to aircraft operating against the Ho Chi Minh Trail

standard sensor fairings

standard sensor fairing

loran navigational antenna

standard sensor canoe

electronic intelligence operators' station

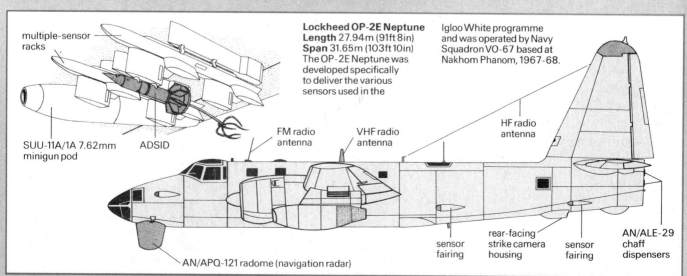

Lockheed OP-2E Neptune
Length 27.94m (91ft 8in)
Span 31.65m (103ft 10in)
The OP-2E Neptune was developed specifically to deliver the various sensors used in the Igloo White programme and was operated by Navy Squadron VO-67 based at Nakhom Phanom, 1967-68.

multiple-sensor racks

SUU-11A/1A 7.62mm minigun pod

ADSID

FM radio antenna

VHF radio antenna

HF radio antenna

rear-facing strike camera housing

sensor fairing

sensor fairing

AN/ALE-29 chaff dispensers

AN/APQ-121 radome (navigation radar)

maximum advantage in order to avoid detection. The Patricia Lynn aircraft, eventually numbering four, remained in Vietnam until 1971 by which time they had carried an enormous variety of equipment including optical cameras developed for spy satellites and terrain-following radars.

The level of night activity, combined with the local geography, led to greater and greater effort being put into sensor systems which could operate in total darkness. It was at this point that a clear division began to appear in the USAF's reconnaissance effort between 'in-country' work, that is the monitoring of communist activity in the South and along the Ho Chi Minh Trail, and strategic support for the growing bombing offensive against the North. In this latter category, January 1964 saw the arrival of a detachment of the 4080th Strategic Wing at Bien Hoa bringing with it a number of the infamous U-2 'spy planes'. The exact nature of their work is still unclear but it is known that one of their aircraft identified the first surface-to-air missile site in North Vietnam during April 1965 and that others were equipped to monitor signals traffic. The U-2 remained in Southeast Asia until 1976 when the U-2R aircraft of the 99th Strategic Reconnaissance Squadron left U Tapao in Thailand to return to the United States.

The discovery of missile defences in North Vietnam led to the deployment of yet another reconnaissance type, the RB-66 Destroyer. This aircraft differed radically from those so far described in that it was equipped for electronic reconnaissance, that is the detection and classification/identification of hostile electro-magnetic emissions. Operating from Tan Son Nhut, RB-66 aircraft of the 363rd Tactical Reconnaissance Wing were used to plot North Vietnamese radars from 1965 onwards.

Standard photo-reconnaissance sorties flown over the North during this period remained in the hands of the 460th's Voodoos. Operations continued until 1967, by which time the type was becoming increasingly vulnerable to the enemy's defences. This vulnerability led to the RF-101s being replaced by the RF-4C Phantom. In addition to being better able to look after itself, the reconnaissance Phantom carried a vastly more sophisticated sensor 'fit', including infra-red detectors and side-looking radar in addition to a spread of three cameras mounted in the nose. By the time of the American withdrawal from Vietnam, the RF-4C had completely replaced the RF-101 and was operated by a total of four squadrons.

The problem of reconnaissance aircraft vulnerability over the North was tackled in two ways; by the Buffalo Hunter programme and by the use of America's most potent and secret reconnaissance aircraft, the SR-71 Blackbird. Buffalo Hunter was the use of unmanned, remotely piloted vehicles (RPVs) for photo-reconnaissance sorties. Such devices were air-launched from DC-130 Hercules carriers, flown automatically to and from a designated target and then retrieved in mid-air by specially modified HH-3E helicopters.

As far as is known, three types of reconnaissance RPV were used in Vietnam – the AQM-34L, M and P – all of which appear only to have carried cameras. The launch aircraft were operated by the 100th Strategic Reconnaissance Wing based at Bien Hoa, while the recovery helicopters flew from Da Nang. RPV operations began in late 1964 and continued until 1973, completing over 2500 sorties.

The Mach 3 SR-71 high-altitude reconnaissance aircraft arrived in Southeast Asia during 1967 when Detachment 1 of the 9th Strategic Reconnaissance Wing began operating three aircraft out of Kadena on Okinawa. These extraordinary aeroplanes were, and still are, almost immune from interception, flying at over Mach 3 at 25,000m (80,000ft). Equipped with extremely high-powered cameras, they contributed vital intelligence to the American war effort for the remainder of the conflict.

While such operations were taking place over North Vietnam, the main effort in the South was going into the Igloo White programme. Igloo White was, quite simply, the sensory 'trip-wiring' of the Ho Chi Minh Trail. Operations began in the mid 1960s and were divided into two clear areas, the airborne placement of the various sensors followed up by the aerial reception and onward transmission of the information they provided.

Five types of sensor were used, two of which operated acoustically (activated by sound), the remaining three functioning seismically (activated by ground vibrations), both seismically and acoustically, and organically. The two acoustic types were named Spikebuoy and Acoubuoy: Spikebuoy buried itself in the ground, while Acoubuoy was dropped by parachute and hung in the jungle canopy. The seismic device, named Adsid, buried itself in the ground but deployed a small antenna shaped like a tropical plant above the earth. Acousid was similar to Adsid but combined the acoustic and seismic functions and was triggered from an airborne control. The last device, known as the 'People Sniffer', was the most extraordinary in that it used a live bedbug to indicate the presence of human beings.

Most of these sensors were delivered from the air by USAF transports, fighter-bombers and helicopters or by the navy's Lockheed OP-2E Neptune (belonging to Observation Squadron VO-67 which was based at Nakhom Phanom, Thailand, between 1967 and 1968). The information gathered was recorded by air force EC-121R Constellation and Beechcraft QU-22 aircraft of the 553rd Reconnaissance Wing, again based at Nakhom Phanom. It is interesting to note that, like the Buffalo Hunter vehicles, the QU-22 could be operated without a pilot.

All the material was retransmitted from the orbiting

Below: Personnel detection sensors, which were used extensively during the intelligence-gathering Operation Igloo White, are mounted on the release pods of a USN OP-2E aircraft.

Above: The outstanding US high-altitude reconnaissance aircraft, the SR-71 Blackbird. This aircraft has a maximum speed of Mach 3.32 and was first deployed for duty in Vietnam during 1967.

relays of EC-121Rs and QU-22s to the Infiltration Surveillance Center at home base where it was computer-processed into a coherent picture and passed on to the various operational commands for offensive action. The Igloo White programme was extremely expensive and its results were disputable. The 'People Sniffers', for example, proved unfortunately responsive to animals as well as people, and false alerts outnumbered genuine ones.

Apart from the Igloo White operations, both the USAF and the US Army put considerable effort into the airborne location of Viet Cong units operating in and around the South. Under the Combat Cougar and Cobra Hood programmes, USAF EC-47s were used to locate enemy radio transmitters along the western borders of South Vietnam, a task in which they were aided by US Army RU-21, AP-2E and RP-2E Communications Intelligence (COMINT) aircraft. Once the source of these transmissions had been located, air or ground strikes would be organised against them.

Again, US Army OV-1B and OV-1C Mohawks equipped with, respectively, side-looking radar and infra-red sensors, were employed to monitor night-time activity on the roads and trails of both South Vietnam and Laos. Even the navy managed to get in on the act with a detachment of EA-3Bs (Skywarriors adapted for electronic reconnaissance) operating from Da Nang against the Ho Chi Minh Trail between 1965 and 1969, backed up by RA-3Bs (camera reconnaissance Skywarriors) of VAP-61 and VAP-62 squadrons which provided infra-red and 'real time' video photography of the area.

The previously described Patricia Lynn aircraft were heavily involved in these 'in-country' operations and are described as providing up to 90 per cent of the useable reconnaissance material during the latter part of their tour in 'Nam'. Of an equally experimental nature were the Lockheed Q-Star aircraft used by both the USAF and US Army during 1969 and 1970. Essentially powered sailplanes, these aircraft were extremely quiet and are reported to have

been able to deploy their infra-red sensors within 30m (100ft) of the ground without detection.

It should not be forgotten that both the US Navy and Marine Corps were also heavily involved in the intelligence gathering business in support of their own seaborne operations, quite apart from their participation in the ground war in the South. From 1964 onwards, carrier strikes were mounted against the Northern heartland from what was known as Yankee Station in the Tonkin Gulf. Photo-reconnaissance support for these operations was provided by the RF-8 Crusaders of VFP-63 squadron and the RA-5C Vigilantes of RVAH-5 squadron amongst others. The RF-8 was a derivative of the Crusader shipborne interceptor equipped with five cameras in a modified nose section. VFP-63 squadron began operations in May 1964 and was still providing photographic cover at the time of the withdrawal in 1973. During these nine years the squadron lost 20 aircraft to the North Vietnamese defences. The Vigilante was an altogether more sophisticated system and was used by the navy for deep penetration reconnaissance sorties over the North. Derived from the A-5 nuclear bomber, the RA-5 carried vertical, oblique and split-image cameras, electronic intelligence equipment and side-looking radar. With a dash speed in excess of Mach 2 the Vigilante provided the navy with a reconnaissance tool as good as any in Southeast Asia.

With its involvement in the bombing of North Vietnam, the navy needed accurate information concerning the enemy's radar cover and to this end fielded two Marine Corps types, the EF-10 and the EA-6A, to provide the necessary electronic intelligence. The EF-10 was derived from the Douglas Skynight interceptor and, operated by VMCJ-1 squadron from Da Nang, provided intelligence and jamming cover for both USAF and Navy strikes between 1965 and 1969. The Grumman EA-6A Intruder entered service, again with VMCJ-1, during the latter part of 1966.

The range of advanced optical and electronic reconnaissance equipment deployed by the Americans in Vietnam might have been expected to have a decisive effect on the outcome of the conflict, but it did not. It was a prime example of the general US problem in Vietnam – that the world's most technically advanced armed forces were not suited to take on the enemy they faced. **Martin Streetly**

1039

The air support of ground forces in Vietnam involved a massive concentration of tactical aircraft, ranging from the piston-engined light planes of the forward air controllers (FACs), through piston-engined attack aircraft and jet fighter-bombers to the eight-engined B-52 heavy bomber. At the peak of American involvement in the Southeast Asia conflict an average of 800 sorties per day was flown by the tactical air forces. About one half of this effort came from the United States Air Force (USAF), with the US Marine Corps air wings providing another one third of the sorties and the South Vietnamese Air Force (VNAF) and carrier-based fighter-bombers of the US Navy contributing the remainder.

The first American close air support missions of the war were flown by the North American T-28Ds and Douglas B-26 Invaders of the USAF Air Commandos' 'Farm Gate' detachment (a special crew-training squadron attached to the VNAF). These elderly piston-engined attack aircraft were intended to perform the dual role of supporting ground forces and providing combat training for South Vietnamese airmen. Although they were flown by USAF pilots, they carried a VNAF second pilot and were marked as VNAF aircraft. From October 1961 until the first deployment of USAF jet aircraft to South Vietnam in 1965, the aircraft of the Farm Gate detachment were the only close air support (CAS) forces available to the South Vietnamese. However, by the mid 1960s their replacement had become a matter of urgency, as the T-28Ds' airframes were approaching the end of their useful lives and the B-26s had been grounded after suffering structural failure. The replacement was the Douglas A-1 Skyraider piston-engined naval attack aircraft, large numbers of which were transfer-

red from the US Navy to USAF Air Commando (later Special Operations) squadrons and to the VNAF. The great advantage of the Skyraider as a CAS aircraft was its heavy weapons load, 3600kg (8000lb) of ordnance plus four 20mm cannon in contrast to the T-28D's two 0.5in machine guns and 800kg (1800lb) of ordnance.

With the build-up of American ground forces from 1965 onwards, the USAF deployed jet fighter-bomber equipped Tactical Fighter Wings to South Vietnam to support them. The North American F-100 Super Sabre was the first jet fighter to operate in the combat theatre and it became the most important CAS aircraft of the war. McDonnell Douglas F-4 Phantoms also flew in this role, although the fast and relatively unmanoeuvrable jets were ill-suited to striking the often fleeting targets presented by North Vietnamese Army and Viet Cong forces in the South. Nevertheless, it was the jets that bore the brunt of the CAS work. In 1969 F-100s flew 52,699 combat sorties in South Vietnam, F-4s flew 19,185, while the A-1s' share was only 2055 sorties.

Modifying for attack

As the war progressed, more specialised support aircraft were deployed to Vietnam. These were generally existing aircraft designs, modified to the requirements of the Southeast Asia conflict. For example, the A-37B Dragonfly attack aircraft was based on the T-37 basic jet trainer. As such it was ideally suited to the needs of the VNAF, whose relatively inexperienced pilots were required to undertake an ever-increasing share of air support duties as President Richard Nixon's policy of 'Vietnamization' of the war took effect. In 1969 the VNAF operated three squadrons of Dragonflies, while by the end of 1972

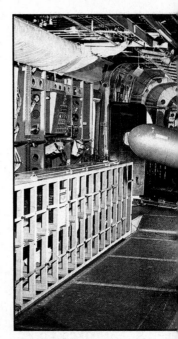

Above: Four 7.62mm miniguns mounted in the interior of an AC-119G gunship with ammunition racks to the left of the picture. These weapons, each with a cyclic rate of 6000 rounds per minute, could entirely blanket a large area if brought into action together. By flying in a sustained circle complete areas could be cleared.

Fire from
US close-support missions

Below: The replacement for the ageing T-28D was the A-1 Skyraider which could not only carry a huge amount of ordnance (3000kg – 8300lb) but also mounted four 20mm cannons. Here two Skyraiders, specially equipped for low-altitude attack with bombs, rockets or napalm, fly in at zero feet to deliver their bomb loads.

this force had tripled in strength. Another important modified type was the AC-47D gunship, basically a Douglas C-47 transport aircraft fitted with a broadside armament of three rapid-firing 7.62mm Miniguns, giving a rate of fire of 18,000 rounds per minute. With the aircraft in a precisely-judged turn, the fire from these weapons could be concentrated into a small area with devastating effect. Using the radio call sign Spooky, AC-47Ds operated at night over South Vietnam, providing fire support for isolated outposts when they came under attack from the Viet Cong. The fixed-wing gunship also became a very effective night interdiction aircraft operating over the Ho Chi Minh Trail.

The heaviest air strikes of the war were flown by Strategic Air Command's Boeing B-52 Stratofortresses. These so-called 'Arc Light' missions flown over South Vietnam were under the control of Combat Skyspot ground-based radars, which could direct the B-52s' bombing with greater accuracy than the bombers' own radars. The first Arc Light mission was flown from Guam in June 1965 and two years later B-52s based at U Tapao in Thailand joined in the campaign. The B-52D variants of the Stratofortress received the 'Big Belly' modification which allowed each aircraft to lift up to 108 340kg (750lb) bombs. The effects of a formation attack by B-52s could be devastating, not least because the high flying bombers gave no warning of their approach. Accuracy was considered good enough to permit bombing within 275m (300 yards) of friendly troops. However, the Arc Light missions had their critics, who considered this massive application of aerial fire power to be wasteful and often ineffective. Indeed, there is reason to believe that some of the early

missions failed to find a worthwhile target. Nevertheless, General William Westmoreland considered that it was the B-52 bombing missions which broke the North Vietnamese Army's assault on the besieged Marine outpost at Khe Sanh in 1968. In that year the bombers flew an average of 1800 sorties per month over South Vietnam.

Although close air support was the mission of the USAF rather than the army, the latter's Bell AH-1G Huey Cobra gunships, armed with machine guns and rockets, could provide a measure of fire support to the ground forces. The Cobras were especially useful in combating Viet Cong 'hugging' tactics, where the separation between enemy and friendly forces was insufficient to allow conventional CAS aircraft to be used with safety. The US Marine Corps' ground operations in Vietnam were generally supported by the tactical aircraft of the Marine Aircraft Groups, which were equipped in the main with A-4 Skyhawks, F-4 Phantoms and A-6 Intruders. However, whenever the ground situation demanded a timely and effective response by CAS aircraft (as at Khe Sanh in 1968), air resources were allocated as available and irrespective of the service to which they belonged.

Napalm and cluster bombs

Over half of the CAS sorties flown were preplanned, so that the pilots could be briefed on the objective in advance and the aircraft armed with appropriate ordnance. For example, it was found that napalm and cluster bomb units were most effective against troops in the open, whereas 230kg (500lb) or 340kg (750lb) high explosive bombs would be needed to penetrate jungle foliage or to deal with enemy bunkers. Not all CAS requirements could be anticipated, however,

the sky

and so a number of aircraft were held on ground alert, armed with a variety of ordnance. This system allowed a call for air support to be met within some 40 minutes. If the situation was so critical that a faster response was needed, then aircraft already in the air would be diverted from other missions.

All CAS missions, and indeed all tactical air operations over South Vietnam, were closely controlled from the ground. The Tactical Air Control Center at Tan Son Nhut airbase outside Saigon monitored all combat aircraft operating over South Vietnam. It was generally responsible for allocating air resources to the various ground commanders on a routine basis and in an emergency it could rapidly redeploy tactical air units from one military region to another. The actual control of CAS missions was delegated to Direct Air Support Centers, which were attached to each corps-sized army formation. This system had the great advantage of flexibility, as all air resources were monitored from a control centre with the authority to allocate them according to the needs of the moment.

Controlling from the air

When the CAS aircraft arrived over their target, they came under the control of a Forward Air Controller (FAC). The FAC was himself airborne in a light observation aircraft such as the Cessna 0-1 Bird Dog, 0-2 Skymaster, or later in the war the specially developed North American-Rockwell OV-10 Bronco. In contrast to World War II and Korea, there were no well-defined battle lines and so it was essential that all air strikes be directed by a FAC, who was better placed than the pilots of fast jets to locate friendly forces and to pick out the enemy positions and mark them with a smoke rocket. He would maintain radio contact with both the attack aircraft and the ground commander and, being an airman with recent experience of service with a Tactical Fighter Wing, he could give the attacking pilots an expert on-the-spot briefing on their target. The usefulness of the FAC did not end with the direction of strike missions, however. Apart

from those FACs assigned to ground combat units, there were others operating within all of South Vietnam's 44 provinces who performed a general reconnaissance and intelligence-gathering mission. As these pilots were assigned to a particular area, they soon became familiar with the terrain and the pattern of life in the local rural communities. Consequently, they could generally spot any unusual signs that might give a clue to enemy activity. If they detected enemy troops the FACs could then lead a ground patrol to the area or direct an air strike.

Close air support may have seemed at times wasteful and inefficient, but it was notable that in spring 1972 it was the presence of US aircraft in the support role which held up the North Vietnamese drive into the South, whereas when the US failed to provide air support under similar circumstances in 1975, the ARVN collapsed and South Vietnam fell.

Anthony Robinson

Top left: A Cessna 0-1 Bird Dog observation aircraft directs fire, either artillery or airborne, onto enemy positions in North Vietnam. It was from aircraft such as these that Forward Air Controllers (FAC) directed US fire missions. These piston-engined craft, which were considerably slower than the jet-engined strike aircraft, utilised their lack of speed in such tasks as accurately marking enemy locations with smoke rockets. Above: A US door gunner saturates enemy ground positions with a 0.3in calibre machine gun from his UH-1B Iroquois helicopter.

THE BOEING
B-52

The massive, eight-engined B-52 Stratofortress strategic bomber has had one of the longest service careers of any aeroplane. The XB-52 prototype first flew in October 1952 and the bomber entered US Air Force service in 1955; the subsequent B-52G and B-52H versions are scheduled to remain in front-line service until the end of the present century and beyond. The key to the Stratofortress's amazing longevity is the adaptability of the basic design. In the course of its USAF service the B-52 has been switched from high to low-level bombing missions; it has been modified on numerous occasions to carry new armament, avionics systems and other equipment; and its structure has been strengthened to such a degree that large portions of the wing and fuselage of later aircraft have been virtually rebuilt.

The original military requirement that was to result in the B-52 was issued in 1945. At that time a turboprop long-range bomber was envisaged, but in 1948 it was decided to substitute turbojet power-plants. This decision meant that when the B-52 replaced the piston-engined B-36 long-range bomber, Strategic Air Command (SAC) would be an all-jet force. SAC's primary role was to deliver nuclear weapons on Soviet strategic targets and until the advent of the ICBM (intercontinental ballistic missile) at the end of the 1950s the manned bomber was the most effective nuclear delivery system. Unlike SAC's first jet bomber, the Boeing B-47, the B-52 had the range to fly its combat missions from bases in the United States, rather than having to operate from forward bases in Europe, North Africa and the Far East in order to bring strategic targets within range.

The B-52 is an enormous aircraft by any standards,

with a wing span of over 56m (185ft), a length of nearly 48m (157ft) and an all-up weight of 229,066kg (505,000lb) in the B-52H version. The eight engines, Pratt & Whitney J57 turbojets on most models, are mounted in pairs beneath the swept wings. Much of the wing's internal volume is given over to fuel and yet more is carried in drop tanks carried underwing between the outboard engine nacelles and the wing-tips. The fuselage, too, accommodates fuel tanks, with the main tank mounted above the internal weapons bay, an aft tank immediately behind this and a forward tank between the forward crew compartment and wing centre section. Fuel capacity is some 181,700 litres (48,000 gallons), giving the B-52G an unrefuelled range of 11,750km (7300 miles). In-flight refuelling can extend this range still further. This is accomplished by the B-52 flying a tight formation beneath the tanker aircraft, allowing its boom operator to make contact with the B-52's refuelling receptacle mounted atop the fuselage just aft of the cockpit.

The normal crew complement of the B-52 is six members, comprising pilot, co-pilot, navigator, radar navigator, EW (electronic warfare) officer and tail gunner. The forward crew compartment is arranged on two levels, with the flight deck on the upper level and the EW officer's position behind the pilots' seats. The two navigators are positioned side by side at a lower level, seated on downward-firing ejection seats. In the early B-52 models (A to F), the gunner was seated in his isolated tail turret over 30m (100ft) away from the other crew members and his only contact with them was over the intercom. However, in the B-52G and H models he was moved forward into the main crew compartment, occupying

Previous page: A classic view of the B-52 in flight revealing the aircraft's four pairs of Pratt & Whitney turbofans. Above: While possessing massive internal fuel tanks the B-52 nevertheless has the facility for in-flight refuelling which provides it with enormous strategic range.

Right: Besides its massive bomb-load capacity the B-52 is also able to launch the Boeing AGM-86A cruise missile.

Left: The B-52D featured an improved fire-control system for the rear armament of four 0.5in machine guns. This variant had extensive combat experience over Vietnam.

Left: The B-52H was the final model in the Stratofortress series. The tail-mounted machine guns of earlier models were replaced by a single multi-barrel cannon, operated by a gunner relocated in the forward crew compartment.

Left: A B-52G stands on the runway armed with 12 Boeing cruise missiles attached to the inner-wing pylons in two tandem triplets. A further eight missiles can be carried on a rotary launcher within the fuselage.

a position beside the EW officer and operating his guns by remote control.

The B-52's offensive weapons load can be carried both in the internal weapons bay and on underwing pylons. Up to eight nuclear free-fall bombs can be lifted, but the B-52s currently in service generally carry a mix of free-fall weapons, SRAMs (short-range attack missiles), and ALCMs (air-launched cruise missiles). Twelve SRAMs can be carried on underwing pylons and a further eight are housed in a rotary launcher fitted in the weapons bay. A similar internal launcher is being developed for the ALCM. The earlier AGM-28B Hound Dog ASM (air-to-surface missile), which was in service from 1961 until 1976, was carried singly beneath each wing. Its 3400kg (7500lb) thrust J52 turbojet could be started up to augment the B-52's own engines on take-off. Another pylon-mounted strategic weapon intended for the B-52 was the GAM-87A Skybolt air-launched ballistic missile, four of which could be carried. This missile was, however, cancelled in 1962 before it entered service. Although its primary role was as a nuclear bomber, the B-52 can carry conventional ordnance and, indeed, the B-52D with the special 'Big Belly' modification can lift no fewer than 108 340kg (750lb) bombs. Sea mining is another mission which the bomber can undertake, the B-52D being able to carry more than 80 225kg (500lb) mines.

All B-52s carry a rearward-firing defensive armament mounted in a radar-directed tail turret. The radar is able to search for enemy fighters and, once the target is acquired, the fire-control system computes the lead angle for the guns. The standard B-52 tail armament comprised four 0.5in machine guns, but on the B-52H they were replaced by a single 20mm multi-barrel cannon with a 4000 round-per-minute rate of fire. Other means of defence include an extensive electronic countermeasures system, which includes radar warning receivers to detect hostile radar emissions, and jammers and chaff dispensers to deal with them. Flares can also be ejected to decoy infra-red homing missiles. An ingenious counter-measure employed by the B-52 force from 1960 until 1978 was the GAM-72 Quail decoy. Four of these miniature aircraft could be carried in the B-52's weapons bay in addition to the bombload. When launched the Quail followed a pre-programmed flight path at a speed and altitude similar to that of a B-52 and, as the Quail's radar beacons produced a signal similar to that of the parent aircraft, enemy radar operations would be unable to distinguish between decoys and real B-52 bombers.

One noteworthy feature of the B-52 design is its undercarriage. Because it would have been difficult to design main wheel undercarriage members to retract into the high-mounted wing, the main wheels are fuselage-mounted. They comprise four twin-wheel units, mounted in tandem pairs. This arrangement makes it necessary to fit additional outrigger wheels on the outer wing just inboard of the auxiliary fuel

Above: Despite the fact that the B-52 had originally been designed as a nuclear bomber the Vietnam War demonstrated that it was well suited to carrying out a conventional bombing role. Opposite above: The enormous wingspan of the B-52 can be appreciated as this example claws its way skyward. Opposite: A B-52 lands at a US airbase in Thailand after a bombing mission over South Vietnam.

tanks to prevent a wing tip being accidentally dug-in during taxying.

In order to carry out its demanding mission, the B-52 is packed with a mass of avionics equipment, ranging from radars for navigation, target acquisition and terrain avoidance to satellite communications sets. The defensive avionics have already been described; the offensive systems include the forward-looking attack and terrain avoidance radars, an inertial navigation set, attitude heading reference set, doppler velocity sensor, radio altimeter and weapons management computers. The offensive avionics systems enable the aircraft to navigate to its target and once there to deliver its warload accurately, while the defensive systems deal with the enemy air defences en route.

The initial B-52As were test aircraft and only three were built. So it was the B-52B which entered service with SAC, the first unit to receive this aircraft being the 93rd Bombardment Wing. This unit demonstrated the B-52's global range when three aircraft successfully completed a 39,150km (24,325 mile) around-the-world flight between 16 and 18 January 1957. Fifty B-52Bs were completed, including 27 RB-52B reconnaissance aircraft. The C model (35 built) had a greater all-up weight, while the B-52D (170 built) dispensed with the earlier aircrafts' reconnaissance capability. Improved bombing and navigation equipment needed for low-level penetration of enemy airspace was introduced on the B-52E (100 built), while the F model (89 built) had more powerful engines to boost take-off power. Major improvements incorporated into the B-52G (193 built) included a redesigned tail fin, integral wing fuel tanks and the relocation of the gunner in the forward crew

compartment. The ultimate B-52 variant, the H model (102 built) was powered by 7711kg (17,000lb) thrust Pratt & Whitney TF33 turbofans, which gave greater fuel economy than the earlier bombers' J57 turbojets. Although both G and H models had the same fuel capacity, unrefuelled radius of the H was 4510 nautical miles compared with the earlier aircraft's 3785 nautical mile radius.

One of the most significant milestones in the B-52's operational service was the change in tactics from high-level to low-level penetration of enemy airspace. The B-52 Stratofortress, as its name implied, was designed for high altitude operations where its large, high aspect ratio wing would encounter little turbulence. At low level it was a very different story and at heights of 100m (330ft) the big bomber could receive a severe buffeting. This unforeseen change in operating environment, necessitated by improvements in Soviet air defences in the late 1950s, led to airframe fatigue problems and required numerous modifications. For example, an EVS (electro-optical viewing system) – a TV and infra-red sensor – was fitted to help with low-level navigation and target damage assessment. Another change in operating procedures came when SAC switched from airborne alert to ground alert. One modification that this made necessary was the fitting of individual cartridge starters to each engine to speed start-ups prior to a scramble take-off.

The high point of the B-52's service career came with its involvement in the Vietnam War. Operating from Andersen AFB on Guam and U Tapao in Thailand, B-52s flew 126,615 Arc Light sorties during the 1960s against suspected enemy troop concentrations. Critics of the bombing effort claimed that all that had been achieved was to turn portions of Indochina into a lunar landscape; certainly, the military gains of this operation were minimal overall, for despite the enormous levels of destruction the object of cutting the Viet Cong supply lines was never achieved. However, it was the eleven-day Linebacker II campaign in December 1972 which gave the B-52s their greatest challenge. During this period B-52 squadrons – operating with improved navigation and bombing electronics – flew 729 sorties, often into the heavily defended Hanoi and Haiphong areas. Fifteen B-52s were shot down by North Vietnamese SA-2 SAMs, but to achieve these kills approximately 1000 missiles were fired (estimates vary from 884 to 1242) and by the end of the campaign North Vietnamese SA-2 stocks were exhausted. No USAF bombers were shot down by enemy interceptors, but two B-52 gunners were credited with shooting down a MiG-21 apiece.

At the end of the 1960s SAC controlled over 500 B-52s; by 1980 B-52 numbers stood at around 300 aircraft and with the phase-out of the B-52D in the early 1980s it was to be reduced to 200. However, the useful lives of the surviving B-52Gs and B-52Hs are likely to extend into the 21st century. This is because, when converted to cruise missile carriers, they will be able to attack Soviet targets at long stand-off ranges and so will be spared the rigours of a low-level mission. Until the Rockwell B-1B becomes operational, the B-52 will remain the mainstay of the USAF's strategic bombing force. After several decades of sterling service with the US Air Force the B-52 has proved itself to be one of the most devastating weapons in the arsenal of the Western powers.

Top: The radar-controlled 20mm multi-barrel cannon installed in the tail of the B-52H. Above: Pilot and co-pilot at the controls of a B-52. Above right: The left-hand turret of the ASQ EVS on a B-52H standing on the runway at Greenham Common in the UK.

B-52H Stratofortress

Type Long-range strategic bomber
Dimensions Span 56.39m (185ft); length 47.85m (157ft); height 12.4m (40ft 8in)
Weight Maximum take-off load 229,066kg (505,000lb)
Powerplant Eight 7711kg (17,000lb) Pratt & Whitney TF33-P-3 turbofans

Performance Maximum speed at 12,192m (40,000ft) 1014km/h (630mph); cruising speed 909km/h (565mph)
Range 16,000km (10,000 miles) maximum
Ceiling 16,760m (55,000ft)

Armament One 20mm T-171 multi-barrel cannon in the rear gun position; up to 47,630km (105,000lb) of ordnance including SRAM and ALCM missiles, and free-fall bombs (nuclear and conventional)

The age of the missile

Naval developments, 1955-70

Between the development of the world's first missile-armed cruiser in 1955 and the laying-down of the first Soviet aircraft carrier, the *Kiev*, in 1971, there was a revolution in naval technology. The missile, not only in its tactical defensive and offensive modes, but also as a submarine-launched strategic nuclear weapon, came to dominate naval thinking in place of the aircraft. There were few major actions during the period, the main ones being the Anglo-French descent on Suez in 1956 and the involvement of the US Navy in the Vietnam War, but there were several important minor incidents, such as the sinking of the Israeli destroyer *Eilat* by Soviet-made missiles in 1967 and the capture of the USS *Pueblo* by the North Koreans in 1968, while profound changes took place in the balance of world naval power, as the British and French fleets declined and the Soviet Navy began its great expansion under Gorshkov.

It was 1 November 1955 when the USS *Boston* was recommissioned after conversion to the world's first missile-armed cruiser. She had been completed in 1943 as a heavy cruiser (CA-69), armed with nine 8in guns, but during her $30 million reconstruction at Camden, New Jersey, the after triple gun turret was replaced by two twin launchers, two massive tracker radars and magazines containing 88 Terrier surface-to-air missiles. She and her sister *Canberra*, redesignated CAG-1 and CAG-2 respectively, were to provide the fleet with 'area defence' against Soviet bombers, while retaining a considerable surface gunnery capability.

Although the first-generation guided missiles were by no means perfect, they offered a reasonable chance of protecting carriers and large surface warships against air attack. They could defend a so-called 'middle layer' area around the fleet, leaving the 'outer layer' to carrier aircraft, which now had their own air-to-air guided missiles. This combination seemed to be the answer to the bomber threat that had dominated the thinking of the previous decade. Big carriers were now free to roam the oceans, and the US Navy was therefore able to reverse the 1949 verdict of

Above left: A US Navy Polaris ballistic missile is fired from the submerged submarine USS *George Washington*. The Polaris missile is almost 10m (31ft) long, weighs close to 16,000kg (35,000lb) and has a range of 4630km (2880 miles).

Congress that had cancelled the new carrier *United States*. In October 1955 the USS *Forrestal* was commissioned, the first of an eventual total of eight 'super carriers' each displacing over 60,000 tons. In August 1957 the first nuclear-powered aircraft carrier, the 76,000-ton USS *Enterprise* was ordered, further proof that the US Navy continued to believe in the power of the carrier task force, not only as an instrument for peacekeeping and political leverage, but also as a strategic weapon, using the carriers' twin-engined bombers to deliver nuclear weapons against the Soviet Union.

More guided-missile ships were also built, a series of large destroyers (some called destroyer leaders or frigates, designated DLGs) and more cruisers, three of the latter new nuclear-powered ships but the rest converted from World War II light and heavy cruisers. Although there was talk of converting battleships in similar fashion, nothing came of these plans for the cost proved too much. Other navies followed the American lead, notably the British, who ordered their first 'County' class DLGs in 1955, but everyone soon realised that the new reliance on sophisticated electronics was bound to push up the cost of warships.

The Russians, faced with the threat of nuclear attack from all four ocean areas, reacted by developing anti-ship missiles to give their ships some chance of knocking out the carriers before they could get within striking distance. In 1957 work started on converting four Kotlin-type destroyers into missile ships armed with a ramp aft for launching SS-N-1 Strela missiles. Although credited with a range of more than 100km (60 miles), it is unlikely that the Strela could have hit any target over the horizon, but when it first appeared at sea in these converted destroyers (which were code-named Kildin by Nato) it caused consternation in Western navies. The next class, the 3650-ton Krupny class, were armed with two Strela launchers, but in 1960 work started on four 4800-ton cruisers, designed from the keel up as

raketny kreiser or 'rocket cruisers'. This Kynda class had a much more potent armament of 16 SS-N-3 Shaddock missiles. Although great emphasis was placed on anti-ship missiles the Soviet Navy quickly realised that its surface warships needed to defend themselves against air attack, so that, for example, the Kynda class was fitted with SA-N-1 Goa anti-aircraft missiles.

The US Navy was also experimenting with long-range missiles, but intended to use them as strategic weapons to supplant the manned bomber. Several firings of the Regulus I and Regulus II missiles took place from carriers and cruisers, as well as submarines. The Regulus was an air-breathing missile which had to be launched from a surfaced submarine, but by 1958 progress on developing underwater launching had reached a point where the first nuclear ballistic missile submarines (SSBNs) could be ordered. The US government wanted to develop a strategic 'triad' of land-, air- and sea-launched strategic nuclear missiles as an insurance against a pre-emptive attack by the Soviet Union, and if part of the deterrent could be based underwater it might be virtually indestructible, at least for the foreseeable future. Despite formidable technical problems the A-1 Polaris missile came through its development and trials programmes in time for the commissioning of

Above: Massive sheets of flame belch from the muzzles of the USS *New Jersey*'s 16in guns as she fires a broadside. This battleship joined the US Sixth Fleet in the Mediterranean in 1983 to reinforce US troops in Lebanon.

Opposite above: HMS *Antrim*, a County-class destroyer which was part of the Task Force despatched to the Falklands in 1982. Her Seacat and Seaslug missile systems are augmented by a Westland Wessex helicopter located toward the rear of the ship.
Opposite below: HMS *Ocean* stands alongside a French hospital ship during the Suez crisis of 1956. The helicopters on board were some of the first ever used to deploy troops against a conventional enemy.

Naval strengths 1970-71

navy	ballistic-missile submarines	other submarines	attack aircraft carriers	other aircraft carriers	cruisers	destroyers, frigates and ocean-going escorts
USA	41	102	15	15	13	260
USSR	53	327	0	2 helicopter carriers	18	200
UK	3	25	3	2	1	62
France	1	19	2	2 helicopters carriers	2	44

Source: International Institute for Strategic Studies, London and Janes Fighting Ships

the first SSBN, the USS *George Washington* (SSBN-598), at the end of 1959.

Submarine building generally continued apace. The trials of the nuclear submarine USS *Nautilus* had proved so successful that five more of improved type were under construction by mid-1956, with many more planned. The British laid down their first nuclear submarine, HMS *Dreadnought,* early in 1959, using an American reactor to make up for delays in their own nuclear programme, and the first Soviet November class was started a year after that. Other Western navies hoped to follow the American lead, for there could be no doubt about the potential of nuclear submarines, but the cost proved so high that in many cases plans were shelved. Instead diesel-electric boats continued to be built, and it was soon discovered that for working close inshore they had certain advantages, being quieter and more manoeuvrable.

The new submarines naturally stimulated defence measures, and a number of modern anti-submarine escorts began to replace obsolete World War II tonnage in Western navies in the 1950s. Their main purpose was to defend shipping against attacks from the numerous Whiskey and Zulu class diesel-electric submarines built for the Soviet Navy at that period. The size of this programme, a total of more than 150 boats, caused great alarm in the West.

The lessons of Suez

In fact, however, the first naval actions of the period were conducted by the West in November 1956, when the British and French launched their ill-considered attack on Egypt to secure the Suez Canal. Far from being a success which was thwarted only by American interference (the popular misconception in the UK), the amphibious operation mounted by the British showed up a number of serious weaknesses in their capabilities. For one thing, the amphibious lift capability had been run down quite severely, so that the vital convoys carrying heavy material took a long time to set sail, and for another the Fleet Air Arm was still badly under strength. In spite of the difficulties, however, a series of brilliant improvisations showed what could be done. The US Marine Corps had been experimenting with 'vertical envelopment', using helicopters to ferry assault troops ashore, but the Royal Marines were given the chance to test the concept in action. Two hastily converted light fleet carriers were able to land 500 Marines in Port Said on 6 November, and in spite of the lack of experience and the unsuitable helicopters, casualties totalled only 11 killed and 52 wounded.

The recent advances in radar and weaponry had little effect on the Suez operation, for very little of the new equipment had become operational. Cruisers and destroyers carried out shore bombardments as they had in 1945, and although some British ships were attacked by aircraft (including some Israeli planes in error) the ships proved capable of defending themselves. Submarines had no effect, and apart from the Royal Marines' brilliant effort at Port Said, the amphibious operations were little different from World War II landings. As the Korean War had shown, carrier air power was vital to success, and it enabled powerful surface forces, including the French battleship *Jean Bart,* to operate off the Egyptian coast with impunity.

We cannot say with certainty what effect the Suez

operation had on Soviet naval plans, but clearly it reaffirmed the danger posed by Western naval air power, even close inshore. The Soviet Navy was already strong in coastal forces, with large numbers of motor torpedo boats in existence. Work was already in hand on anti-ship missiles and if Western intelligence sources are to be believed, work started in 1959 on the first of a new type of small warship, the missile boat. By 1961 the first of the Komar class was ready, a 75-ton diesel-engined craft armed with two SS-N-2 Styx missiles. The Komar was only an interim solution to the problem of coastal defence for it was a conversion of the existing P-6 motor torpedo boat hull. Shortly afterwards the first of an improved type, the 160-ton Osa class, appeared. These had four Styx missiles, and with a powerful defensive armament were clearly a tough opponent for anything but a major air strike.

The Styx threat

Western opinion tended to ignore the Komar and Osa classes, for neither the US Navy nor its allies was contemplating inshore operations against the Soviet land mass. However, they also chose to ignore the threat posed by the Styx missile to any forces lying close inshore supporting amphibious operations such as the Port Said landings. Work was proceeding in a desultory fashion on anti-ship missiles in all Western navies, but it was widely assumed that carrier aircraft could deal with small strike craft, when and if they were encountered. It should be remembered that the Komar and Osa boats were no better than their predecessors in operating outside coastal waters, and no Western carrier task force would encounter a squadron of Osa boats in mid-ocean.

Western complacency received a nasty jolt on 21 October 1967, when the Israeli destroyer *Eilat* was sunk off Port Said by three Styx missiles, fired from behind the breakwater by a pair of Komars. Immediately Western navies became obsessed by the 'Styx threat', ignoring the unusual circumstances under which the *Eilat* had been sunk. She had been patrolling far too close inshore, on a regular basis. In spite of her age (she was launched in 1943) and her lack of any modern anti-aircraft defence it took three Styx to sink her. Not for another seven years would anyone appreciate the limitations of the Styx guidance system, and for the moment all that Western navies could do was to push ahead with their own missiles and to investigate countermeasures as fast as they could. The French company Aérospatiale had a missile on the drawing board, and the Royal Navy soon made the crucial decision to buy it, launching the MM-38 Exocet on its remarkably successful career. The American McDonnell Douglas company also received funds for its Harpoon missile, while Israel speeded up work on the small Gabriel, and Norway went ahead with the Penguin.

None of these missiles was operational by the end of the 1970s, but their existence had begun to shape not only the pattern of naval warfare but the design of ships. The impact of electronics became even more crucial, with more internal volume dedicated to electronic equipment. Even a subsonic missile approaches its target within seconds of being detected and so information has to be handled by electronic means and the commander needs, above all, accurate processing of all the radar contacts. One immediate result of this increased emphasis on electronics was a reduction of weapons to make room for the computers and displays needed to control the battle.

It was no use merely firing defensive missiles to fend off an enemy missile attack, and attention had to be paid to 'electronic warfare' as a means of defending against missile attack. The British and Americans were quickly off the mark with 'chaff dispensing' systems. These were simply rockets packed with what the RAF had termed 'Window' in World War II, strips of metallic material which created a false radar echo to fool the radar seeker in the nose of the missile.

The Pueblo Incident

On 23 January 1968 the US Navy's 'spy ship' *Pueblo* was boarded and captured off the coast of North Korea by North Korean patrol boats. She had been carrying out electronic surveillance from outside territorial waters, in a manner which both Soviet and Western ships had sanctified by usage for many years.

The '*Pueblo* Incident' as it was soon called, came at a bad moment for the Americans, who felt that it constituted a blatant attempt to distract them from the Vietnam War and to tie down South Korean and US forces. To this day nobody has been able to understand the North Korean government's motives.

The resulting stalemate had particularly harsh consequences for the prisoners taken aboard the *Pueblo*. They were held captive in barbarous conditions while the North Koreans demanded an apology. After 11 months of wrangling the US government was forced to accept the conditions, as the only way for the prisoners to be released.

The incident underlined the apparent ease with which a minor nation can humiliate a superpower if the conditions are right.

Below: The USS *Pueblo*, the intelligence-gathering ship captured by the North Koreans in 1968. Left: A crewman of the *Pueblo* shortly after his release from captivity.

By that date, the US Navy was deeply involved in the Vietnam War. The navy's role was in many ways a repetition of the Korean War experience, a weary round of gunfire support missions and air strikes. But as the United States became more deeply embroiled in the land war and troops were committed in large numbers, close air support was required. Although the North Vietnamese Air Force was unable to score any successes against the American ships lying offshore the occasional attacks gave the air defence organisation the chance to test its techniques. Most of the attacks were beaten off by the carriers' combat air patrols, but two cruisers were credited with the destruction of MiG-21s at extremely long range. This was the first occasion on which shipborne surface-to-air missiles were fired in anger.

Like the US Air Force, the Navy and Marine aircrew found that surface-to-air missiles made deep-penetration raids ever more costly. The experience taught the US Navy important lessons about electronic countermeasures and evasive manoeuvring to shake off missile attacks, invaluable knowledge which a decade later would give the Israelis a decisive advantage against the latest Soviet technology in air combat with the Syrians.

As the 1960s drew to a close there was increasing evidence that the aircraft carrier no longer enjoyed unchallenged superiority. The United States could now boast that it had 41 ballistic missile submarines and the Soviet Union had matched them with their first Yankee class boats. The seaborne deterrent was now firmly established underwater rather than in the weapons carried by carrier-borne aircraft, while the new generation of missiles was again posing a threat to the capital ship.

The most basic change of the period, however, lay in the changing balance of world naval power rather than in the changing technological mix. By 1970 the Soviet Navy was unrecognisable from the force of the mid 1950s, while the French and British fleets that had carried out the Suez landings had slipped far behind those of the two superpowers.

The French continued to maintain a balanced fleet, with the full panoply of sea power from nuclear ballistic missile submarines to aircraft carriers and amphibious forces but the Royal Navy found the price unacceptably high. In 1966 it was decided that the long-overdue replacements for the 50,000-ton aircraft carriers *Eagle* and *Ark Royal* would not be built, and the Fleet Air Arm would hand all fixed-wing aircraft over to the RAF. It was a bitter blow to the Royal Navy, for it had pinned its faith on the carrier not just as a strike weapon but as the vital shield for the rest of the fleet. By 1970, however, the navy that had ruled the seas a century before was in painful decline.

Antony Preston

The first US multi-platform anti-ship missile, the Harpoon (below being launched) can be fired from ships, aircraft or submarines and provides the attacking craft with an ability to hit a target beyond the horizon (inset below, a target ship after a direct hit by a Harpoon missile). Despite early Western complacency over the development of anti-ship missiles, the sinking of the *Eilat* in 1967 by three Soviet-made Styx missiles spurred development of the anti-ship missile which led to the production of Harpoon.

The bear gets webbed feet

Soviet naval expansion under Admiral Gorshkov

The Soviet Union emerged from World War II with a huge land army but practically no navy. During the war the Soviet Navy had played a relatively minor, supporting role in the confrontation with Nazi Germany and in doing so had lost nearly half the ships in its pre-war inventory. Even before the war the navy had been allotted a secondary role in Soviet strategy, and a building programme belatedly aimed at creating a 'blue-water' (deep sea) fleet was interrupted by the German invasion. By the time the war was over the destruction of the principal Soviet naval bases and shipbuilding yards and the catastrophic state of the Soviet economy in the immediate postwar years, made the speedy revival of Soviet naval power impossible. In 1946 the independent Commissariat of the Navy was integrated into the Commissariat of Defence, and the Commissar, Admiral N. Kuznetsov, was dismissed. Nevertheless Stalin decreed that Russia was once again to have a large, conventional surface fleet that would be 'still stronger and more powerful'.

At that stage Stalin and his naval strategists were thinking primarily in terms of defence. Stalin was deeply impressed by what the Americans had achieved in their amphibious assaults in Europe and the Pacific, and he feared that similar actions might be launched against the Soviet Union. The Soviet plan for defence against any such seaborne invasion involved three lines of defence: an arc of submarines guided by long-range reconnaissance aircraft; extensive minefields in the approaches to possible invasion sites; and a mobile force of cruisers, destroyers and torpedo boats covered by land-based aircraft. The Soviet Army was expected to be able to deal with any enemy forces that might survive the seaborne defences. The plan involved the construction of 1200 submarines, 35 cruisers and 175 destroyers over a period of 20 years.

While the Russians were concentrating on the creation of an 'anti-amphibious' force, the Americans and British were busy retiring or mothballing their amphibious craft. The US Navy's capability in this field was reduced from 1256 ocean-going ships in 1945 to just 91 in 1950. Anxious nevertheless to retain a strategic role comparable to the US Air Force's bomber programme, the US Navy began to experi-

Above: Gunnery teams aboard the Soviet cruiser *Mikhail Kutuzov* practise anti-aircraft drill on naval exercises in 1967. Until the late 1960s all Soviet naval exercises had been held within their territorial waters but in 1968 the Soviet Navy held its first manoeuvres outside home waters, reflecting its growing confidence and a new interest in global maritime affairs.

The Soviet Navy 1955/1970

date	strategic submarines equipped with medium- or long-range ballistic missiles	post WWII patrol submarines displacing 700 tonnes or more	coastal submarines displacing less than 700 tonnes	major surface warships – missile armed	major surface warships – conventionally armed	patrol boats, torpedo boats and gunboats – missile armed	patrol boats, torpedo boats and gunboats – conventionally armed
1955	0	215 conventional	269	0	256	0	516
1970	24 nuclear 25 conventional	58 nuclear 283 conventional	22	39	206	150	600

ment with nuclear-equipped aircraft aboard its carriers. This faced the Russians with a new and much more serious threat: nuclear-armed jet attack-aircraft operating from mobile carrier strike groups in the Pacific, the Mediterranean and the North Sea. It was a threat which the Soviet 'anti-amphibious' force could not deal with.

Soviet strategic planners were clearly confused about the problems of the postwar, nuclear world, and they were in any case subject to Stalin's overriding decisions. In 1951 he again separated the Navy Commissariat from Defence, reappointed Kuznetsov and ordered the big-ship building programme to go ahead. But in 1953 Stalin died, and almost immediately his successors countermanded the Stalin plan and brought the building programme practically to a halt for two or three years. In 1956 Kuznetsov was again dismissed and replaced by Admiral Sergei Gorshkov, who was given the task of devising a naval strategy to meet the demands of the new situation. Gorshkov's appointment marked the end of a purely defensive phase in the postwar history of the Soviet Navy.

Gorshkov's promotion to commander-in-chief – at the age of 46 – was a turning point in the history of the Soviet Navy. Nikita Khrushchev, who then dominated the Soviet scene, was obsessed by the potential of nuclear missiles. For him the navy's principal function was to serve as a mobile missile-launching pad,

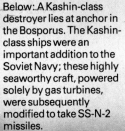

Below: A Kashin-class destroyer lies at anchor in the Bosporus. The Kashin-class ships were an important addition to the Soviet Navy; these highly seaworthy craft, powered solely by gas turbines, were subsequently modified to take SS-N-2 missiles.

which meant, in practice, building a huge submarine fleet. Khrushchev let it be known that he considered the surface fleet was good only for 'taking the admirals around' and might as well be scrapped. Gorshkov went along with Khrushchev's plans for expanding the submarine fleet and for arming the navy with guided missiles but quietly scotched plans for dismantling Russia's surface fleet. He managed to save six cruisers from the scrap-yard and to have ten new ones laid down.

An 'anti-carrier' policy

Gorshkov's immediate task was to devise an effective 'anti-carrier' policy. The Soviet naval staff formulated a 'three wave' approach to the problem. In the primary stage, the carrier strike force was to be located and monitored by long-range reconnaissance aircraft, supplemented by a bomber force equipped with air-to-surface missiles capable of attacking the carriers (from 1958 the bombers were to be augmented by nuclear submarines armed with torpedoes). The second line of defence was to consist of conventional submarines armed with missiles, while the third would consist of cruisers and destroyers equipped with missiles launched out of range of American attack aircraft. The principal weakness of this strategy was the Soviet Navy's lack of overseas bases for its aircraft and ships.

The new role allotted to the Soviet Navy necessi-

tated a rapid programme of shipbuilding and conversion which took place from 1956 to 1961. Four partially-completed Kotlin class destroyers were converted for their new task by mounting missile launchers in place of their aft gun turrets and fitting 57mm anti-aircraft guns amidships. Ten Krupny class destroyers were fitted with SS-N-1 and SS-N-2 missiles, and a Sverdlov class cruiser had SS-N-1s mounted on her quarterdeck. Submarines, with which the navy was well supplied, were armed with SS-N-3 missiles.

In the second phase of the 'anti-carrier' programme, which lasted until 1965, came the construction of cruisers of the Kynda and Kresta classes, armed with surface-to-surface missiles, and of Kashin class destroyers equipped with surface-to-air missiles. At the same time, the Juliett conventionally powered submarine, armed with the SS-N-3 missile, was put into large-scale production. These additions to the navy, plus the adaptation of Bear and Badger bomber aircraft, gave the anti-carrier strike force a range of 3000 nautical miles.

In the final phase of their anti-carrier programme the Soviet strategists found themselves faced with a new problem in the shape of the United States nuclear-powered carrier, the USS *Enterprise*, which had greater range and mobility. To deal with this problem the Russians decided to equip the hulls of the Juliett submarines with nuclear reactors from the Hotel class submarines. This produced the Echo class submarine which had sufficient speed and range to shadow the carrier strike groups and the missiles to hit the carriers.

The submarine threat

At this point, in 1960, when the Russians believed that their efforts to overcome the carrier threat had been successful, they learnt that the first American nuclear-powered submarine equipped with ballistic missiles, the USS *George Washington*, had begun to patrol the Soviet coastline. By August 1961 there were five of these Polaris-armed submarines in service, capable of maintaining continuous patrols in the Arctic Ocean from their new base in Holy Loch, Scotland. With the addition of another base at Rota, in Spain, the Polaris was able to move into the eastern Mediterranean. Most of European Russia was now within range of Polaris.

The Soviet naval staff was caught unawares by the speed with which the Americans had developed their nuclear-powered submarines. Their first reaction was

to adapt surface ships to act as 'submarine hunters' with the addition of helicopters and various anti-submarine and anti-aircraft devices. But this policy was abandoned when the Americans developed the Polaris A-2 and A-3 missiles with ranges of 1600 and 2400 nautical miles, thus enabling them to operate far beyond the reach of the Soviet hunters. The Soviet naval chiefs were then forced to adopt a rather desperate tactic: their cruisers and submarines would shadow the American carrier force and, if a major conflict broke out, they would strike the carriers before they could launch their aircraft, even though this would also mean the loss of the shadowing cruiser. In an effort to reduce the threat of the Polaris SSBN force, development of the Hotel class was pushed ahead by Soviet naval chiefs and it was not until 1964 that the first one came into operation. The problem was not solved however, as these submarines still needed to surface in order to launch their missiles and were thus vulnerable.

Gorshkov was not content, however, with a purely defensive role for the Soviet Navy. Apart from the major role it would have to play in the event of nuclear conflict – providing the mobile submarine launching pads for strategic missiles – he saw the navy playing

Above: Soviet warships on a friendly visit to Cuba in 1969. Such visits were part of the new Soviet naval policy that the Soviet Navy should make its presence felt around the world.

Below: A Foxtrot-class submarine patrols open waters alongside a Kashin-class destroyer. In all, some 60 Foxtrot-class submarines have been built since they first appeared in 1958. Below right: A Riga-class frigate. These ships are of fairly conventional design and are armed and equipped to carry out anti-submarine warfare duties.

an equally important role in peacetime in support of the Soviet government's worldwide ambitions. This meant the construction of a large 'blue-water' surface fleet involving the use of huge funds and resources which the Soviet political leaders were loath to allot.

It was the Cuban crisis of 1962 that turned the tide of opinion in the Kremlin in Gorshkov's favour. The US Navy's blockade which forced Khrushchev to abandon his attempt to install missiles in Cuba also convinced the Soviet leaders that however powerful their nuclear armoury might be, it would be ineffective without overall command of the seas. Henceforth the Soviet Navy was to make its presence felt in the oceans of the world, and Gorshkov made no secret of the fact that, from being a purely defensive force, the navy had become 'an instrument of state policy'. He boasted of his country's achievement in building 'an ocean fleet fully capable of defending our country in this atomic century' and of converting it into 'a real force capable of ensuring the State interests of the Soviet Union in the world ocean'.

The first evidence of this new policy came in 1964, with the stationing of a small Soviet naval squadron in the Mediterranean, capable of monitoring the activities of the American carrier and submarine forces. Between 1964 and 1967 the number of Soviet warships passing through the Dardanelles increased from 91 to 250.

Cruising further afield

The next stage in the forward deployment of the Soviet Navy took place in the Indian Ocean, where Soviet vessels began making regular goodwill visits to the ports of the surrounding countries, notably India, Pakistan, Iraq, Yemen, Ethiopia, Somalia and Ceylon. In 1969 the Russians made their presence felt even further afield. Two missile-armed destroyers made six-month runs to ports along the Atlantic coast of Africa, and small groups of missile-armed cruisers, destroyers, submarines and support ships began showing the Soviet flag in the Caribbean, making especially long visits to Cuba.

These mainly 'diplomatic' operations were accompanied by a more serious development in the shape of naval manoeuvres. Until the late 1960s, each of the Soviet fleets (Black Sea, Baltic, Pacific and Northern) had conducted all its manoeuvres separately, in Soviet waters and behind a strict security screen. In 1968, however, the Soviet Navy held its first manoeuvres outside home waters, and in 1970 Admiral

Admiral Gorshkov

Admiral of the Fleet Sergei Georgievich Gorshkov, who became commander-in-chief of the Soviet Navy in 1956, is the acknowledged architect of the new Soviet Navy, and has devoted the whole of his life to the navy and to Russia's recovery of sea power. The navy and naval power are his overriding passion.

Gorshkov was born in 1910 in the Ukrainian town of Kamenets-Podolsk, the son of a Russian schoolteacher. At the age of 17 he entered the exclusive Naval Academy in Leningrad, where he excelled at his studies and did not even find it necessary to join the Communist Party, which is the usual path of advancement in the Soviet Union.

After graduation he served first in the Black Sea Fleet and then in the newly-formed Pacific Fleet. Stalin's purges of the 1930s, which marked the end of many a military and naval career, served only to clear the way for Gorshkov's promotion, so that when Hitler attacked Russia in 1941 Gorshkov was already a rear-admiral with the Black Sea Fleet, where he remained for the duration of the 1941-45 war. In 1942, in the middle of the war, he finally joined the Communist Party.

In 1951 Gorshkov took command of the Black Sea Fleet and in August 1956 became First Deputy to Admiral Kuznetsov, at that time commander-in-chief of the navy. Six months later Khrushchev got rid of Kuznetsov, who had ideas about a more independent role for the navy, and put Gorshkov in his place. At the time Gorshkov kept his own views to himself. When Khrushchev was removed from power in 1964 Gorshkov was not disturbed and remained in command of the navy, apparently trusted and respected by the navy and the politicians alike. He became a deputy defence minister, a member of the Central Committee of the Communist Party, a deputy to the Supreme Soviet and a Hero of the Soviet Union. In October 1967 he was promoted to the rank of 'Admiral of the Fleet of the Soviet Union' – the first person ever to hold this new rank.

Gorshkov has been described as primarily a 'naval politician'. He has never had the chance to command his fleets in action, and is not, as far as is known, a great administrator. His major achievement lay in bringing the men in the Kremlin round to his point of view: in formulating the theories and arguments that persuaded them of the need for sea power in the nuclear age and then in obtaining the enormous funds necessary for the building programme. But he had in exchange to surrender to the General Staff a good deal of the navy's autonomy.

Gorshkov's writings on naval theory and practice have been very influential. His major work is *The Sea Power of the State* (1976).

Left: The Soviet Navy tends to mount heavy armament on its warships. Seen here on the *Moskva* is one of the two twin SA-N-3 mounts, while above it are the two 'headlight' radars used to control the surface-to-air missiles. Below: A Kresta II-class cruiser with its resident helicopter airborne. A feature of the Kresta II is the amount of electronics and armament crammed into its small hull. Bottom: Easing carefully under a bridge, the Soviet intelligence ship *Kosmonaut Yuri Gagarin* heads for the Mediterranean.

Gorshkov went out of his way to demonstrate to the world the extent of Soviet naval power. Ships from the various Soviet naval fleets joined together in Exercise Okean, displaying a highly sophisticated command network on a global scale. The Soviet Navy had arrived on the world scene.

The rapid expansion of the Soviet fleet had been a remarkable achievement, enabling Gorshkov to declare: 'The flag of the Soviet Navy now flies over the oceans of the world. Sooner or later the United States will realise that they are no longer masters of the seas.' A German naval authority, Professor Eckehardt Opitz, paid tribute to the Russian achievement in these words: 'The Soviet Navy has been converted in the shortest time from being a defensive coastal maritime force to being an offensive sea-power adapted to the oceans of the world.' Admiral Davis, Commander of the US Pacific Fleet, put it more succinctly: 'The Russian bear has gotten webbed feet.'

The new flag-showing role of the Soviet fleet certainly did something for Soviet prestige in the Third World. But Gorshkov knew very well that his forces could not survive far from land-based air cover in the event of a conflict with the US Navy and its carrier strike forces. Consequently, after having once declared that 'the sun has set' on the aircraft carrier, in 1968 Gorshkov performed a remarkable U-turn and announced that the carrier still had an important part to play in modern naval warfare. He changed his mind, apparently, because of the development of vastly more efficient means of defending large capital ships and of recognition of the part they could play as

bases for anti-submarine aircraft. So Gorshkov persuaded the Soviet leaders that, if the Soviet Navy was going to compete with the US Navy, it must have aircraft carriers.

The first Kiev class carrier was laid down in 1971 and became operational in 1976, providing the navy with a modest intervention ability and the means of displaying Soviet aircraft in flight far from Soviet territory. Bigger and more powerful carriers were to follow, as well as new escort vessels – the Kirov class nuclear-powered cruiser – and amphibious vessels – the Ivan Rogov class. This combination indicated that Soviet plans were not limited merely to showing the flag to client nations around the world. In Gorshkov's words: 'The growing sea-power of the Soviet Union guarantees the successful realisation of its foreign policy.' Far from scorning what used to be called 'gun-boat diplomacy', he claimed: 'By showing the fleet it has been possible on many occasions to achieve political objectives without having to resort to armed warfare.'

A strategic role

By the early 1970s Soviet naval vessels were operating in every ocean of the world, and Gorshkov had converted what had been after World War II a purely defensive force, subordinated completely to the Soviet Army, into a powerful navy with an important role to play both in peacetime and in war. Gorshkov recognised that in a major war the Soviet Navy would no longer play the traditional role of a navy, fighting battles with fleets of enemy warships, but would be part of the strategic attack on the enemy's mainland and would therefore be subordinate to the overall command of the Ministry of Defence. In his major work, *The Sea Power of the State*, published in 1976 and now obligatory reading for naval officers in the West, Gorshkov described the modern navy he had built in the following terms: 'The main components of our navy today are submarines and naval aircraft, while our principal weapons are ballistic and cruise missiles with nuclear warheads.' Gorshkov thus gained for the Soviet Navy a major role in modern warfare and also gave it an important peacetime role. His achievement is to have effected the most far-reaching alteration in the balance of naval power since World War II.   **David Floyd**

Showing the flag

In the troubled years after 1945 the US Navy found it necessary to reinforce the small squadron of ships in the Mediterranean, known as Naval Forces Mediterranean. So diminutive was the squadron at the time that Vice-Admiral Bieri USN flew his flag from a destroyer tender berthed in Naples. The first major warship sent as a reinforcement, the light cruiser USS *Dayton*, became the flagship in August 1947. The following year the force changed its name to Sixth Task Fleet, and the present name US Sixth Fleet was bestowed in 1950.

As so many of the post-1955 naval incidents have been centred on the Mediterranean, the US Sixth Fleet has often been called into action. Its first major operation came in October 1956 when its various units stood by to evacuate US nationals from Egypt during the Anglo-French invasion of Suez. As the US government was not supporting either the British or the French there was some initial friction when Sixth Fleet units interposed themselves between the Anglo-French task force and their objective, but no serious incidents occurred.

More direct action took place in July 1958 when the Lebanese government appealed for help. A force of Marines landed unopposed to help support the Chamoun regime, and then withdrew without seeing any action. In 1967 the fleet went to full alert when Israeli aircraft attacked the electronic surveillance ship USS *Liberty*, but as in the Jordanian Crisis of 1970 and the Arab-Israeli Yom Kippur War of 1973 the fleet's presence was purely to discourage Soviet intervention.

Following the Yom Kippur War the Sixth Fleet took part in a multi-national (including Russian) effort to clear sunken ships and mines which were thought to have been laid along the Suez Canal.

Evacuations of refugees and foreign nationals have also formed a large part of the fleet's activities. In July 1974 and in June-July 1976 personnel were evacuated from Cyprus and the Lebanon respectively. In June 1982 the hostilities in Lebanon required immediate naval evacuation for foreign nationals.

In August 1981 the Sixth Fleet faced its most serious challenge to date. Colonel Muammar Gaddafi, the ruler of Libya, declared the Gulf of Sirte in the central Mediterranean to be Libyan territorial waters, a unilateral decision which would deny free movement not only to the US Navy's ships but to those of all nations. President Reagan and his Defense Secretary Caspar Weinberger declared their intention of keeping the disputed waters open and the giant nuclear-powered carrier USS *Nimitz* was ordered to pass through the Gulf of Sirte, adhering to the internationally recognised open sea. After some shadow-boxing, the Libyans inexplicably chose to order two Sukhoi-22 (Nato code-name Fitter) ground support aircraft to fire their air-to-air missiles at the F-14 Tomcat fighters of the carrier's Combat Air Patrol. It was militarily suicidal to match these slow and elderly Russian aircraft against the world's finest carrier-borne interceptors, and when the Libyan ground controller ordered his pilots to open fire outside the range of their own missiles, the result was predictably the destruction of the two Su-22s. Fortunately no

Above: Photographed from a launch, the USS *Forrestal* lies at anchor. The *Forrestal* was the first US carrier to be fitted with steam catapults and to be built with an angled flight deck which was set at eight degrees to the norm.

Composition of the US Sixth Fleet

The strength of the US Sixth Fleet which operates in the Mediterranean, has been continually reviewed and increased since the late 1940s. In the 1980s, the Commander of the Sixth Fleet has normally had the following formations under his command:

Carrier Striking Force	CTF-60
Amphibious Force	CTF-61
Landing Force	CTF-62
Service Force	CTF-63
Ballistic Missile Submarine Force	CTF-64
Special Contingency Force	CTF-65
Area Anti-Submarine Force	CTF-66
Maritime Surveillance and Reconnaissance Force	CTF-67
Special Operations Force	CTF-68
Submarine Force	CTF-69

The ballistic missile submarines are based on Maddalena in Sicily, with CTF-69 and Submarine Group 8. The Landing Force (CTF-62) is a reinforced Marine battalion embarked in CTF-61. The Sixth Fleet is commanded by a vice-admiral while the Carrier Striking Force is under a rear-admiral.

Below: CTF-60 in formation.

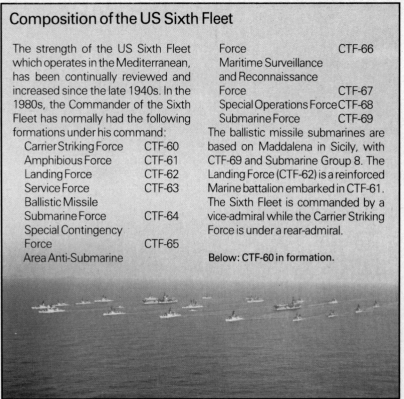

The US Sixth Fleet in the Mediterranean

further action was taken against the USS *Nimitz* and, as a result of her presence, the Gulf of Sirte is still open to international shipping.

Since June 1982 the Sixth Fleet has become steadily more embroiled in the Lebanon crisis, and the landing of US Marines as part of the multi-national peacekeeping force marked a new development in America's policy towards the Middle East. By September 1983, US destroyers offshore were firing their 5in guns against Druze artillery positions in an effort to suppress enemy artillery attacks against the Marines' ground positions on the mainland. At one stage it looked as if Beirut might

feel the full weight of 16in gunfire, when the newly refitted battleship USS *New Jersey* was ordered to reinforce the Sixth Fleet. Her arrival, however, coincided with a ceasefire agreement between the Christian and Druze militia-men.

Despite the non-aggressive nature of some of its Mediterranean activities, the US Sixth Fleet is first and foremost a military unit prepared to adopt an aggressive role at any time. The normal composition of the fleet is that of a carrier task force, with an additional amphibious force made up of US Marines and their specialised craft. The carrier, either a nuclear-powered unit such as the USS *Enterprise* or USS *Nimitz*, or oil-fired such

Below: A vital element of any naval task force is the troops it carries. The versatility of the Sixth Fleet is illustrated by the fact that these US Marines coming ashore in Lebanon in 1982 could rely upon the guns of the force's warships to cover the amphibious landing and subsequently to suppress enemy attacks.

as the USS *America*, is protected by missile-firing cruisers and destroyers. The firepower of the 90-odd aircraft of the carrier's Air Group is sufficient to wipe out the Soviet ships in the Mediterranean, but in addition there are the anti-ship missiles and guns of the carrier's escorts, and from time to time attack submarines may operate in support.

In an enclosed sea area such as the Mediterranean, there is always the fear of a large-scale enemy air strike, which accounts for the number of air-defence ships allocated to the fleet. The other possibility is a pre-emptive strike, and to guard against being taken by surprise the Sixth Fleet rarely cruises in a single large formation. It never visits any port as a major formation; apart from the impossibility of accomodating such a vast assemblage of ships in one harbour, dispersing small detachments for overhaul or leave reduces the risk of a pre-emptive strike.

Commanding the fleet

On average the fleet numbers 30 ships and up to 100 aircraft. The personnel totals roughly 20,000 men and women. When it operates under the direction of Nato (in wartime) its main role is the defence of southern Europe. Should war break out the Sixth Fleet commander would become Commander, Naval Striking and Support Forces; he would report to the Commander-in-Chief, Allied Forces, Southern Europe (CINCSOUTH), who is based at Naples. During peacetime the fleet is part of the US chain of command, and comes under the Commander-in-Chief, US Naval Forces, Europe (CINCUSEUR) in London.

The last of the cruiser flagships was withdrawn in the late 1970s, and since 1980 the flag has been flown once more in a destroyer tender, the USS *Puget Sound*, which is based at Gaeta in Italy.

Apart from the battleship USS *New Jersey*, already mentioned, the largest guns in the Sixth Fleet are 5in guns, but the main surface striking power lies in the enormous weight of ordnance which the Carrier Air Groups can deliver. Against surface targets there are also Harpoon anti-ship missiles capable of hitting vessels at a range of up to 97km (60 miles). These are scheduled for future support from Tomahawk cruise missiles, capable of hitting targets nearly 483km (300 miles) away. The Tomahawks will be fired from the

torpedo tubes of submarines as well as from surface ships. The carriers' aircraft are all capable of delivering nuclear weapons, but strategic bombers no longer form a part of the force. The nuclear capability extends from tactical bombs down to depth-charges but in any conflict short of all-out war conventional weapons would be used.

Travelling around the Mediterranean today the observer is likely to see units of the Sixth Fleet almost anywhere. The enormous natural harbour at Villefranche, near Cannes, has long been a favourite for ships giving leave, but individual ships put into such places as Port Mahon in Minorca to take on fresh water. As the primary purpose of the Sixth Fleet in peacetime is to stabilise the area, great stress is laid on that oldest of naval activities, 'showing the flag', and ships are detailed to visit as widely as possible. Although in theory the home port of the Sixth Fleet is Norfolk, Virginia, repair facilities are provided in friendly harbours. The main repair base is at Naples but in an emergency the repair facilities of allied navies are available.

Today there is a danger that the Sixth Fleet has become an institution, but we would be foolish to underestimate its striking power, as Nikita Khrushchev did when he threatened to turn its ships into steel coffins. The history of the past few years shows how volatile the Mediterranean area still is, and nowhere in the world does the United States have such powerful forces close to the likely scene of conflict. It is this closeness which has made the Sixth Fleet so effective in crisis management. **Antony Preston**

Above: The world's most powerful carrier-borne interceptor is the F-14 Tomcat, photographed here on the deck of the USS *Nimitz*. One of the Tomcat's outstanding features is its Phoenix air-to-air missile which when used in conjunction with the AWG-9 radar can select and destroy a chosen aircraft from a formation at a distance of 160km (100 miles).

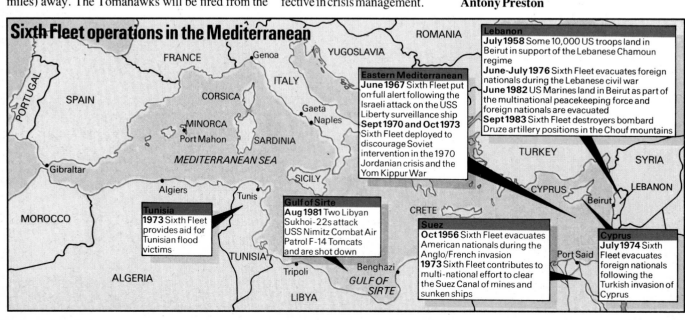

Sixth Fleet operations in the Mediterranean

PORTUGAL — SPAIN — Gibraltar — FRANCE — Genoa — CORSICA — ITALY — MINORCA — Port Mahon — SARDINIA — Gaeta — Naples — *MEDITERRANEAN SEA* — SICILY — ROMANIA — YUGOSLAVIA — Algiers — MOROCCO — ALGERIA — Tunis — TUNISIA — Tripoli — *GULF OF SIRTE* — Benghazi — LIBYA — CRETE — TURKEY — CYPRUS — Beirut — SYRIA — LEBANON — Port Said

Tunisia
1973 Sixth Fleet provides aid for Tunisian flood victims

Gulf of Sirte
Aug 1981 Two Libyan Sukhoi-22s attack USS Nimitz Combat Air Patrol F-14 Tomcats and are shot down

Eastern Mediterranean
June 1967 Sixth Fleet put on full alert following the Israeli attack on the USS Liberty surveillance ship
Sept 1970 and Oct 1973 Sixth Fleet deployed to discourage Soviet intervention in the 1970 Jordanian crisis and the Yom Kippur War

Suez
Oct 1956 Sixth Fleet evacuates American nationals during the Anglo/French invasion
1973 Sixth Fleet contributes to multi-national effort to clear the Suez Canal of mines and sunken ships

Lebanon
July 1958 Some 10,000 US troops land in Beirut in support of the Lebanese Chamoun regime
June-July 1976 Sixth Fleet evacuates foreign nationals during the Lebanese civil war
June 1982 US Marines land in Beirut as part of the multinational peacekeeping force and foreign nationals are evacuated
Sept 1983 Sixth Fleet destroyers bombard Druze artillery positions in the Chouf mountains

Cyprus
July 1974 Sixth Fleet evacuates foreign nationals following the Turkish invasion of Cyprus

Key Weapons

NATO GPMGs

During World War I heavy and medium machine guns dominated the battlefield, but in the inter-war years military thinkers gradually came to realise that the employment of such weapons in 1914-18 was applicable only to trench warfare, and that mobile warfare required a different approach. Most countries therefore adopted two machine guns; a medium gun, belt-fed and usually water-cooled, for the prolonged supporting fire demanded in set-piece battles, and a light, magazine-fed gun capable of being carried by one man, used with the rifle section in the fluid battle.

The German Army, however, looked at the problem from a different angle: its theorists disliked the manpower drain demanded by medium machine guns which were used only occasionally, and they had no intention of allowing infantry to get bogged down in positional warfare if it could be avoided. They therefore reached the conclusion that one properly designed machine gun could fill both roles. Equipped with a bipod and iron sights it could function as the squad automatic or light machine gun, or, mounted on a tripod and with an optical sight, it could act as the sustained-fire support machine gun. In both roles it would be belt fed, and it would have a removable barrel so that when the barrel got hot (as it would, not being water-cooled) then it could be quickly changed for a new one. The result of this thinking was the MG34 and subsequently the improved MG42. The military record of these weapons made such a favourable impression during World War II that soon after the end of hostilities allied designers were examining the guns and tacticians were discussing their role in modern warfare.

As a result of these deliberations four GPMGs (general purpose machine guns) came into service

with Nato: the French M1952 (AAT Mle52); the German MG3; the Belgian FN MAG; and the American M60. In spite of talk of standardisation there was never any chance that all Nato would adopt the same weapon, and in fact the French even managed to avoid adopting the 7.62mm Nato standard cartridge for many years.

The French M1952 first appeared in 7.5mm calibre, this having been the standard French military round since 1929; in recent years, though, manufacture in 7.62mm has taken place and many of the earlier guns have been converted to the Nato cartridge. The M1952 is unusual in being a delayed blowback weapon; the bolt is not rigidly locked to the barrel during firing. In order to provide some safety, the bolt is a two-part unit with the front part carrying a lever which engages in a recess in the body of the gun. On firing, the cartridge case attempts to blow itself out of the chamber, forcing the bolt head backwards. This puts pressure on the lever, and in order for the bolt head to move the lever must rotate and disengage from its recess, which it does at a considerable mechanical disadvantage, so slowing the opening of the bolt. As soon as the lever is disengaged, both parts of the bolt (the rear section is comparatively heavy and slow moving) are blown backwards against a return spring.

Another drawback with the M1952 is that although a hot barrel can be quickly changed for a cool one, the bipod is attached to the barrel, so that once the barrel is removed the gunner has to hold the hot gun off the ground until the new barrel and bipod are fitted.

For sustained fire the M1952 can be mounted on a tripod. For the light machine gun role it is fired from the shoulder using the bipod; there is also a small monopod attached beneath the shoulder stock which

Previous page: US troops try out the M60 GPMG during firing trials at an army range in California. Above and above left: The forerunner of the GPMG was the World War II German MG34 which could either be used as a light support weapon, with a bipod, or in a sustained fire role on a tripod. Top: In 1942 the complex MG34 was replaced by the simpler MG42 which was later to become the basis for the West German Army's own MG3.

M1952 (AAT Mle 52)

Calibre 7.5mm/7.62mm
Length (stock extended) 116.6cm (45.9in)
Weight 15kg (33lb)
Operation Blowback
Feed system Belt
Rate of fire 700rpm (900rpm with 7.62mm ammunition)
Muzzle velocity 820mps (2690fps)

can be lowered to give a solid support and which can be adjusted for height so as to control the elevation of the gun. There is a micrometer scale on the monopod so that settings can be recorded and repeated so, for example, a target can be engaged by day, the setting recorded, and the gun set up at night to fire on the same target without the firer actually seeing it.

The German MG3 is the wartime MG42 with some minor variations, the most significant being the change from 7.92m to 7.62mm Nato calibre. The Germans subjected a variety of machine guns to a series of severe tests and found nothing that they liked so much as the MG42; but by the late 1950s, when the Bundeswehr came into being, the original drawings of the MG42 had vanished and it was necessary for them to acquire a handful of original MG42 guns, tear them to pieces, measure them, and 'reverse engineer' these dimensions into drawings from which new guns could be made.

The MG3 uses a roller-locked breech mechanism of great strength and reliability, and a roller on top of the breech bolt operates the belt feed mechanism. Operation is by recoil; the barrel and locked breech recoil together until shaped cam tracks in the gun body press in the locking rollers and disconnect the bolt from the barrel; the barrel then stops and the bolt moves back against a return spring. On its forward stroke it loads a cartridge into the chamber and as it does so the cam tracks move out two rollers and locate them in recesses in the gun body, so locking the breech to the barrel. Only when the rollers have moved into the locked position is it possible for the firing pin to pass through the centre of the bolt and fire the cartridge.

Since the barrel recoils about 20mm (0.8in) after each shot it is necessary to hold it in a support; this is a

Above: The French response to the GPMG requirement, the M1952, featured a monopod underneath the metal stock and a calibre of 7.5mm. Left: A bipod-mounted MG3 fitted with a muzzle cap. Below: MG3s on a twin anti-aircraft pedestal mount. Its high rate-of-fire is an obvious asset in this role. Below: An MG3 mounted on a West German Jpz 4-5 tank destroyer.

MG3

Calibre 7.62mm
Length 122cm (48in)
Weight 11.5kg (25.51lb)
Operation Recoil
Feed system Belt
Rate of fire 700-1300rpm
Muzzle velocity 756mps (2480fps)

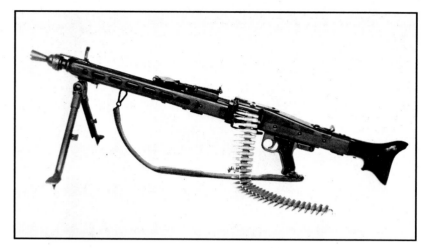

perforated jacket which helps the airflow around the barrel and which is slotted on the right side to allow the barrel to be slipped out and changed. The MG3 can be fired from a bipod or from a tripod, and there are also a variety of specialised mountings for anti-aircraft defence or for firing from vehicles.

The Belgian FN MAG (Fabrique Nationale Mitrailleuse d'Appui Générale) was designed in the early 1950s as a gas-operated and belt-fed weapon, and has been widely adopted throughout the world; it is used in Britain as the GPMG L7A1 and the tank machine guns L8A1 and L37A2, and in the USA as the tank machine gun M240. It has also been made in other calibres, notably for Sweden as the 6.5mm M58 GPMG. A major factor in the FN company's success has been its excellent export record.

The mechanism of the FN MAG is rather unusual; it has a gas piston which is connected to the breech block by a toggle link. As the unit goes forward the block forces a cartridge from the belt into the chamber, and the toggle then drops across a bar in the gun body, so that any rearward movement of the bolt is locked by pressing the toggle against the solid bar. As the round is fired, so a small portion of the cartridge gas is tapped from a hole in the barrel and drives the piston rearward; this straightens out the toggle, unlocks it from the bar, and then withdraws the bolt to extract the empty case and begin the reloading cycle once more. A regulator in the gas cylinder allows additional pressure to overcome dirt or lack of lubrication in the mechanism and can also be used to adjust the rate of fire to between 600 and 1000 rounds per minute. As with other GPMGs the gun can be used on a bipod or on a tripod.

Above: The direct relationship of the MG3 to the wartime MG42 can be clearly discerned in this photograph.

Left: The FN MAG can be carried ready-to-fire by the average infantryman and yet can still be utilised to lay down long-range interdiction fire. Below: A two-man crew of British infantry prepare to fire an FN MAG from a well-concealed position.

FN MAG

Calibre 7.62mm
Length 126cm (49.7in)
Weight 10.88kg (24lb)
Operation Gas
Feed system Belt
Rate of fire 600-1000rpm
Muzzle velocity 855mps (2800fps)

Right: The complete kit for the British FN MAG showing cleaning kit and spare barrels. When tripod mounted the stock is normally removed. Below: A member of the British Task Force blasts away with his FN MAG against Argentinian positions on the Falklands.

M60

Calibre 7.62mm
Length 111cm (43.7in)
Weight 10.43kg (23lb)
Operation Gas
Feed system Belt
Rate of fire 550rpm
Muzzle velocity 855mps (2800fps)

The American M60 was the result of development which began in 1944 by copying a German MG42; consequently it still uses some elements of the MG42 feed mechanism, though other aspects are somewhat different from the German gun. The bolt mechanism resembles that of the old-time Lewis gun, a gas piston carrying a vertical post which engages with the bolt and, by a curved slot in the bolt, rotates and withdraws the bolt on its backward stroke and then rotates it once more to lock into the barrel on the forward stroke. The bipod is, though, attached to the barrel, and the most important piece of equipment is the asbestos glove with which the gunner's mate removes the hot barrel, since there is no handle. Once again the gunner has to hold the gun off the ground until a new barrel and

Left: Prior to the real thing British troops tried out their FN MAG machine guns on Ascension Island to improve marksmanship and fire control.

bipod are fitted.

There is a tripod mounting for sustained fire, and there are also minor variant models of the gun for mounting in armoured vehicles or helicopters. Evaluation is currently in progress for a new lightweight model which has several improvements, notably the attachment of the bipod to the gun body and a handle on the barrel, making barrel-changing much easier.

Several armies are now beginning to question the whole GPMG concept, particularly since many have gone over to the 5.56mm cartridge for their standard rifle. It now makes sense to equip the infantry platoon with a light machine gun taking the same cartridge as the rifle, and several armies (notably the British and American) are in the process of adopting 5.56mm

Below right: A squad of M16-armed infantrymen support their M60 machine gun team during a battalion exercise. Below: The M60 in combat conditions – a sergeant in the 173rd Airborne Brigade defends his unit perimeter during fighting near Dak To in 1967. Like most other machine gunners in Vietnam he carries copious supplies of ammunition as well as a bottle of cleaning fluid held within his helmet band.

light machine guns. And as the 5.56mm bullet does not have the power for long-range machine-gun fire, some armies have stated their intention of staying with the heavier 7.62mm bullet, though perhaps adopting a lighter machine gun for the infantry squad. It now seems likely that the GPMG will be replaced by a dual system of 5.56 and 7.62mm machine guns.

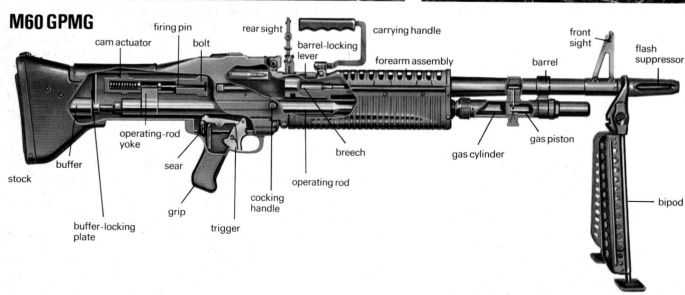

M60 GPMG

cam actuator · firing pin · bolt · rear sight · barrel-locking lever · carrying handle · forearm assembly · front sight · flash suppressor · barrel · gas piston · gas cylinder · breech · operating rod · cocking handle · trigger · grip · sear · operating-rod yoke · buffer · stock · buffer-locking plate · bipod

Shambles and stalemate

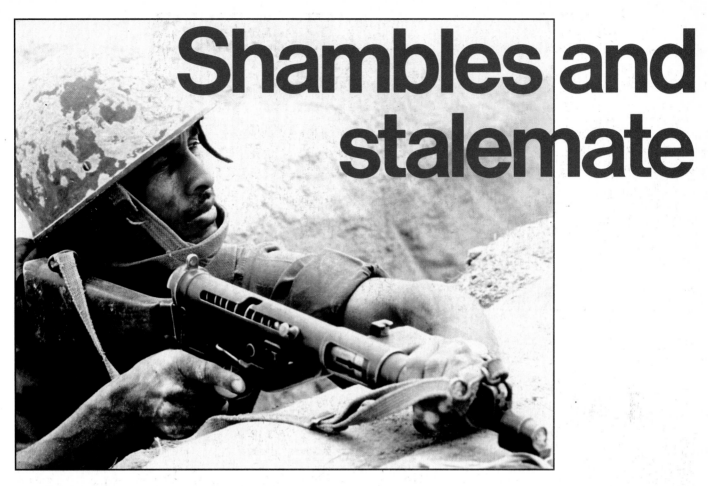

The war between India and Pakistan in 1965

The confused fighting of 1947-48 left the state of Jammu and Kashmir (popularly known simply as Kashmir) divided between Pakistan and India along a supposedly temporary ceasefire line. Both sides agreed in principle that a plebiscite would settle the future of the state, but no plebiscite was ever held. Kashmir was strategically too important to both India and Pakistan for either to accept its loss. Pakistan gradually integrated the government and forces of Azad Kashmir (Free Kashmir) into its own army and political system, while the pro-Indian government in the Kashmir state capital, Srinagar, not only confirmed the state's accession to India in 1957, but permitted India to erode the state's special semi-autonomous status.

Meanwhile, militarily weak and politically divided, Pakistan sought international support. The army commander, General Ayub Khan, was authorised to open negotiations with the United States and in 1954 secured modern equipment worth $1500 million. In return, Pakistan abandoned non-alignment and joined pro-Western military alliances such as the Baghdad Pact and Seato. The New Delhi government's original attitude of disdain towards Pakistan was now overlaid with alarm, and it was mortally offended by the sudden appearance of the Cold War on its non-aligned borders. Nor were its fears eased when a coup installed a military government, under General Ayub Khan, in 1958.

Defeat in the Sino-Indian War of 1962 revealed embarrassing weaknesses in India's armed forces. India responded to the Himalayan debacle with a massive rearmament programme, to which the Soviet Union became a major contributor, seeing in India a potential ally against an increasingly assertive China. Pakistan, meanwhile, established closer links with China, which effectively recognised Pakistan's claim to north Kashmir in an agreement concluded in 1963.

Attempts to negotiate a solution to the Kashmir problem came to nothing when talks broke down in May 1963, and in the next six months Jawaharlal Nehru accelerated the process of integrating the state into India. During 1964 tension between India and Pakistan increased and during the autumn there was a mutual expulsion of diplomatic missions. Thwarted in its efforts to seek a negotiated settlement, Pakistan felt that military force was the only option to prevent the irrevocable absorption of southern Kashmir by India.

Ayub Khan perceived a narrow window of opportunity before Indian rearmament got into its stride and while New Delhi was still devoting a major part of its forces to its Himalayan border with China. The window seemed to be opening when civil unrest developed among Muslims in the Vale of Kashmir during 1964 and 1965, protesting at the policies of the state government. The early 1960s were a period of considerable interest in, although little understanding of, the concept of 'wars of national liberation', and the Kashmir disturbances seemed to offer an excellent opportunity to create such a war. For Ayub Khan and his advisers, the crucial unknown factor was the probable reaction of India's new premier, Lal Bahadur Shastri, who had taken over on Nehru's death in

Top left: Armed with a MkV Sten sub-machine gun, an Indian soldier peers over a low parapet in search of enemy patrols in the Rann of Kutch. Top: General Ayub Khan who came to power in Pakistan after a coup in 1958. Above: The Indian Prime Minister Lal Bahadur Shastri.

May 1964. They soon found an opportunity to put him to the test.

The opportunity came at the opposite end of the border, on the mudflats of the Rann of Kutch, which are almost uninhabited but were nonetheless disputed between the two sides. In January 1965, border forces clashed after the discovery that a track inside Indian-claimed territory was being used by Pakistani policemen. On 9 April the Karachi government committed an army brigade to an assault on the poorly-defended frontier. Although the Indians responded by sending two brigades to confront them, fighting never became intense (total Indian casualties were 93 in six months). Shastri was obviously content to ignore popular calls for war and adopt a low profile response, although Indian forces were mobilised in the Punjab (Operation Ablaze) to test Pakistan's defensive strategy. Ayub Khan mistook Shastri's caution for timidity and secretly decided upon covert military action in Kashmir. He seized the opportunity of the Commonwealth Conference in London, during June 1965, hastily to end hostilities in the Rann of Kutch. The two leaders agreed to return to the pre-1965 situation pending arbitration and on 1 July fighting ended. Final demarcation of the border was scheduled for a foreign ministers' meeting in New Delhi to be held on 20 August, but by then events in Kashmir had driven the Rann of Kutch affair into the background, and the meeting never took place.

The American-trained Pakistani Special Forces had been ordered, in May 1965, to create a guerrilla force which would spearhead the revolt of Kashmiri Muslims against Indian rule. The first of four training camps opened at Murree on 26 May. Gibraltar Force, as it was known, came under Major-General Akhter Hussain Malik, commander of the 12th Infantry

Division in Kashmir, but it was quite distinct from the Azad Kashmir units of the Pakistani Army. Eventually 5000-6000 men were recruited from regular soldiers, paramilitary forces and civilian volunteers. They were given six weeks training for a short campaign which was supposed to end with a call from the 'oppressed' Muslims for deliverance from Indian rule, providing the pretext for an invasion by Pakistani regular forces. But the Pakistanis made the same fatal mistake as many other students of unconventional warfare in the early 1960s in assuming that the mere presence of armed men is the basis of guerrilla warfare.

Guerrilla war

On 5 August irregulars began crossing the 16-year-old ceasefire line through mountains and forests to start a campaign which lasted into October. They harassed Indian forces and communications, and held the town of Mandi, near Punch, from 7-11 August, but they had no political infrastructure to rally popular support and the anticipated popular uprising never occurred. Nevertheless, the Indians had to commit the 13th, 25th and 26th Infantry Divisions and the 191st Independent Infantry Brigade before they were able to contain the guerrillas' activities within a 15km (10 mile) belt of the ceasefire line. Ten days after the operation began, Pakistani artillery opened up in support of the guerrillas and this gave India's Kashmir-based XV Corps under Lieutenant-General K. S. Katuch an excuse to cross the ceasefire line itself and seize key points to cut infiltration routes. Skirmishes between the regular forces escalated, and on 26 August India captured the Haji Pir Pass close to the Azad Kashmir capital of Muzaffarabad. To relieve pressure on this extremely sensitive spot Malik took

the fateful decision to stage a diversion, Operation Grand Slam, into the Chhamb salient 30km (20 miles) from Akhnur, through which ran the main Indian supply line into western Kashmir.

During the ceasefire period UN observers had maintained peace by keeping each side informed of the other's movements and intentions, usually with the unofficial assistance of each army. So it was natural that as Malik's 12th Infantry Division, with two armoured regiments of the 6th Armoured Division (led by Major-General Abrar Hussain), assembled on 31 August, UN observers reported it to the commander of the nearby Indian 26th Infantry Division. He in turn telephoned Srinagar where Lieutenant-General Katuch happened to be meeting the army chief of staff, General J. N. Chaudhuri, a man all too conscious of his country's military weakness. The garrison in the Chhamb salient, 191st Infantry Brigade, was too weak and too far forward to be able to offer serious resistance, but Chaudhuri insisted Katuch hold Akhnur.

The following day's attack, by seven Pakistani battalions with armour, overwhelmed the four Indian battalions west of the Munawar Tawi River. The defending ground forces were not helped by the disastrous intervention of their own side's air force, which lost four Vampires and mistakenly attacked its own men. The diversion had been spectacularly successful. General Mohammed Mura, the Pakistani Army commander, found the temptation to advance further across the plain to Akhnur irresistible. He compounded this error by assigning the task to a fresh formation, 7th Infantry Division headquarters under Major-General Agha Mohammed Yahya Khan, which did not arrive until a day later. By the time the attack was renewed the Indian defence had begun to pull itself together with the arrival of two fresh infantry brigades, and although the attackers were able to bring Akhnur under artillery fire on 7 September they could progress no further. By then events to the south were distracting attention and resources.

Planning Operation Riddle

Indian strategy in the Punjab had assumed a defensive posture since 1954, but when Lieutenant-General J. S. Dhillon had taken over XI Corps in the Amritsar salient he had advocated a more active defence. He especially proposed lopping off the Chawinda salient which threatened communications into Kashmir. His arguments were accepted by Western Command (Lieutenant-General Harbakhsh Singh) following Operation Ablaze, which had revealed that Pakistani strategy was based on holding and fortifying the newly-constructed Ichogil Canal, a 40m (140ft) wide, 4m (14ft) deep irrigation canal which ran parallel to the frontier a few kilometres inside Pakistan, linking the Ravi and Sutlej Rivers. Harbakhsh Singh accepted Dhillon's concept of an offensive but modified it as Operation Riddle. Dhillon's XI Corps was to seize the eastern bank of the canal and bridges across it, while I Corps (under Lieutenant-General P. O. Dunn) was to attack the Chawinda salient from the north using Major-General Rajindar Singh Sparrow's 1st Armoured Division. Dhillon would have at his disposal the 2nd Independent Armoured Brigade, comprising a regiment of Centurions and four regiments of Shermans.

However, when open war began on 1 September 1965, General Chaudhuri, as army chief of staff, was extremely reluctant to authorise an advance in the Punjab. Indeed, he was in a state of considerable anxiety for he was all too well aware of the Indian

Above left: Indian troops man a position overlooking a valley near Srinagar with a .303in Vickers machine gun covering the left flank. Note the use of individual and two-man foxholes to increase the gun's field of fire.

Left: Pakistani infantry advance at the double in the Rann of Kutch. It was border conflicts in this area that preceded the outbreak of full-scale hostilities, although the Rann of Kutch itself is a region of desolate mudflats of little value to either nation.

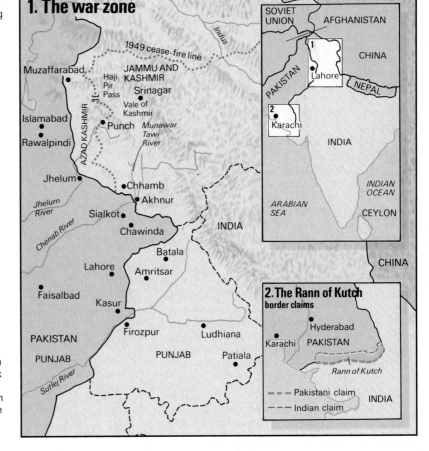

1. The war zone

SOVIET UNION
AFGHANISTAN
CHINA
Lahore
NEPAL
PAKISTAN
Karachi
INDIA
ARABIAN SEA
INDIAN OCEAN
CEYLON
CHINA

1949 cease-fire line
Indus
Muzaffarabad
Haji Pir Pass
JAMMU AND KASHMIR
Srinagar
Vale of Kashmir
Islamabad
Punch
Munawar Tawi River
Rawalpindi
AZAD KASHMIR
Jhelum
Chhamb
Akhnur
Jhelum River
Sialkot
Chenab River
Chawinda
Batala
Lahore
Amritsar
Faisalbad
Kasur
PAKISTAN
Firozpur
Ludhiana
PUNJAB
PUNJAB
Patiala
Sutlej River

2. The Rann of Kutch
border claims
Hyderabad
Karachi
PAKISTAN
Rann of Kutch
--- Pakistani claim
--- Indian claim
INDIA

Army's deficiencies; he overestimated Pakistani capabilities and feared Chinese intervention. An offensive in the Punjab would consume his strategic reserve with little hope of result, for his forces would face an equal number of enemy divisions which could compensate for any numerical inferiority with more modern equipment. Only five of the Indian Western Command's armoured regiments had the modern Centurion Mark 5 with an 84mm gun; the remainder were equipped with old Mark 3, Mark 4 and Mark 5 Shermans with 75mm and 76mm guns, or light tanks such as the AMX13 and PT76. By contrast, six Pakistani armoured regiments had the M47 Patton tank with a 90mm gun, three regiments had M24 Chaffee light tanks, and the rest were similarly equipped with Shermans. Consequently Chaudhuri advocated a defensive posture and changed his mind only after an unpleasant scene with Prime Minister Shastri.

Punjab offensive

It was the need to relieve pressure on Akhnur that led, on the night of 5/6 September, to the order to execute Operation Riddle. It was also intended to cripple enemy military power and pre-empt an expected advance on Amritsar. In fact Pakistan had intended only to defend its territory and General Musa placed his forces on full alert only on 4 September when Indian civil radio reports led him to suspect that an attack was imminent. IV Corps' 15th Division defended Sialkot supported by four armoured regiments (160 tanks) and the brigade-size 6th Armoured Division (120 tanks) was stationed west of Chawinda. In front of Lahore was I Corps' 10th Infantry Division with six infantry battalions holding fortifications along the Ichogil Canal, supported by the equivalent of two battalions in reserve with an artillery brigade. To the south were elements of 11th Infantry Division with four battalions around Kasur, while in strategic reserve was Major-General Nasir Ahmed's 1st Armoured Division (comprising 4th and 5th Armoured Brigades) with 200 Pattons and Chaffees.

The Indian XI Corps' operation, which began on 6 September, went badly. In a vain effort to achieve surprise Dhillon brought up his three divisions directly from their peacetime stations and then struck out on diverging axes; the 15th and 7th Infantry Divisions converged on Lahore through Dograi and Barki while the 4th Mountain Division, anxious to avenge its recent Himalayan defeat by the Chinese, advanced from Khem Keran upon Kasur.

The advance on Lahore across the extensively irrigated plain was a shambles. Poor staff work meant units were short of transport, radios, recoilless guns and ammunition, accurate intelligence was sparse and there were neither photographs nor maps of the main objective, the canal. Air and artillery support was miserly, the corps having only one heavy artillery regiment. By the time the divisions reached the canal all 70 bridges had been blown up and no sooner had the 15th Division reached Dograi, 12km (8 miles) from Lahore, than it was forced to retreat by heavy shelling. Its commander, Major-General Niranjam Prasad, lost touch with one brigade and, in discovering a Pakistani bridgehead east of the canal, at Bhasin, was almost captured. He was soon relieved of his command. The Pakistani 10th Division used the bridge-head to launch counter-attacks which split the Indian 15th Division, driving one brigade back across the border in panic. The Indians could not stabilise the

situation until 13 September with the despatch of two infantry brigades and the 2nd Armoured Brigade. But renewed attempts to take Bhasin failed and it was not until the night of 21/22 September, on the eve of the eventual UN-sponsored ceasefire, that Dograi was recaptured. Meanwhile the Indian 7th Division had made similar heavy weather of its advance on Barki, 20km (12 miles) from Lahore. Barki did not fall until 10 September, the Indian battalion commander leading the attack having served with the defending battalion before Partition. The capture of Barki and Dograi gave the Indians control of 50km (30 miles) of the canal, but the objectives had been hard gained and could not be exploited.

If anything, the attack on Kasur went even worse for the Indians. The six battalions of 4th Mountain Division had to travel 240km (150 miles) from Ambala to their jump-off point and quickly encountered strong resistance east of the canal from the newly raised and similarly sized Pakistani 11th Division, supported by the 5th Armoured Brigade. The Indians succeeded in advancing to within 300 metres of the Ichogil Canal before the defenders, supported by 140 guns, contained them. A Pakistani counter-offensive on 7 September led to a retreat which quickly became a rout. The flight was stopped only at Khem Keran, where new positions were prepared on the road to Amritsar only 50km (30 miles) away. General Musa decided to exploit his success by committing the remainder of Nasir Ahmed's 1st Armoured Division and for two days the 4th Mountain Division fought a

Below right: Indian troops, some armed with 7.62mm FN FALs, advance across a track as they approach a Pakistani position. Heavy defensive fire forces them to move with caution. Although infantry were subordinate to armour during the 1965 war – both sides deploying large tank formations as the cutting edge of their attacks – infantry formations suffered heavy casualties in defence, most notably the Indian 4th Mountain Division when it successfully held the road to Amritsar.

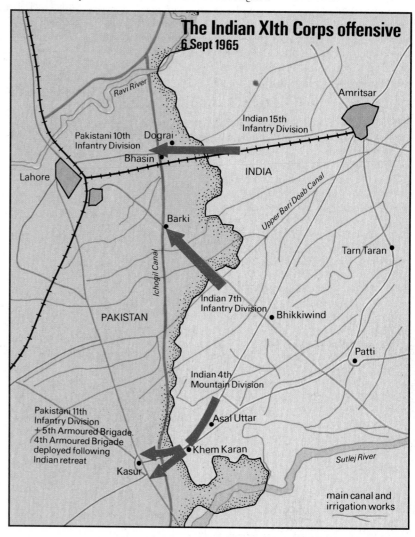

The Indian XIth Corps offensive
6 Sept 1965

desperate battle to contain the Pakistani armoured thrust. Fortunately for the Indians, the attacks were constricted by the numerous irrigation channels, flooded areas and fields of sugar cane 3m (9ft) high. The defenders' artillery was used to devastating effect, disrupting inter-arm coordination and hindering the attackers' logistic support. By 10 September Dhillon had succeeded in disengaging the 2nd Armoured Brigade from the Lahore front and sent them south. Their Shermans now replaced by some 150 AMX13s and PT76s, they clashed with Nasir Ahmed's regiments around the village of Asal Uttar. The lighter Indian force triumphed after enticing the enemy into an ambush which cost the Pakistanis some 40 tanks. Twenty-eight were captured intact, some with their engines still running – they had outrun their support and then been trapped. The 4th Armoured Brigade suffered especially badly; both its commander and Nasir Ahmed were killed. Pressure on Sialkot led the Pakistanis hastily to withdraw 4th Armoured Brigade and transfer it north that same night, but Khem Keran remained in Pakistani hands. Clumsily-organised attacks by fresh Indian brigades failed in the face of the defenders' air and artillery superiority.

Divisions in disarray

The Indian attack on the Chawinda salient, which began on the night of 7/8 September was code-named 'Nepal'. Lieutenant-General Dunn failed to define the tasks of his three divisions, 1st Armoured, 26th Infantry and 6th Mountain, who were restricted to a series of limited advances involving four infantry battalions of 6th Mountain Division and 300 Centurions and Shermans, across a flat, dry plain which was soon cut up by the 3000 vehicles. The 26th Division made a separate advance on Sialkot from the east. Two battalions of the Pakistani 11th Division in the salient were consequently permitted to make a fighting withdrawal. In the north the 15th Division, now under Major-General Tikka Khan, staged a reconnaissance in force that caused such confusion that the Indian attackers were forced to halt, losing a dozen Centurions in skirmishes. The Pakistani 6th Armoured Division was late arriving because of false reports of parachute drops and the consequent

The Air War

The Indian Air Force enjoyed a clear numerical superiority over its Pakistani opponents – 775 combat aircraft against 141 – but its equipment was of poorer quality and its forces more widely dispersed. India's 130 obsolescent Vampire jet fighters were withdrawn from combat after four had been shot down in the first serious engagement of the air war on 1 September 1965. India deployed MiG-21s against Pakistan's F-104 Starfighters – the first time that Mach 2 fighters had met in combat – but their involvement in the fighting was marginal. The battle for air superiority was fought between Pakistan's F-86 Sabres and India's Folland Gnats, Hawker Hunters and Mystères. Some of Pakistan's Sabres were equipped with Sidewinder missiles.

The major combats took place on 6-7 September, as each side tried to knock out its enemy's forward airbases. The Pakistani raids were the more successful. After heavy losses sustained in attacks on Pakistan's Sargodha airbase on 7 September, the Indian Air Force retreated into a defensive role, leaving Pakistan in control of the air over the land battlefield. Indian armoured formations consequently suffered heavily.

By the end of the war, India had lost at least 35 aircraft, including some 14 Hunters, nine Mystères and three Gnats. Pakistani losses totalled 19 – 13 Sabres, two Starfighters, and four Martin B-57s.

A PAF pilot (left) and the two main fighters of the air war, the Sabre (below) and the Gnat (bottom).

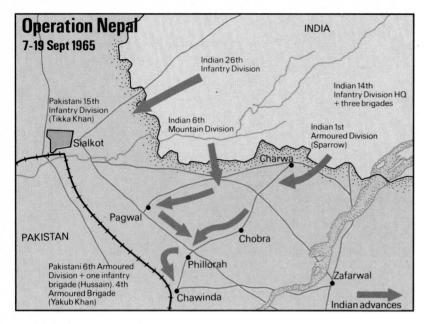

Operation Nepal
7-19 Sept 1965

INDIA

Indian 26th
Infantry Division

Pakistani 15th
Infantry Division
(Tikka Khan)

Indian 14th
Infantry Division HQ
+ three brigades

Sialkot

Indian 6th
Mountain Division

Indian 1st
Armoured Division
(Sparrow)

Charwa

Pagwal

PAKISTAN

Chobra

Phillorah

Pakistani 6th Armoured
Division + one infantry
brigade (Hussain). 4th
Armoured Brigade
(Yakub Khan)

Chawinda

Zafarwal

Indian advances

Below: Only hours before
the ceasefire in 1965, a
Pakistani tank recovery
vehicle hauls an
Indian-Army British-made
Centurion tank away from
the battle zone in the Khem
Keran sector. Fierce
armoured engagements
had taken place in this area.
The armoured forces of
both sides had suffered
heavy losses, the Indians
losing some 375 tanks and
the Pakistanis 350.

two-day pause, while Dunn brought up 14th Infantry Division headquarters with three brigades to protect his rear in the salient, was extremely valuable to Pakistan.

The Indian advance was renewed on 11 September with the objective of taking first Phillorah with its nearby crossroads, and then Chawinda. The defending forces under the 6th Armoured Division commander Abrar Hussain were unable to prevent the fall of Phillorah, but with strong air support they managed to prevent Sparrow's 1st Armoured Division from exploiting its success. By delaying the advance they bought time for Pakistan's 4th Armoured Brigade to reach the front by train, although this delaying action cost half 6th Armoured Division's tanks. Sparrow, who was senior to Dunn, wished to stage a classic armoured thrust, but the cautious Dunn refused and ordered him merely to press on to Chawinda where he was to cut the railway line to Sialkot. After a three-day pause the Indian armour clattered forward and cut the railway north of Chawinda. But they were unable to enter the town, which was defended by the 6th Armoured Division reinforced by an infantry brigade. Then Pakistan's 4th Armoured Brigade, now

under Major-General Yakub Khan and reduced to some 75 tanks, staged a successful ambush as Sparrow tried to envelop the town from the west. The Indian armour was forced to retreat with the destruction of 13 tanks. This ended the war of movement. Dunn henceforth contented himself with trying to take Chawinda by a series of clumsy frontal attacks involving the 6th Mountain Division. The last of these was beaten off on the night of 18/19 September.

Meanwhile, both India and Pakistan were under extreme diplomatic pressure to stop the fighting. Both the United States and Britain cut off all military supplies to both sides. This, coupled with financial exhaustion and the military stalemate, persuaded the combatants to accept a ceasefire on the morning of 23 September, although the front flared and flickered throughout the rest of the year. Losses of personnel had been heavy, each side suffering 5000-6000 casualties including some 1000 dead, but it was the material destruction which was most serious. India lost 375 tanks (175 destroyed or captured) and 35 aircraft, compared to Pakistan's 350 tanks (200 destroyed or captured) and 19 aircraft, although both were soon making good their material losses. Russian offers of military assistance to both sides led them to accept a peace conference in Tashkent in the Soviet Union from 4-10 January 1966. Largely through the efforts of Soviet Premier Alexei Kosygin, a face-saving agreement was hammered out permitting military disengagement and a return to the pre-war situation. The strain of negotiation proved fatal to Shastri who died a few hours after signing the agreement.

Pakistan's Kashmir gamble had failed but there was to be no complete return to the pre-war situation. The authority of the military regime was weakened, leading to growing discontent, especially in East Pakistan. Having been unsupported by its patrons, China and the United States, the Karachi government began to look to the Middle East for backing at a time when the Islamic religious revival was getting under way. India too had not received the support it expected either from the United Kingdom or the United States and under its new premier, Indira Ghandi, turned increasingly to the Soviet Union. Within six years, India and Pakistan would be at war once more.

E. R. Hooton

Biafra

The tragedy of the Nigerian Civil War

The Nigerian Civil War of 1967-70, fought over the secession of Biafra, resulted in one of the great human tragedies of the postwar era. The very name of Biafra became synonymous with mass starvation; human suffering was used as a political counter by both sides to the conflict. By the end, perhaps one million people were dead, only a small proportion as a direct result of military action.

Nigeria is by far the largest black African state in terms of population – over 50 million in the 1960s – and has important oil reserves in the delta region of the River Niger. At independence in 1960 the country became a federation of three regions – North, West and East – increased to four two years later when a Mid-Western Region was formed out of part of the Western Region. The Federal capital was at Lagos. The dominant tribes in the regions were the Muslim Hausa and Fulani in the North, the Anglican and Muslim Yorubas in the West, and the Catholic Ibos in the East, although other minority tribes made up about 50 per cent of the total population. Tribal rivalries were intense, especially between the Northerners and the traditionally more educated and advanced groups in the south – most notably the Ibos of the Eastern Region.

The British left behind a civilian democratic system of government. But democracy functioned poorly, with political parties tied to tribal and regional power bases competing for the material spoils the elite could expect from independence. In 1966, amid mounting disturbances, the army intervened.

The first coup, on 15 January, was headed by a group of young army officers, most of them Ibos, appalled by the ballot rigging and blatant corruption of many leading politicians which had brought the country to the brink of chaos. In Kaduna, the Northern capital, troops stormed Government House, killing the regional premier and the local garrison commander. In Lagos insurgents assassinated Nigeria's prime minister, the finance minister, and the three most senior Northern officers, but the army commander, Major-General Johnson Aguiye Ironsi, escaped from the city in his Land Rover, driving to the garrison town of Ikeja. There he was able to rally the garrison and organise a counter-attack which had little difficulty in overwhelming the rebel forces.

The outcome of this failed revolution was the installation of a military regime under General Ironsi. The new ruler was an Ibo and surrounded himself with Ibo advisers. It was believed in the North that the coup attempt had been a plot to install Ibo domination. Much resentment was felt at the lenient treatment of

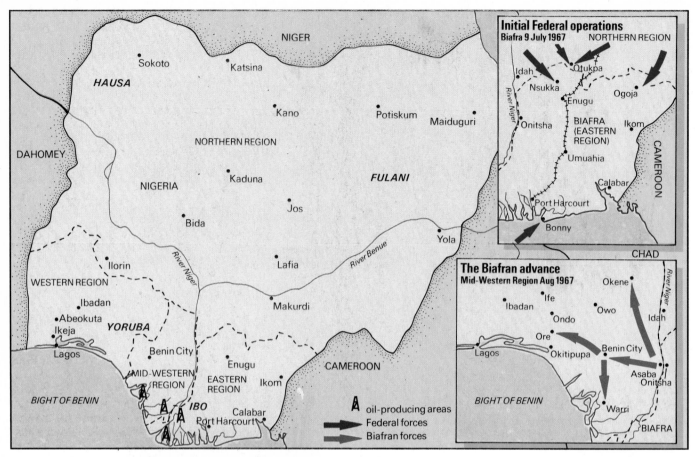

Initial Federal operations
Biafra 9 July 1967

The Biafran advance
Mid-Western Region Aug 1967

A — oil-producing areas
→ Federal forces
→ Biafran forces

Page 1075: The real victims of the war, Biafran civilians in the grip of famine. Right: A few days before the declaration that was to throw Nigeria into a bloody civil war, Lieutenant-Colonel Ojukwu addresses the Eastern Nigerian Consultative Assembly.

Below left: Federal troops from Colonel Adekunle's 3rd Commando Division come under fire from rebel units as they advance towards enemy positions.

the young Ibo rebel officers, not one of whom was brought to trial and whose imprisonment amounted to little more than house arrest. General Ironsi quickly announced the replacement of the federal system by a 'United Central Government', a move which aroused widespread resentment.

The second coup, launched on the night of 28/29 July, has often been referred to as 'the revenge of the North'. The first town to be affected was Abeokuta in the Western region. At 2300 hours, two platoons of Northern troops broke into the officers' mess where a party was in progress. Everyone present was mown down. The rebels then stormed the arsenal before carrying on to murder every non-Northern soldier on sight. The following morning at Ibadan, the Western capital, General Ironsi was captured by insurgents, tortured and machine-gunned to death. At Ikeja and at Kaduna the pattern of mass murder, torture and executions was repeated.

An end to chaos?

On 10 August, with power firmly in their hands, the Northerners called a halt to the killing. The murdered General Ironsi was succeeded as head of state by the most senior Northern officer, Lieutenant-Colonel (soon promoted Major-General) Yakubu Gowon, who had not participated in the coup. Gowon sought to end the chaos, but through September thousands of Ibo civilians in the North were massacred. Ibo army officers and men had already returned to their own areas in the East and Mid-West; after the September massacres, some 700,000 Ibo civilians trod the same path to the safety of their homeland.

The military governor of the Eastern Region, Lieutenant-Colonel Chukwuemeka Odemegwu Ojukwu, was determined to reject General Gowon's authority as head of the Federation. Whether he really wished for more independence for the East or rather to replace Gowon as head of the central government is unclear. Prolonged negotiations between Gowon and Ojukwu failed to produce a formula which would allay Eastern fears and, on 27 May 1967, Gowon unilaterally announced a new structure for Nigeria with 12 states to replace the previous four regions. One of his aims was to appeal to minorities in the East against the Ibos; the oil-producing regions would henceforth be in states controlled by minority groups, not the Ibos. On 30 May Ojukwu retaliated by declaring Eastern Nigeria the independent Republic of Biafra.

General Gowon described Ojukwu's declaration as an 'act of rebellion'. On 6 July, in the face of Ojukwu's refusal to negotiate or retract, the Federal Army was mobilised and ordered to carry out what was described as 'a surgical police operation and not a civil war'. An economic blockade of the East was announced and on 9 July Federal troops began a cautious advance. First to fall were the towns of Ogoja and Nsukka. Then the 3rd Commando Division led by Colonel Benjamin Adekunle took the oil terminal at Bonny in a well-executed amphibious assault. This was a crucial success, since it dissuaded the oil companies from any temptation to pay their revenues to Biafra rather than to the central government.

The Federal advance was going according to plan, but Ojukwu had devised a devastating surprise counter-stroke. On 9 August the Biafrans launched an attack across the Niger at Asaba, led by a Yoruba officer, Lieutenant-Colonel Victor Banjo. A column

The rival forces

In January 1966 the Nigerian Army numbered 9000 men, the Navy 1500 and the Air Force 1000. During the war, however, the Federal Army expanded to 120,000 and the Biafran Army to about 40,000. This rapid expansion meant that most troops were poorly trained and experienced officers were spread very thinly. Since independence the 228 British officers had been replaced by promoted Nigerians in an 'Africanisation' programme. Moreover, almost half of the Nigerian officers ranking major and above were killed in the 1966 coups. Not surprisingly, rapidly promoted young officers frequently showed deficiencies in leadership; the standard of NCOs was correspondingly poor.

Both sides had difficulty obtaining arms and private arms dealers had a field day. Despite the shortage of ammunition, both armies showed a tendency to fire recklessly and wastefully. Most of the war consisted of skirmishes and slow cautious movement. Communications and logistic support were neither fast nor efficient. The dedication of officers to the struggle was often less than complete. Military historian Zdenek Cervenka writes: 'At all stages of the war, no matter how fierce the battles were parties were always held. Officers would arrive from places on the front, change into civilian and traditional clothes and accompanied by their girlfriends, drink and dance to the highlife music.'

The Federal Army fielded two infantry divisions and a Marine commando division. The 1st Infantry Divison, comprising six brigades, was a much more efficient fighting forma-

tion than the 2nd which was hastily raised on the opening of hostilities. Only three brigades strong, the 2nd Division was so poor in training, morale and leadership that it was sometimes looked upon more as a liability than an asset. It was the 3rd Commando Division which stole the limelight. Led for most of the time by a talented but over-ambitious officer, Colonel Benjamin Adekunle, it ended the war with by far the most distinguished battle record.

The Biafrans claimed to have mobilised five divisions but this was deceptive since each division was little more than a brigade group in strength. Later the 4th Commando Brigade was formed, led by European mercenaries under the command of 'Colonel' Rolf Steiner, a German ex-*caporal-chef* of the Foreign Legion, who had lost a lung at Dien Bien Phu and had later fought with the OAS in Algeria. Biafra also raised a small hand-picked unit, the Biafran Organisation of Freedom Fighters (BOFF), whose speciality was behind-the-lines operations.

The Federal side had a monopoly of naval power, boasting a frigate, a submarine chaser, two seaward defence vessels, three coastal patrol boats and landing craft. Initially, both air forces were very weak: the Federals had only trainers and the Biafrans one B-26 bomber. Britain refused a Federal request to supply jet fighters, but the Russians eventually supplied 12 Aero L-29 Delfins, 10 MiG-17s, six MiG-15s and three Ilyushin Il-28 bombers. DC-3s and DC-4s were used for night bombing. In 1969 Biafra obtained Swedish Minicons and Harvard AT-6s. On both sides, aircraft were mostly piloted by foreigners – chiefly Egyptian pilots for the Federals and Swedish pilots for Biafra.

Friends and enemies

Above: General Yakubu Gowon.

Above: Colonel Ojukwu.

The Nigerian Civil War was in part a conflict between two men of strikingly different characters – General Yakubu ('Jack') Gowon and Colonel Chukwuemeka Odumegwu Ojukwu. Both were young for the roles they assumed – Gowon was 32 and Ojukwu 34 when the fighting began. Both received their officer training in Britain. Both had served in the Congo with the Nigerian UN contingent. Until the fighting broke out the two men were good friends and on first name terms.

Their backgrounds and characters were, however, very different. Gowon was a northerner from the minority Anga tribe, a devout Christian, son of an evangelist. His only education had been at a secondary school in the Muslim north of Nigeria. Ojukwu was an Ibo, son of a self-

made millionaire, a Roman Catholic, he was educated at King's College, Lagos (Nigeria's 'Eton') and at Oxford University.

Gowon was deeply committed to the cause of a united Nigeria and to the Nigerian Army. No great intellectual, he was nevertheless capable of listening to and taking advice from those around him. The fact that he belonged to a minority tribe helped his stance as leader of a united Nigeria.

Ojukwu was a far more outgoing and self-confident man, quick-witted and a skilful diplomat. He was more a politician than a military leader, and he quickly came to personify the Ibos' longing for independence. He was not, however, very open to advice. But he was undoubtedly a popular, charismatic figure, whereas Gowon was respected rather than loved.

of 100 vehicles, many of them 'home-made' armoured cars – soft-skinned vehicles with steel plates added – raced to Benin City, capital of the Mid-Western Region. Before their arrival, mutinous Ibo officers seized control of the town, and Banjo's column entered unopposed. The rebels broadcast an appeal to the people of the West – chiefly Yoruba like Colonel Banjo himself – to rise up against Northern domination, but the appeal fell on deaf ears. Still, the Biafrans pressed on across the Western Region border to threaten both Lagos and Ibadan; Lagos was subjected to a raid by Biafra's single B-26 bomber, piloted by a Czech, 'Kamikaze' Braun.

With their supply lines overstretched, however, the Biafrans were forced to halt at Ore, allowing the Federal Army time to regroup and call up reinforcements. Realising that the suppression of the rebellion would be no easy task, General Gowon called for 'full-scale military operations', declaring that 'no mercy will be shown to the rebel clique'.

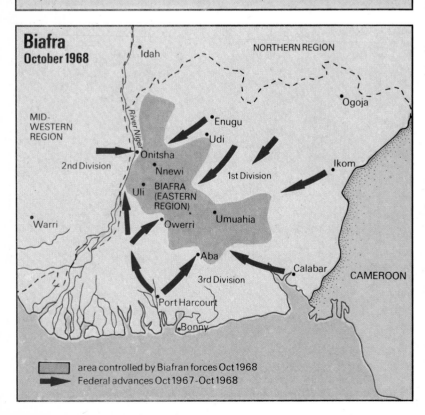

Biafra
October 1968

- Idah
- NORTHERN REGION
- MID-WESTERN REGION
- River Niger
- Ogoja
- Enugu
- Udi
- Onitsha
- 2nd Division
- Nnewi
- Ikom
- 1st Division
- Uli
- BIAFRA (EASTERN REGION)
- Warri
- Umuahia
- Owerri
- Aba
- 3rd Division
- Calabar
- CAMEROON
- Port Harcourt
- Bonny

□ area controlled by Biafran forces Oct 1968
➤ Federal advances Oct 1967 – Oct 1968

On 15 August a Biafran attempt to resume the offensive was stopped dead after fierce fighting and the Federal troops moved over to the attack. By mid-September the Biafrans had been driven out of most of their early gains and were back in the Eastern Region. Though this reversal of fortune was due largely to the superior weight fielded by the Federal side, there was also in-fighting between the Biafrans which proved fatal. Colonel Banjo, who had promoted himself brigadier, had ambitions to supplant Ojukwu. He had declared a short-lived 'Republic of Benin' in the Mid-West, and had also been in contact with Lagos. When the Federal advance came, Benin was evacuated without a fight. Colonel Ojukwu had Banjo and three other suspected conspirators arrested and shot, but the damage was done. The Biafrans would never again come within sight of victory and now had to fend off impending defeat.

On 4 October Enugu, the Biafran capital, fell. Ojukwu transferred his headquarters to the town of Umuahia. Then, on 19 October, Adekunle's commandos took Calabar after an aerial and naval bombardment. To the east, Ikum had fallen by the end of 1967, cutting the main route to the Cameroon.

Premature promises

These spectacular gains encouraged General Gowon to make a rash promise over Lagos radio during his New Year's Day (1968) broadcast, that it 'would all be over by 31 March'. At first it appeared he might be right. Through January more major towns fell. The Biafran Republic was being squeezed inexorably into an ever-shrinking perimeter, its communications with the outside world more and more restricted, the threat of famine looming. But in February resistance stiffened. The Federal advance was halted, in some places pushed back; there was no possibility of Gowon's promise being fulfilled.

On 21 March Federal forces launched a major assault on Onitsha, Biafra's second largest town. Supported by a mortar barrage, 7th Brigade advanced on the town from the southeast while 6th Brigade crossed the Niger on light craft. After five hours bitter struggle the town fell. Then, on 18 May, Adekunle's commandos took Port Harcourt, not only depriving Biafra of its last sea port but also of its major airport. General Gowon stepped up air attacks with Ilyushin Il-28 bombers provided by Russia in April – an estimated 2000 Biafrans were killed by bombing between May and October 1968. Yet the Federal forces still could not deliver a decisive blow.

Meanwhile, the plight of the Biafrans had become a matter of intense public concern throughout the world. Ojukwu had cleverly engaged a public relations firm, Markpress of Geneva, to organise a propaganda campaign on Biafra's behalf. At first Markpress played the religious card, representing Biafrans as Christians resisting Muslim attack, but although this had some success in US Catholic circles, the well-known fact that Gowon and most of his troops were also Christian undermined the campaign's credibility. With the growing famine in 1968, however, as the Biafrans fled the most fertile parts of their homeland and were squeezed into an ever tighter area, cut off from outside supplies, Markpress changed their campaign to a humanitarian appeal against 'genocide by starvation'. Pictures of starving children provoked indignation and an immediate humanitarian response. By August 1968 a group of international religious charitable organisations had initiated a major airlift of relief food supplies into Biafra.

As well as humanitarian aid and public sympathy, Biafra won important political backing. In Africa, Tanzania, Zambia, the Ivory Coast and Gabon recognised the Biafran Republic in April 1968, although they had no material aid to offer. But in September France, which had previously provided only a small measure of covert backing, came out in favour of Biafra. The French began to channel weapons to Biafra through Gabon and the Ivory Coast.

The only airfield left under Biafran control was at Uli. This was no more than a widened and hardened

Below: Rebels pose for the camera during a break in operations from their jungle base. The man in the foreground is armed with a 7.62mm Nato general purpose machine gun.
Below right: Federal troops man an artillery piece in support of an armoured advance. The Federal Army procured most of its arms from Great Britain and the USSR, while Biafra found France the most reliable supplier of armaments.

Von Rosen's Flying Circus

One of the most unlikely episodes of the Biafra War concerned Count Carl Gustav von Rosen, an ageing Swedish aristocrat who had flown for the Ethiopians against Mussolini's Italians in the 1930s and for the Finns against the Russians a few years later.

Like many adventurous pilots, he was engaged by a charitable organisation to fly food supplies into Biafra, running the Federal blockade. But out of a long-standing sympathy for the underdog, he determined to take things further. At his instigation seven Malmö Flyg Industri training aircraft called 'Minicons' were delivered from Sweden via France, where they were secretly fitted with weapon stations. Each was then capable of carrying twelve 76mm MATRA rockets. Since they could fly low enough to escape radar detection, they were able to deliver surprise attacks; they could also operate from improvised jungle airstrips.

Von Rosen got together a group of Swedish and Biafran pilots to fly the planes, and launched his attack. On 24 and 25 May 1969 the Minicons raided Federal airfields at Port Harcourt, Enugu and Benin, destroying two MiGs and one Ilyushin on the ground. Later they effected such a devastating strike on the refinery at Port Harcourt that the Federal government found itself faced by a temporary oil crisis.

From October the increased vigilance of the Federal MiG fighters inhibited the activities of Von Rosen's men; in any case, Biafra was by then a lost cause. The Count survived the debacle, however, only to die a few years later in a desperate bid to save Ethiopian Imperial princesses from that country's revolutionary regime.

Left: Count Carl Gustav von Rosen whose small Biafran-based air force recorded some startling successes.
Top: Von Rosen's 'Minicon' fitted with MATRA rockets.

tarmac road, but as transport planes carrying both arms and relief food supplies swept in by day and night, Uli became one of the busiest airports in Africa.

Still, on 27 August 1968 General Gowon told a BBC reporter that the last rebel strongholds would fall 'within four weeks'. Federal troops were advancing on two fronts: from the south 5000 men of the 3rd Commando Division supported by Saladin and Ferret armoured vehicles were pushing in the direction of Umuahia, while in the north the 1st and 2nd Divisions pressed towards Nnewi. On 4 September the commandos took Aba and 12 days later they occupied Owerri, a vital centre on the approaches to Umuahia. This double blow reduced viable Biafra to an area of 100km by 50km (60 miles by 30 miles). A further

Left: The devastation wreaked in Aba by Federal air strikes as the government forces closed in on the rebels. Below left: A Biafran soldier strips the bloodstained webbing belt from a Federal soldier after a successful ambush. In general, the Biafrans never seriously considered the option of a sustained guerrilla campaign; they preferred a conventional-style war in which small-scale ambushes and hit-and-run raids had little part.

advance by the Federals brought Uli airstrip within reach of their guns.

Biafra seemed on the point of collapse. Refugees clogged the roads and over 6000 civilians a day were dying of starvation. But at this point Colonel Ojukwu called on 4th Commando Brigade, under the mercenary 'Colonel' Rolf Steiner, for a last desperate effort to avoid total collapse. Despite the fact that it had lost 1800 men in the battle for Aba, the brigade responded. Not only was the pressure on Uli relieved, but two oil wells, the loss of which had threatened the basic mobility of the Biafran forces, were regained. In October, equipped with French-supplied ammunition and arms flown in from Gabon and the Ivory Coast, including the latest anti-tank weapons, the

Above: Colonel Rolf Steiner, leader of the mercenary force which fought with the Biafrans, and a young bodyguard take a break during a lull in the fighting.

Below: Colonel Benjamin Adekunle, commander of the Federal 3rd Commando Division, stands with his men shortly before the final assault against Port Harcourt.

Biafrans went over to the offensive, recapturing a number of small towns and villages, and effectively halting tentative Federal counter-moves.

But internal dissent once more interrupted Biafran progress. Steiner was involved in a violent quarrel with Ojukwu whom he accused of 'murdering' his mercenaries by employing them in frontal assaults on enemy positions. The same night, Steiner was seized and flown out of Biafra. The incident marked the end of mercenary participation in the army on any significant scale.

On the ground, 1969 opened quietly, but Federal air raids were increasingly heavy. Reports of indiscriminate bombing and of Nigerian efforts to stop food supplies to the starving Biafrans outraged world opinion. Belatedly, Gowon tried to improve Nigeria's public image. In April 1969, at the special urging of British Prime Minister Harold Wilson, whose government was under pressure to withdraw support from the Federal side, Gowon ordered bombing attacks to be limited to military targets. More importantly, he tried to negotiate an agreed method for delivering food aid which could not be used as a cover for military supplies. Ojukwu's evasive response to all such proposals disillusioned many of his humanitarian supporters.

Occupation and counter-attack
In late April the Federal forces launched an assault on Umuahia. Using tracked vehicles for the first time, they occupied the town. Colonel Ojukwu was forced to move his headquarters to Nkwerre, some 40km (26 miles) from Uli airfield. Yet once more the Biafrans demonstrated their remarkable resilience. No sooner had Umuahia fallen than they staged a sudden counter-attack to the south, recapturing Owerri and inflicting a sharp defeat on the supposedly invincible 3rd Commando Division. General Gowon seized the opportunity to deprive the dangerously popular Colonel Adekunle – 'The Black Scorpion' – of his command.

From May to October 1969 the limelight was monopolised by Count Carl von Rosen and his Swedish 'Minicon' air force, whose air strikes against the Federal side succeeded in destroying part of the Nigerian Air Force and two major oil refineries. But this was just delaying the inevitable. In two years the actual territory under Ojukwu's control had shrunk to less than one-tenth of its size at the outbreak of

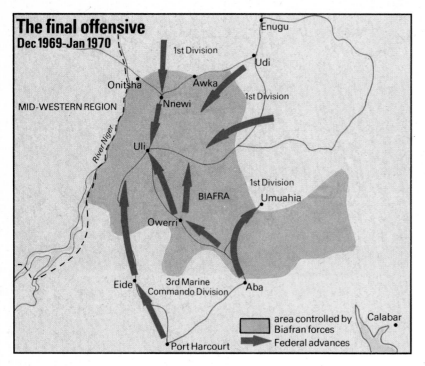

The final offensive
Dec 1969-Jan 1970

MID-WESTERN REGION

Enugu
Udi
1st Division
Onitsha
Awka
1st Division
Nnewi
River Niger
Uli
BIAFRA
1st Division
Umuahia
Owerri
Eide
3rd Marine
Commando Division
Aba
Port Harcourt
Calabar

area controlled by
Biafran forces
Federal advances

Below: Biafran troops carry the body of their mercenary commander back from the front. Mercenaries fought on both sides during the war, but they were most important for the rebels. Rolf Steiner's 4th Commando Brigade staved off collapse in September 1968.

road, was attained on Christmas Day. Instead of sitting down to consolidate this gain, the commandos then pushed on to link up with the 1st Division in Umuahia. Biafra was now split in two.

Possibly because so many previous announcements had proved premature, Lagos did not broadcast its first victory communiqué until 10 January 1970. It simply stated that 3rd and 1st Divisions had achieved their liaison. It could, however, have announced news of the end. Biafran morale, having stood up to so many trials, suddenly collapsed. Soldiers, discarding arms and uniforms, mingled with refugees.

The last meeting of the Biafran cabinet, held on 10 January, was reported as 'a long and sad affair'. Eventually, having been persuaded to leave the country after handing over to his chief-of-staff, Major-General Effiong, Colonel Ojukwu was able to reach Uli and take off at 0300 hours on the morning of 11 January for the Ivory Coast. By then Federal troops were only 5km (3 miles) distant.

On 12 January, General Effiong broadcast to announce the Biafran capitulation. On the same day General Gowon also broadcast, giving his official acceptance of the surrender and ending: 'We must all welcome, with open arms, the people now freed from the tyranny and deceit of Ojukwu and his gang.'

However unrealistic this assessment of Ojukwu's relation to the Ibo people may have been, there is no question that the Nigerian government and army treated the former citizens of Biafra in an exemplary manner, completely disproving claims that they intended to wipe out the Easterners. A large degree of national reconciliation was achieved in a remarkably short time after the conflict. But nothing could eradicate the scars of a war that had cost about one million lives.
Patrick Turnbull

hostilities. In June a Federal offensive was repelled, but the Biafrans were too weak to follow up the enemy retreat. The few vehicles still operational were wearing out. There were few spare parts or replacements. Meanwhile the Federal side received fresh MiG fighters and Soviet 122mm artillery pieces. In December, the final offensive began.

The onslaught was spearheaded by the 3rd Commando Division, now led by Colonel Obosanjo. Its first objective, the securing of the Aba-Umuahia

Key Weapons

SMART BOMBS

Smart weapons – that is, free-falling or gliding munitions which have a guidance system – first appeared during World War II in response to the need for increased accuracy of aerial bombing against important targets that were difficult to hit. Two very similar types, the American Azon and the German Fritz-X, were used operationally and these established the modern smart formula of a standard iron bomb with a strap-on guidance system and control/flight surfaces. The Azon was based upon the 450kg (1000lb) M-65 bomb fitted with a special tail unit which allowed it to be steered in flight. Guidance commands were passed to the weapon via a radio link with the bomb aimer on the carrier aircraft. Once the target had been acquired in the bomb sight, the bomb aimer could direct the Azon onto it. The Azon also had a flare mounted in the tail unit to maximise visibility from above. Likewise, the German Fritz-X used the Luftwaffe's PC-1400 armour-piercing bomb, mated to a steering unit. Control was again via a radio link and a tail flare was used for visual tracking.

Both these weapons were fairly successful, the Azon being used most effectively against bridges in Burma, whilst the Fritz-X made a spectacular operational debut with the sinking of the Italian battleship *Roma* on 9 September 1943. The need to track the bombs visually throughout their fall, however, left the carrier aircraft open to anti-aircraft fire during the necessarily long and steady bombing run, while the use of radio as the guidance link rendered the system vulnerable to jamming.

These operational and technological limitations virtually halted smart-weapon development in the years following 1945 and it was not until the late 1950s that interest in the concept re-awakened. By this time, the transistor was beginning to revolutionise electronics through miniaturisation and for the first time it was possible to consider a television system as an alternative to radio for guidance. Television could offer a high degree of accuracy combined with the capacity to function a long way from the target. As long as the signal emitted from the weapon could be picked up, it did not matter where the carrier aircraft was; the target could still be seen. A further advantage was that the VHF/UHF frequencies used for television transmissions were much harder to jam.

The practicality of such a system, now known as EO (electro-optics) and the stimulus of the war in Vietnam, prompted the Americans to develop a second generation of smart weapons, many of which are still in service today. The first operational EO type was the US Navy's AGM-62 Walleye which came into service in Southeast Asia in 1967/68. Guidance for the Walleye was provided by a TV camera mounted in the weapon's nose which transmitted target information back to the carrier aircraft. The operator could either lock on to the target prior to launch or 'fly' the weapon during the course of its gliding trajectory. Initial enthusiasm for the Walleye led the US Navy to describe it as 'the most accurate and effective air-to-surface conventional weapon ever developed', but more sober evaluations showed it to have too small a warhead to deal with certain 'hard' targets, and to be lacking in range.

These limitations were recognised quite early on in the weapon's development and were tackled in a number of programmes culminating in the Walleye II system which appeared in the early 1970s. The new model carried a much larger warhead and was provided with enlarged wings which more than doubled the range capability of the earlier model to 56km (35 miles). Even these improvements were not considered sufficient and, in 1972, the type was further modified to incorporate a data link which allowed it to be launched at extreme range and to be controlled remote from the carrier aircraft if required. A total of five such Extended Range/Data Link Walleye IIs, as the new model was known, were launched operationally in Vietnam with encouraging results and, since 1978, some 3800 early-model Walleyes have been brought up to this standard.

While the US Navy was developing Walleye, the United States Air Force (USAF) was working on its own EO programme, code-named Pave Strike. Research and development resulted in the GBU-8 HOBOS (homing bomb system) family which became operational in Vietnam in February 1969. Unlike the navy weapon, HOBOS reverted to the strap-on philosophy pioneered by the Azon and Fritz-X, the initial models being based on the Mk84 or M118 iron bombs. The GBU-8 family was also designed to carry

Previous page: A Paveway II LGB demonstrates its astonishing pin-point accuracy. Comparative tests against conventional free-fall bombs have shown that the LGB, while improving accuracy by a factor of 200, also represents a massive saving in ordnance costs, since targets which would normally require the use of hundreds of free-fall bombs can be knocked out by only a few well-placed LGBs. Above: An early example of a smart weapon, the Tarzon, was a 5450kg (12,000lb) bomb fitted with the Azon's steering gear. The Tarzon was suspended in 1951 after one blew up its B-29 carrier on release.

Above: A prototype of the first operational EO smart weapon, the AGM-62 Walleye, which uses a TV camera mounted in the nose of the bomb to relay directional information back to the carrier aircraft. Left: A sequence of photographs showing a US Navy pilot's view of the Ninh Binh bridge in North Vietnam through the TV-guidance eye of a Walleye bomb as he steers the bomb onto the target, seconds before impact with the superstructure.

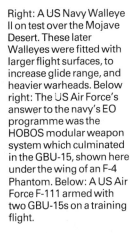

Right: A US Navy Walleye II on test over the Mojave Desert. These later Walleyes were fitted with larger flight surfaces, to increase glide range, and heavier warheads. Below right: The US Air Force's answer to the navy's EO programme was the HOBOS modular weapon system which culminated in the GBU-15, shown here under the wing of an F-4 Phantom. Below: A US Air Force F-111 armed with two GBU-15s on a training flight.

a range of homing systems in addition to the standard television link to maximise its operational flexibility. The most important of these alternatives was an infra-red unit which allowed HOBOS to be used in low-light conditions.

In Southeast Asia, GBU-8 was used with considerable success by the 8th Tactical Fighter Wing (TFW) flying F-4 Phantoms, especially during the 1972 Linebacker I campaign against North Vietnamese communications, when it was used against important bridge links. Indeed, the HOBOS' performance was so impressive that, in 1972, the USAF initiated another development programme which resulted in what is perhaps the most advanced EO weapon, the GBU-15.

The new programme laid emphasis on extended range and on the provision of blind-attack facilities. To achieve these goals, the GBU-15 was designed from the start as a modular weapon in which various component groups could be mixed and matched to suit a specific operational need. To this end, two warhead options, the Mk84 iron bomb or the SUU-54 cluster munition, were provided which could be coupled with one of three sets of flight/control surface packages. For guidance either EO, laser, or thermal-imaging (the use of infra-red radiation to produce a visual image) could be employed. In addition, a data link system was fitted as standard to give the same sort of range performance as the navy's Extended Range/Data Link Walleye II.

Still in production in the 1980s, the latest model of the GBU-15 is known as the CCW (cruciform wing). The type is based around the Mk84 bomb or the CBU-75 cluster munition and uses EO or thermal-imaging guidance. In practice, the GBU-15 CCW is launched at low or medium altitude with the operator aiming it directly at the target when using thermal-imaging guidance, or in its general direction using EO with the weapon controlled via the data link until visual contact is acquired. This use of the data link allows the carrier aircraft to employ terrain-hugging tactics for surprise against heavily defended targets and provides a launch window well outside the range of the enemy's defences. Indeed, such tactics often involve the use of a second control aircraft standing off to allow the carrier to make the quickest of escapes and are reported to be flown at extremely low level.

Effective as the EO-guided bombs have proved to be, they nevertheless have certain inherent limitations, not the least of which is that they nearly always require daylight to function effectively. This was clear even at the start of EO development in America and from the outset smart-weapon designers were looking for alternatives. The breakthrough came in 1960 when Bell Telephones produced the first practical gas laser. In such a device, producing as it does a

Paveway series

Paveway I

Paveway II

Paveway III

Left above: A US Air Force 435th Tactical Fighter Squadron F-4D Phantom, armed with Paveway I LGBs, on a bombing raid over North Vietnam. Left: An Australian Mirage IIIO carrying test-round Paveway IIs during the Australian Air Force's evaluation trials of the Paveway LGB system.

continuous, very intense and very sharply defined beam of infra-red light, the weapon designers saw an extremely efficient targeting capability. The secret of the laser's value in this role lies in the coherence of the light beam it produces, even when that beam is reflected. This being the case, the highly directional nature of laser light meant that a target could theoretically be marked to an accuracy of centimetres and its equally coherent reflection could be used to guide an air-dropped weapon with the same degree of accuracy. Better still, laser-designation target-marking would be as effective at night as it was in daylight and the laser source could be remote from the carrier. In effect, ground troops could mark a bridge or installation while the bomb homed in on the reflected light (known as the 'basket'), and followed through to the target with minute accuracy.

The exciting possibilities of lasers in this area were quickly realised and the Pave Alpha programme to develop LGBs (laser guided bombs) was initiated and successfully tested in 1965. Work on the designator equipment proved to be more difficult but was eventually successful and the first Paveway LGB was used in Vietnam in May 1968. The Paveway bomb retained the strap-on approach developed by the USAF in its HOBOS EO weapons, in that each weapon was a standard iron bomb modified to accommodate a laser-seeker unit on the nose and a set of flight/control surfaces. The Paveway family is very large, now being in its third generation, but in every case the operating principle is the same. Once launched, the seeker head, a silicon detector divided into four quadrants, aligns itself with the direction of flight. Each of the quadrants is searched in turn for reflected laser light and when detected, a linked on-board computer generates guidance commands for the con-

trol surfaces to direct the weapon towards the light source. The system is simple and effective and any fighter or bomber can carry an LGB on its standard munitions racks. There is no need for the installation of control equipment in the carrier and a single designator, be it air or ground based, can control the weapon.

The end of the Vietnam War saw no slackening of pace in the development and use of the Paveway family, and in the early 1980s the weapon equipped

Above: A Paveway I drops from a Teledyne Ryan AQN-34 remotely-piloted vehicle over Vietnam. Below: The Paveway III, the latest addition to the Paveway family. Inset: With accurate designation it can destroy its target with minute precision and devastating effects.

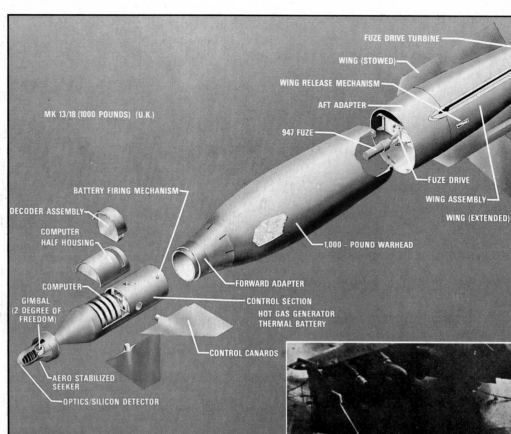

FUZE DRIVE TURBINE

WING (STOWED)

WING RELEASE MECHANISM

AFT ADAPTER

947 FUZE

MK 13/18 (1000 POUNDS) (U.K.)

FUZE DRIVE

WING ASSEMBLY

WING (EXTENDED)

BATTERY FIRING MECHANISM

DECODER ASSEMBLY

COMPUTER
HALF HOUSING

1,000 - POUND WARHEAD

COMPUTER

FORWARD ADAPTER

GIMBAL
(2 DEGREE OF
FREEDOM)

CONTROL SECTION

HOT GAS GENERATOR
THERMAL BATTERY

CONTROL CANARDS

AERO STABILIZED
SEEKER

OPTICS/SILICON DETECTOR

Left: An exploded view of the British Royal Air Force Paveway Mk 13/18 laser-guided smart bomb. The Mk 13/18's laser-seeking unit is strapped onto a 455kg (1000lb) warhead, a combination which proved highly successful in precision strikes against Argentinian troop positions on the Falklands. Below: Armed with the Mk 13/18 LGB, a British GR3 Harrier stands-by on the flight deck of the carrier HMS *Hermes*.

the air forces of no less than 15 countries, including the British Royal Air Force who are the most recent users of the type in combat. During the 1982 Falklands War, the Harriers of No 1 Squadron used Paveway bombs on at least three occasions, the first of which was an abortive attack on Port Stanley airport. This mission failed due to a lack of adequate designators, but by June suitable equipment was available and two strikes were made on Argentinian positions on Mount Tumbledown with devastating success.

There can be little doubt that, with the entry into service of the EO GBU-15 and the Paveway III LGBs, the smart bomb has come of age. Despite continuing limitations in certain areas, the class as a whole looks certain to have a place in the armouries of the world's air forces for the foreseeable future, providing as it does a solution to one of aerial warfare's oldest problems: how to bomb a target accurately.

Smart weapons

Weapons	Year	Length	Span	Guidance system	Warhead	Range
Fritz-X	1943	3.26m (10ft 8in)	1.35m (4ft 5in)	line of sight/ command radio	PC 1400 1400kg (3080lb)	up to 9km (5.6 miles)
Walleye I	1967	3.44m (11ft 3in)	1.16m (3ft 9in)	electro-optics	high explosive 371kg (825lb)	up to 26km (16 miles)
Walleye II	c.1970	4.04m (13ft 3in)	1.3m (4ft 3in)	electro-optics	Mk84 bomb 900kg (2000lb)	up to 56km (35 miles)
GBU-8 HOBOS	1969	3.78m (12ft 7in)	1.3m (4ft 3in)	electro-optics or infra-red	Mk84 bomb or M118 bomb 1360kg (3000lb)	
KMU-351A/B Paveway 1 family	1968	4.27m (14ft 3in)	1.14m (3ft 9in)	laser	Mk84 bomb	
GBU-15 CCW	1983	3.91m (12ft 10in)	1.49m (4ft 11in)	electro-optics or thermal-imaging	Mk84 bomb or CBU-75 cluster	up to 8km (5 miles)

Countdown to conflict

The outbreak of the Six-Day War

It is obvious that the existence of Israel was at the root of the Six-Day War but it would over-simplify the issues involved to claim that it was the cause of the war. The war grew out of a number of long-standing problems, many of them purely internal questions within the states involved, which erupted into a serious crisis in May 1967. Once involved in the crisis governments were unable to control its progress, their actions being misunderstood by friend and foe alike.

Within the Arab world there were two camps. The 'traditionalist' element, led by King Faisal of Saudi Arabia, included Jordan, Tunisia and the smaller Gulf states. The 'revolutionary' states included Egypt, Syria, Iraq and Algeria, all broadly socialist regimes. In the 1950s the revolutionary grouping had made most of the running under the leadership of President Nasser of Egypt. Nasser's prestige had been enhanced by the humiliation of the British and French governments in the 1956 Suez Crisis and he was a leading member of the non-aligned movement in world affairs. But during the 1960s, his position was challenged from several directions. The United Arab Republic (UAR), a federation of Egypt and Syria, broke up in 1961 and the Ba'athist, army-run regime in Syria continually complained about Nasser's failure to act against Israel; his attempt to support the revolutionary regime in the Yemen led to involvement in a long counter-insurgency campaign against the Saudi-backed monarchists, while at home promises of economic progress had proved hollow and Egypt was struggling with an increasing burden of foreign debts.

Since 1956 Nasser had been content to play down the Israeli question. In 1964 and 1965 he instigated a series of Arab summit conferences which generally favoured long-term solutions to the problem. An Arab Unified High Command had been established under an Egyptian general; and he reported that there was no immediate prospect of military action. But by 1967 Israel was the only issue on which the Arabs were united and which could divert attention from Nasser's internal problems.

The traditionalist states were also becoming more influential, thanks to Faisal and Saudi Arabia's increasing oil wealth. They had little time for Nasser, whom they justifiably suspected of supporting opposition groups. Among these states Jordan was the most vulnerable, divided between the Palestinians of the West Bank and the Bedouin in the rest of the country. King Hussein could count on the loyalty of the Bedouin only and had had to fight off several attempts to overthrow him.

A new element among the Arabs was the creation of a Palestinian 'entity' at the Cairo Summit of January 1964, which developed into the Palestine Liberation Organisation (PLO). The PLO set up a Liberation Army based in Gaza in Egypt and armed by the Egyptians, but received little positive support from the other Arab states. Syria, suspicious of Egypt's influence in the PLO, created El Fatah ('struggle') which carried out a series of guerrilla raids into Israel.

Within Israel these raids created political as well as security problems for the government of Levi Eshkol. The Israeli opposition parties attacked Eshkol's tired-looking coalition for its inactivity in the face of El Fatah raids and Syrian artillery attacks on settlements in the north. Eshkol was aware that retaliation might compromise American support or provoke the Soviet Union into more active assistance to the Arabs, but he could not altogether resist the calls for military action. Moreover, Israeli military doctrine had no place for purely defensive action. Because of the vulnerability of their small country the Israelis believe in fighting on their enemy's territory and in pre-emptive action. From the very first Arab raids onto their territory the Israelis had not been content to try to defend their settlements but had struck back against the guerrilla

Below: Despite Israel's declared intention of going to war to maintain a right of passage through the Straits of Tiran, political pressures forced Nasser to impose a blockade of Israeli shipping passing through this area in an announcement on 22 May 1967. Here Israeli torpedo boats patrol the Straits in early 1967.

bases in the neighbouring states. In 1956 this policy had culminated in the invasion of Sinai in order to 'cleanse' the Gaza Strip. Now there was a similar pattern of heavier and heavier military strikes. In 1965 the Israelis struck at Jordanian and Lebanese villages suspected of being El Fatah bases. In November 1966 an Israeli battalion group crossed into Jordan and attacked the village of Es Samu near Hebron, killing 14 Jordanians. On 7 April 1967 an artillery duel on the Syrian border led the Israeli Air Force to intervene. Six Syrian MiG fighters were shot down without Israeli loss. This was followed by increasingly hard-line statements from the Eshkol government. On 13 May Eshkol declared that Israel would respond 'at the place, the time and in the manner we choose' to violations of her borders.

This statement could only be seen as threatening in the Arab capitals, but might have passed as simple rhetoric if it had not been for reports of Israeli troop concentrations against Syria. It appears that the Soviet Union definitely warned Syria that the Israelis had concentrated 11 to 13 brigades against them. Although there is no evidence of real Israeli preparations on that scale, which would have required a major mobilisation, it is possible that some lesser punitive strike was being contemplated.

Thoroughly alarmed, the Syrians called for help. Nasser was taunted by both Syrians and Jordanians because of his failure to act at the time of the Es Samu raid and the April air battle. If he failed to act now his claim to leadership of the Arab world might vanish. It is hard to avoid the conclusion that from this point in the crisis Nasser's primary concern was the impact his actions would have among the Arabs and the rest of the world. He also seems to have believed his own propaganda, for Cairo Radio was claiming that the Israeli Defence Forces were little more than a home guard who could 'not take part in battles involving regular armies'. Certainly Nasser seems to have been

Above left: After signing the defence treaty, which sealed a degree of Arab unity by placing the Jordanian forces under an Egyptian general, King Hussein (left) and President Nasser (right) leave the Kubbeh Palace. Above right: Levi Eshkol, the Israeli prime minister, who had to take the final decision as to whether Israel should initiate war by attacking Egypt. Eshkol's decision was heavily influenced by the fact that Israeli military doctrine concentrated on offensive rather than defensive action, and his generals urged a pre-emptive strike.

excessively foolhardy in relying on Israeli passivity.

His first step was to deploy Egyptian forces into Sinai on 16 May 1967. This was a fairly obvious move, but would not have satisfied the Arab world by itself. Nasser therefore simultaneously insisted that the United Nations Emergency Force (UNEF) withdraw from its positions in Sinai. UNEF had held observation posts along the Egyptian-Israeli border since 1956, and Nasser had often been accused by his Arab critics of sheltering from the Israelis behind this force; his demand to the UN Secretary-General was basically a gesture to quieten those critics. In Israel, however, the move could be seen as evidence that Egypt was planning an attack in Sinai.

Closing the Straits
The withdrawal of UNEF may have brought Egypt into direct confrontation with Israel, but it did not satisfy the Arabs. Amman Radio asked, on 21 May, whether Nasser would go on to close the Straits of Tiran to Israel. The Israelis had made it clear that they would go to war to keep the Straits open. Egyptian troops replaced United Nations observers at Sharm el Sheikh, which dominated the Straits. If Nasser had failed to impose a blockade all his previous moves would have been revealed as mere sabre-rattling, and on 22 May he announced that Israeli ships would not be allowed to pass through the Straits. It is still not clear whether, in taking this step, Nasser was ignoring the risk of war that could result, or whether he had included it in his calculation.

Israel immediately appealed for international support. The United States, Britain and France had guaranteed freedom of passage for Israeli ships in 1957. The embarrassed Western powers procrastinated and sought diplomatic compromises. America was heavily involved in the Vietnam War and Britain and France were unwilling to worsen relations with the Arab world. As it became clear that nothing substantial would be done by the international community, pressure grew within Israel for unilateral action. On 1 June Eshkol was forced to make Moshe Dayan minister of defence and bring two more opposition leaders, Menachem Begin and Joseph Saphir, into a new Government of National Unity. The newcomers strengthened the opinion within the Cabinet that Israel's only option was an early war.

In the Arab world Nasser's closure of the Straits had raised him to a new height of popularity. Enthusiastic anti-Israeli demonstrations in every Arab country drove their governments to patch up their differences, although this appearance of unity came rather late in the day. For example on 23 May, after a terrorist bombing in a Jordanian town, Jordan had broken off relations with Syria. However, Hussein's position was increasingly precarious and he was forced to make a gesture of his own. On 30 May he flew to Cairo and signed a defence pact with Egypt that set up a joint command under an Egyptian general and included Syrian participation. Iraq joined within days and Iraqi forces began to move into Jordan. Saudi Arabia deployed armoured brigades near her border with Jordan, intending to move them closer to Israel. Algeria announced that it was sending a brigade to Egypt. The Egyptian force in Sinai reached a strength of seven divisions, 100,000 men.

These diplomatic and military moves were accompanied by a torrent of calls for the overthrow of Israel.

PLO leader Ahmad Shukeiri announced on 28 May 'Zero hour has come.... The UAR Army alone is capable of destroying the Israeli aggressor within a few hours.' On 29 May Nasser announced: 'Preparations have been made. We are now ready to confront Israel.' He warned that the issue was not the Straits of Tiran but 'the entire Palestine question'. Arab radio stations were filled with threats to Israel. It is far from certain that Nasser intended to attack Israel; he may even have been so confident of Israel's weakness that he was prepared to let the Israelis start the war. This would earn Israel international condemnation and Nasser may have believed that the Egyptians could defeat any Israeli attack.

The Israelis were not inclined to give Nasser the benefit of the doubt. They could hear the chorus of hatred, they could see the growing strength of the Arab armies on their borders. The Israeli armed forces were fully mobilised by the end of May, but could not be maintained at full strength without crippling the economy. The balance of forces could only grow even more unfavourable. By 4 June the High Command was able to convince the Cabinet that war was coming and, from the Israeli point of view, it must come as soon as possible.

Michael Orr

Below: El Fatah commandos atop a hill during a break in training in the Jordanian countryside. Raids into Israel by Fatah guerrillas had contributed greatly to the rise in tension in the Middle East, and had put great pressure on Israeli Premier Levi Eshkol, who was being urged to take decisive action against them.

The Middle East 1967

Face to face

The rival forces in the Middle East, 1967

As the Middle Eastern crisis of 1967 grew closer to open war, many of Israel's allies and all her enemies were convinced that the balance of forces was over-whelmingly stacked against her. The speed and completeness of the Israeli victory therefore appeared to be exceptionally dramatic and even miraculous. In reality the situation in June 1967 is an excellent illustration of the complexity of the factors which have to be considered in assessing a military balance. Such balances are never static but capable of con-siderable variations, particularly in response to tactic-al circumstances. A state which seizes the initiative can create its own military balance.

Thus, those who relied on figures such as those in Table 1 could easily paint a gloomy picture of Israel's chances. Israel's tiny population of two and a half million seemed likely to be swamped by the tens of millions of the Arab nations. But Israel mobilised over 10 per cent of her population in the armed forces. Egypt might have mobilised, in time, total forces approaching 500,000 but most of these would have been capable only of static internal security duties in the interior of the country. In forces actually available for combat on 5 June 1967 Israel outnumbered any individual Arab state. Arab protestations of unity and mutual assistance were impressive and in a long war might have been significant. However, in the six days that the war lasted only Egypt, Syria and Jordan took an active part. Saudi troops never reached Jordan and although an Iraqi armoured division was deployed into Jordan its leading brigade was destroyed by Israeli air attacks, halting the division's progress long before it reached the battlefield.

Inequality in numbers

Even so, the figures indicate that Egypt, Syria and Jordan between them outnumbered Israel in man-power and were superior by two-to-one in tanks, eight-to-one in artillery and three-to-one in aircraft. But this Arab superiority was never committed simul-taneously against Israel. Holding the initiative and exploiting the smallness of their country, its excellent roads and the comparative slowness of the Arabs, the Israelis shuffled their forces from front to front to achieve a far more equal balance on the battlefield. This is reflected in Table 2, which attempts to show the balance of forces in each of the three theatres of war. It must be said that such figures can only be approximate because even now reliable information is hard to find. The Israelis in particular have never released a detailed order of battle. Yet, despite this, it is clear that in operational terms the Israelis were only out-numbered in the Sinai. Elsewhere they achieved at least a rough equality.

Numbers are the most easily assessed aspect of a military balance. Subjective factors, quality rather than quantity, are more significant but very difficult to assess except with the benefit of hindsight. The

Israelis were obviously overwhelmingly superior in 1967, but where did this superiority lie? A key factor was that from the first hours of the war the Israelis had total command of the air. The advantage in terms of firepower that this gave them was crucial and soon became a moral advantage too. The spirit of the Arab armies was sapped by their feeling of hopeless vulner-ability to the Israeli Air Force.

In terms of the quality of equipment neither side had a great advantage. All the armies had a mix of obsolete World War II weapons and more modern equipment. Some weapons, such as Centurion and M48 tanks, were deployed by both sides, although most Arab equipment was Soviet in origin while the Israelis relied on Western manufacturers. In neither

Top: Reservist soldiers of the UAR Palestine Liberation Army shoulder their .303in Lee Enfield bolt-action rifles during training in Cairo.

case were the weapons designed specifically for the Middle East, although the Israeli tanks proved to be better suited to desert warfare. Another Israeli advantage lay in the superior technical skills of their soldiers and the higher standards of equipment maintenance achieved in the Israeli Army. Probably at least 20 per cent of Arab tanks and aircraft were out of action when the war began.

National survival

Most crucial were the fighting qualities of the rival armies. The Israelis had the tremendous boost of national unity and the belief that the army was fighting for national survival. On the Arab side unity was no more than a veneer. Jordan had been bitterly at odds with Egypt and Syria until a matter of days before the war started. A joint High Command was appointed, but it hardly functioned. There were also serious divisions within individual Arab nations. Thus the Palestinian element in Jordan felt little loyalty to King Hussein, who relied on the Bedouin majority within the army to stay in power. The Syrian Army was heavily involved in politics and a succession of purges had resulted in a substantial weakening of its officer corps.

There were good soldiers in the Arab armies: the Bedouin units of the Jordanian Army were highly

regarded and several Egyptian units performed well in the circumstances. However, the leaven was too thinly spread to counterbalance the Arabs' deficiencies. The average Arab soldier was poorly educated and the day-to-day life of, for example, an Egyptian *fellahin* provided little preparation for the unit discipline and group loyalty required by the armed forces. In static positions Arab soldiers could fight stubbornly, but they relied heavily on their officers and lacked the initiative which was so characteristic of the Israelis. Nor were Arab officers good at 'thinking on their feet'. They were extremely defensive-minded and relied too much on written orders. There was, generally speaking, a vast gulf between officers and men and officers felt little personal responsibility for the welfare of their soldiers. In Chaim Weizmann's words: 'Their officers are too fat and their soldiers are too thin.' Such leadership contrasted unfavourably with that of the Israeli Army, where leadership from the front was stressed. The cost of this was high; 23 per cent of Israeli casualties were officers. At every level the Arabs failed in leadership, whether it was battalion officers, middle-ranking staff officers or generals. Ultimately the greatest imbalance in the Middle Eastern military balance lay in the quality of individual officers and soldiers in the respective armies. **Michael Orr**

Above: Israeli tank commanders and their crews parade with their Centurion tanks in front of their commanding officer in the field, shortly before launching an offensive against Egyptian positions.

Arab-Israeli balance of forces 1967

Table 1: The overall balance

	Israel	Arab total*	Egypt	Syria	Jordan	Ìraq
total population	2,500,000	41,700,000	26,000,000	5,500,000	2,000,000	8,200,000
total armed forces	275,000	395,000	190,000	65,000	58,000	82,000
total ground forces	204,000	340,000	160,000	60,000	56,000	70,000
tanks-total modern obsolescent	1000 450+ 550	2450 1350 1100	1200 500 700	550 350 200	200 200 0	500 300 200
artillery pieces	200	1550	1000	300	250	
combat aircraft-total mach 2 first-line fighters supersonic aircraft subsonic fighter bombers light/medium bombers	260 90 20 150 0	760 200 120 440 106	470 120 100 180 70	120 20 20 60 20	20 0 0 20 0	150 60 0 80 16
naval forces personnel destroyers and frigates fast attack craft fast attack craft (missile armed) submarines	4000 3 9 0 3	14,000 7 61 22 12	13,000 7 44 18 12	1000 0 17 4 0		

*in addition Saudi Arabia, Kuwait and Algeria offered small contingents which never reached the combat zone

Table 2: The theatre balances

	Sinai	West Bank	Golan
Arab	7 armoured brigades 1 mechanised brigade 19 infantry/parachute brigades total ground forces 100,000 tanks 900	2 armoured brigades 7 infantry/parachute brigades total ground forces 45,000 tanks 200	2 armoured brigades 2 mechanised brigades 5 infantry/parachute brigades total ground forces 35,000 tanks 350-400
Israeli	6 armoured brigades 5 infantry/parachute brigades total ground forces 70,000 tanks 650	2 armoured brigades 1 mechanised brigade 6 infantry/parachute brigades total ground forces 45,000 tanks 275	4 armoured brigades 4 infantry/parachute brigades total ground forces 40,000 tanks 300-350

Operation Dawn
The Israelis destroy the Egyptian Air Force

The Six-Day War of June 1967 marks the high point of Israel's military fortunes during the 30 years of intermittent conflict with neighbouring Arab states which followed the creation of the state of Israel in 1948. And the successes gained against Egypt in Sinai, as well as the advances into Jordan and Syria to the north, were largely due to the Israeli Air Force (IAF) winning air superiority at a single bold stroke at the outset of the war.

Israel's chief antagonist in 1967 was Nasser's Egypt which, at least on paper, had superior air power. The IAF's tactical fighter force consisted of nearly 200 aircraft, all of which had a dual air-to-air combat and ground attack capability. The most modern fighter, which equipped three squadrons, was the Dassault Mirage IIICJ. Less modern French warplanes made up the balance of the force, with one squadron flying the Dassault Super Mystère B2, three squadrons flying the Dassault Mystère IVA and two employing the Dassault Ouragan. In addition there was a single squadron of Sud Vautour twin-engined attack aircraft and more than 70 Fouga Magister jet trainers, which could be employed for light attack missions. This force totalled 297 combat aircraft, although not all would be available for operations at any one time.

The Egyptian Air Force's 450 combat aircraft were all supplied by the Soviet Union. They comprised six squadrons of MiG-21 air superiority fighters, which had only a limited ground attack capability, and four squadrons of MiG-19s, also primarily intended for air-to-air combat. Ground attack was undertaken by five squadrons of MiG-17s and MiG-15s, with a single squadron of the newer Sukhoi Su-7 on strength. The bomber force consisted of three squadrons of Ilyushin Il-28 light bombers and two squadrons of Tupolev Tu-16 medium bombers. The Tu-16s represented a particularly serious threat to Israel's densely populated cities. The air forces of Syria, Iraq, Jordan,

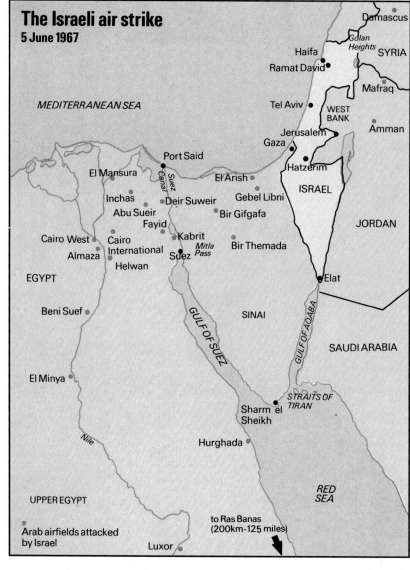

The Israeli air strike
5 June 1967

MEDITERRANEAN SEA

Damascus
Golan Heights
SYRIA
Haifa
Ramat David
Mafraq
Tel Aviv
WEST BANK
Amman
Jerusalem
Gaza
Hatzerim
Port Said
El Arish
ISRAEL
El Mansura
Suez Canal
Gebel Libni
Inchas
Deir Suweir
Bir Gifgafa
JORDAN
Abu Sueir
Fayid
Cairo West
Kabrit
Bir Themada
Cairo International
Mitla Pass
Almaza
Suez
Helwan
Elat
EGYPT
GULF OF SUEZ
SINAI
GULF OF AQABA
Beni Suef
SAUDI ARABIA
El Minya
STRAITS OF TIRAN
Sharm el Sheikh
Nile
Hurghada
RED SEA
UPPER EGYPT
to Ras Banas
(200km-125 miles)
Arab airfields attacked by Israel
Luxor

Algeria and the Lebanon could contribute a further 370 warplanes to the overall Arab air strength.

However, what the IAF lacked in numbers of aircraft it compensated for in the morale, motivation and training of its combat pilots. The Egyptian Air Force's pilots, by contrast, were trained under the rigid and unimaginative constraints of Soviet Air Force doctrine and tended to lack initiative and aggressiveness in combat. Similarly, while senior Egyptian Air Force officers were stereotyped in their thinking, the IAF commanders showed both originality and audacity. No clearer illustration of these traits can be found than the preliminary planning for the air strike on Egyptian airfields that was to open the Six-Day War.

The plan to knock out the Egyptian Air Force on its own bases would only work if the Israeli pilots could coordinate their attacks. As they would be operating from different bases and flying aircraft with dissimilar cruising speeds, this requirement was by no means as straightforward as might have been supposed. However, unless the initial air strikes all went in at the same time, surprise would be lost and the Egyptian defences alerted. Also, the need to fly at low level throughout the mission to avoid detection by enemy radar made navigation especially difficult. Thus the Israeli air strike was only feasible because of the high calibre of its pilots. It also relied for its success to a large degree on the predictable behaviour of the enemy air force. The initial attack was carefully timed to catch the Egyptians at a disadvantage. It was known that their fighters were put on alert to counter a possible dawn attack and that air patrols were also flown at this time. By attacking at 0745 hours Israeli time (0845 hours Egyptian time), the Israelis were confident that the Egyptian air

Above left: The view through the bomb sights of an IAF bomber clearly shows plumes of smoke rising from an Egyptian airbase after an attack by IAF planes. Above inset: General Mordechai Hod, the commander of the IAF. He advocated the pre-emptive strike which destroyed the Arab air forces on the ground and gave air superiority to the Israelis. Below: Israeli Centurion tanks halt their advance as an IAF French-made Sud Vautour bomber swoops low over their position.

patrols would have landed and the fighters on ground alert would have stood down. Furthermore, the Egyptian commanders and staff officers would not reach their offices until 0900 hours, 15 minutes after the initial attacks.

The Israeli Mystères and Ouragans, the oldest fighters in the inventory, attacked four major airfields in Sinai – Bir Gifgafa, Bir Themada, El Arish and Gebel Libni – on 5 June 1967. Two of the airfields – El Arish and Gebel Libni – were spared the destruction of their runways; the Israelis believed that their own army would soon overrun eastern Sinai and these bases could then be speedily returned to use as forward airfields for the IAF. The approach flight to the Sinai targets followed the direct route from the airbases in southern Israel. But the Super Mystères and Mirages which attacked airfields in the Canal Zone, the Nile Delta and the Cairo area flew in a wide sweep out into the Mediterranean, before swinging in over the Egyptian coast. This brought them over their targets from a totally unexpected direction, attacking out of the sun.

The Israeli air strike achieved complete tactical surprise. Egyptian aircraft were discovered lined up on their hard-standings with little attempt to disperse them around the airfield. This was by no means simply the result of short-sightedness on the part of the Egyptians, since operating from a flight line rather than from dispersal sites gave greater efficiency in aircraft servicing and maintenance. This was the way in which most air forces operated in the 1960s.

Nevertheless, the result was disastrous for the Egyptians. Many aircraft were destroyed by cannon and rocket fire where they stood, although at least eight formations of MiGs were knocked out on their taxiways as they attempted to take off.

For the Israeli pilots, the clear morning light and the still air conditions of the early day, before the sun's heat had created the low-level turbulence usually associated with desert flying, made the task of weapons aiming considerably easier. The enemy runways were a priority target. Once these had been cratered, the Egyptian Air Force was effectively grounded and could be dealt with at leisure. The Israeli fighters were armed with a special runway-cratering bomb of French manufacture. Weighing 550kg (1200lb), it comprised a 360kg (800lb) warhead and two rockets. One of the rockets fired immediately after the bomb's release to retard the weapon's forward momentum, a drogue parachute then deployed to stabilise its downward flight and finally

Carnage at Beni Suef

'In those first instants of the Israeli assault everything was completely confused. Even before we realised what was happening, the attack was over. Everything was damaged. It was incredible. Despite dummy planes and camouflage the Israelis seemed to know exactly which targets to hit. In those moments I was in terror of my life and the scream of the jets as they flew in low to attack was more frightening than the explosions or the guns. We were caught in complete surprise and had no chance to defend. The planes which were actually on the runway were completely destroyed, the buildings were burning and for the first time in my life I saw war casualties. It was terrible. Blood was everywhere and people were trying to hold on to limbs that were falling off. I saw one man who had been cut in half by machine gun fire trying to scoop his intestines back into his body. Everywhere people were running around shouting orders but nobody knew what was happening or what to do.

'Of course, that was bad. We had only two aircraft that could be repaired but that would take days and also there was more death to come. The runway had been hit many times with a special bomb. At first we did not understand it. We laughed because their bombs had not exploded and we would soon mend the runway but we learnt very quickly that this was a different type of bomb. It was a delayed fuse and as soon as we tried to move them they would go off. We lost many men in human sacrifice as we tried to clear the bombs away, sometimes they would just go off when you got near them. We could do nothing. We were destroyed and we could not get operational. But above all, we were completely shocked, astonished, by the ferocity and speed with which our unit was annihilated. They had come and gone without us firing a shot in defence and they had left us shattered with no equipment and many men dead or dying.'

Left: Three Egyptian MiG-21s destroyed by accurate IAF bomb runs.

Account by an Egyptian eye-witness of the Israeli dawn raid on Beni Suef airfield, 5 June 1967.

the second rocket ignited to drive the bomb into the runway's concrete surface, where the warhead detonated to create a 2m (6ft) deep crater. The Egyptians' task of runway repair was hampered by the inclusion of a number of bombs fitted with delayed-action fuses in the warload.

Flying in formations of four aircraft, the Israelis attacked in relays. Because the outward flight to the target airfields had to be made at low level, where fuel consumption is high, the attacking fighters needed to carry auxiliary fuel tanks. This reduced the bomb load that the fighters could carry and so forced them to rely on their built-in cannon armament. Once their attacks were completed, the Israeli fighters returned to their airfields to refuel and rearm and by 0845 hours (Israeli time) were ready to launch a second wave of attacks.

Completing the destruction

The 10 airfields hit during the first wave of the Israeli attack were naturally the Egyptian Air Force's main bases, but follow-up attacks on airfields of lesser importance were needed to complete the work of destruction. Although the Tu-16 bombers' base at Cairo West was one of the initial targets, it was reported that some of the Tu-16s had been dispersed to Cairo International Airport and so this airfield was added to the target list. The IAF succeeded in destroying all 30 Egyptian Tu-16s before they could go into action. Not all Egyptian aircraft were grounded, however, and an air battle between 16 Mirages and 20 MiG-21s took place over Abu Sueir airfield in the Canal Zone, four MiGs being shot down.

Two airfields in Upper Egypt, Ras Banas on the

Red Sea and Luxor, were beyond the range of the Israeli fighter aircraft. A long-range strike was mounted against them by the twin-engined Vautours. Operating from the bases at Ramat David and Hatzerim, the Vautours flew down the Gulf of Aqaba and across the Red Sea to attack their targets.

The effective destruction of the Egyptian Air Force was accomplished within a period of two hours, allowing the Israelis to turn their attention to the other Arab air forces and to the task of ground support. At 1100 hours the Jordanian Air Force had launched an attack on the Israeli airfield at Kfar Sirkin. The IAF counter-attack against Jordanian airbases at Mafraq and Amman was devastating. Eighteen of Jordan's 22 British Hawker Hunters – the air force's only effective fighting strength – were lost on 5 June. The Syrian Air Force also launched an attack, a bombing raid on the Haifa oil refineries, with similar results – a strike against Syrian bases which destroyed 45 of their 142 aircraft.

It is a measure of the Israelis' success on 5 June that of the 254 Egyptian aircraft destroyed during the Six-Day War, no fewer than 240 were lost on the first day. Nearly 1000 sorties were flown by the Israelis and 20 of their aircraft were shot down. Most of the losses were due to ground fire, the only aircraft to be destroyed in air combat being a Vautour. The air superiority gained on the first day of the war was never seriously challenged, although on 6 June the Algerian Air Force despatched a squadron of MiG-21s to the combat zone and these went into action over Sinai. Sporadic air engagements took place over all fronts, but the air battle had been decided on the first day and

Above right: A three-shot sequence taken from an IAF Mirage shows a Syrian MiG caught in the sights, being hit and then exploding. Above far right: A Soviet-made SA-2 Guideline missile is guarded by two Syrians on the Golan Heights. Right: An Egyptian Air Force MiG-17 lies shattered at the edge of its airfield.

thenceforth the Six-Day War was fought primarily on the ground.

The initial Israeli ground assaults had been supported by attack sorties flown by Magister armed trainers, as these were the only Israeli warplanes which had not been committed to the pre-emptive strike against the Egyptian Air Force. But from 6 June the IAF was able to concentrate on close air support of the army. This proved to be especially effective against Egyptian forces retreating through the Mitla Pass in Sinai, where several hundred vehicles were destroyed in air attacks. The virtual elimination of enemy air opposition also allowed the Israelis to employ airborne forces and helicopter-borne assault troops in operations behind Egyptian lines, one notable success being the capture of Sharm el Sheikh – the key to the strategically-important Straits of Tiran. Ground-support missions over the heavily-fortified Syrian positions on the Golan Heights were tougher going. Here the Israeli pilots for the first time encountered Soviet SA-2 Guideline surface-to-air missiles.

In the final reckoning, the IAF accounted for the destruction of some 350 Arab combat aircraft for the loss of 31 of its own during the Six-Day War. In the wider perspective, the Israelis' success in destroying aircraft on the ground pointed to a lesson that few air commanders could afford to ignore.

Anthony Robinson

War in the shadows

Mossad and the Israeli intelligence network

Every state concerned to preserve its independence and security must have an efficient intelligence service. Only then can a government know the resources and intentions of its enemies, actual or potential. Intelligence is an essential element of defence, and no government has been in greater need of a good intelligence service than has the state of Israel since it came into existence in 1948, surrounded by openly hostile Arab nations. Fortunately for Israel it has, and has had since its foundation, an intelligence service which is the envy of most other nations and which ranks with the American CIA and Russian KGB in the quality and quantity of the information it acquires.

Even before Israel became an independent state in 1948 the leaders of the Jewish population in Palestine had recognised the importance of intelligence gathering. In the 1930s the Haganah – the Jewish self-defence force in Palestine – built up an underground intelligence organisation to collect information about the plans both of the British mandatory power and of the Arabs who were stepping up their actions against the Jewish settlers. At the same time Jews employed in the British administration learnt a great deal about intelligence and secret work from police officials and the military, who included such masters of the trade as Orde Wingate, later famous as leader of the Chindits in Burma in World War II.

Once World War II was over Zionists were able to turn their full attention once again to the task of forcing the British out of Palestine and creating their own independent state. Apart from operations within the Mandate itself, the Haganah created a highly efficient organisation for smuggling Jews out of the displaced persons camps in Europe and North Africa and into Palestine in the face of active opposition by the Royal Navy, while Israeli agents were busy in Europe and America buying up arms and shipping them secretly to Palestine. It was all first-class experience for the men who would later form the core of Israel's secret service.

In all these activities the Jews enjoyed, and still enjoy, one tremendous advantage over most other nations: there is a Jewish community in almost every country, living not as foreigners but as assimilated members of the society of their adoption. Even if such people usually feel a greater loyalty to the country where they or their ancestors have found refuge than to Zionism or the State of Israel, many of them are still ready to support the Jewish cause with information, money or the use of influence.

The peacetime Israeli intelligence service developed naturally out of the pre-1948 organisations. Its creation was primarily the work of Ben Gurion, first prime minister of Israel, who took great pains to ensure that the new intelligence service was firmly under the control of the government and did not serve any factional purposes.

The organisation which eventually emerged had three main branches. The first was the Directorate of Military Intelligence, known as the Aman (from Agaf Modlin or Information Bureau), which is concerned only with the collection of military information abroad. The second was the Shin Beth (an abbreviation of Shereth Bitakhon or Security Service), which is mainly a counter-espionage organisation but which has also come to supervise the whole intelligence operation. It has to grapple with the difficult problems created by the large Arab population living in Israel and the numbers of Jewish immigrants entering Israel from Russia and eastern Europe. Both these groups might be infiltrated by Arab or Soviet agents.

The third branch was the Mossad, known properly as the Mossad Le Aliyah Beth, meaning the Institution for Intelligence and Special Services, which is the oldest of the intelligence organisations and is responsible for Israel's intelligence operations throughout the world. It is the Mossad which mainly accounts for the high esteem in which the Israeli secret service is held by other intelligence organisations.

These three branches of Israeli intelligence overlap in some areas: they cooperate with each other and sometimes compete. But their work is coordinated by

the head of the service, known as the Memuneh, who is answerable only to the prime minister and the Knesset (parliament). While Ben Gurion presided over the foundation of the Israeli intelligence service it was Isser Harel, the first Memuneh, who put Ben Gurion's ideas into practice and gave the service its worldwide connections and a global outlook.

One of the first major operations involving the Mossad was a strictly 'local' affair arising out of Israel's running conflict with neighbouring Egypt. It was anything but successful and came to be known as the 'Lavon affair', after Pinchas Lavon, the defence minister who was ultimately forced to resign in 1955 after what turned out to be a disaster for Israel. The operation was prompted by Israeli suspicions, apparently well founded, that after the British withdrawal from Egypt, scheduled for completion by 1956, the Americans might give their full support to Nasser as a 'bulwark against communism'. Operation Suzanne was conceived in 1954 with the aim of exposing the fundamental hostility to Britain and America that inspired the revolutionaries in Egypt.

It was a crude plan which deserved the disaster in which it ended. Israeli agents were to organise attacks on British and American property in Egypt for which either communists or the ultra-right-wing Muslim

Left: Elie Cohen (alias Kamal Amin Tabet), the Mossad spy, dangles from a rope after being hanged in the main square of Damascus in Syria.

Above: Pinchas Lavon, the Israeli defence minister who was forced to accept responsibility for Operation Suzanne, the abortive Mossad operation in Egypt in 1955.

Far left: Isser Harel, the first head of the Israeli intelligence services, who was accountable only to the prime minister and the Knesset. Under his direction the Israeli intelligence service became a powerful force with a global outlook.

Brotherhood would be blamed. The Egyptian police would have to crack down on them; civil disorder would follow; the Egyptian government would be discredited; the West would withdraw its support and British forces would remain in Egypt. The operation was to be carried out by a Special Service Unit called 'Unit 131'. Lavon, who had only recently been made minister of defence and knew little of military affairs, gave the plot his enthusiastic support.

The plot failed hopelessly as a result of a mixture of sheer inefficiency and treachery. Bombs were planted but failed to explode, and the details of the whole operation were betrayed to the Egyptians by one of the leading conspirators. The whole of the Israeli spy network in Cairo and Alexandria, which had taken years to build, was wiped out. Lavon resigned, still protesting that he had not given the order for the operation to go ahead. A later enquiry cleared him but he was not reinstated. In the long term the principal

Operation Noah's Ark

Of all the many daring operations carried out by the Israeli secret service in various parts of the world none was more dramatic, or more successful, than their snatching of five powerful gunboats from under the very noses of the French in December 1969. It was in fact a joint operation by the Mossad and the Israeli Navy, which needed the boats to make it an effective naval force in the Mediterranean. Twelve of them were being built to Israeli specifications by a French firm in the shipyards in Cherbourg. Five of them were completed and delivered to Israel in 1968.

At the end of 1968, however, the Israelis made a reprisal raid on Beirut airport which provoked General de Gaulle into imposing a complete embargo on all deliveries of arms to Israel. The Israeli reaction was swift: the sixth boat immediately slipped out of Cherbourg harbour as soon as the embargo was announced, and the seventh followed three days later. That left five unfinished boats locked in the yard, guarded by the French Navy. De Gaulle gave strict orders that they were never to reach Israel.

But the French president had not reckoned with the skill and determination of General Yariv, the head of Military Intelligence, and Admiral Mordechai Limon, who headed the Israeli purchasing mission in France. Between them they set in motion Operation Noah's Ark which was to extract the gunboats from Cherbourg by stealth.

The 'plot' which they concocted was fairly straightforward. The Israelis were to give the impression that they had accepted the loss of the boats and were concerned only to obtain compensation for them. At the same time they were to arrange for the boats to be sold to a nominally Norwegian company secretly controlled by Israel. It was a very thin 'cover' for the operation, but it was just sufficient to persuade the French to give permission for the boats to leave.

It was an immensely complex operation. Europe had to be scoured for the additional equipment necessary to make the boats fit for a 3000-mile journey; food for the trip had to be collected quietly and loaded aboard; extra crew had to get from Israel to Cherbourg unnoticed; the French authorities had to be put off their guard; and the weather had to be favourable.

The day chosen for the escape was 24 December – Christmas Eve, the time when most French families would be enjoying their Christmas dinners and when vigilance would be at its lowest. Admiral Limon arrived in Cherbourg from Paris in the morning and booked a table for a party that evening in one of the best restaurants in the town to allay any suspicions the French might have. Limon decided that the flotilla should aim to leave at 2030 hours in the evening.

But at 2030 hours a gale-force wind from the southwest made the departure impossible – and it was not until 0200 hours on Christmas Day that the boats cut their way through the harbour and out to sea.

Once outside the harbour the boats headed westwards and made for the Bay of Biscay, Gibraltar and the Mediterranean, where Israeli ships were stationed at regular intervals ready to provide fuel and victuals. The gunboats all reached Haifa safely on the evening of 31 December 1969.

Below: The first of five Israeli-manned gunboats arrive from France at the port of Haifa.

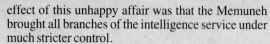

effect of this unhappy affair was that the Memuneh brought all branches of the intelligence service under much stricter control.

There were, however, brilliant successes to offset the Lavon affair, two of them, significantly, the work of talented individuals who nevertheless could not have succeeded without the backing of the enormous resources of the Mossad. In the early 1960s the Mossad had agents operating at the very centre of the ruling regimes in Egypt and Syria. They were Wolfgang Lotz and Elie Cohen, two of the most daring and successful spies to penetrate enemy security in this century.

Lotz was born in Mannheim, Germany, in 1921; his father was a theatrical producer in Berlin and his mother a Jewish actress who emigrated to Palestine with Wolfgang in 1933. By 1939 the boy was fluent in English, German, Hebrew and Arabic; he fought with the British Army in North Africa; and, after World War II, with the Haganah and the Israeli Army.

Lotz was picked by the Mossad as the ideal man to infiltrate Egyptian high society and gain the confidence of Egypt's top military leaders. Lotz not only looked like a German, he *was* German according to his documents. It was a relatively simple matter to provide him with a satisfactory cover: that he had fought with Rommel in the Desert War of 1941-42 and that after the war, as a Nazi, he found life too unpleasant in Germany and so had emigrated to Australia.

Socialite and spy

Lotz was amazingly successful. He quickly established himself as a popular figure, something of a playboy, in Cairo society, and was soon sending a stream of information about Egypt's armament programme back to Tel Aviv each day by the radio concealed in his flat. Thanks to the parties he gave, the generous gifts he distributed and the riding school he established, Lotz built up a circle of contacts among senior officers in the Egyptian intelligence service, the army and the police, and the government. There was little of real importance in the field of armaments in Egypt that Lotz was not in a position to know.

It was probably Lotz's very success and the consequent length of his radio transmissions that eventually led to his undoing. Apparently Egypt's Russian military advisers began to suspect the presence of a spy in high places in Cairo and brought their latest detection apparatus to Egypt. One day in February 1965 Lotz returned to his home in Cairo to find officers of the Egyptian security services lying in wait for him. His game was up: the 'champagne spy' was caught. But his 'cover' was so effective that even under interrogation he did not reveal his true allegiance, and his life was spared. Following the Six-Day War in 1967 he and the Lavon group were released in exchange for 500 Egyptian POWs, including nine generals.

The other great name in Israeli intelligence work – Elie Cohen – had a more difficult task to perform than Wolfgang Lotz. Cohen was born in Egypt, the son of two Syrian Jews who had emigrated there before World War II. He remained in Egypt until after the Suez campaign of 1956, when he moved to Israel. Cohen had the advantage, from the Mossad's point of view, of being easily capable of passing himself off as an Arab. He was also a highly intelligent and courageous man. In 1958 he agreed to submit to the strenuous course of training that would provide him

both with the tools of the spy trade and a new identity, with which he might be able to win the confidence of the Syrians.

Elie Cohen became 'Kamal Amin Tabet', born in Beirut, whose Syrian parents had emigrated to Egypt in 1933 and then to Argentina in 1947, where he had gone into business and built up a small fortune. By the end of 1960 Elie was ready for action. In 1961 he arrived in Buenos Aires and rapidly acquired a large circle of friends among the many Syrian businessmen there. Then, in 1962, he set out for Syria – a natural move for a patriotic Syrian who longed to return home. Again, it took him very little time to become accepted in the upper reaches of Damascus society and to form friendships among Syrian army officers and politicians. He became a popular host, a broadcaster on Syrian radio and an activist in the ruling Ba'athist party. Where Lotz had been the flamboyant playboy, Cohen was the serious intellectual and earnest Syrian patriot. Lotz had tended to be rather uncritical of the material that came his way; Cohen treated his sources and the information they supplied with caution.

For three years he moved freely in Syrian government circles, gathering more information than he could easily communicate to Tel Aviv each day. He provided the Israeli general staff with a complete picture of Syrian fortifications on the Golan Heights, details of the Syrians' plan to divert the waters of the River Jordan away from Israel, specifications of all the Soviet weapons being delivered to the Syrian Army, and the complete Syrian order of battle.

As in Lotz's case, it was probably Cohen's success and the enormous quantity of information he had to transmit each day by radio to Tel Aviv that brought about his downfall in 1965. He was actually operating his transmitter when Syrian counter-intelligence officers burst into his flat and arrested him. After a trial held mostly behind closed doors Cohen was sentenced to death and the Syrian authorities turned a deaf ear to all appeals for clemency, as well as to an Israeli offer of a million dollars for his release. The sentence was duly carried out, by hanging in the main square of Damascus. Too many Syrian officials had been on friendly terms with Elie Cohen for him to be left alive. As it was, in the aftermath of his trial some 60 Syrian officers were arrested, some cabinet ministers were disgraced, and the government collapsed.

Remarkable though they were, the achievements

An intelligence coup

One of the most remarkable achievements of Israeli intelligence occurred during the Six-Day War of 1967, when an Israeli officer found himself in command of a group of Egyptian tanks.

The Israelis had succeeded in breaking into the Egyptians' communications system and had also broken their codes, so that they received the orders issued by Egyptian commanders as quickly as the officers they were intended for. When a large Egyptian tank formation got lost in the Sinai desert and the commander lost contact with Cairo the Israelis seized the opportunity of replacing Cairo. They told the commander to change frequencies and follow their instructions. They then proceeded to make the Egyptian tanks move backwards and forwards quite harmlessly and far away from any Israeli formations. They continued to do this until the ceasefire, when the controller in Tel Aviv instructed the Egyptian officer to deliver his tanks to the nearest POW camp, which he did.

Although Operation Suzanne was a dismal failure (top right, some of the Israeli intelligence members of the Cairo and Alexandria network who were rounded up by Egyptian security forces), Wolfgang Lotz (top left, assembling a radio transmitter) penetrated Egypt's top military circles and operated successfully until his arrest in Cairo in February 1965 (above, Lotz, centre, awaiting trial at Cairo's Supreme Court).

Right: Elie Cohen moved freely in Syrian government circles for three years until his arrest in 1965. Cohen was executed after a closed trial, but his infiltration of the Syrian High Command was of immense value to the Israelis.

Left: Yuval Ne'eman, one of the three key leaders of Israeli intelligence, was responsible for promoting the use of electronics in intelligence work.

Left: General Aharon Yariv became head of military intelligence (Aman) upon the departure of Meir Amit.

Left: General Meir Amit left military intelligence for Mossad; he managed to encourage cooperation between Mossad and Aman.

of Lotz and Cohen were only a part of the tremendous contribution made by the Israeli secret service to the swift victory in the Six-Day War of 1967. It was a victory made possible by the painstaking intelligence work that preceded it. By the time it started in June 1967 there was practically nothing of any significance going on in the armed forces of Israel's Arab neighbours that was not known by the Israeli general staff. Israeli intelligence was then at the peak of its performance, thanks largely to the efforts of three men: General Aharon ('Ahrele') Yariv, head of military intelligence, General Meir Amit, head of the Mossad, and Yuval Ne'eman, who was both an outstanding scientist and an experienced soldier.

Meri Amit had taken over in 1963 from Isser Harel, the man whom Ben Gurion had put in charge of the Mossad ten years previously. Amit had been head of military intelligence (Aman), and his first job was to end the rivalry that had developed between Mossad and Aman. Yariv, who had been Amit's deputy at Aman, was promoted to succeed him, and since the two men knew and respected each other the way was cleared for smooth collaboration between the two intelligence organisations. But their joint efforts would not have raised Israeli intelligence work to such extraordinary heights if it had not been for the foresight and enterprise of Yuval Ne'eman.

Introducing computers

A scientist applying his knowledge to military intelligence, Ne'eman's great contribution was to foresee in the early 1950s the key role that was to be played by computers in the business of intelligence gathering and analysis. It took much effort and argument to persuade the Israeli government to part with the huge sums of money needed to equip Israel's intelligence organisations with the necessary machinery, but by the 1960s Israel had a computer-linked electronic warning system equal to the best in the world. Into it went the fruits of the vast intelligence network.

In the case of the Six-Day War, the result of the Ne'eman reforms was made abundantly clear when the Israeli Air Force destroyed the air forces of Egypt, Syria and Jordan in a matter of hours. This was made possible by the precision with which Israeli intelligence had pin-pointed every Egyptian airfield and plane. Even the timing of the attack was determined by detailed intelligence on the ground, which showed that between 0730 hours and 0800 hours in the morning the Egyptians were at their most vulnerable: people manning the radar system would be tired at the end of their night shift; aircrews would be strolling from their breakfast canteen to collect their flying gear; ground-crews would have rolled the planes out of the hangars for servicing; and senior officers would most likely be caught up in traffic jams on their way to their offices in Cairo. So Yariv chose 0745 hours (0845 hours Egyptian time) and was proved right.

During the 1970s and 1980s, the Israeli intelligence services were to expand their activities in the face of PLO terrorism and the threat of technological advances in the Arab world; in particular, the possibilities of an Arab atomic bomb were viewed with great suspicion and led to the strike on the nuclear reactor in Iraq (7 June 1981) when the opportunity presented itself during the Gulf War. But it was in the period leading up to 1967, when Israel was at its most vulnerable, that the intelligence gained counted most.

David Floyd

Key Weapons

MODERN DESTROYERS

In common with most other varieties of warship, destroyers have changed so dramatically since 1945 in both size and function that their old designation is now virtually meaningless. In 1939 the destroyer was still well defined both in layout and concept, and despite differences in detail any destroyer would still be recognisable as such. All destroyers carried out similar functions in acting as escorts to the main body of the fleet and in being able, alone or in concert, to mount a torpedo attack against an enemy force. To meet these requirements they featured a lean hull, devoted largely to machinery for generating speeds of 36 to 40 knots. A powerful surface or dual-purpose gun armament was included, usually from four to eight guns of between 4in and 5.9in calibre. Topside layout was dominated by the torpedo battery, generally of two banks, each having three, four or five tubes. Operations were normally at flotilla strength.

During World War II, advances in aviation and submarine warfare ensured that destroyers were rarely called upon to cover the old battle groups, still less to deliver textbook torpedo attacks; typically they would be found escorting convoys, hunting submarines, bombarding shore positions, evacuating garrisons or even transporting essential stores. Having lost their original functions, most nations' destroyers were found to be over-armed and lacking in endurance. This was particularly true in the case of the British who began the process of rethinking the destroyer concept along the lines of long-range lightweight escort vessels. The US Navy, however, still had a role for the destroyer in its traditional form, acting as guards to the fast carrier groups that decided the naval war in the Pacific.

At the end of World War II the destroyer had emerged as an ASW (anti-submarine warfare) and increasingly as an AAW (anti-aircraft warfare) vessel. In the Pacific, victory at sea had resulted largely from an overwhelming use of aviation, and in the decade following World War II the Soviet Union,

ever-mindful of the West's carrier capability, gave priority to research into methods of destroying the carrier forces from a safe distance. In the 1960s ships carrying large SSMs (surface-to-surface missiles) were complemented by long-range maritime aircraft capable of launching ASMs (air-to-surface missiles) from ranges beyond the effective radius of the carrier's combat air patrols. Both missile types have remained a feature of the Soviet weapon inventory.

The West's answer to this threat was to provide an outer ring of escorts armed with SAMs (surface-to-air missiles), their surveillance sets operating in conjunction with the carrier's own AEW (airborne early warning) system. These escorts were termed destroyers and their AAW speciality tended to differentiate them from lower-capability ASW ships, usually identified as frigates. The designation of modern warship types according to function is far from consistent, however, and has changed over time and from country to country. In the Royal Navy destroyers and frigates have both ASW and AAW roles, the major difference between the two types being one of size.

In the immediate postwar years most nations tried to utilise existing designs but by the late 1950s a new generation of destroyers began to emerge. The American Navy required a task-group sea speed in excess of 30 knots, so the leanness of earlier designs was retained, the bulk of the SAM launching and stowage gear demanding a significant increase in length in the first two new classes to see service, the Coontz and Adams. In appearance they had changed considerably, with the addition of a mass of topside electronics dedicated to surveillance, tracking and guidance. For ASW, each relied on the Asroc ballistic weapon. In turn, in the 1960s the Royal Navy introduced the County-class destroyers which, at 6000 tons, displacement, were greatly over normal size, though a bonus of size was the ability to ship a medium helicopter for ASW which put them ahead of their American contemporaries.

Previous page: An ASW helicopter flies off from the deck of HMS *Birmingham*, a Type 42 destroyer of the Royal Navy. Above: British destroyers of World War II on escort duty reveal their heavy topside gun armament; after the war destroyers began to lose their guns in favour of specialised anti-aircraft equipment, notably SAMs and the electronics to bring them into action.

Right: The USS *John King*, a Coontz-class destroyer off Norfolk, Virginia. The twin missile launcher on the vessel's stern is for the Tartar SAM. Additional armament includes two single 5in guns mounted fore and aft.

Above: An Exocet
anti-shipping missile
is launched from the
County-class destroyer
HMS *Norfolk*.

Top: The US Navy
guided-missile destroyer,
the Charles F. Adams.
Above: County-class
destroyer HMS *Glamorgan*
leads an escort flotilla.
The *Glamorgan* suffered
considerable damage
when hit by a land-based
Exocet missile during the
Falklands conflict.

Left: A modified Kashin-class guided-missile destroyer at sea, July 1976. The crowded deck and superstructure typical of Soviet warship design are evident in this photograph. At the stern is a helicopter pad. Left below: The *Svet*, a Kotlin-class destroyer of the Soviet Navy as seen by a Sea King helicopter from HMS *Blake* in the North Sea.

Below: A Soviet Kashin-class destroyer steams alongside a US carrier in the Mediterranean.

During the 1950s the Soviet Union had brought out its first missile-armed destroyers, converted Kotlin-class destroyers redesignated Kildins. Armed with either a single SS-N-1 surface-to-surface missile or with twin SA-N-1 surface-to-air missiles they represented a new trend in Soviet destroyer design that was followed in 1962 by the 4500 ton Kashin class. Significant in being the first all-gas-turbine propelled major warship, the Kashin class was fitted with twin SA-N-1 launchers and a variety of ASW weapons as well as a quintuple set of 21in torpedo tubes.

The success of the Kashin destroyers led to the introduction of the Krivak-class in 1971, which while having a displacement of only 3600 tons is capable of packing a mighty punch by Western standards. Armament consists of a quadruple launcher for the SS-N-14

anti-submarine missile, eight torpedo tubes, and for AAW there are two SA-N-4 launchers and four 76mm guns. Considered to be highly reliable with good sea-going qualities, the Krivak class represents an important addition to the Soviet Navy's escort-ship force.

The British Type 42 and the US Spruance-class destroyers were the West's answer to escort requirements for the 1970s and 1980s. Of these, the Type 42 had its size and fit kept to unrealistically low levels by budget constraints but, even so, had a greatly improved ASW capacity in addition to its area-defence SAM abilities. The Spruance class was built to the simple idea that larger hulls are more easily 'driven' and show improved sea-keeping qualities as well as having plenty of room for future refits, so offering scope for updating. As a result, while the Type 42s are planned never to have a mid-life modernisation, it can be confidently expected that the Spruances will see many changes in form.

Two Type 42 destroyers of the Royal Navy, HMS *Sheffield* (above) and HMS *Glasgow* (below). The Type 42 is distinguished by the two large domes containing the Sea Dart fire-control radars. The large 'bedstead' radar, mounted as high as possible, for air surveillance.

Above: The USS *Oldendorf*, a Spruance-class destroyer in the Pacific. A notable feature is the large helicopter landing pad. One of the *Oldendorf's* two 5in guns is positioned aft, the other forward. Left: Technicians man data-system consoles in the combat information centre aboard the USS *Spruance*. Below: Spruance-class destroyer the *Carron* fires a Sea Sparrow missile, while (below inset) the Sea Sparrow launcher can be seen in detail.

Indeed, the basic form of the Spruance class has been so modified already as to make categorisation virtually meaningless. The bulk of this important class have been provided with a distinct ASW bias with no area defence SAM capabilities; only their 7300-ton full load displacement really militates against their being classed as frigates. There exist two major variants, however, both of which use the same hull and machinery. The more significant group is fitted with the Mk 26 combined SAM/ASM/SSM launcher and with Aegis, a radar and data processing system capable of coordinating the defence of a complete task group. So capable are these ships that they have in fact been given the classification of a cruiser. The other group, the Kidel class, has a similar armament but is without Aegis; these ships are termed destroyers.

Sinai '67:

the preparations

Rival plans and dispositions

As tension rose between Israel and its Arab enemies through the month of May 1967, both sides hastily mobilised their men and equipment. Memories of the 1956 Sinai campaign were still fresh in the minds of the army commanders, and Israel and Egypt deployed heavy forces in anticipation of an armoured duel.

The final Egyptian deployment in Sinai closely resembled that of 1956, although the fortified positions were much stronger and the number of troops involved was far greater (about 100,000). The dispositions were basically defensive and the Egyptian commander-in-chief of the Sinai front, General Abdel Mohsen Mortagui, clearly expected the Israelis to attack first. On the other hand, Mortagui was a keen student of the Montgomery set-piece battle; he was also influenced by the Red Army's concept of a defence in depth intended to wear down an attacker's strength, followed by a strong armoured counter-stroke which would complete his destruction, the whole being reminiscent of the Kursk operations of 1943 which finally put an end to German ambitions in Russia. Given that the Egyptian Army's command, control and communications apparatus, and also its state of training – though not its courage and motivation – were less impressive than the

Israelis', such a strategy might appear sensible enough, had not the value of holding open stretches of desert for their own sake repeatedly proved questionable, from the Sidi Barrani battles of 1940 to the Sinai debacle of 1956. Mortagui must have been aware that it made better military sense to establish his defensive zone in western Sinai, but that would have meant abandoning the Gaza Strip and El Arish. Since national prestige was at stake, such a move could not even be contemplated.

By 4 June Mortagui had the equivalent of seven divisions in position on or close to the frontier. In the Gaza Strip was Major-General Mohammed Hasni's 20th (Palestinian) Infantry Division, with 50 Shermans; Rafah, the Jiradi defile and El Arish were held by the 7th Infantry Division under Major-General Abdel Aziz Soliman, with 100 T34/85s and Josef Stalin (IS) IIIs; the Abu Aweigila/Um-Katef fortified zone was defended by Major-General Sadi Naguib's 2nd Infantry Division, with 100 T34/85s and T54s; and the 3rd Infantry Division, again with 100 T34/85s and T54s, commanded by Major-General Osman Nasser, was deployed in depth behind the 2nd Infantry at Gebel Libni. In the south, the axis El Kuntilla-El Thamad-Nakhl, along which Major-General Ariel

Above: Israeli soldiers man defensive positions on the border of the Gaza Strip a few days before the outbreak of the Six-Day War. Forced to mobilise by pressure from its Arab neighbours, Israel had no intention of fighting a defensive campaign and would soon move onto the attack.

Sharon's paratroopers had advanced to the Mitla Pass in 1956, was held in strength by Major-General Abdel Kader Hassan's 6th Mechanised Division with 100 T34/85s and T54s. The principal counter-attack force, equipped with 200 T55s and based at Bir Gifgafa, was the crack 4th Armoured Division, commanded by Major-General Sidki el Ghoul. A second armoured group, named Task Force Shazli after its commander, Major-General Saad el Din Shazli, was equipped with 150 T55s and positioned on the border between El Quseima and El Kuntilla, its mission being the isolation of the port of Elat and the southern Negev from Israel proper.

Egyptian weaknesses

Ostensibly, Mortagui had done everything possible to prevent the sort of runaway success the Israelis had achieved in 1956. On the other hand, the disposition of his armour can be seriously faulted. Altogether, the Sinai front was defended by 950 tanks and tank destroyers (300 T34/85s, 400 T54/55s, 100 ISIIIs, 50 Shermans and 100 SU-100s), including 150 in immediate reserve, yet of these only 350 were serving in armoured formations, the remainder being allocated to infantry divisions. Again, the weight of the Israeli attack would fall hardest on the older and more expendable Shermans and T34s and it remained an open question whether the modern T55s, leaguered well outside those sectors likely to be threatened, could intervene in time. The T55 itself, armed with a 100mm gun, provided a reasonable combination of firepower, protection and mobility and was a simple machine to operate; its design, however, tended to ignore the human factor and the loader quickly became exhausted due to the lack of headroom in which to perform his heavy task.

The Israelis, too, had digested the lessons of the 1956 campaign in Sinai. They had begun recalling

Far left: Major-General Israel Tal, who commanded an armoured division during the Six-Day War and who was responsible for a considerable improvement in the standard of Israeli tank gunnery through his rigorous training procedures. Left: Israeli tank crews ready to move out in their Centurion tanks. The 0.5in Browning machine gun mounted on the commander's turret was the Centurion's main anti-aircraft defence – for which, as it turned out, the Israelis were to have little use.

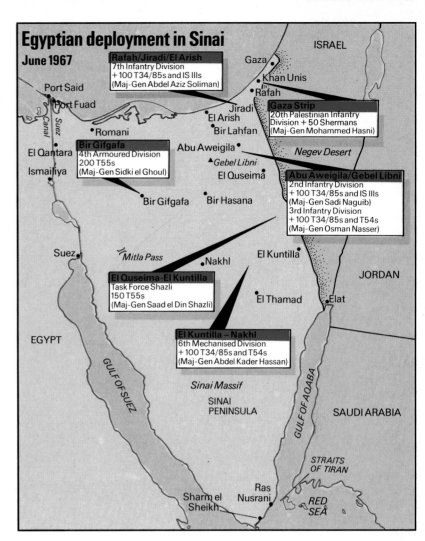

Egyptian deployment in Sinai
June 1967

Rafah/Jiradi/El Arish
7th Infantry Division + 100 T34/85s and IS IIIs (Maj-Gen Abdel Aziz Soliman)

Gaza Strip
20th Palestinian Infantry Division + 50 Shermans (Maj-Gen Mohammed Hasni)

Bir Gifgafa
4th Armoured Division 200 T55s (Maj-Gen Sidki el Ghoul)

Abu Aweigila/Gebel Libni
2nd Infantry Division + 100 T34/85s and IS IIIs (Maj-Gen Sadi Naguib)
3rd Infantry Division + 100 T34/85s and T54s (Maj-Gen Osman Nasser)

El Quseima-El Kuntilla
Task Force Shazli 150 T55s (Maj-Gen Saad el Din Shazli)

El Kuntilla – Nakhl
6th Mechanised Division + 100 T34/85s and T54s (Maj-Gen Abdel Kader Hassan)

reservists on 20 May and were now ready to take the field. The primary objectives of the Southern Command, under Major-General Yeshayahu Gavish, were the destruction of the Egyptian Army in Sinai and an advance to the Suez Canal, which would thereafter serve as a natural military frontier. The nature of Egyptian dispositions was fully understood and the operation itself, code-named Red Sheet, would follow the classic pattern of blitzkrieg, applying concentrated force during the break-in phase followed by an acceleration in the operational tempo as the armour debouched across Sinai towards its strategic objectives. The one element which would be absent for much of the critical first day's fighting would be direct air support, as the Israeli Air Force (IAF) would be fully engaged in its own pre-emptive strike against the Arab air forces.

The Israeli Defence Force (IDF) unquestionably regarded the tank as the weapon of decision and it had formed four armoured divisions which were organised on the flexible American system, permitting all-arms battlegroups to be detached for specific missions at short notice. The level of individual crew training was high and the Armoured Corps' most recent director, Major-General Israel Tal, had improved the overall standard of tank gunnery beyond recognition.

Tal was now commanding an armoured division which was deployed opposite the Gaza Strip and Rafah. This included the crack regular 7th Armoured Brigade and was equipped with a mixture of Centu-

rions, M48s, Shermans and AMX13s, the total tank strength being 250. Opposite Abu Aweigila was a second armoured division commanded by Major-General Sharon, with 150 tanks (Centurions, Shermans and AMX13s). Between Tal and Sharon, lying in immediate reserve, was a third armoured division under Major-General Avraham Yoffe, equipped with 200 Centurions; the task of this division was to prevent intervention in the break-in battle by the Egyptian 4th Armoured Division or Task Force Shazli. The Israeli armoured build-up in Sinai was completed by two small independent armoured brigades, Colonel Amnon Reshef's brigade with 30 AMX13s near Gaza, and Major-General Avraham Mandler's brigade with 50 Shermans in the southern Negev.

Thus the entire Southern Command tank strength of 680 (with 70 in reserve) was, in sharp contrast to the Egyptian dispositions, employed in armoured formations. Again, while the best Egyptian tanks were to be committed only after the battle had been joined, the Israelis intended leading with their Centurions. Armed with a powerful 105mm gun supported by good gun-control equipment, and offering excellent protection to its crew, the Centurion was looked upon at the time as queen of the battlefield.

As the sun set on 4 June the Israeli tank crews knew that on the morrow they would be fighting one of the most critical battles in their country's history. They knew, too, just how much depended on the outcome; as Tal himself put it to them, 'If we do not win, we have nowhere to come back to.' **Bryan Perret**

Sinai '67:

the attack
Armoured warfare in the desert

The start of Operation Red Sheet, the Israeli offensive in Sinai, was timed to coincide with the Israeli Air Force (IAF) strike against Egyptian airbases. At 0815 hours on 5 June, Major-General Israel Tal's armoured division and Colonel Raphael Eitan's paratroop brigade, the latter with Colonel Amnon Reshef's AMX13 battalion in support, sliced into the base of the Gaza Strip. Their objectives were Rafah and Khan Yunis. This was a difficult country of tortuous lanes, stone walls and cactus hedges, all of which inhibited

Above: An Israeli Sherman rolls forward into the Sinai. Below: Israeli troops watch as Fouga Magister jets sweep in to attack Egyptian positions. Right above: An Egyptian truck burns fiercely.

the tank commanders' vision. The Egyptians had dug anti-tank ditches across the principal approach routes as well as laying multiple minefields, and they had also had plenty of time in which to camouflage their positions. To avoid disclosing the location of individual guns, their anti-tank batteries fired in unison.

The Israeli armour came under heavy fire almost immediately. Tal's 7th Armoured Brigade, commanded by Colonel Shmuel Gonen, consisted of a Centurion battalion, an M48 Patton battalion, and a mixed Sherman/AMX13 battalion. Leading from the front, Gonen pushed his two heavier units through Khan Yunis and then swung south to Rafah, taking casualties but brushing aside the piecemeal intervention of the Palestinians' Shermans. The battle was one of

innumerable small tactical encounters which demanded a high degree of personal initiative, and sometimes self-sacrifice, from the Israeli troop and squadron commanders. The one thing Gonen had to maintain, whatever the cost, was the momentum of the assault.

Meanwhile, Eitan's paratroopers were pinned down by heavy artillery and automatic weapon fire. The IAF's major combat aircraft were all fully committed elsewhere but, conscious of the importance of operations in the Gaza Strip, it had armed its Fouga Magister jet trainers for a ground attack role and these now swept in to rocket the Egyptian gun positions. With the easing of pressure, the paratroopers began working their way into the heart of the defences, fighting hand-to-hand against bitter Egyptian resistance. Tal, however, could not afford to become involved in cleaning out the Strip and capturing Gaza itself – that would have to be left to Eitan and Reshef. His own mission demanded that he break out along the coast road to the west in the shortest possible time. As the morning wore on the 7th Armoured Brigade captured the important road junction southwest of Rafah but was then counter-attacked by the major part of the Egyptian 7th Division's armoured element, including most of its ISIIIs. This impressively armoured vehicle, equipped with a 122mm gun, had originally been designed for the break-in role but was quite unsuited to the sort of fast-moving action about to take place, and the lack of tank radios prevented the Egyptian commander exercising adequate tactical control. While the Centurions engaged from the front, the Pattons moved to a flank, catching their opponents in a fire trap. Tal's emphasis on accurate long-range gunnery quickly paid off and by noon the ISIIIs and their accompanying T34s had been reduced to burning hulks.

The tanks roar on

Gonen quickly got his brigade moving again, with the Centurion battalion leading. They took the defenders of the Jiradi defile by complete surprise and roared straight through, keeping them pinned down with a hail of HESH rounds and machine-gun fire. By the time the Patton battalion appeared, however, the Egyptians had manned their weapons and were putting up a spirited defence. With difficulty, the Pattons managed to fight their way through, losing several of their number in the process; the battalion commander, Major Ehud Elad, was killed, three of his squadron commanders wounded, and every surviving vehicle bore scars from the encounter.

Both battalions continued their advance and secured El Arish so far ahead of the Red Sheet timetable that a parachute drop and amphibious landing designed to assist Tal take this objective were hastily cancelled. But the Egyptians stubbornly refused to relinquish their grip on the Jiradi defile. It would have been suicidal for the lightly armoured tanks of Gonen's 3rd Battalion to try to fight their way through and Tal, whose division now stretched all the way from El Arish back to Rafah, realised that it would take a set-piece attack to reopen the road. The light tanks and one mechanised infantry battalion moved into the dunes to menace the Egyptian position from the south but became stuck in soft sand. At midnight a second mechanised infantry battalion, with a reserve Centurion squadron in close support, launched a frontal assault in the wake of artillery preparation and

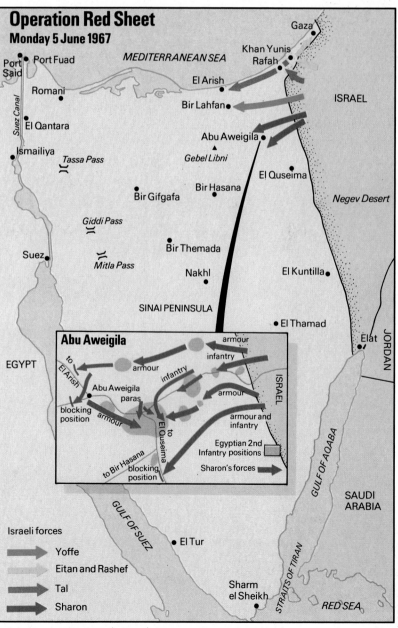

Operation Red Sheet
Monday 5 June 1967

MEDITERRANEAN SEA

Gaza
Khan Yunis
Rafah
El Arish
Bir Lahfan
ISRAEL
Abu Aweigila
Gebel Libni
El Quseima
Port Said
Port Fuad
Romani
Suez Canal
El Qantara
Ismailiya
Tassa Pass
Bir Gifgafa
Bir Hasana
Negev Desert
Giddi Pass
Bir Themada
Suez
Mitla Pass
Nakhl
El Kuntilla
SINAI PENINSULA
El Thamad
Elat
EGYPT
JORDAN

Abu Aweigila
armour
infantry
to El Arish
armour
infantry
infantry
armour
Abu Aweigila
paras
ISRAEL
armour
blocking position
armour
to El Quseima
armour and infantry
Egyptian 2nd Infantry positions
Sharon's forces
to Bir Hasana
blocking position

GULF OF SUEZ
El Tur
GULF OF AQABA
SAUDI ARABIA
STRAITS OF TIRAN
Sharm el Sheikh
RED SEA

Israeli forces
→ Yoffe
→ Eitan and Rashef
→ Tal
→ Sharon

took the position after a ferocious four-hour battle. The division was now ready to resume its advance to the west.

Some way to the south Major-General Avraham Yoffe's armoured division had also crossed the frontier and had been moving steadily west throughout the day. Its route had crossed a wide area of deep dunes which the Egyptians considered to be tank proof – as indeed it was, to any tank but the Centurion. By dusk the first 25 tanks were through and had taken up ambush positions covering the track junction at Bir Lahfan. It had been anticipated, correctly, that the Egyptian 4th Armoured Division would launch a

Victors and vanquished. Israeli tank crews (right) take their first rest after their successful campaign while a seriously wounded Egyptian (right below) lies slumped in the road. Egyptian casualties in the Sinai campaign were extremely heavy – about 10,000 dead and 20,000 wounded.

No hiding place

This interview with an Israeli who was caught in one of the rare Egyptian air strikes shows vividly the devastating effect air attacks could have on the morale of troops caught in the exposed desert landscape, and brings home the vital importance of Israeli air superiority achieved in the first hours of the war.

'I can tell you when I was frightened, though – when four MiGs strafed us. This time I felt that I had had it. We had heard planes approaching occasionally but hadn't even looked up.... We feel sure that today, the third day of the war, there just can't be a single Egyptian plane left intact. Anyway, this plane opens fire and an officer yells, "MiGs! spread out quickly!" We run like mad among the sand dunes. The plane circles over us and fires. It was just like it is in the films – you hear *pap, pap, pap*. We look up and see more of their planes, three more MiGs getting into formation ready for the strike. We run like mad and throw ourselves down on the sand....

'When you're lying on the sand and there's no cover, no place to hide, no shelter, you just wait for the planes to come at you and they come, and you see this monster getting nearer and bigger, a terrific noise. They begin to fire when they're still some distance away and there's nothing you can do

about it. You just lie there. That's when you feel this is really the end....

'Anyway, the first plane comes over, fires. The second plane, the third, the fourth – the minutes seem like hours – and then they've all passed. You lift your head up, completely dazed, and look to see if you're still alive. Really: you look to see if your hands and legs are still there and that you're not wounded. Is it possible you're still alive?.... you suddenly remember that you must look around to see if anyone's wounded or not. It was then that I got up and looked around. The boys shouted: "Get down, get down, they're coming back"....

'The first plane passes over. It fires. The shots ricochet between me and one of the first-aid men who's with me. I feel as if death had brushed past me. The second plane comes up. A deafening noise. It doesn't fire, it doesn't do anything. The third one drops a napalm bomb and a terrific pillar of smoke shoots up. We can hardly see anything at all. The fourth plane shoots again. And the whole thing is over in a matter of minutes....Then you notice that they're preparing for a third round; this really shakes you. You look around and you try to do something – perhaps you can find better cover, some little hole to crawl into. What wouldn't I have given for some little hole – and there's nothing. Just the sand, and that's all....'

counter-attack against Tal at El Arish and must pass through Bir Lahfan on its way forward from its base at Bir Gifgafa.

Major-General Ghoul, commanding the Egyptian 4th Armoured Division, was not alone in being surprised by the Israeli offensive, and it had taken him all day to prepare his counter-stroke. It was quite logical that he should embark on a night march which would place him in position to attack at first light, yet utterly inexplicable that he should do so with headlights blazing. His column, consisting of a T55 brigade and a mechanised infantry brigade, was spotted approaching the Bir Lahfan junction at 2300 hours. Yoffe's gunners had plenty of time to set their sights and opened fire at extreme armour-piercing (AP) range. In an instant 14 T55s erupted in flames, as did several lorries carrying ammunition and fuel. The Egyptians scattered, switching off their headlights, but they were now fighting on a brilliantly illuminated battlefield, whereas the Israelis were hidden by dark-

Above: Major-General Sharon, whose armoured division captured the desert stronghold of Abu Aweigila. Below: Israeli infantry advance in half-tracks.

ness, identified only by their muzzle flashes. The Egyptian losses continued to mount but, despite the fact that the T55s were fitted with night-fighting equipment, only one Centurion was hit. Tal, aware of the situation, despatched the 7th Armoured Brigade down the track from El Arish and by first light it was in action against the Egyptian left flank. The remnants of Ghoul's counter-attack force, caught between two fires, broke and fled towards Gebel Libni with the Israelis in hot pursuit, their retreat constantly harried by the IAF, which had begun to play a steadily increasing part in the land battle since the previous afternoon.

Sharon's armoured division, the smallest of the three, had in the meantime captured the desert stronghold of Abu Aweigila in an epic, tortuous struggle. During the day a Centurion battalion, commanded by Colonel Natke Nir, worked its way through what the Egyptians considered to be the impassable dune country to the north of the position, fighting a series of hard actions on the way, and by evening had cut the tracks to El Arish and Gebel Libni. Simultaneously, an AMX13 battlegroup cut the track to Kusseima in the south, while the Egyptian eastern defences were engaged at close range by the division's Sherman battalion. It was against these eastern defences that Sharon intended putting his main assault. At dusk three infantry battalions marched up to their start lines and snatched a few hours' rest.

The Israeli bombardment which began at 2230 hours on 5 June was the heaviest in the army's history to date, being carried out by two 25-pdr battalions, one 155mm howitzer battalion, one 160mm mortar battalion and two 120mm mortar battalions. As the Egyptian artillery began to reply, Sharon played his trump card. A parachute battalion was lifted by helicopter to a point just behind the enemy's gun positions, which were promptly stormed. The Israeli infantry, equipped with coloured flares to indicate their progress, then fought their way into the eastern defences with close Sherman support, while to the west the Centurion battalion joined forces with the paratroops. A fierce close-quarter infantry/tank night battle ensued and ended with the two Israeli groups meeting in the centre of the position, putting the surviving Egyptians to flight. The central Sinai axis was now open.

On the morning of 6 June, Major-General Yeshayahu Gavish, the General Officer Commanding Southern Command, met his three divisional commanders to outline future strategy, the essence of which was that Tal and Yoffe should advance through the retreating enemy and seize the three passes – the Tassa, the Gidi and the Mitla – leading from the Sinai plateau to the Suez Canal. In the north one of Tal's brigade groups would continue its advance westwards from El Arish towards the Canal. Another, with assistance from Yoffe, whose primary objective was the Mitla Pass, would eliminate the Egyptian 3rd Infantry Division at Gebel Libni and also the remnants of Ghoul's 4th Armoured Division. Sharon still had some tidying up to do around Abu Aweigila, but once this had been completed he would advance south to Nakhl and drive the Egyptian Task Force Shazli and the 6th Mechanised Division onto the blocking position which Yoffe would establish at the Mitla Pass, so destroying them.

The Israelis were now understandably very tired and a short period had to be allowed for rest so that the advances made throughout 6 June were comparatively short. Nonetheless, the brigade group on the coast road pushed on for 64km (40 miles) without meeting significant opposition and, together, Tal and Yoffe routed the Egyptian 3rd Infantry Division from its positions around and to the south of Gebel Libni.

Duels and destruction

On 7 June the tempo of the battle quickened again. The battlegroup on the coast, commanded by Colonel Israel Granit, was joined by some of Eitan's paratroopers, who had driven west at top speed following the fall of Gaza. Mortagui clearly recognised the vulnerability of this axis, and at his request armoured reinforcements had been sent across the Canal to block it. Granit's battlegroup encountered these fresh forces between Romani and El Qantara. Granit halted his tanks and engaged in a long-range duel with the Egyptian armour while the paratroops' half-tracks and jeep-mounted recoilless rifles swung out to hook wide onto the enemy's flank. Caught between two fires, the Egyptian tanks were destroyed and Granit drove on through their wreckage to become the first Israeli commander to reach the Canal.

The remainder of Tal's division, led by Gonen's 7th Armoured Brigade, had pounced on the remnants of 4th Armoured Division at Bir Gifgafa, the Centurion and Patton battalions mounting converging attacks which virtually destroyed Ghoul's command in a two-hour tank battle. During the night, however, the AMX13 battalion, occupying a blocking position a few kilometres to the west of the division, came under simultaneous pressure from Egyptian troops trying to escape from Sinai and reinforcement armour attempting to enter it. Several light tanks were lost before a company each of Shermans and Centurions arrived to restore the situation. Next morning Tal, realising that he now faced only disorganised local opposition, secured the northern pass and drove

Operation Red Sheet
Tuesday 6 – Wednesday 7 June 1967

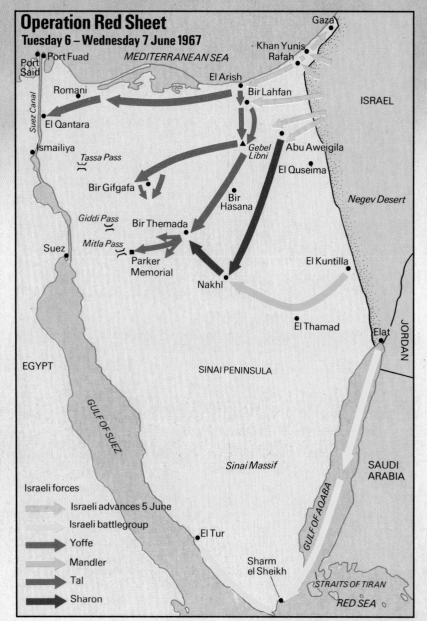

Gaza
Khan Yunis
Rafah
Port Said
Port Fuad
MEDITERRANEAN SEA
El Arish
Romani
Bir Lahfan
ISRAEL
El Qantara
Ismailiya
Gebel Libni
Abu Aweigila
Tassa Pass
El Quseima
Bir Gifgafa
Negev Desert
Bir Hasana
Giddi Pass
Bir Themada
Suez
Mitla Pass
Parker Memorial
El Kuntilla
Nakhl
El Thamad
Elat
JORDAN
EGYPT
SINAI PENINSULA
GULF OF SUEZ
Sinai Massif
SAUDI ARABIA
GULF OF AQABA
El Tur
Sharm el Sheikh
STRAITS OF TIRAN
RED SEA

Israeli forces
Israeli advances 5 June
Israeli battlegroup
Yoffe
Mandler
Tal
Sharon

Above: Israeli soldiers reload a machine gun on their Centurion tank before moving on an offensive operation against Egyptian positions. Right: A Centurion thunders into action. The Centurion proved to be highly effective during the Sinai campaign, crossing dunes thought impassable to armoured vehicles. Below: The results of an Israeli airstrike against an Egyptian transport column caught in the open with no air cover and no effective air defence.

through to the Canal, where he was joined by Granit's battlegroup at El Qantara.

Yoffe's axis of advance to the Mitla Pass, on which the remains of Mortagui's army were also converging, took him through Bir Hasana and Bir Tamada. His advance guard, commanded by Colonel Yiska Shadmi and consisting of two Centurion battalions and an armoured infantry battalion, frequently caught up with Egyptian columns and ploughed through them, guns blazing. The Egyptians abandoned their vehicles and their weapons to scatter across the sand. The IAF now dominated the battlefield completely but in one respect its very efficiency came perilously close to being counter-productive, for its constant strafing left a tangle of wrecked and burning vehicles through which Shadmi's column had to force its way. Fuel was in critically short supply and, as the Centurions had already been put to hard usage, vehicle after vehicle began to drop out, either out of fuel or with mechanical problems. When Shadmi finally arrived at the eastern entrance to the pass his battlegroup had been reduced to nine Centurions (of which two were already on tow and three more had to be towed into position, having exhausted their fuel on arrival, while

the turret of a sixth vehicle had been jammed when hit by a 122mm round), two armoured infantry platoons and three 120mm mortar half-tracks.

Shadmi established a roadblock near the Parker Memorial. The Egyptians began converging on this towards dusk and from that time onwards Shadmi's tiny force beat off continuous attacks by the enemy's armour. Some engagements took place at a range of only 100 metres, but the only vehicle to break through to safety was a solitary SU-100 tank destroyer. As each attack failed its wreckage inhibited the success of further attacks, and the IAF continuously bombed, strafed and rocketed the 5km (3 mile) log-jam of convoys which had built up around the entrance to the pass. A subsequent count revealed no less than 157 destroyed or abandoned Egyptian fighting vehicles in this area. When, at dawn on 8 June, the remainder of Yoffe's division arrived and began driving through the pass to the Canal, Shadmi's four surviving Centurions were down to their last few rounds, but their incredible stand had served its purpose.

Trapped at the Mitla Pass were elements of the Egyptian 4th Armoured Division, the 3rd Infantry Division, the 6th Mechanised Division and Task Force Shazli. Many hundreds of their transport vehicles had been destroyed by air strikes or gunfire and Sharon's armoured division was closing in on their rear from the east, quickly encircling them. Sharon had driven south from Abu Aweigila throughout 7 June and next day effected a junction with Mandler's armoured brigade, which had driven west from El Kuntilla. Near Nakhl the Egyptian rearguard, consisting of an armoured brigade and an infantry brigade belonging to the 6th Mechanised Division, was overwhelmed with the destruction of 60 tanks, 100 guns and 300 vehicles. The trap was now firmly shut on the survivors of Mortagui's army and those who had been unable to escape as individuals or in small groups were forced to surrender.

The final act in the Sinai drama was the opening of the Straits of Tiran. Yoffe, who had led the 9th Infantry Brigade in its remarkable march from Elat to the Straits in 1956, despatched a battlegroup down the western coast of the peninsula to link up with a paratroop force which had been dropped on Sharm el Sheikh. There was no fighting, for on 7 June Israeli torpedo boats discovered that the Egyptian garrison had gone.

Operation Red Sheet
Thursday 8 June 1967

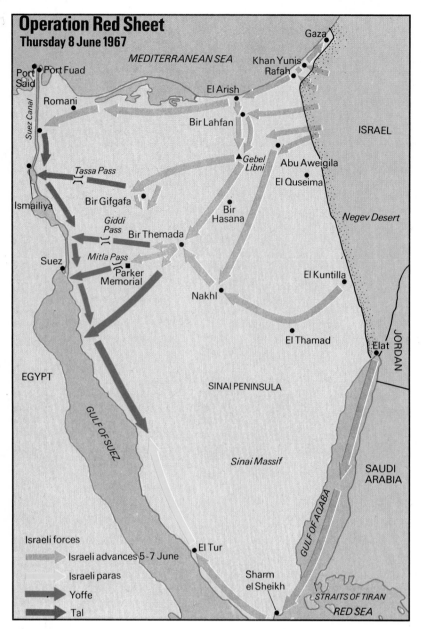

Israeli forces

- Israeli advances 5–7 June
- Israeli paras
- Yoffe
- Tal

Right: Tortured and twisted metal in the burning wastes of Sinai, the wreckage of Egypt's Army abandoned in the face of the Israeli advance towards Suez. In the background stands an abandoned T55. Centre right: After the crushing defeat of Major-General Mohammed Hasni's 20th (Palestinian) Infantry Division, in the Gaza Strip, Israeli commanders accept his surrender. Far right: A captured Egyptian SA-2 missile. So total was the Egyptian debacle that much of their equipment was captured intact.

Seldom in the history of war has so complete a victory been achieved in so short a space of time; it had taken a mere four days to wipe an army of seven divisions from the map. Some 10,000 Egyptians were killed, 20,000 wounded and 5500 captured; 500 tanks were destroyed and 300 captured intact (some were later converted for Israeli use); 450 artillery weapons of various calibres were also taken, along with 10,000 vehicles of different types. It was later admitted that 80 per cent of the Egyptian Army's equipment holdings had been lost in the Sinai. Israeli losses amounted to 275 killed and 800 wounded. Since the Israelis retained possession of the battlefield, they were able to repair most of their battle-damaged tanks.

To the average Egyptian the defeat came as a tremendous psychological shock, made worse by the fact that for the first two days of the fighting the Cairo media had reported victories in Sinai. Much of the blame was placed on inferior equipment, training and doctrine, and since these had all been inherited from the Soviet Union, the disaster caused equal dismay in the Kremlin. The Soviet government was in serious danger of losing face throughout the Arab world, and this it sought to combat in three ways. First, it made good the Egyptian losses almost immediately. Secondly, it embarked upon a world-wide publicity campaign designed to demonstrate the Soviet Army's invincibility. And thirdly, in the longer term, it sought to create the appropriate conditions for an Arab victory in the next war with Israel.

There remained for the Egyptians the question of leadership. Most Israelis admitted to having some admiration for the Egyptian soldier's quiet brand of stoical courage, but at the same time expressed contempt for certain self-seeking sections of the Egyptian officer corps. During its final advance Sharon's division came across an entire brigade of ISIIIs, abandoned with all their equipment in full working order. The brigade commander, captured by Yoffe's division, pleaded that he had received orders to retreat, but none regarding the destruction of his vehicles to prevent their falling intact into Israeli hands. Sadly for the Egyptians, this officer's attitude was not untypical of senior commanders, a number of whom deserted their men and fled to safety. Some were court-martialled and severely punished and Field-Marshal Abdel Hakim Amer, commander-in-chief of the Egyptian Army, committed suicide rather than face trial. Nasser, however, survived. In the aftermath of the defeat he offered his resignation, but the popular demand for him to stay was overwhelming.

The Sinai campaign of 1967 fully justified the Israeli concept of mechanised war. In assessing its lessons, however, the Israelis placed too much emphasis on the tank as the prime battle-winner and reduced the relative strengths of the infantry and artillery elements within their armoured formations. The future would prove this decision to be a serious error of judgement, arising directly from the over-confidence inspired by easy victories. **Bryan Perret**

Above: Huge palls of smoke fill the sky after a direct hit on the Suez oil refineries by Israeli artillery. Left: Deputy Chief of Staff Bar-Lev and Yoffe meet in the Sinai in victorious mood. Right: Captured Egyptian soldiers, stripped of their uniforms, are transported in a truck to a prisoner of war camp while an Israeli armoured convoy moves through the Sinai desert.

Surprise has always been a critical element in warfare – from the destruction of the Persian fleet at Salamis in 480 BC to the German attack in the Ardennes in 1940, examples abound of how campaigns have been decided by one unexpected blow. In the modern world, surprise has come to occupy an even more central place than formerly, mainly because the destructive power of modern weapons means that all an enemy's retaliatory power may be destroyed in one stroke. The counter to this has been the development of ever more sophisticated forms of technical surveillance to prevent an enemy gaining such an advantage; but all such systems – and their human operators – are fallible.

In some instances surprise can result from a straightforward failure of surveillance and the intelligence agencies. Prior to the Japanese attack on Pearl Harbor in December 1941 the American intelligence organisation was insufficiently coordinated to interpret Japanese intentions correctly. Similarly, Nato's surprise at the Soviet takeover of Czechoslovakia in August 1968 owed much to the breakdown of communication systems at all levels. US President Lyndon B. Johnson was informed of the Soviet action not by his intelligence services but by the Soviet ambassador, while other Nato officials first heard from news broadcasts.

More often than not, intelligence of an opponent's intentions is received but it is not evaluated correctly. Thus, in the Arab build-up to the attack on Israel in the Yom Kippur War of October 1973, many indicators of Arab intentions were misinterpreted by Israeli intelligence. Syrian troop concentrations were ascribed to defensive plans and Egyptian movements to routine manoeuvres, with no correlation being made between the two. Nor was any significance

attached to the evacuation of the families of Soviet technicians from Egypt two days before the attack was to begin. Some intelligence officers were concerned but their superiors remained unconvinced. The failure of Israeli intelligence to anticipate the attack was matched by that of American intelligence. When a crisis management team was assembled in Washington on the day the war started, several members, including the Secretary of Defense, the Chairman of the Joint Chiefs of Staff and the Director of the CIA, had been given to understand that it was Israel that had attacked the Arabs.

Frequently, however, the failure to act on intelligence warnings lies in the capacity of military and political leaders for self-deception rather than in the mistakes of their intelligence advisers. In the Korean War in October 1950, the many warnings from the Chinese of their impending intervention were regarded as mere bluff. When evidence was detected of a gradual Chinese military concentration inside North Korea, it was supposed that the Chinese had limited aims which would not extend to an offensive against UN forces. The Israelis were firmly convinced in 1973 that the Egyptians would not risk another war until at least 1975.

What may contribute to the surprise resulting from such failures of intelligence or evaluation is, of course, the deception practised by one's opponent. At a strategic level, part of the reason why the North Korean build-up for the invasion of South Korea in June 1950 went undetected was that there had been constant frontier violations in the past. In October 1956 the Israelis lulled the Egyptians into a false sense of security by appearing to threaten action against Jordan rather than in the Sinai, while just before the

Below: Three US battleships lie burning at anchor after the Japanese strike against Pearl Harbor on 7 December 1941, the most famous example in modern times of a pre-emptive air attack.

First strike

Right: US Marines in Grenada in 1983. Below right: Soviet forces move into Czechoslovakia in 1968. Bottom right: Egyptian aircraft destroyed by the Israelis in 1967.

Surprise and the unexpected in modern war

Israeli attack in June 1967 Moshe Dayan stated that it was too late for Israel to react militarily to the closure of the Straits of Tiran and that action would not in any case be contemplated until diplomacy had run its course.

In turn, the Egyptians misled the Israelis in appearing to mobilise fully or partially on some 20 different occasions between December 1972 and October 1973. One major Egyptian mobilisation in May 1973 cost the Israelis £4.5 million to match, against the advice of their chief of intelligence, General Eliahu Zeira, who believed it a feint. When confronted by similar evidence in October Zeira remarked, 'I told you then that nothing was going to happen, but you didn't believe me. I tell you again, nothing is going to happen.' In Zeira's defence it must be said that crises are rather more common than wars and that 'crying wolf' is an occupational hazard of intelligence services. The Soviet invasion of Czechoslovakia in August 1968 was also marked by attempts to deceive others as to military intentions. At the time of the invasion a series of manoeuvres on the Czechoslovakian frontier had ended and the troops had apparently begun to disperse, while the Soviets noted that President Johnson had retired to his ranch for the summer in the belief that nothing would now occur.

Tactical misinformation

Surprise may also be achieved at a tactical level. In 1956 the initial Israeli parachute assault on the Mitla Pass was announced as a 'reprisal' to mislead the Egyptians into believing that it was an isolated act. In seeking to destroy the Egyptian Air Force at one stroke on 5 June 1967, the Israelis were careful to avoid attacking at dawn or dusk, when such an attack might be expected, and timed their attack for 0845 hours Egyptian time, when the Egyptians would have been stood down from early morning alert. No electronic countermeasures were employed, to avoid creating suspicion that any operation was under way, and initially Egyptian communications were deliberately left alone. The Israelis were equally taken by surprise tactically in October 1973 by the Egyptian employment of high-pressure water hoses to break through the banks of the Suez Canal and, of course, by the extensive Arab use of anti-tank and anti-aircraft missiles. Tactical ploys utilised by the Soviets included flying in the first paratroopers to Prague in August 1968 in civilian aircraft.

Surprise is mostly associated with the beginning of wars when it can gain important advantages in the vital first hours of conflict if it succeeds. Indeed, surprise need not be total to achieve spectacular success. The Israelis had belatedly realised in 1973

that an attack was imminent and ordered full mobilisation at 1000 hours on 6 October, but four hours proved insufficient time to react positively to the Arab threat. In the midst of war surprise may be harder to achieve but, again, it has proved possible on many occasions. During World War II the Western allies were able to deceive the Germans in the invasion of Normandy in June 1944 when the Germans were well aware that an invasion was coming. Both the Inchon landings by the UN forces on 15 September 1950 during the Korean War and the North Vietnamese Tet offensive against South Vietnam in January 1968 achieved considerable surprise. The Israeli success in June 1967 is the more impressive by virtue of the fact that both sides had been fully mobilised for four days.

The continuing possibility of achieving surprise in modern war has particular significance for Nato, Soviet doctrine having stressed the value of surprise ever since the failure to perceive German intentions in June 1941. It was once supposed that Nato would receive at least three weeks warning of any offensive in central Europe but the increase in Warsaw Pact capabilities in recent years now enables the Soviets to launch an attack from a 'standing start' without prior mobilisation. Sufficient warning time is vital to Nato in view of its numerical inferiority and lack of the territorial depth which might be traded to win time for the defence.

Nato deploys an impressive range of advanced technological devices in an attempt to probe Warsaw Pact intentions. Although the constant flow of satellite pictures to intelligence centres could reveal unusual activity, more faith is put in the monitoring of Eastern bloc communications, a constant task for sophisticated equipment at locations in western Europe such as Cheltenham in Britain. There are two kinds of intelligence involved – the identification and classification of transmitters and other military electronics, and the interception and decoding of messages. While a careful enemy should be able to avoid giving the game away by broadcasting instructions for an attack that can be picked up by the other side, it would be more difficult to get around the need for a sudden unusual pattern of communications between and within formations.

But whatever the sophistication of electronic and optical technology to keep watch upon the other side every minute of the day, the possibility of surprise and deception remains. Someone will still have to take the agonising decision – is this an attack or a feint, is this mobilisation or just manoeuvres? The luck or judgement of military commanders and politicians will always ultimately decide the chances of a successful surprise attack. **Ian Beckett**

Above: Jet-assisted take-off from a DEW Line radar site in Greenland for a C-130D. In the present era of advanced military technology, the possibility of a surprise nuclear 'first strike' has led to the development and the global dispersion of early warning stations such as the DEW Line.

The A-7 CORSAIR II

Taking its name from the famous F4U Corsair fighter of World War II, the Vought A-7 Corsair II proved to be one of the US Navy's most effective close support and strike aircraft during the Vietnam War. Like the F-4 Phantom, it provided an example of a very good navy aircraft later being built in numbers for the US Air Force. The A-7 Corsair II had its origins in a US Navy design competition started on 17 May 1963 for a subsonic carrier-based single-seat light attack aircraft to carry a substantially greater load of non-nuclear weapons than the Douglas A-4E Skyhawk, and to supplement the latter in service. The navy specified an in-service target date of 1967, and to meet this date and cut costs to a minimum it was also stipulated that the new aircraft should be based on an existing design. These two requirements between them led to only four firms submitting proposals and the entry submitted by Chance Vought Aircraft Incorporated was named as the winner on 11 February 1964.

To meet the very rapid time-to-service schedule demanded by the navy, Vought's design team based the A-7 Corsair on the Chance Vought F-8 Crusader single-seat carrier-based fighter which had entered navy service in 1957. The F-8 Crusader had a shoulder-mounted variable-incidence wing – to enable the landing speed to be reduced without the aircraft · assuming too nose-high an attitude – and a nose radome mounted above the engine air intake. The A-7 Corsair II retained the distinctive nose radome, but had a fixed as distinct from variable-incidence wing, mounted in the same position but with less sweepback. Because of this the A-7's span was slightly greater but its fuselage was shorter than the F-8. Unlike the F-8, the A-7's wing had outboard ailerons for lateral control. The engine of the initial production variant, the A-7A, was a Pratt & Whitney TF30-P-6 turbofan.

The A-7's structure was strengthened to carry a weapons load of up to 6800kg (15,000lb) or about four times as much as the F-8 (some versions of which carried bombs or rocket projectiles). The A-7 was built with eight weapons pylons in all, two on the fuselage sides, two under the wings (inboard) and two on each of the outer wings. These could take almost any weapon in the navy's armoury at the time of the A-7's design, and over 200 different combinations of external 'stores' were subsequently claimed to be

possible. These included both air-to-air and air-to-ground missiles, bombs, rocket projectiles in pods, gun pods and (on the USAF's A-7D version) Pave Penny AN/AAS-35 laser target-designation pods. A typical load of the many combinations that could be carried consisted of two 1135 litre (300 US gallon) drop-tanks on the inboard wing pylons, 12 226kg (500lb) bombs in two clusters of six on the centre pylons, three 113kg (250lb) bombs under each outer pylon and four Zuni rocket pods on the fuselage pylons. Among the missiles carried were the Shrike air-to-surface missile for use against enemy radar installations, the Martin AGM-12B Bullpup air-to-surface missile and the Martin Walleye television-controlled 'smart' bomb. In addition to its formidable external loads, the A-7A was fitted with a fixed armament of two 20mm cannon in the fuselage.

On 19 March 1964 a contract was awarded for three YA-7A Corsair II prototypes and an initial order was placed for 39 production A-7As. The YA-7A made a successful first flight on 27 September 1965 and that month a further 140 A-7As were ordered, with a repeat order for 17 placed later bringing the total of this variant built (including the prototypes) to 199; the last A-7A deliveries were made in the spring of 1968.

The first operational tactical A-7A squadron was VA-147, commissioned on 1 February 1967, which made the first carrier landings with the type on the USS Ranger in June that year. The ship later sailed for

Previous page: A pilot boards an A-7E Corsair II on the flight deck of the US carrier Coral Sea. The A-7's distinctive nose cone and air intake are clearly visible in this photograph. Above: An A-7A prototype is made ready for the US Navy.

Below: Two A-7s bracket an F-8 Crusader, the ancestor of the highly successful A-7 series of support and strike aircraft.

the Gulf of Tonkin, where VA-147 took the A-7A into combat for the first time over Vietnam on 4 December 1967. During six months operational service in Southeast Asia, VA-147 lost only one A-7A in combat.

The next version of the Corsair II was the A-7B, which differed from the A mainly in having a slightly more powerful Pratt & Whitney TF30-P-8 turbofan of 5450kg (12,200lb) thrust. The first production A-7B made its maiden flight on 6 February 1968 and altogether 196 were built, the last A-7B being delivered to the navy on 7 May 1969. By this time 15 A-7A and A-7B squadrons had been trained and 11 of these had seen action in Vietnam, the B variant first entering combat there on 4 March 1969. Among the duties entrusted to the A-7s was the laying of corridors of 'chaff' consisting of millions of pieces of silver foil cut to the right length to interfere with enemy radar frequencies and the launching of SAMs. If the corridor was correctly sown (the 'chaff' was carried in underwing dispensers), strike aircraft could fly through the corridor with no threat from SAMs. But this task meant flying in formation at reduced speed, straight and level, which made the 'chaff'-sowing aircraft vulnerable to SAMs and attack by MiG fighters. The A-7s in this role also carried ECM (electronic countermeasures) pods to jam the SAM radars, but had to have fighter escort to protect them from MiGs. After their service in Vietnam A-7Bs had

Above: Armed with bombs and air-to-air missiles an A-7A Corsair prepares for launch from USS *Constellation* during the Vietnam War. Right: An A-7C painted in the distinctive 'stinger' markings of VA-113.

Right: One of the A-7s used for test flight purposes at the Edwards AFB in California.

Right: The two-seat TA-7C trainer. Both The US Navy and Air Force found the A-7 effective in a variety of different roles.

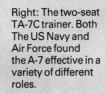

Left: A unit of A-7Es maintains strict formation while flying over a winter landscape.

their engines modified to the TF30-P-408 version of 5900kg (13,400lb) thrust.

The Corsair II's success in Southeast Asia attracted the interest of the USA, for whom the next version to fly, the A-7D tactical fighter, was built. This differed chiefly in having an Allison-built version of the Rolls-Royce Spey turbofan; designated TF41-A-1, this US-built powerplant was of 6500kg (14,500lb) thrust. The D variant was also fitted with a single multi-barrel M61A-1 Vulcan 20mm cannon in the port side of the fuselage in place of the two single-barrel cannon of earlier versions; this Vulcan gun had 1000 rounds of ammunition and firing rates of 4000 or 6000 rounds per minute could be selected by the pilot. More complete avionics were featured for blind or automatic weapons delivery under all weather conditions. Inertial/doppler navigation equipment was also fitted, as was a Marconi-Elliott head-up display.

The first A-7D was accepted by the USA on 23 December 1968 but the D variant waited until October 1972 before going into combat over Southeast Asia. Altogether 459 A-7Ds were built, the last of this version being completed in December 1976, or just over ten years after the first order for the D variant was placed. From mid-1978 modifications were made to a total of 383 A-7Ds to fit them to carry a Pave Penny AN/AAS-35 laser target-designation pod, mounted under the air intake duct lip.

The navy were sufficiently impressed with the A-7D to order their own version of it with the same basic engine, designating it the A-7E. But because of production delays with the Allison TF41-A-2 powerplant for the E variant the first 67 A-7Es were delivered with the TF30-P-8 turbofans that had powered the A-7Bs. With these engines they were redesignated A-7Cs late in 1971 to avoid confusion with the TF41-powered A-7Es. The designation TA-7C had originally been reserved for a two-seat operational trainer version of the A-7A that was never built. Later the TA-7C designation was revived for 40 A-7Bs and 41 A-7Cs earmarked for conversion into two-seater trainers, retaining the same guns and weapons pylons

Above: An A-7 drops its load of Mk 82 high drag bombs. Light, manoeuvrable and yet capable of carrying an impressive bomb load, the A-7 found its true role as a strike aircraft in Vietnam.

and flight refuelling capability as before. The first TA-7C made its maiden flight on 17 December 1976 and TA-7Cs entered service in 1978.

The first flight of an A-7E was on 25 November 1968 and the first delivery of this variant was made on 14 July 1969. The A-7E entered combat service in Southeast Asia in May 1970 with attack squadrons VA-146 and VA-147 aboard the carrier USS *America*, and these units flew nearly 3000 combat sorties (totalling 5700 hours) without losing an aircraft. Altogether 551 A-7Es were built, and early in 1977 the A-7E FLIR (forward-looking infra-red) variant began to come off the line. This had a pod under the starboard wing housing a Texas Instruments FLIR

Above right: Crew work on an A-7 on USS *Coral Sea*, preparing the aircraft for another flight mission. As the nose cone is in the up position the 10-mode APQ-126 radar can be seen.
Right: Two Corsairs from the USS *Enterprise* in flight.

Left: With its deck arresting hook down, an A-7 comes in to land after completing a bombing mission over Vietnam.

A-7E Corsair II

Type Subsonic single-seat light attack/close support fighter-bomber
Dimensions Span 11.80m (38ft 9in); length 14.06m (46ft 1½in); height 4.90m (16ft)
Weight Empty 8668kg (19,111lb); maximum take-off 19,050kg (42,000lb)
Powerplant One 6800kg (15,000lb) Allison TF41-A-2 turbofan

Performance Maximum speed at sea level 1112km/h (691mph); maximum speed at 1525m (5000ft) with 12 Mk 82 bombs 1040km/h (646mph)
Range Ferry range with maximum internal and external fuel 4604km (2861 miles)

Armament One 20mm M61A-1 Vulcan multi-barrel cannon; a total weight of over 6800kg (15,000lb) of bombs, missiles and other 'stores' can be carried on six under-wing pylons and two fuselage weapon stations. Strike camera in lower rear fuselage for damage assessment.

sensor, and a modified cockpit head-up display for improved night attack capability. The RA-7E was a proposed tactical reconnaissance version which carried cameras in under-wing pods.

The A-7G was a model proposed for the Swiss Air Force but during evaluation trials was rejected in favour of the Northrop F-5E. Greece placed the first export order, for 60 of a land-based version of the A-7E designated A-7H for the Hellenic Air Force, which also acquired five TA-7H two-seat trainers. The A-7H first flew on 6 May 1975, and was delivered to Greece between August 1975 and mid-1977; this version retained the upward-folding outer wing panels of earlier A-7s.

In 1980 the US arranged to supply 20 ex-navy A-7As to the Portuguese Air Force under the designation A-7P. These were refitted by Vought with the A-7E's navigation and weapons delivery avionics and uprated TF30-P-408 engines, and they equipped two squadrons in 1983. The latest Corsair II variant is the two-seat TA-7K combat trainer built for the US Air National Guard.

Although not an export success like the Starfighter the A-7 has been ordered by Greece and Portugal. The Hellenic Air Force has bought both the single-seat version (top left) and the two-seat trainer (top). In 1980 the Portuguese ordered 20 A-7Ps (left) to equip an attack squadron. Above: The two-seat YA7-H completes a landing with the aid of a parachute. Below: An A-7K undergoes detailed inspection by ground crew. Built for the National Guard, this variant was the last in the Corsair II series.

Sword of David

The Israeli conquest of the West Bank

Of the three major Arab armies to participate in the Six-Day War, the Royal Jordanian Army was, for its size, the most formidable, having maintained the high standards of discipline, training and battlecraft imparted to the Arab Legion by its former British officers. On 4 June 1967 the bulk of the army was deployed around the perimeter of the Jordanian-held West Bank of the River Jordan as follows: in the north, and occupying positions in the Jordan valley itself, was the 36th (El Kadasia) Infantry Brigade, with one squadron of M47 tanks under its command; to its left was the 25th (Khaled el Walid) Infantry Brigade, plus an M47 battalion, based on Jenin; the narrow waist of Israel was covered by the 1st (Emira Auya) Infantry Brigade at Nablus and the 2nd (Hashemite) Infantry Brigade at Ramallah; the Jerusalem sector was held by the crack 3rd (King Talal) Infantry Brigade, which had been reinforced; and the Hebron sector was controlled by the 29th (Hittin) Infantry Brigade and a Centurion battalion. Two armoured brigades, the 40th and the 60th, each equipped with 88 M48 Pattons, were positioned centrally at the Damiya Bridge and Jericho. In immediate reserve were the 12th (Jarmouk) Infantry Brigade at the Damiya Bridge and the 4th (Hussein Ibn Ali) Infantry Brigade at the Allenby Bridge, the general reserve being provided by the 27th (Imam Ali) Infantry Brigade. Two Egyptian commando units joined the Jordanian Army on the eve of the war, as did General Abdel Muneim Riadh, the Egyptian officer King Hussein had agreed to accept as commander-in-chief following his reconciliation with Egypt's President Gamal Abdel Nasser.

Hussein had designs on Israeli territory and knew that alone his country was no match for Israel, but even so he had been extremely reluctant to join the other Arab leaders in making war. Had he not done so, however, Jordan would instantly have been branded a traitor to the Arab cause, such was the war hysteria sweeping the Middle East. The Israeli prime minister, Levi Eshkol, was fully aware of the King's dilemma and on 5 June, while the Israeli Air Force (IAF) was destroying the Egyptian Air Force on the ground, he informed Hussein through the medium of General Odd Bull, the United Nations commander in Jerusalem, that if Jordan refrained from hostilities Israel would do likewise. Nonetheless, during a telephone conversation with Nasser, the King was told that the Israelis had already suffered crippling air losses and that Egyptian divisions were rolling across the frontier into the Negev; simultaneously, Field Marshal Amer, commander-in-chief of the Egyptian Army, was giving General Riadh a similar erroneous version of events. Hussein had no way of verifying these statements, but his radar stations confirmed intense air activity over Israel and at 1100 hours he reached a decision, ordering his aircraft to attack targets across the border while his artillery opened fire along the front, the heavy batteries dropping shells on Tel Aviv itself.

The Israeli forces deployed around the West Bank salient were drawn from the Central and Northern Commands, under Major-General Uzi Narkis and Major-General David Elazar respectively. One infantry brigade, the 16th, under Colonel Eliezer Amitai, with a 30-strong Sherman battalion under command, was at Jerusalem; others were in position at Latrun, Qalqiliya, Nathanya and Nazareth. Major-General Elad Peled's armoured division was in immediate reserve in Galilee with 120 Shermans and AMX13s.

Above: Arab refugees crowd the wrecked Allenby Bridge on the River Jordan. Below: General Moshe Dayan. Bottom: Major-General Uzi Narkis, commander Israeli central forces.

In general staff reserve was the Harel Armoured Brigade, equipped with 50 Shermans and Centurions, under Colonel Uri Ben-Ari who had led the 7th Armoured Brigade with such distinction in the Sinai campaign of 1956. Altogether, the Israelis could field a total of 200 tanks against the Jordanians who had 250, not including the substantial Iraqi contingent which was assembling at Mafraq.

The Jordanians had two offensive options. The first was to sever the Jerusalem corridor, the effect of which would be to place the Israeli community in the newer part of the city under immediate siege. The second was a drive to the Mediterranean, crossing the northern sector of Israel's narrow waist; this would isolate Galilee from the rest of the country and render it extremely vulnerable to an attack by Syria. As the day wore on, however, the IAF not only eliminated the Royal Jordanian Air Force but also strafed the Arab Legion's artillery positions to such good effect that a Jordanian offensive became increasingly unlikely. Further, General Mordechai Gur's 55th Parachute Brigade, its drop on El Arish having been

cancelled following Major-General Israel Tal's unexpectedly rapid capture of the town, was freed for operations on the Jordanian front. Seeing the balance of the situation turning in their favour, the Israeli general staff decided to seize the initiative.

From the coastal plain the land rises steadily into the hills of Judaea and Samaria and then drops sharply into the Jordan valley. The tactically important high ground was all in the possession of the Jordanians. Nonetheless, the Israeli general staff planned to launch two simultaneous offensives into the West Bank. In the centre, Jerusalem would be isolated and Jericho captured, cutting off the Jordanian troops in Hebron, who would be placed in the impossible position of having to fight with their backs to the Dead Sea. In the north a thrust from the Jezreel valley into the shoulder of the West Bank salient would capture first Jenin and then Nablus, both important road junctions, and then roll up the remaining Jordanian positions in Samaria.

Some fighting had already taken place in the Central Command sector. In Jerusalem the Jordanians

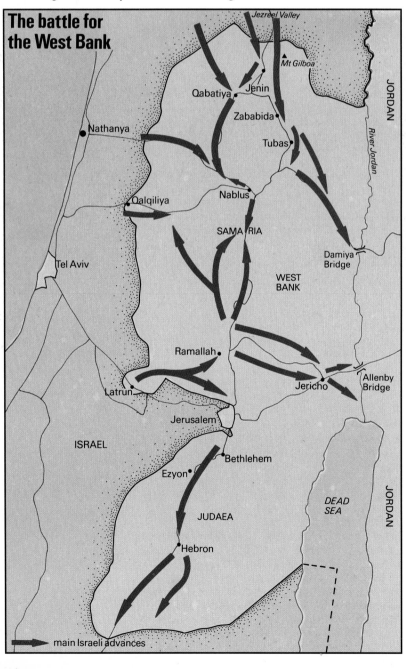

The battle for the West Bank

Jezreel Valley · Mt Gilboa · JORDAN · River Jordan · Qabatiya · Jenin · Nathanya · Zababida · Tubas · Qalqiliya · Nablus · SAMARIA · Tel Aviv · Damiya Bridge · WEST BANK · Ramallah · Allenby Bridge · Jericho · Latrun · Jerusalem · ISRAEL · Bethlehem · Ezyon · DEAD SEA · JORDAN · JUDAEA · Hebron

main Israeli advances

had occupied the enclave surrounding Government House, formerly the residence of the British High Commissioner in Palestine and now the headquarters of the United Nations observation team, but after heavy fighting they had been pitched out by the Israeli 16th Brigade, which had gone on to sever the road leading south to Bethlehem and Hebron. To the west Colonel Moshe Yotvat's infantry brigade had routed the Egyptian commandos, whose mission had been to raid airfields and other installations in Israel, and had captured Latrun.

During the afternoon of 5 June, Ben-Ari's armoured brigade moved up the Jerusalem corridor and swung off the road at three points in order to scale the high ground to the north. The Arab Legion had spared no effort in fortifying its positions, but these were blasted apart at close range by the tanks and cleared out by the infantry. Having taken Radar Hill, Ben-Ari moved east along the ridge, cutting the Jerusalem-Ramallah road. At Tel El Ful, where King

Hussein was having a palace built, a weak counter-attack by a handful of Jordanian M48s was easily brushed aside. The brigade had now isolated Jerusalem from the north and was in a position to dominate the Jericho road to the east.

The Pattons encountered at Tel El Ful belonged to a sub-unit of the Jordanian 60th Armoured Brigade and formed part of the Jerusalem garrison. The remainder of the brigade was now moved forward from Jericho to intervene. It never arrived, however, for the IAF ambushed its columns and strafed them without mercy, continuing to attack after dark by the light of parachute flares. The same fate awaited part of the El Kadasia Brigade, which had also been ordered to converge on Jerusalem.

The availability of Gur's 55th Parachute Brigade meant that the Israeli plan could now include the capture of Jerusalem. During the evening its three battalions deployed between Ben-Ari's position and the walls of the Old City. After thorough artillery

preparation the Israeli formations crossed their start lines at 0230 hours on 6 June with the 16th Brigade's detached Sherman battalion in close support, their objectives illuminated by searchlights. Throughout that night and the following day the Israelis fought a long and bitter battle against the King Talal Brigade for possession of the northern and eastern suburbs; particularly savage fighting took place at the Police School and on Ammunition Hill, where the defenders died to a man. By nightfall the Jordanian commander, Brigadier Ata Ali, had reached a decision. The reinforcements he had been promised had not arrived and although his brigade was fiercely contesting every foot of ground, it was being forced steadily back. He broke contact and conducted a most skilful withdrawal, so that when two Israeli parachute battalions launched an attack on Augusta Victoria Hill and the Mount of Olives at 0830 hours on 7 June, they met little opposition. Gur's third battalion had meanwhile been working its way along the walls from the Rocke-

Top left: Jordanian gunnery teams of the Jordanian Royal Artillery demonstrate their skills during an exercise in the Jordan valley. Top: Wearing steel helmets and battle order webbing, Jordanian troops prepare to move up to the Israeli frontier. Above: Sherman tanks of the Israeli Defence Force thunder across open ground as they move against Jordanian positions.

Right: An Israeli soldier stands guard over a holy place in the newly captured city of Jerusalem. The battle for the Holy City cost Israel 195 killed and 1131 wounded but for the Israelis, the capture of the city was a great victory.

feller Museum and, led by the brigade commander himself in his half-track, broke into the Old City through St Stephen's Gate. By 1000 hours they had reached the West Wall (Wailing Wall) of the Temple Mount.

During the battle the 16th Brigade had continued to mop up the southern suburbs of the city from Mount Zion to the Dung Gate. It now advanced rapidly to the south, taking Bethlehem, Ezyon and Hebron in quick succession. Of the Jordanian Hittin Brigade, which had contributed one battalion to the defence of Jerusalem, there was little trace save for abandoned equipment, including most of the Centurions belonging to its tank battalion.

In the meantime Yotvat's infantrymen had moved forward from Latrun and relieved Ben-Ari's armoured brigade on the high ground north of the city. Ben-Ari advanced to Ramallah and then despatched two of his battalions to Jericho, where the speed of their attack swamped limited Jordanian resistance and carried them through the town to seize the Jordan bridges a few miles beyond. The Harel Brigade's third battalion was directed north to Nablus, effecting a junction with troops from the Northern Command on the way.

The battle for Samaria had been equally fierce and at one point an Israeli defeat seemed a distinct possibility. Peled's armoured division had begun its attack on Jenin at 1700 hours on 5 June, led by a brigade battlegroup under the command of Colonel Moshe Bar-Kochva. However, the Jordanian Khaled el Walid Brigade, and its M47 battalion, put up the most determined resistance throughout the night and by dawn possession of the important Qabatiya road junction was still being bitterly contested. At this point Bar-Kochva was informed that large numbers of Jordanian M48s were converging on Qabatiya from two directions and in the circumstances he had no alternative but to abandon his attack and take up defensive positions.

Tank duel at Qabatiya

The M48s belonged to the 40th Armoured Brigade. Its commander, Brigadier Raken Inad el Jazi, had advanced one of his battalions through Tubas and another through Nablus, hoping to trap Bar-Kochva between them. The plan was well conceived, but its final execution was marred by the fact that the two battalions attacked at different times, thereby enabling Bar-Kochva's Shermans to bring each to a halt independently. Nonetheless, further Israeli progress through Qabatiya was now firmly denied.

To resolve the stalemate Peled despatched a second brigade battlegroup, commanded by Colonel Uri Ram and consisting mainly of AMX13s, along an axis to the east of Jenin. This involved a laborious climb along a goat track on the slopes of Mount Gilboa and the elimination of an anti-tank position, but resulted in Ram emerging on the Jordanian flank at Zababida, where he cut the Tubas-Qabatiya road and destroyed a number of M48s and armoured personnel carriers (APCs).

At dawn on 7 June the tanks of both sides renewed their hull-down gunnery duel at Qabatiya, in which the IAF intervened with decisive effect. The Jordanian 40th Armoured Brigade, reduced through casualties to half strength, was now in serious difficulty, with Ram operating against its rear areas and

---

The battle for Jerusalem

to Ramallah
Tel El Ful
Radar Hill
ISRAEL
Ammunition Hill
Augusta Victoria Hill
Old City
to Jericho
Jerusalem
JORDAN
main Israeli advances
Bethlehem
to Ezyon and Hebron

Ammunition Hill
Police School
Augusta Victoria Hill
Rockerfeller Museum
Mount of Olives
OLD CITY
St Stephens Gate
Wailing Wall
Dung Gate
Mount Zion

Left: Israeli paratroopers stand by the Western (Wailing) Wall, as they await orders for a final advance against Jordanian troops still within the city.

Below: Israeli soldiers take cover behind a wall during close quarter fighting for Jerusalem, and give first aid to a wounded soldier, using field dressings to deal with a shrapnel wound.

Israeli infantry formations closing in on its lines of communication. At this point King Hussein, shaken by the loss of Jerusalem and the total defeat of the Egyptian forces, ordered a general withdrawal to the east bank of the Jordan. For the 40th Armoured Brigade, still enmeshed in battle, this was easier said than done. Its line of retreat was marked by a litter of wrecked or abandoned tanks, self-propelled guns and APCs. Only eight of its Pattons crossed the Damiya Bridge before Bar-Kochva's pursuit closed this last available vehicle exit from the West Bank. Many of its men, and the survivors of the Arab Legion's infantry brigades, managed to scramble to safety, but their equipment had to be left behind.

Israel and Jordan both accepted the United Nations call for a ceasefire and hostilities ended at 2000 hours on 7 June. In a war lasting only 57 hours, Israel had completely eliminated the threat from the West Bank and secured a natural frontier on the Jordan River itself. Jordanian casualties amounted to over 6000 killed and missing, plus an unverifiable number of wounded. On the other hand, the Arab Legion had never broken and it had inflicted on the Israelis the heaviest losses incurred on any front during the Six-Day War: 550 killed and 2500 wounded.

Hussein was never to forgive the Egyptian deception which had led him into the war, nor the Syrian failure to honour specific promises of support. It must, therefore, have been with very mixed feelings that he learned on the second day after his ceasefire that an Israeli offensive had been launched into Syrian territory. **Bryan Perrett**

'Murder and

This account of the experiences of a young Israeli paratrooper, who fought in the battle to drive the Jordanian Arab Legion out of the old city of Jerusalem, was recorded soon after the war ended and gives a vivid impression of the intensity of feeling on both sides.

❝We lay there and they threw everything at us. We could see the guns flicker from the embrasures. But it's a funny thing: when you first go into battle, you don't believe that you can die. You just can't imagine ending, *bom*, just like that. You think, well, who would ever take over my life. Later it's different, I'll come to that. And another thing: they don't send new troops straight into battle. They wouldn't be able to do a thing. It's the enemy who gives you your courage, you see. You don't just pick courage up from nowhere: the enemy gives it to you. You see your own boys dying around you, your friends, and you get mad. And all the time you hear the bullets and shells screaming and whining around you. Then there was one long scream that sounded as if it would never stop, it just kept coming straight at me. The shell landed about a metre away. It killed the boy next to me and I felt a stinging on my cheek. Just for a tiny moment. I put my hand up and felt the blood, running down, cool, on my face. They told me to put my bandage on it. It didn't hurt; it just burned for a while, but it made me so mad. That's when I got my courage.

They told us to charge – we had a few tanks supporting us, but they couldn't touch those deep dug-outs. In a charge it's every man for himself. You see people falling all round you, but you still don't believe it can happen to you. The second time, though, you know it can and your body is rigid the whole time, just waiting for the bullets to go thudding into you. You just go on, running like hell. And a few metres in front is the officer. However fast you run, you can never catch up with him. That's why so many of them were killed.

You find you've reached a dug-out and you throw in hand grenades and hose it out with your Uzi. And that's it, till the next one. All the time you begin to get more and more scared and more and more angry. They gave us a rest when we'd finished that and then we were sent into the Old City. I remember when we rested I began to think what I'd done and I remember at one point – I think it must have been then – hearing that my kibbutz had been shelled. So all at the same time, I was scared but I wanted to get at the bastards all the more.

We went into the Old City and from then on it was hand-to-hand and house-to-house. That's the worst thing in the world. In the desert, you know, it's different. There are tanks and planes and the whole thing is at a longer range. Hand-to-hand fighting is different, it's terrible. I killed my first man there. Well, I suppose I must have killed before, but as far as I'm concerned that was the first, because the others I didn't see. All of a sudden I saw this man coming out of a doorway, this gigantic Negro. We looked at each

other for half a second and I knew that it was up to me, personally, to kill him, there was no one else there. The whole thing must have lasted less than a second, but it's printed in my mind like a slow-motion movie. I fired from the hip and I can still see how the bullets splashed against the wall about a metre to his left. I moved my Uzi, slowly, slowly, it seemed, until I hit him in the body. He slipped to his knees, then he raised his head, with his face terrible, twisted in pain and hate, yes, such hate. I fired again and somehow got him in the head. There was so much blood . . . I vomited, until the rest of the boys came up. A lot of them had been in the Sinai Campaign and it wasn't new to them. They gave me some water and said it's always like that the first time, not to worry. I found I had fired my whole magazine at him. It's true what they said: you grow more and more callous as you go along, and at the same time, you get used to the gun and miss less. But I'll never forget that moment . . . .

But as we went on fighting, I began to care less. For the whole three days that we fought I was sick and vomiting, but it meant less and less to me. All my friends were going down and I grew madder and madder. I wanted to kill them, all the time that I didn't want to see them. I wanted to get a wound and get out; that's what we all wanted – anything to get out. You just went from house to house, up the stairs, on to the roof, saying to yourself: one more house and I'll get out, then another. Gradually you get fatalistic. Either you'll be killed or you won't – there's nothing you can

Above: An Israeli infantry section crouches low behind a wall as they take cover from Arab Legion snipers. Outnumbered by three to one, the Israelis were hard pressed in the initial fighting for Jerusalem.

fear'

do about it yourself, so you just go on, scared and hating . . . .

As we grew angrier, we stopped being human beings. You start out shouting, but by this time, we were all just machines for killing. Everyone's face is set in a snarl and there's a deep growl coming from your belly. You want to kill and kill. You grow like an animal, you know – no, worse than an animal. Things were happening . . . I can't tell you about them. Once, one of our NCOs gave a drink of water to a prisoner. The Jordanian drank and then he pulled a knife and slit the NCO's throat, like a chicken. Things like that. We killed the prisoner, you can't blame us. But you've got to understand what things like that did to us. We hated and hated. And all the time we were thinking what they would do to us and our families if they got us . . . .

Then we got to St Stephen's Gate and we could see the Western Wall, through an archway. We saw it before, but this time it was right in front of us. It was like new life, as though we had just woken up. We dashed down the steps; we were among the first to get there, but a few had already got there and I could see them, men that were too tired to stand up anymore, sitting by the Wall, clutching it, kissing the stones and crying. We all of us cried. That was what we had been fighting for. It goes so deep this emotion we felt when we reached the Wall. What they did in Sinai and Syria, sure it was marvellous, but it wasn't the same. Getting to the Wall meant everything.

That was about it, except that we had to go back and clean out the snipers. There were a lot of them – they killed a whole lot of women and children in the next few days, people coming to see the Wall. We had to clean them out and it wasn't easy.

The worst was after we had a rest. We couldn't eat or sleep, thinking about the fighting. We just drank and thought. I used to look at my Uzi, lying next to me. It looked so innocent, just a piece of shining metal. So innocent. Like a person with a smirk on his face. Then we'd be ordered to get up and go in again. We were so scared, then. But we had to get up and face it again, somehow. You get a sharp pain in your guts, just like the feeling you get before you jump from a plane . . . .

I've got to respect the Legionnaires (Arab Legion). They fought like tigers. They fought fantastically. They were fighting for their own homes, you see. But we were fighting for our existence, that's why we won, though they outnumbered us three to one in the Old City.

I came back without any joy. The victory didn't mean anything to me. None of us could even smile, though the people were cheering us when we came through the Mandelbaum Gate. But we had lost 50 per cent of our company. Another company – 50 men – came back with four alive. I never want to go back. I've had enough of the place. I'll tell you in two words what the battle was: murder and fear, murder and fear. I've had enough, enough . . . . **"**

Top: Still stunned after the battle, one of the first Israeli soldiers to enter Jerusalem after its capture, shows clearly his relief and disbelief that the battle is over.

The road to Damascus

The fight for the Golan Heights

Despite having played a leading role in provoking a Middle East conflict, Syria contributed little military support to her principal allies at the outbreak of the Six-Day War. On the morning of 5 June her air force mounted a raid against the Israeli oil refineries at Haifa, but was destroyed as a fighting entity by an Israeli Air Force (IAF) counter-strike that same afternoon. Syrian activities were then confined to the shelling of Israeli settlements in Galilee and to several company-sized raids against *kibbutzim*, though these were quickly beaten off. It is possible that Syria intended to attack once the Israeli Defence Force (IDF) had been whittled down by Egypt and Jordan, but following the disasters in Sinai and on the West Bank this strategy changed to one of passive defence. The Syrian Army was unlikely to succeed where its allies had failed and it was probably for this reason that the Syrian high command declined to despatch

Above: Israeli artillery hits Syrian positions on the northern Golan Heights. Although the Israelis continuously shelled the Syrians, the bombardment had little effect against their well protected positions.

Below: Syrian artillery overlooking Israeli settlements in the valley below the Heights. Above right: Israeli field guns, their sights trained on Syrian positions, pounded the enemy night and day.

the reinforcements promised to King Hussein, since this could have been construed as the final provocation which might initiate an all-out attack by Israel on Syria itself.

The Israeli/Syrian frontier was only 80km (50 miles) long. Approximately one-third of this border was formed by the Sea of Galilee. To the north towered the long chain of the Golan Heights, culminating in the 2750m (9000ft) high Mount Hermon massif. Like the Egyptians, the Syrians were armed by the Soviet Union and favoured the Russian concept of defence in depth. Syria had so thoroughly fortified the Golan, which provided panoramic views across Israeli territory, that its bunkers were proof against artillery and air attack, and would need to be stormed by ground forces.

The Golan defensive perimeter was manned by three infantry brigades, the 8th in the north, the 11th in the centre and the 19th in the south, each with a 30-strong T34 tank/SU-100 tank destroyer battalion in immediate support. Additionally, 30 ancient but still formidable PzKpfwIV tanks of World War II vintage were dug in along the front. A second line of defence was provided by the 8th Infantry Brigade at Mas'ada, the 123rd Infantry Brigade at Quneitra and the 32nd Infantry Brigade at Rafid, each again with 30 T34/SU-100s. The counter-attack force consisted of the 17th Mechanised Brigade (40 T54s) at Q'ala, the 44th Armoured Brigade (90 T54/55s) at Quneitra and the 14th Armoured Brigade (90 T54/55s) at Kfar Nafekh. Altogether, the Syrians could muster 450 tanks with a further 200 in reserve, and their plentiful artillery had every potential target area on the Golan approaches zeroed to the inch.

Israel had initially been reluctant to launch an attack on Syria since it was felt that this might draw the Soviet Union into the conflict. However, with the defeat of Egypt and Jordan this danger receded and it was decided to seize the Golan Heights, which would serve in the future as a natural frontier.

The Israeli offensive was mounted under the direction of Major-General David Elazar's Northern Command. To support those troops already on the spot, battle-hardened formations were redeployed from both the Sinai and the West Bank. This process continued throughout the battle so that eventually Elazar commanded the following formations: Colonel Yona Efrat's Golani Infantry Brigade, one of the best in the Israeli service but thus far unblooded in the war, with a Sherman battalion in support; two further infantry brigades, one at Bnot Ya'aqov Bridge and the other near the Sea of Galilee; Colonel Avraham Mandler's armoured brigade, arriving tired from its pursuit of the Egyptian Task Force Shazli across the Sinai; Colonels Uri Ram's and Moshe Bar-Kochva's armoured brigades, fresh from their success against the Jordanian armour at Qabatiya; and Colonels Mordechai Gur's and Danny Matt's parachute brigades from, respectively, Jerusalem and Abu Aweigila.

Of the three roads crossing the Golan Heights, one, the southernmost, passed along the narrow corridor of land between the Sea of Galilee and heavily fortified positions on the Jordanian border; the second ran straight across the hills from Bnot Ya'aqov Bridge, but was covered by two unassailable Syrian positions; the northern route crossed the lower slopes of Mount Hermon and it was here that Elazar decided to launch his principal thrust, for although the approach was covered by the fortified citadel of Tel Azzaziat, the Syrian anti-tank defences were less numerous. The object was to open the road through Baniyas and Za'ura to Mas'ada and thus unhinge the entire Syrian front. The attack would be made by the Golani Brigade with Mandler's armoured brigade on its right, the mission of the latter being to storm the fortified complex at Q'ala. In overall command of the operation was Brigadier-General Dan Laner, the Northern Command's chief of staff.

Onto the attack

The offensive began on the morning of 9 June with concentrated strikes by the IAF against the Syrian defences, which absorbed tremendous punishment without a visible reduction in their capacity to resist.

Two Golani battalions, with Shermans in support, crossed their startlines a little to the north of Kfar Szold *kibbutz* and began climbing the slopes, leaving Tel Azzaziat to their left. A frontal assault on this fortress would have been quite pointless, but it had been discovered that Tel Azzaziat was vulnerable to an attack from the rear. Approach from this direction was covered by another fortified position at Tel Faher, and it was against this that the assault was directed.

The advancing troops were immediately blanketed by Syrian artillery fire, while individual Shermans became the target of dug-in tanks and anti-tank guns. Mines further eroded the Israeli tank support, but a few vehicles did succeed in reaching the plateau. Here the nature of the Syrian defences became fully apparent. Tel Faher was a warren of bunkers, trenches, machine-gun posts and anti-tank positions surrounded by three double-apron wire entanglements with minefields covering the approaches. Nonetheless, this was very much a grudge fight for the Golanis; for too long their families had lived in fear of the Syrian guns and now they sought only to come to grips with their tormentors. Men threw themselves

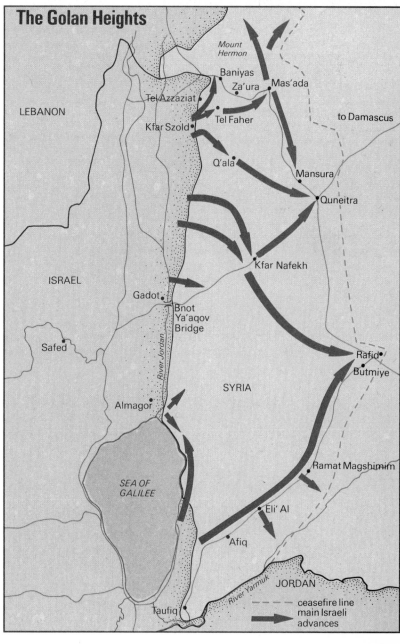

The Golan Heights

onto the wire, forming human bridges across which their comrades rushed, hurling grenades and blazing away with their Uzi sub-machine guns. Efrat committed the brigade's reconnaissance unit to the savage fighting, which spilled from the trenches down into the bunkers. Battalion, company and platoon commanders were killed but their places were instantly taken by junior officers and NCOs. The battle raged throughout the day and by 1800 hours Tel Faher was in Israeli hands. Simultaneously, the third Golani battalion had been working its way north along the summit of the Heights. As dusk fell it launched an attack, with tank support, into the vulnerable rear defences of Tel Azzaziat, overwhelming them.

To the south Mandler's armoured brigade fought an equally stiff battle. Its startline was close to that of the Golani Brigade. It climbed the mountain road in single file, hammered continuously by Syrian artillery. Several tanks were knocked out but their crews joined the mechanised infantry battalion, which itself lost a number of half-tracks. Leading the attack was an engineer company equipped with unarmoured bulldozers, and this not only had the task of clearing the enemy's obstacles from the track, but also of pushing aside wrecked and burning Israeli vehicles.

On reaching the summit the leading tank battalion, commanded by Lieutenant-Colonel Biro, struck southeast across the plateau towards Q'ala, having already suffered severely during the climb. Mandler's plan recognised that the western defences of Q'ala were the most formidable and involved an indirect approach from the north, through Za'ura. However, because of the dust and smoke thrown up by the artillery fire of both sides, Biro's battalion missed the vital track junction and continued on the direct route to Q'ala, running head on into the Syrian defences. In the fierce exchange of fire which followed, Biro was seriously wounded and command of the battalion passed to Lieutenant Natti of the leading

Right: Israeli Sherman tanks pass a knocked-out AMX13 as they claw their way across the Golan Heights. Right below: Israeli field armour, here showing an SPG in the foreground and an APC to the rear, on exercise along the Golan Heights.

Below: A lightly armed Israeli foot patrol approaches a hovering helicopter to exchange intelligence reports. The wide open spaces of the Heights meant that small groups of infantry could observe a wide area without detection. Below right: An upgunned Israeli Sherman receives a direct hit from a Syrian phosphorous shell. During the battle for the Golan Heights, much of the Israeli armour came under intense anti-tank fire, and Israeli armour casualties were comparatively high.

squadron who, believing that the rest of the brigade would be arriving shortly, continued to attack.

Although Mandler was now aware that a mistake had been made, he decided to proceed with his original plan with the remainder of the brigade. Meanwhile, Natti continued to attack against impossible odds. As the light began to fade he requested an air strike to relieve the pressure on his two surviving tanks. Minutes later Mandler advised him that the brigade was through Za'ura and closing in fast from the north. Worried by the prospect of encirclement, the Syrians withdrew from Q'ala during the early hours of darkness.

Still further south, an infantry attack across the River Jordan had succeeded in securing the high ground north of Bnot Ya'aqov Bridge and Ram's armoured brigade, hill-climbing for the second time in a week, passed through to capture the village of Rawiye. Simultaneously, paratroops had eliminated a Syrian position east of Darbashiya. The central route across the Golan Heights, connecting Quneitra with Bnot Ya'aqov, was then severed by an Israeli armoured thrust to the southeast, effectively isolating those Syrian units still in position to the west.

The following morning the Israeli offensive gathered momentum. In the north Bar-Kochva's armoured brigade, newly arrived from the West Bank, passed through the Golani Brigade, part of which was successfully lifted by helicopter onto the lower peak of Mount Hermon. Quickly taking Baniyas and Mas'ada, Bar-Kochva's tanks swung south to Mansura on the road to Quneitra, towards which Mandler's armoured brigade was also advancing from the direction of Q'ala. Ram, meanwhile, was pushing past Kfar Nafekh and was driving on Quneitra from the southwest, thus virtually encircling the town from which the only route of escape lay eastwards, along the road to Damascus.

Mopping up

Elsewhere, mopping up operations were taking place along the Golan Heights and on the eastern shore of the Sea of Galilee, while a new sector had been opened in the narrow corridor between the latter and the Jordanian border. Here, operations were controlled by Major-General Elad Peled's division, which still retained some of its armour although it now consisted mainly of infantry formations, including Gur's paratroop brigade. A set-piece attack with concentrated air support captured Taufiq, thereby opening the corridor. The paratroops were then deployed forward by helicopter into the Yarmuk valley, eventually reaching Butmiye.

The Syrians had fought hard and well the previous day but by mid-morning on 10 June they had lost heart, partly because the IAF dominated the skies and the Israeli ground troops seemed to be growing stronger by the hour, and partly because their own high command seemed incapable of responding to the situation. A general withdrawal through Quneitra was turned into a panic-stricken rout as the IAF strafed the converging columns from end to end, and soon the three Israeli armoured brigades found themselves advancing through the now familiar scenes of wrecked and abandoned vehicles. Mandler won the race for Quneitra, entering the town unopposed at 1400 hours on the same day.

It seemed to the shaken Syrian administration that an advance on Damascus was likely and, through the Soviet Union, a request was made for the United Nations to impose a ceasefire. The Israelis, who already had all the Syrian territory they needed, agreed to this the same evening.

The battle for the Golan Heights had cost Syria 2500 killed, 5000 wounded, approximately 100 tanks and 200 artillery weapons. Israeli casualties amounted to 115 killed and 306 wounded; material losses were relatively high, but a large proportion of battle-damaged tanks were repaired and returned to service. It remained only to turn round the defences on the Heights and make them secure against the Syrian counter-offensive which, given the nature of Arab/Israeli relations, was bound to come in the course of time.
Bryan Perrett

Where angels fear to tread

Superpower involvement in the Middle East

The crucial strategic objective of the superpowers (the United States and the Soviet Union) in the Middle East is control of the oilfields of the Gulf, source of essential energy supplies to the industrial West. Yet since World War II the superpowers have been sucked into a dangerous involvement with the local politics of an area of far less importance, the eastern Mediterranean. The prolonged confrontation between the Israelis and the Arabs has escaped the control of the superpowers, drawing them into entanglements often contrary to their broader global interests.

Up to the end of World War II neither the US nor the USSR had any major involvement in the region. Britain was the dominant regional power, with France in a subsidiary role. The focus of US and Soviet attention in the immediate postwar period was on Turkey and Iran rather than on Palestine, where Britain faced mounting pressure for the creation of a Jewish state. Perhaps surprisingly in view of much that has followed, the USSR was the most outspoken supporter of the creation of Israel among the major powers. It was the first state to give Israel full legal recognition in 1948 and it supplied arms and aircraft through its satellite Czechoslovakia to the infant state. Many Israeli military personnel, like the mastermind of the 1967 Israeli pre-emptive air strike, Major-General Mordechai Hod, received their training in Czechoslovakia.

American support for the formation of the new state was comparatively uncertain. Some leaders were against it – in 1948 Secretary of State Dean Acheson claimed that the creation of a Jewish state would 'imperil not only American but all Western interests in the Middle East' (a view undoubtedly shared by the Soviets – hence their support for Israel). Official backing for Israel prevailed, however, and in March 1949 the Israeli Knesset (parliament) adopted a statement of basic principles which included a declaration of 'friendship with all freedom-loving states, and in particular with the United States and the Soviet Union'.

This honeymoon with the Soviet Union was short-lived. Stalin's anti-semitic policies in the early 1950s caused the first deep rift between the two countries. Then, after Stalin's death in 1953, the USSR's new leaders made a reassessment of the Middle East situation. Support for Israel had been based on that country's hostility to Britain and, in lesser part, on the socialist orientation of the early Israeli state. Stalin's policymakers had believed the Arabs to be natural allies of the Western imperialists, but the successors

in the Kremlin were impressed by the emerging Arab nationalist movements. The traditional ruling powers in the region, Britain and France, were part of the Western bloc, and so the nationalist regimes established in Syria in 1950 and in Egypt in 1952 were inherently anti-Western. Since the Soviet aim was to break up the West's solid hold on the region, backing Arab nationalism looked a good bet. This analysis was confirmed in 1953 when an attempt by US Secretary of State John Foster Dulles to promote a Middle East Defence Organization, which would have linked all regional states in an alliance against Soviet influence, was rejected by the Arabs, who were on the whole more fearful of Western than of Soviet interference.

The rise to power of Gamal Abdel Nasser in Egypt in 1954 opened a new phase in Middle East politics. The Western powers were extremely suspicious of Nasser and the French began secret arms supplies to Israel. In the autumn of 1955, since the US refused to supply him with arms, Nasser negotiated a deal with the Soviet Union for military supplies via Czechoslovakia. The Suez conflict the following year marked the end of the role of Britain and France as dominant regional powers. Motivated largely by hostility to colonialism, the US refused to support the action of its Western allies and subsequently joined with the USSR in pressing Israel to withdraw from the Sinai. From that point forward, the US took over the task of maintaining Western interests in the eastern Mediterranean.

Defending Western interests

Western interests certainly needed defending, as a tide of radical nationalism swept the Arab world. Fearing that pro-Western governments might fall, in 1957 President Dwight D. Eisenhower enunciated the Eisenhower Doctrine, stating US readiness to intervene militarily if invited to do so by a threatened friendly government in the region. In July 1958 a coup in Iraq overthrew a pro-Western regime that was one of the pillars of the anti-Soviet Baghdad Pact, and in the same year the US and Britain were forced to send troops into the Lebanon and Jordan respectively to preserve pro-Western governments against radical opposition. The Soviet Union was able to stand aside while events drifted its way, developing a solid friendship with the increasingly nationalist regimes in Syria, Egypt and Iraq without the need for any military intervention.

Israel offered the Americans an obvious counter-

Superpowers and their clients: above: Israeli Defence Minister Moshe Dayan with US President Richard Nixon; above right: Egypt's President Nasser meets Soviet Premier Khrushchev.

Below: A Czech-manufactured MG37 medium machine gun in use by Israeli troops during the 1948–49 Arab-Israeli War. Eastern bloc arms supplies were vital to Israel's survival in these early years.

weight to Soviet influence in the radical Arab states. US governments were also under domestic pressure to back Israel – there are more Jews in New York than in any city in Israel and their votes count heavily in presidential elections. There was also a cultural identification in the US with the Israelis, seen as hard-fighting democratic frontier people, a favourite image from America's own past. But on the other side of the balance there was always the counter-pressure from oil: any action which alienated Arab oil producers or disrupted peace in the Middle East was a threat to the West's oil supplies. As a consequence, the US supported Israel, but urged peace and moderation.

Neither the US nor the USSR wanted the war that eventually broke out in 1967. The Soviet Union was certainly guilty of encouraging Syria and Egypt to build up a confrontation with Israel, but war was not in its plans. The Soviets were almost certainly dismayed by Nasser's decision to block the Straits of Tiran and surprised by Israel's aggressive response. Nor were the Americans a party to the Israeli attacks, as the Arabs claimed. Indeed, one of the main precipitating factors of the war was Israel's perception that US and West European support was lukewarm. When the West responded to the closing of the Straits of Tiran by urging moderation, rather than compelling Egypt to lift the blockade, Israel assumed that its fate was in its own hands. It could not depend on the US to guarantee its security and must therefore have recourse to military action.

The superpower game

For the superpowers, the crisis of the war came when Israeli troops closed on Damascus. The Soviet Union made it clear that an Israeli occupation of Damascus would overstep the limits of the superpower game. The US accepted that it must discipline its associate and leaned on the Israelis to accept a ceasefire (which as it happened they were not reluctant to do).

In the aftermath of the war, both superpowers confirmed and extended their presence in the region. The war had been won by Israel using much French equipment, but Israel now found itself the object of an arms ban imposed by President Charles de Gaulle (indeed, in 1970 France was to supply 110 Mirage fighters to Israel's enemy Libya). Along with other European powers, France was keen to avoid further upsetting Arab oil-producers and had little sympathy with Israeli expansionism. Thus the US emerged as Israel's almost exclusive source of military aid and diplomatic support – often an uncomfortable situation for the Americans.

Meanwhile the Soviet Union was turning defeat into victory. The collapse of the Soviet-armed and trained Arab forces in 1967 was a blow to Soviet prestige, but the war left Egypt and Syria even more dependent on the support of their superpower backer. In a remarkably short time the USSR had re-equipped the decimated armies. By the end of 1968 Egypt had received an estimated $1000 million-worth of military aid, and Syria and Iraq between them had been given around $1500 million-worth. In return, the Soviets were given, amongst other advantages, naval base rights at the Egyptian ports of Alexandria and Port Said.

Spiralling commitment

By the end of the decade the two superpowers seemed involved in an irreversible upward spiral of commitment. In December 1968 President Richard M. Nixon had raised the technological level of armament in the area to a new height by sending Israel 50 F-4 Phantoms, the most powerful strike aircraft in the world at that time. In March 1970 Israel received a massive US arms shipment, valued at around $500 million. In the same year the number of Soviet military and technical advisers in Egypt was raised from 300 to 20,000, including fighter pilots, and the Soviet Union supplied SA-3 and ZSU-23-4 anti-aircraft weapons for the first time. It was obvious that any further conflict between Egypt and Israel – and such a conflict seemed almost certain to occur at some point in the future – could precipitate a disastrous superpower confrontation. An Arab-Israeli war had become a favourite opening to scenarios for World War III.

Yet both superpowers recognised one another's legitimate concerns in the region – as witnessed by talks between the US and USSR in 1969 to seek out a solution to the Israeli-Arab problem. Neither superpower had any real interest in war in the Middle East, especially not the US with its need to placate Arab oil states. The danger to world peace lay not in superpower rivalry as such, but in the superpowers' inability to control their client states. Israel on one side and Egypt and Syria on the other now had the power, in pursuing their own local conflict, to pull the US and the USSR into a confrontation that neither wished for.

R.G. Grant

The mystery of the Liberty

President Nasser and other leaders of Arab states which took part in the Six-Day War were convinced that the United States collaborated with Israel in the planning or execution of offensive action. But the uncertainty of relations between Israel and the United States during the 1967 war was never more clearly seen than in the attack on USS Liberty.

The Liberty was a US ELINT (Electronics Intelligence) vessel assigned to a surveillance mission off the Sinai coast. On 8 June it was following a northwesterly course 14 nautical miles north of El Arish when it was attacked by Israeli motor torpedo boats and strike aircraft. Through a mixture of luck and good seamanship, the Liberty was kept afloat and reached port in Malta on 14 June, but 34 of her crew were killed and 164 wounded. US Navy fighters from USS America scrambled to help the Liberty but no clashes with Israeli fighters took place.

No explanation of this extraordinary event has ever been produced by either the Israeli or US governments. The Liberty was identified by flags and signals as a US vessel. Even if a mistake had been made at the outset, the Israelis must have realised they were dealing with an American warship long before the attack was ended. Among many speculations about the affair, it has been suggested that the Liberty was acting in association with a Polaris submarine, the Andrew Jackson, which had instructions to hit Israeli missile installations should an Israeli missile attack on the Egyptians be threatened.

The US government took a surprisingly lenient view of the attack, which did not affect relations with Israel. The Israelis never officially apologised for the loss of life caused, although it did offer financial compensation to the victims.

Below: The USS Liberty in dry dock in Malta, showing the extent of damage to her hull.

Right: Members of American Jewish organisations express their hostility to the PLO in a demonstration in New York. The scale and intensity of Jewish support for Israel in the United States was a major factor in deciding successive American governments to back Israel against its Arab neighbours, despite the West's crucial need for secure supplies of Arab oil.

Key Weapons

CRUISE MISSILES

The concept of the cruise missile – defined as a 'long-range pilotless delivery system whose flight is wing-supported in atmosphere' – is not new; a range of such weapons was produced from the mid-1940s onwards. The three families of weapons known by the name today began life in 1970 when the US Department of Defense gave Boeing the go-ahead to build the AGM-86 SCAD (sub-sonic cruise armed decoy).

SCAD was intended to complement the existing AGM-69 SRAM (short-range attack missile) carried by the B-52 fleet. Up to 20 SCADs could be carried by a single B-52, a percentage of which would be armed with nuclear warheads. It is fairly obvious what effect a shot-gun scatter of such missiles would have on an enemy's defences: each SCAD would have to be dealt with individually, giving the SRAM-carriers that much greater chance of getting through to the target.

In military terms, SCAD made a lot of sense but its cost militated against Congressional approval and it was never put into production. The existing project was not, however, wasted as the USAF quickly realised that the design could be readily adapted to become a true ALCM (air-launched cruise missile). The need for such a weapon was pressing as the B-52s were becoming increasingly vulnerable to interception by the latest generations of Soviet interceptors and SAMs (surface-to-air missiles).

With a range of around 1200km (750 miles) the AGM-86 seemed to offer the quickest and cheapest solution available to the problem, and in 1973 the AGM-86A ALCM was revealed. The new model was based very closely on SCAD, differences mainly involving increased fuel capacity, a permanent nuclear warhead and a more sophisticated guidance system. The most important element of this latter package was the McDonnell Douglas DPW-23 TERCOM which has gone on to become the cornerstone of most subsequent American cruise developments.

Standing for TERrain COMparison, TERCOM originated in an E-Systems' patent of 1958 and offered a guidance system which could be accurate to within tens of metres of a target over very long ranges. This latter fact is the real key to the system's usefulness. Previously, most attack missiles used IN (inertial navigation) systems for guidance. IN, that is the use of gyro-stabilised accelerometers to give a read-out of present position related to that at launch, is very accurate over short ranges, but as the duration of the flight increases that accuracy falls away. This phenomenon, known as 'drift rate', can be as much as 750m (820yds) per hour and means that an IN-guided missile launched at the ranges AGM-86 is capable of flying, would impact kilometres away from a designated target – clearly useless when that target was, for example, a hardened missile silo.

TERCOM, on the other hand, generates guidance commands by making direct comparisons between what it should be flying over and what it is flying over in reality. This is done by programming an on-board computer with a series of digital spot-height grids corresponding to specific locations on the missile's flight path. At each location, a radar altimeter is used to produce a similar grid showing the actual terrain below the missile. The two are compared and if an exact match is found, the missile is on course. If not,

Previous page: A Tomahawk cruise missile flies over the Mojave Desert during an exercise to test a prototype vertical launcher. Above: The distinctive shape of the Boeing cruise missile in flight.

Opposite page: A helicopter dangles a US Air Force ALCM with parachute brake trailing at the rear, while (inset) the ALCM can be seen in flight. Below: A cluster of ALCMs are slung under the wing of a B-52G. Further cruise missiles can be carried within the B-52's fuselage.

the computer instructs the weapon to execute a search until the match is found.

The use of specific way-points rather than continuous comparison is so as not to overload the available computer memory. IN is used to navigate the legs between points, with the TERCOM being used to update the IN system periodically and correct any 'drift'. It will be seen that such a combination offers almost limitless range, the only constraints being the amount of fuel carried by the missile and the number of TERCOM grids the on-board computer can hold.

The promise held out by TERCOM led to the creation of America's second current cruise weapon, the General Dynamics Tomahawk. This missile was developed for the US Navy initially as an SLCM (ship-launched cruise missile) to be fired from both submarines and surface ships. Two companies, General Dynamics with the BGM-109 and Ling-Temco-Vought with the BGM-110, were instructed to produce prototypes during 1972. General Dynamics' contender flew in 1976 and was chosen as the basis for the production weapon during the following year. At the same time, it was recommended that the type should be further developed as a GLCM (ground-launched cruise missile) for the USAF.

It would have been surprising if the development of weapons of the complexity of Boeing and General Dynamics' cruise missiles had been trouble-free, but as both programmes progressed, it became apparent that something more than minor teething troubles was at work. Test rounds fell out of the sky with alarming regularity and costs began to soar. Equally, as the failure rate increased, so did the political pressure. Congress became strident in its demands to know what was going wrong and, more importantly, as prices spiralled, began seriously to question the wisdom of producing two independent systems.

Against this background, Boeing found itself having to compete in an unwanted 'fly-off' between its AGM-86 (which had first flown on 5 March 1976) and an air-launched Tomahawk, the AGM-109A. President Carter's cancellation (later rescinded) of the B-1 bomber in June 1977, however, gave Boeing a way out as it opened up the possibility of a 'super' ALCM, the AGM-86B. The original model was designed to fit the existing AGM-69 carrying racks in the B-52 which meant that its fuel capacity was limited. Following the withdrawal of the B-1, range became of even greater importance if the venerable B-52 was to remain operationally viable into the 1980s and beyond. As early as 1976, Boeing had suggested equipping the AGM-86A with a ventral auxiliary fuel tank, but with this new impetus they sold the USAF a bigger missile.

Some 30 per cent bigger than its predecessor, the AGM-86B offered a considerable range improvement with the same W-80 200KT nuclear warhead, combined with numerous internal modifications shown to be advantageous during the earlier test programme. The new missile could no longer be carried internally by the B-52, however.

The 'fly-off' began on 17 July 1979 with a planned total of 19 launches. By the end of December, 16 had been fired, of which eight failed to function correctly. The tests ended in March 1980, at which time the AGM-86B was declared the winner and Boeing was awarded a $141 million contract for the first 225 ALCMs (the total 'buy' being pegged at 3400). The

Above: A sequence of three photographs showing a General Dynamics Tomahawk anti-ship cruise missile hitting a target ship. The missile was launched over 160km from the target.

Below: A Tomahawk cruise missile is launched from its TEL (transporter erector vehicle) as part of an air force programme to improve its tactical nuclear capability. A typical air force GLCM unit will have four TELs, each capable of firing four missiles.

failures experienced during the USAF 'fly-off' give a good indication of the problems both companies were facing in trying to make cruise work, but they were as nothing compared with what General Dynamics was about to face. With the decision to proceed with the AGM-86B ALCM, Tomahawk development concentrated on the BGM-109A nuclear SLCM, the BGM-109B conventional anti-shipping weapon, the BGM-109C conventional land-attack weapon and the BGM-109G nuclear GLCM. The BGM-109A and G used the described IN/TERCOM guidance system which by now was a fairly mature and reliable package. The BGM-109B was fitted with IN combined with the active radar seeker from the Harpoon missile, whilst the BGM-109C used IN/TERCOM combined with a terminal guidance system known as DSMAC (digital scene matching area correlation). DSMAC uses the same digital comparison method as TERCOM but with 'real time' information coming from an electro-optical unit rather than a radar altimeter.

Although the four variants used a common airframe their detail differences, especially in the various guidance systems, were very obviously overloading General Dynamics' research and development capacity. If this were not enough, the company had also involved itself in the development of the AGM-109H (USAF) and the AGM-109L (USN) Tomahawk derivatives for the MRASM (medium-range air-to-surface missile) programme. Costs continued to rise, test and production schedules slipped, and inflight failures continued (by January 1981, 56 Tomahawks had been launched of which 11 had failed). Back in the Boeing

camp, work on the AGM-86B was progressing more smoothly and the first ALCM-equipped B-52 became operational during December 1982.

The current operational mode is for the B-52s to launch their ALCMs from points 350km (220 miles) or more from the Soviet coast. All AGM-86-carrying B-52s will be fitted with FROD (functionally-related observable-differences) wing-root strakes to make them visible to Soviet satellites in accordance with the provisions of the (unratified) SALT II treaty.

Boeing is already looking to the future with a proposed AGM-86C which would offer a 10 per cent range improvement over the B combined with an improved powerplant, and is working on an advanced cruise missile for the late 1980s. Such work is deemed worthwhile as, with the re-instatement of the B-1 by the Reagan Administration, the USAF sees cruise as a viable weapon into the 1990s. As currently planned, the 1986 production B-1B will carry 14 ALCMs externally and eight internally.

As 1983 opened, the various strands of the Tomahawk programme seemed finally to be bearing fruit. The US Navy's conventionally-armed BGM-109Bs and Cs entered service with the submarine fleet late in 1982. The submarine-launched weapons are fired either from the standard torpedo tubes or from vertical launchers carried in the bows. The largest surface vessels currently envisaged as carrying SLCMs are four Iowa-class battleships.

The nuclear-tipped BGM-109A will be launched from both submarines and line ships whilst the most infamous member of the family (oddly, also the most reliable in test firings), the BGM-109G GLCM has been deployed in the UK. The ground-launched Tomahawks are organised into 'flights' which com-

prise 16 missiles loaded onto four TEL (transporter/ erector/launcher) vehicles, accompanied by two LCC (launch control centre) vehicles. The GLCMs are described as being capable of 'selective or general nuclear release', that is, strikes on specific targets such as airfields or 'shotgun' attacks on troop and tank concentrations. In action, the TELs and LCCs will deploy from holding bases to pre-planned sites in order to launch their missiles, making them that much harder to knock out.

It must be stressed that the US sees GLCM as a theatre weapon and has structured the launch system accordingly, with the TEL/LCC vehicles being armoured against smallarms fire and being capable of operating in a radioactive or chemical/biological warfare environment.

The MRASM Tomahawks are currently far less certain to see service. Indeed, the US Navy pulled out of the whole programme in 1981, preferring a modified Harpoon to fulfill the requirement. Department of Defense pressure has forced them back into the project. Currently, the USAF is considering the AGM-109H (MRASM weapons all being air-launched) and the navy the AGM-109L. The H is intended for airfield attacks and uses conventional sub-munitions and laser-gyro IN/TERCOM for guidance. The L is designed as a dual-role conventional weapon for use against ships and land targets. Guidance is provided by IN/TERCOM combined with DSMAC or imaging infra-red terminal homing. The navy is still not enthusiastic about its MRASM Tomahawk and no forward progress on the project seems likely in the near future.

The controversy generated by the whole 'cruise' issue has tended to obscure and distort many of the

Right: A Tomahawk cruise missile undergoes testing on a prototype launching system being developed for the US Navy. Spruance-class destroyers will be able to take this new missile launcher.

Below left: An SLCM is fired from an armoured box launcher on the USS *Merril* in 1982. Such a weapon represents a considerable increase in a small naval vessel's offensive capability. Below right: A Tomahawk SLCM emerges from the water (with boost motor power) following a launch from the nuclear-powered attack submarine USS *Guitarro*.

Cruise missiles

Designation	Length	Weight	Range	Speed (approx)	Engine	Guidance	Warhead
AGM-86B	6.32m (20ft 8in)	1450kg (3197lb)	2500km (1553 miles)	805km/h (500mph)	F107-WR-100 turbofan	IN/TER	Nuclear 200kt yield
AGM-109H	5.90m (19ft 5in)	1400kg (3087lb)	450km (281 miles)	805km/h (500mph)	Teledyne CAE turbojet	IN/TER DSMAC	HE
AGM-109L	4.90m (16ft 1in)	1000kg (2705lb)	450km (281 miles)	805km/h (500mph)	Teledyne CAE turbojet	IN/TER/IIR	HE Sub-munitions
BGM-109A	6.40m (20ft 10in)	1200kg (2646lb)	2500km (1553 miles)	805km/h (500mph)	F107-WR-100 turbofan plus rocket launch boost	IN/TER	Nuclear 200kt yield
BGM-109B	6.40m (20ft 10in)	1200kg (2646lb)	450km (281 miles)	805km/h (500mph)	F107-WR-100 turbofan plus rocket launch boost	IN/AR	HE
BGM-109C	6.40m (20ft 10in)	1270kg (2800lb)	1500km (932 miles)	805km/h (500mph)	F107-WR-100 turbofan plus rocket launch boost	IN/TER DSMAC	HE
BGM-109G	6.40m (20ft 10in)	1200kg (2646lb)	2500km (1553 miles)	805km/h (500mph)	F107-WR-100 turbofan plus rocket launch boost	IN/TER	Nuclear

facts about the weapons. Not the least important of these distortions is the answer to the simple question, will cruise work as advertised? The answer is problematic, but there is growing evidence that it will not.

Throughout the development of both the AGM-86 and the Tomahawk, various aspects of their capabilities have been questioned. Quite early on, the low operating speed of the various weapons suggested that they might be vulnerable to interception. In January 1979, such unease goaded the Pentagon into a public denial of Russia's capability to shoot a cruise missile down. This was almost certainly the case then, but the Soviet Union has had a good deal of time since to ponder the problem and is close to introducing a new generation of interceptors with a much improved 'look-down, shoot-down' radar capability of the sort needed to destroy the low-flying missile. In fairness, it must be said that current American radars have quite a problem dealing with such a target and the Russians almost certainly lag some way behind in this area.

The biggest question mark, however, lies over the TERCOM guidance system. That it works is not in doubt; what is worrying the air force and the navy is whether it can be provided with adequate data to allow it to work effectively. In 1982, the US General Accounting Office came to the remarkable conclusion that adequate pre-flight mapping for the system would not be available before 1986 (the necessary information coming from spy satellites) and that in any case, seasonal variations such as snow and the annual leaf-shedding by deciduous forests would

seriously affect TERCOM's ability to recognise a way-point even when it was positioned directly over it. Further indirect evidence of the system's limitations has been revealed by the admission that for TERCOM to work when launched from stand-off B-52s, only limited routes are available because of the missile's inability to register coastlines devoid of particularly striking geographical features.

Whatever the strengths and weaknesses of 'cruise' may be, it certainly has found a place in current history as the cause of a change in Western public attitudes towards nuclear weapons generally and, more significantly, towards the competence of politicians and the military in their handling of such weapons of mass destruction.

Below: A Tomahawk II cruise missile mock-up is shown with two F-16 fighters at Edwards air force base in California. The Tomahawk II programme is an attempt to provide the US Air Force and Navy with a stand-off weapon that can be delivered by a variety of aircraft, including the lightweight F-16.

Friends and helpers

America's allies in Vietnam

The Vietnam War was a struggle fought for the allegiance of some 19 million Vietnamese living south of the 17th parallel; it was prosecuted by forces both from within South Vietnam itself – the communist Viet Cong and the South Vietnamese government – and by the armed forces of North Vietnam and the United States. But these were not the only combatants. The US was concerned to use whatever allies it could in the struggle, and was able to call on two separate sources of manpower. The first source lay in America's allies in the Pacific and Asia – Thailand, the Philippines, South Korea, Australia and New Zealand – but the second lay in Indochina itself, in the hill people, the so-called 'Montagnards', who were dragged into a conflict with most tragic consequences.

Put in more flags

In the early 1960s South Vietnam's President Ngo Dinh Diem had been unwilling to accept much outside help. But by 1964, as communist insurgency increased, US President Lyndon Johnson called for 'more flags' to come forward to support an endangered ally. The obvious source for such aid was the South East Asia Treaty Organization (Seato) of which South Vietnam was a member; but other members, such as France, were strongly against committing Seato forces, and after April 1964 this was not considered as an option.

By the end of 1964 the USA was urgently seeking involvement from other nations, and by mid 1965, as US ground troops were for the first time deployed to South Vietnam in large numbers, the Americans began a major drive to secure help. US motives were mixed; partly the Americans were anxious to demonstrate that the US build-up was supported by other nations in the area, but they were also genuinely in need of extra combat troops. The South Vietnamese initially took little part in this search for more allies and certainly saw it as a cosmetic exercise; they were content with American help. On 6 April 1965 a National Security Action Memorandum asked the State Department to explore the possibility of South Korean, Australian and New Zealand forces fighting in Vietnam, and at the Honolulu Conference of the same month these deployments were agreed.

All the nations that sent forces into Vietnam relied on US logistics to supply their men. The various countries were subject to differing internal pressures that made them either more or less willing to provide the forces that they had agreed. As with the American troops, some units acquitted themselves well, while

others proved to be less effective than was hoped.

The most important foreign contingent came from South Korea, which, by its very nature, had always been disposed to support any anti-communist governments in Asia (the Koreans had even offered to send troops to support the French in Indochina in 1954). A Korean hospital unit was sent to South Vietnam in 1964, and early in 1965 the 2500-strong 'Dove Unit' (officially composed of non-combatants) arrived. During the spring of 1965 there were long discussions between the US and Korea over the terms on which Korean combat troops would be provided; the Korean government wanted the Americans, among other things, to modernise the entire South Korean armed forces in return for the deployment of troops to Vietnam. By August the bargaining had been completed and a bill authorising the despatch of a Korean division was passed through the Korean National Assembly. By November the Capital Division and a Marine brigade were in position, the former near Qui Nhon and the latter near Tuy Hoa.

In all, South Korea despatched 47,872 military personnel to Vietnam, including the 'Dove Unit' of

A New Zealand artilleryman, wounded in the chin by a sniper's bullet, receives treatment from a US medic in November 1965. The New Zealand contingent in Vietnam had just combined with Australian and US forces to conduct a sweep around the town of Bien Hoa, north of Saigon, an area notoriously strong in communist forces. Not until the massive operations of the spring of 1967 – Cedar Falls and Junction City – was the communist hold on this area shaken. The New Zealand artilleryman shown here was one of the first to arrive in Vietnam, belonging to the 105mm battery that began its tour of duty in July 1965.

1965, the Capital Division, the 2nd Marine Brigade, the 9th Division (which arrived in 1966 and was stationed near Ninh Hoa), a Marine battalion that was sent in 1967, and aircrew who arrived in 1969.

Operational control of the Koreans was at first somewhat problematic, as they did not wish to be seen as acting as 'mercenaries' for the US and wanted their independent role to be recognised. In effect, however, they came directly under General Westmoreland's operational control, and their logistic back-up was always supplied by the US.

The Korean tour of duty in Vietnam was one year, and the troops selected were all volunteers, while the Capital Division (often called the 'Tiger' Division) was generally recognised as one of the best formations in the Korean Army. The Koreans, therefore, performed very effectively in action; a US Department of the army study concluded that: 'In Vietnam, it may be unequivocally stated, the Korean forces handled themselves with proven competence in both tactical and tactical-support operations.' The thoroughness of Korean sweeps and their aggression in combat were also favourably remarked upon; in many circles they were considered the best combatants of the allied forces in Vietnam.

The problem with Korean troops was that they were much less efficient in the other side of counter-insurgency warfare – winning the 'hearts and minds' of the local population. They were unwilling to get involved in programmes of civil improvement; there were many reports of corruption on the part of Korean officers and, most important of all, the Koreans had a well-founded reputation for brutality, torture and acting without regard for the possessions or personal safety of the local population. There must be, therefore, serious qualifications in any assessment of overall Korean effectiveness.

Electoral complications

The situation of Australian forces in Vietnam was always complicated by the fact that the Vietnam War was very unpopular with large sections of the Australian public. The first Australian combat troops arrived in Phuoc Tuy Province in June 1965. By 1966, Australian troops were being used in offensive operations, notably in a sweep into the 'Iron Triangle' near Saigon in February 1966. A further increase in the Australian forces deployed was held up until after the Australian elections of November 1966, since the government feared this might prove unpopular.

By October 1967 there were over 8000 Australian troops in Vietnam, the destroyer HMAS *Hobart* was integrated into US Navy operations and Australian Canberra bombers were being deployed. Australian troops were very successful; their specialised units, such as the SAS, had had long experience in anti-guerrilla operations in Malaya and Borneo; the Australian Army was an all-volunteer, highly-trained force, and they were, in general, concerned to build up good relations with the local population. Australian forces were withdrawn in 1971, as US force levels began to run down.

New Zealand forces in Vietnam served with the Australians. In July 1965 a combat force consisting of a 105mm gun battery arrived, and this was increased in size in March 1966. By 1967 there were New Zealand SAS forces in action, and with the addition of two infantry companies the New Zealand contingent reached a total of 517 men; New Zealand forces left with the Australians in 1971.

Over 10,000 troops from Thailand fought in Vietnam from 1967 to 1971. They were assigned to an area of low Viet Cong activity to the east of Saigon. They took part in few large-scale operations, and in general found it difficult to coordinate with US artillery and air support.

President Marcos of the Philippines declared his opposition to sending combat troops to Vietnam in 1966, but was prepared to deploy a 'civic action group' which would provide its own security while initiating medical and civil aid projects within four provinces to the north and west of Saigon. There was considerable internal opposition within the Philippines to the deployment of any Filipino troops in Vietnam, however, and in 1969 the 'civic action group' was withdrawn.

The Filipino, Thai, Australian, New Zealand and South Korean forces involved in the Vietnam War were all there because their governments had decided – for whatever reasons – that their participation was desirable. And they were all eventually withdrawn as the American commitment wound down. America had other allies in the Vietnam War, however, who could not withdraw with the GIs. These were the hill people, the Montagnards, of the Central Highlands.

The vast majority of the population of South Vietnam were Vietnamese, who had begun moving into the area in the Middle Ages, displacing the Khmers and Chams, who still formed sizeable minorities by the 20th century. These races mainly inhabited the fertile coastal plains and the Mekong Delta, however; the mountains that formed so much of the land area were the preserve of the hill tribes, who numbered about 670,000 in the early 1960s. These had traditionally been hostile to the Vietnamese (who called them *moi* – savages) and until the French colonial administration had halted the process in 1932, the Vietnamese, with a more settled form of agriculture, had been steadily encroaching into the Highlands. When the Republic of South Vietnam was set up, this encroachment recommenced and refugees from the North were given land there.

Mountain war

The vast, wild expanses of the Central Highlands were clearly the strategic key to South Vietnam, and major fighting took place there in 1965-68, 1972 and 1975. As the full weight of American analysis was brought to bear on the problems of Vietnam, the advantages of establishing an effective presence in the sparsely populated region became evident. From 1961 onwards, therefore, US Special Forces began working closely with the local people. This attempt to mobilise the Montagnards received little encouragement from the South Vietnamese government.

The Montagnards were very susceptible to American persuasion. The provision of arms, medical assistance and economic aid, and the prospect of earning previously unheard-of amounts of money by serving in units such as the Civilian Irregular Defense Groups (CIDG), were an alluring bait, and, ultimately, the Montagnards had little choice but to accept, for they were, in any case, located in a region in which hostilities were steadily building up.

The results of being drawn into the centre of the war were, however, disastrous for the people of the Central Highlands. First of all, the camps that were set up for them, or the re-ordering of existing villages,

Above: Korean Marines storm into a village in 1967. The first Korean Marines arrived in November 1965. The troops here are armed with M1 rifles, the standard US infantry weapon at the end of World War II; the US had to maintain a delicate balancing act to avoid antagonising its Asian allies, who all wanted their troops to be given the new M16. Right: Men of the 7th Royal Australian Regiment go into action in 1968. Below: Lines of Australian troops wait to be deployed by US transport. The US provided its allies with almost all their logistic support.

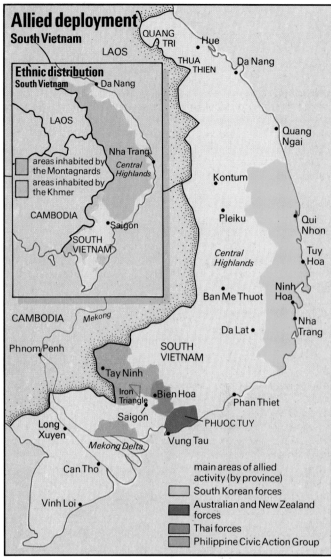

Allied deployment
South Vietnam

Ethnic distribution
South Vietnam

□ areas inhabited by the Montagnards
□ areas inhabited by the Khmer

main areas of allied activity (by province)
□ South Korean forces
■ Australian and New Zealand forces
■ Thai forces
■ Philippine Civic Action Group

altered their traditional methods of agriculture, and in spite of undoubted US efforts to respect their lifestyle, they became more and more dependent upon outside aid merely to exist. Then, as US interest shifted from a supposedly 'pacified' area, and South Vietnamese forces took over, deep-rooted antipathies reasserted themselves. There were even some Montagnard uprisings against the South Vietnamese government forces. From the other side, the communist forces were often prepared to exact a terrible price from villages that were a thorn in their flesh, and many isolated camps fell victim to Viet Cong attacks.

The Montagnard population fell dramatically during the period – from almost 700,000 to about 500,000. The Brou people, for example, were 38,593 strong in 1959; they inhabited Quang Tri and Thua Thien provinces. By September 1972, there were no Brou at all in Quang Tri, and figures were unknown for Thua Thien.

As the Americans withdrew from Vietnam in the period 1968-72, the Montagnard units had to be transferred to direct South Vietnamese control, or 'converted' as the jargon had it. On paper this was successful, with 14,534 of the 17,057 CIDG troops joining South Vietnamese Ranger battalions, but in practice they became identified with a regime that was about to collapse. The Montagnards were irretrievably sucked into a catastrophe. **Ashley Brown**

The Green Berets

US Special Forces in Southeast Asia

US Army Special Forces personnel began operating in Vietnam as early as 1957. On temporary duty assignment from the newly-established 1st Special Forces Group based on Okinawa, Special Forces soldiers served as trainers and advisers to elements of the Army of the Republic of Vietnam (ARVN). Most of that earliest contingent were stationed at the Vietnamese Army Commando Training Center, Nha Trang, which soon became Special Forces headquarters.

From 1961, the US armed forces held high-level strategy and planning sessions to discuss counter-insurgency. The outcome was a directive instructing each service to establish a unit to spearhead its counter-insurgency effort. The US Army already had such a unit in the Special Forces. New guidelines were drawn up, defining their counter-insurgency role as the planning, conducting and supporting of unconventional warfare and internal security operations. For these tasks highly qualified, trained and cross-trained personnel were a necessity and the Special Forces provided just that with their airborne-qualified selected volunteers. Only after training and cross-training in five specialist areas – weapons, communications, combat medicine, intelligence and engineering – and further courses in such areas as escape and evasion, survival and land navigation (among many others) was a candidate given his green beret.

Newly-minted Special Forces soldiers were assigned to the basic Special Forces tactical element, the A Team (or A Detachment), consisting of two officers and 10 enlisted men. Beginning in 1961 these A Teams became involved in what was to become one of the most successful programmes of the Vietnam War, the Civilian Irregular Defense Group (CIDG) project. The CIDG programme evolved from the ideas of International Volunteer Service member David Nuttle as he worked among Montagnard tribesmen of Vietnam's Central Highlands. Nuttle had perceived that with appropriate encouragement and assistance the Montagnards could be turned into a bastion of anti-communism in the region. He shared the idea with Gilbert Layton, a CIA operative, who used it as the basis for a combined village defence and improvement programme. After consultation with Special Forces personnel the idea was fleshed out and in early 1962 A Team-113 began the first CIDG effort among Rhade tribesmen in Buon Enao.

A cursory look at a map of South Vietnam will reveal how strategically important the Central Highlands were. Not only was the region South Vietnam's vital mid-section, but it also bordered Cambodia and Laos, massive sanctuary and infiltration sites for communist troops. The people of the Central Highlands – known as the Montagnards – had traditionally been hostile to the Vietnamese, and they, together with the two other main minorities (the Cham and the Khmer), felt little loyalty towards the state of South Vietnam. Under French rule Vietnamese expansion into the Central Highlands had been forbidden, but

after 1954 many Vietnamese refugees from the North were settled there. In 1953 the Vietnamese population of the Central Highlands was only 20,000; by 1974 it had grown to 500,000. This process was accompanied by discrimination against Montagnard culture – in Dorlae Province, for example, Montagnard dress was abolished. It was, therefore, a very sensitive area, both geographically and politically, in which the US Special Forces were operating.

The Special Forces used classic counter-insurgency techniques to win the trust of the Montagnards. Through self-help, village improvements and civic action – most importantly in respect for traditions – Special Forces CIDG cadres assured the protection of Montagnard lifestyles and enabled the villagers to defend themselves against communist intimidation; they offered a considerable rise in the standard of living, and distributed large quantities of arms. By August 1962 some 200 villages had been incorporated into the CIDG programme with new camps being added weekly, so that they soon extended into all four military regions of South Vietnam. The triangular-shaped CIDG camps, each constructed near a Montagnard village, housed A Team facilities within a defensive structure. These far-flung outposts would, in many cases, become sites for future battles as they proved tempting targets for enemy forces.

In September 1962 HQ US Special Forces (Provisional) Vietnam became operational. It assumed command of all unconventional operations and the CIDG programme. It consisted of one C Detachment

Above: President Lyndon Johnson presents the Congressional Medal of Honor to Captain Roger Donlon of the Special Forces. Right: Training irregulars in fieldcraft was a major part of Special Forces' duties. Below: Special Forces personnel show Montagnards how to operate a 57mm recoilless cannon.

Kennedy's command

The celebrated green beret was first chosen as Special Forces wear by a committee of officers and NCOs at Fort Bragg in 1954, a year after the formation of the Special Forces. The beret was modelled on that of the British Royal Marine Commandos. The berets were first worn publicly in June 1955 and in December of that year the 77th Special Forces Group ordered all its personnel to wear the beret. This order was countermanded in the early months of 1956, however, because of a feeling in the army command that elite units should not be encouraged.

In spite of a vigorous campaign to have the beret reinstated, the official veto on its parade use remained until 1961. In October of that year President Kennedy visited Fort Bragg, and inspected the 5th and 7th Special Forces Groups with the men wearing the berets at his request. He telegraphed back from Washington that he was sure the beret would be a mark of distinction 'in the trying times ahead', and in December the green beret was made official headgear for all Special Forces.

(HQ Command), overseeing three B Detachments (Operations Control) under which 26 A Detachments carried out their various duties. Temporary duty personnel from 1st Special Forces Group (SFG) Okinawa and 7th SFG Fort Bragg continued to serve.

As US force levels in Vietnam began to grow and the Central Highlands developed into a major area of combat, it became obvious that some use other than village defence could be found for the CIDG forces. Among the first indigenous forces to be used in a wider role were trained 'mountain scouts' from the Hoa Cam people who were sent on long-range missions in remote areas, gathering valuable intelligence. Additionally, 'trailwatchers' carried out surveillance missions in their local areas near the borders with Cambodia and Laos. These trailwatchers were deployed after eight weeks training at Da Nang.

CIDG Camp Strike Forces (CSF–'Strikers') evolved from early self-defence units and signalled a switch to more offensive operations. Strikers were trained and armed by Special Forces personnel after volunteering for duty. They supported village militias and carried out aggressive patrolling over a wide operational area. They could be called in to help repel enemy attacks, they set up ambushes to trap communist patrols and they regularly checked village defence procedures. Strikers were organised into platoons and companies and were paid the same wages as compara-

ble soldiers in the ARVN. A CSF Company consisted of 150 enlisted men, arranged in a 10-strong Company HQ, three 35-man rifle platoons and a 35-man weapons platoon. Armaments included 0.3in M1 carbines, 60mm mortars, Browning automatic rifles and .45in M3 sub-machine guns. Special Forces command established a target of 20,000 Strikers to be trained and deployed by mid-1964. At the same time, Strike Forces were given the task of border surveillance. They were used for long-range patrolling in these sparsely-populated areas, building up intelligence and seeking to root out any communist presence, especially along the infiltration routes from Cambodia and Laos.

The first Mobile Strike (MIKE) force was formed in October 1964. MIKE forces were capable of conducting raids, ambushes, combat patrols and other small unit combat operations either independently or in conjunction with other CIDG units, as well as in support of conventional forces. A typical MIKE company consisted of 150 personnel; all were airborne-qualified.

One of the reasons for establishment of CSF and MIKE forces was the vulnerable position of far-flung CIDG camps, which was dramatically illustrated on 6 July 1964 at Camp Nam Dong. At approximately 0300 hours, enemy forces launched a surprise attack from several directions preceded by an intense mortar

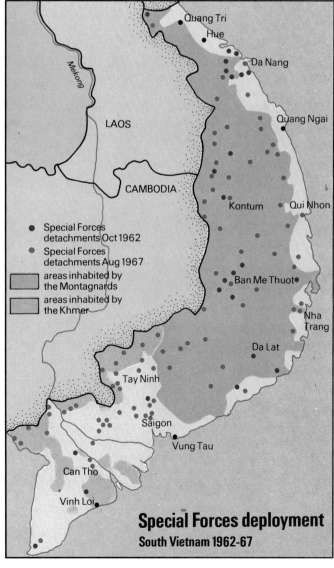

Special Forces deployment
South Vietnam 1962-67

- Special Forces detachments Oct 1962
- Special Forces detachments Aug 1967
- areas inhabited by the Montagnards
- areas inhabited by the Khmer

barrage. It was later estimated that 80 per cent of the casualties were sustained in those first 15 minutes of the attack. What eventually saved Nam Dong were the multi-depth perimeter defences and mutually supporting fighting positions. Local forces fought well in slowing the enemy assault waves which were beginning to breach defences in several areas. Camp commander Captain Roger Donlon, commanding officer of A Team-726, continued to direct the defence of Nam Dong despite suffering multiple wounds. At one point he carried an abandoned 60mm mortar to a new location 30m away where he tended to wounded men who would then service the mortar. Following this he crawled 175m after sustaining another wound to direct 81mm mortar fire from another position. These actions earned Captain Donlon the first Medal of Honor to be awarded during the Vietnam War, the first of 13 earned by Special Forces soldiers.

On 1 October 1964, 5th SFG, 1st Special Forces, was constituted in Nha Trang. 5th SFG replaced the previous Special Forces headquarters, and all temporary duty staff departed. Group strength at the time was five B and 44 A Detachments.

The autumn of 1966 saw two additions to Special Forces operations in Vietnam. In September General Westmoreland directed 5th SFG to establish the MACV (Military Assistance Command, Vietnam) Recondo (reconnaisance commando) School at Nha Trang. The school conducted three-week courses for selected personnel in airborne, escape and evasion, survival, long-range patrolling and other relevant skills. Instructors were drawn not only from seasoned Special Forces veterans but also Australian SAS, New Zealand SAS and other allied forces. Within a year of its establishment the Recondo School was turning out 120 graduates every three weeks.

Mobile Guerrilla Forces were instituted that same autumn as a tactical adjunct to the MIKE forces. They

were organised, trained and equipped to operate deep in what was considered enemy territory. In strategic terms, Mobile Guerrilla Forces were tasked with interdicting enemy infiltration and supply routes, conducting surveillance, hunting enemy forces and camps and collecting intelligence. These guerrilla units were usually inserted by clandestine means into an operational area. They used mobile bases and were capable of operating without resupply for up to 60 days, living solely off the land. Special air-drops of supplies could be requested if required. These units represented ready-reaction forces for Special Forces companies throughout Vietnam and were operationally controlled by the Special Forces commander in each Tactical Zone. Command and control at a tactical level resided entirely with A Detachment commanders. Led by Special Forces personnel, Mobile Guerrilla Forces were manned by local troops.

By the mid-1960s, Special Forces were being used extensively to monitor enemy movements. The four so-called 'alphabet' projects – Delta, Omega, Sigma and Gamma – were set up to further this role. Project Delta evolved from its operational predecessor Leaping Lena and was set up on 15 May 1964. Its objectives were long-range reconnaissance and intelligence-gathering. During its six-year lifespan it became one of the most powerful and effective combat operations of the war. Delta consisted of 12 ten-man reconnaissance teams, six six-man 'roadrunner' teams assigned to long-range reconnaissance of trail networks, one 124-man camp security company drawn from the Nung people, and the ARVN 91st Ranger Battalion. Its missions were varied: location of enemy units, intelligence-gathering, hunter-killer missions, bomb-damage assessment, artillery/air strike coordination, special purpose raids, harassment and deception missions. Delta personnel were trained by Special Forces cadres over a six-week

Below: Lying in wait for the Viet Cong, with M16 at the ready. By 1966, the Special Forces had adopted a more aggressive role than previously, moving into the border areas to curb communist infiltration from Laos and Cambodia.

Above: A Special Forces adviser discusses dispositions and tactics with the commander of a Civilian Irregular Defense Group.

Above: The Special Forces' badge, on which the three bolts of lightning represent their ability to strike by sea, land or air. All Special Forces personnel had to have an initial airborne qualification, and then they were given arduous training and cross-training in a variety of disciplines – the major ones being weapons, communications, combat medicine, intelligence and engineering.

period in base camp and field sites. Based in Nha Trang, highly mobile Delta units could be deployed to any of the four Combat Tactical Zones as needed. Operations continued until June 1970.

Following on the success of Project Delta, 5th SFG established Project Omega in September 1966. Headquartered at Ban Me Thuot, Omega consisted of four (later eight) roadrunner teams, eight (later 16) intensive patrolling teams and three commando companies who served as tactical reinforcement and reconnaissance-in-force units. As with Delta, Omega was assigned a camp security company. Its personnel reflected its Highlands setting with Sedang, Rhade and Jah Montagnard tribesmen making up its contingents. Project Omega was used to keep tabs on enemy movements and intentions along the critical tri-border area of Cambodia, Vietnam and Laos where branches of the Ho Chi Minh Trail funnelled men and supplies into South Vietnam. Omega operated until June 1972. Project Sigma was also established in September 1966 to conduct similar missions. Headquartered at Ho Ngoc Tau, it was composed of ethnic Chinese and Cambodian personnel and was structured like the other projects. It operated until May 1971. Project Gamma, with an authorised strength of 52 personnel, was established by 5th SFG in June 1967 to gather information on enemy logistics in Cambodia. Gamma personnel were headquartered first in Saigon and then in Nha Trang. Its operations ended in March 1970.

Clandestine operations

In addition to these extensions of the CIDG programme and reconnaissance projects, in January 1964 the US MACV established what was called its 'Studies and Observation Group' (SOG). Under that rather academic title were instituted wide-ranging, multi-service clandestine operations, including sabotage, psychological operations and special operations in North and South Vietnam, Laos, Cambodia and southern China. SOG was allocated 2000 US and 8000 indigenous personnel. The majority of the US contingent were US Special Forces, and the indigenous troops were all highly-trained.

SOG had its own aircraft and helicopters in the 90th Special Operations Wing, composed of the US Air Force 20th Special Operations Squadron and their UH-1F 'Green Hornet' helicopters (a more powerful, better-armed version of the UH-1B Huey), a squadron of USAF C-130s, a 'black' (secret) squadron of C-123s piloted by foreign nationals and the Vietnamese 219th H-34 helicopter squadron. By 1967, SOG had been organised into three regional command and control elements, based in Da Nang, Kontum and Ban Me Thuot respectively. From these bases SOG personnel executed cross-border operations and sent agents into North Vietnam.

In the central region, for example, the SOG ran its clandestine operations out of Forward Operating Base Kontum. It consisted of some 30 'Spike' and 'Hatchet' reconnaissance teams and four SLAM (search-location-annihilation mission) companies. They operated in the critical tri-border area and though their operations are still mostly classified, one can assume that a majority of their missions centred on intelligence-gathering, ambushes, interdiction and locating enemy concentrations in the Laotian/Cambodian border areas and along the Ho Chi Minh Trail.

During their eight years of missions, SOG operatives built up a commendable record of professional effectiveness, though their hazardous tasks led to a relatively high casualty rate. The clandestine nature of their missions of course meant that their many heroic accomplishments went unheralded or were misrepresented. SOG operative Staff Sergeant Fred Zabitosky, for example, earned the Congressional Medal of Honor while assistant team leader of Reconnaissance Team Maine during actions in Laos in 1968. A sensitive US government refused to print 'Laos' as the location of the action in the citation.

Although the Special Forces were very effective in all the actions they took part in, and although their exploits have a romantic aura reminiscent of the early days of the American frontier – the small group of rugged individualists, with some loyal native scouts, operating in a remote, hostile terrain against a vicious enemy – Special Forces operations did not achieve all the long-term goals hoped for. One constant difficulty was that cooperation with US Army staff was not always easy; Special Forces operations did not fit into conventional patterns, and, in the words of the official Department of the Army study, 'On the whole, US commanders never really became familiar with the civilian irregulars and their capabilities... Special Forces troops were continually conscious of mistrust and suspicion on the part of many relatively senior field grade US military men.'

The basic problem, however, was that the Vietnamese Army and its Special Forces found dealing with the Montagnards very difficult (there was actually a Montagnard uprising against the government in 1964) and many projects initiated by US Special Forces, such as the original Buon Enao programme, foundered when taken over by the Vietnamese. So the possibility of implementing an effective counter-insurgency programme in the Central Highlands based upon a loyal Montagnard population gradually disappeared.

The main task of US Special Forces after 1964 was to form an interdiction zone along the frontier to slow down or report on communist infiltration. This almost impossible goal was never fully achieved; early on, there were never sufficient forces along the border and later, when numbers had risen (in 1967, there were 40,000 para-military troops and 40,000 regional forces acting with Special Forces advisers) many of the camps proved vulnerable to communist attack as larger North Vietnamese units moved in. During this period, however, MACV estimated that 50 per cent of its intelligence on communist movements came from the Special Forces and the CIDG, and so this part of their task was being effectively fulfilled. After the Tet offensive in 1968, the US Special Forces concentrated on handing over their camps and irregulars to Vietnamese Special Forces, and the level of intelligence declined again because, as we have seen, the Vietnamese were less sympathetic to the Montagnards.

The Special Forces in Vietnam had their successes and their failures. But few would dispute the tribute of former 5th SFG commander Colonel Francis J. Kelly: 'The Special Forces men earned on the battlefield their rightful place in the US Army. Tough, resourceful, dedicated and efficient, the men of the Special Forces stood and fought as well and bravely as those of any fighting unit in our country's history.'

John B. Dwyer

War by proxy
The CIA and the Laotian hill tribes

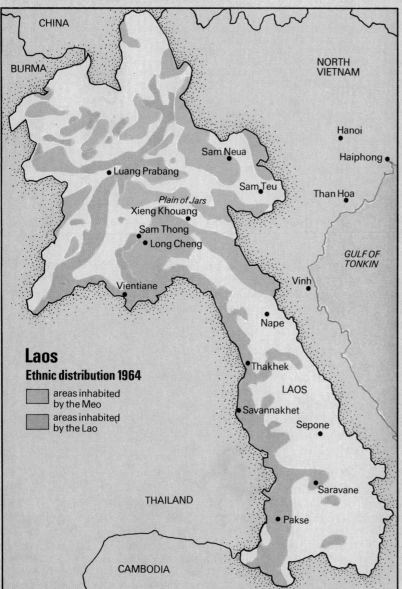

Laos

Ethnic distribution 1964

- areas inhabited by the Meo
- areas inhabited by the Lao

The half-squad of brown-skinned tribesmen returned to their temporary base camp as night fell on the jagged Laotian peak on whose flank they had made their flimsy shelter. On arrival, their leader scrawled a message in the failing light and handed it to the radioman. The radioman encoded it and tapped it out on his key while his assistant cranked the generator. It read, in Lao: 'Seng despatched into enemy territory at 1730 hours today as planned. Just before he disappeared over the ridge in the direction of Sam Neua he turned into a tiger and galloped away. Request helicopter pickup at LZ Romeo tomorrow at daybreak. Acknowledge. Thao.'

Seng was an agent despatched behind Pathet Lao lines to collect intelligence on communist movements around their headquarters at Sam Neua. The message was addressed to Meo headquarters at Long Cheng, in the mountains some 65km (40 miles) north of the Laotian capital of Vientiane. The Thai radio technician at the Long Cheng message centre delivered a copy to General Vang Pao, chief of the irregular forces and at the same time Region II commander of the Royal Lao Army. Another copy was translated into English and delivered to Vang Pao's American adviser, a civilian CIA operative. Both Vang Pao and the American had a good laugh about Seng's transformation into a big cat but attached no significance to it. They quickly agreed to send the helicopter that had been requested by Thao. In a week or so they hoped to begin receiving a series of radio reports from Seng.

This tiny episode took place almost exactly as described (with some allowance for the frailty of human memory) in northern Laos in mid-1964 and sums up, in a way, the bizarre but deadly war that was fought by several hundred thousand Meo and other hill tribesmen against the Pathet Lao (the Laotian communists) and the North Vietnamese in the mountains of Laos from 1961 to 1973. In a unique way the war combined the up-to-date technology of the Americans with the primeval craft, endurance and courage of the tough and rather superstitious Meo people.

It was an accident of history that brought Americans and Meo, as well as Thai troops, together to fight a twilight 'secret' war against the Vietnamese and Lao communists. In the 1960s Laos was officially governed by a neutral coalition government, but in practice the country was split between anti-communist forces concentrated in the south, neutralists, and the communist Pathet Lao in the north. For the Americans, the main consideration by the mid 1960s was naturally the relationship between Laos and the Vietnam War. Laos was the site of the Ho Chi Minh Trail, down which men and supplies poured in to reinforce the communist war effort in the South. The US ambassador to Laos, William H. Sullivan, successfully resisted all suggestions that American regular forces should move into the country to try to block the Trail. Instead, there was a great deal of undercover involvement, whether in the arming of the Meo by the

Opposite: Meo hill-tribesmen of Laos. The Meo had migrated south from China in the 19th century, and had always been hostile to any form of central control. They practised a form of 'slash-and-burn' agriculture, but various of the villages were engaged in the opium trade, with which they augmented their meagre living standards. Hostile to both the communists and the Laotian government, the Meo of northeastern Laos proved useful allies of the Americans, who, in a CIA-run operation, used them as irregulars against the communist Pathet Lao. For the Meo, this had disastrous results. Above: The war in Laos was smaller in scale than the conflict in Vietnam, but it was just as vicious. Here, government forces (well supplied with American equipment) have captured a suspected communist guerrilla and it seems clear that the interrogation will be short and brutal.

CIA, the incursions of Special Forces units into the south of the country, or the large-scale bombing of the Trail by the US Air Force (USAF). The operation among the Meo in the north of the country was merely one among many US initiatives in Laos.

From the American viewpoint, the collaboration was successful. Over a 12-year period, a force of tribal irregulars numbering at its height some 30,000 men, armed and equipped mostly with light weapons but also with artillery, including some 105mm pieces, formidably supported by jet fighter-bombers flying from nearby Thailand and ultimately by B-52s, held off the Pathet Lao and North Vietnamese from the approaches to Vientiane, prevented communist control of the strategic Plain of Jars which dominated these approaches, and insulated the neutralist Lao government from communist pressures. In doing so, it exacted a significant toll of Vietnamese communist soldiers and equipment, contributing to the attrition strategy of the US command in Vietnam.

In the jargon of that time, the effort was highly cost-efficient. At its peak the programme involved but a few hundred American civilians, and combat losses were extremely low. The Americans were augmented by several hundred trainers, technicians and interpreters from Thailand, whose services were contributed by the Thai government in the belief that the effort to keep the communists away from the Mekong (the Thai/Lao border) was in Thailand's interest. Eventually, towards the end of the campaign and in an effort to stave off disaster, the Thais contributed a large body of troops in a successful last-ditch effort to prevent the fall of Long Cheng; Thai losses were also low.

Maize and opium

The Meo, on the other hand, bore the brunt and cannot be blamed if they view the episode as an unmitigated disaster. Their total military and civilian casualties from combat and war-caused disease and disruption may have been as high as 50,000 out of a total population estimated at 250,000 – 300,000.

As far back as anyone knows, the Meo have relied on a 'slash-and-burn' cultivation, moving from place to place every few years as the soil gives out. Seeking more land, groups of them came down from China into Laos in the late 19th century. They preferred life at altitudes of 1100–1500m (3500–5000 feet), a convenient preference since the dominant races of the area preferred the lowlands. In their hills, in sturdy independence, they raised their crops of upland rice, maize and opium – the latter a legal cash crop grown because of the ready market and because the year's product of a village could be transported easily out of the roadless mountains on the back of a man or a horse. They developed a reputation as fierce fighters, and paid little heed to the central government.

In the early 1950s, during their war with France, the communist Pathet Lao and their sponsors, the Viet Minh, came to northeastern Laos, taking over control of most of the province of Sam Neua. Here the Meo lived in large numbers and they quickly began to find communist rule irksome. They learned that it meant the end of their immemorial independence; it meant heavy taxes, the drafting of men to fight or provide labour, and schools that turned children against their elders and the ways of the tribe. Other Meo were organised and trained by the French to fight as irregulars. After the French withdrew, communist control of Sam Neua was confirmed by the Geneva Accords of 1954 and the Pathet Lao began to expand into adjacent areas. At this point, the Americans became involved in Laos and began to work with some of the French-trained Meo to gather intelligence on the communist areas. Finally, in the internal Laotian conflicts of the early 1960s, with the agreement of the anti-communist Meo leadership, paramilitary self-defence forces were underwritten by the Americans to fight the Pathet Lao.

Very quickly the majority of the Meo population became engaged in the war. Their military leader was Vang Pao, initially trained by the French, a regular officer in the Lao Army and, in fact, the highest ranking tribesman in that force. When a village chose to support Vang Pao, the whole population was involved. Young men of military age were recruited, and if the village site was taken by the enemy, the entire population retreated with the fighting men to avoid being separated from their soldiers. In this way, hundreds of thousands of Meo suffered and thousands lost their lives in exodus after exodus. Some villages moved and resettled four times in the years of combat that ensued.

The battleground was a land virtually without roads. The Meo effort became possible only because of the air support that the CIA provided through its own airline, Air America. An entirely civilian operation, with civilian pilots, Air America (together with a private American company called Bird & Son) contracted with the US government to provide air services. And this they did far above and beyond the requirements of their contracts. All the aircraft were propeller-driven, many were STOL (short-take-off and landing), some were helicopters of the old 'flying banana' type. The strips they flew from and to were hair-raising, the weather often abominable, the navigational aids scanty or non-existent. Nevertheless, they had a remarkable safety record while reliably supplying the irregulars with all their needs, moving

them about, hauling knocked-down 105mm howitzers and all the ammunition needed, evacuating wounded, and dropping food and other essentials to a refugee population that sometimes reached a total of 150,000 men, women and children.

The USAF moves in

The urgent needs of this shifting village population, not only for emergency assistance but for resettlement, health care and education, brought into play an unusual effort by the US government's Agency for International Development (AID). Led by an extraordinary Indiana farmer named Edgar 'Pop' Buell, AID succoured the Meo population when they were driven from their homes by the shifting tides of war. More than that, it established a hospital at a village near Long Cheng headquarters, staffed it with doctors and trained Meo nurses. It trained hundreds of Meo medics and staffed dispensaries for them. It helped them to build schools wherever a village asked for one and then created a middle school to provide more advanced education. From here, some Meo went on to the Vientiane *Lycée* and eventually obtained university degrees in France. Briefly, perhaps for a period of about two years, the Meo achieved a standard of living which – although extremely low by Western standards – was considerably better than anything that they had previously enjoyed. Much of the tribal population of northern Laos had simply walked away from Pathet Lao control. At their Long Cheng headquarters, where eventually the population reached 40,000, at the nearby civilian headquarters in Sam Thong, and in a large cluster of villages centred around these two, the Meo briefly glimpsed a prospect of material prosperity.

This future was to be brutally snatched away, however. The immediate cause of the eventual debacle – although almost certainly it would have happened in any case, once the US withdrew from Vietnam – was probably the large role that the US Air

Bottom left: Heavily camouflaged Pathet Lao anti-aircraft positions. The Americans were unwilling to commit ground forces to Laos, but they were quite prepared to use the might of their air power to attack the communist forces, although they attempted to keep the extent of their involvement in Laos secret. Bottom centre: Pathet Lao forces in action. The infantryman hurling the hand grenade is also armed with a French MAT 49 sub-machine gun – a relic of the first Indochina War.

Force began to play in events. At first, the USAF took advantage of Meo forward positions to base large helicopters – the so-called Jolly Green Giants – for rescue missions into North Vietnam to recover US pilots shot down there. At about the same time, a navigational aid was emplaced on a 1500m (5000 foot) mesa called Phou Pha Thi, to assist aircraft bombing North Vietnam. Thirteen USAF personnel manned the beacon, protected by a company of Meo at a location only about 30km (20 miles) from North Vietnam. Meanwhile, at Long Cheng, larger and larger contingents of USAF personnel were stationed to collect air targeting intelligence from the Meo units operating throughout northern Laos. Increasingly, US tactical air power came to the support of irregulars slugging it out for various strategic positions along the frontline. For this purpose, USAF 0-1 spotter planes were also based at Long Cheng, along with their pilots and the mechanics to maintain them. At the peak of these operations, the USAF had about 1000 personnel at Meo headquarters.

It may well have been this concentration of regular US military and their direct involvement in combat only a few kilometres from the back door of North Vietnam that persuaded the North Vietnamese to concentrate the considerable resources necessary to eliminate the threat. It was a lengthy effort because, as the communists increased their troop contingents and improved the roads to permit them to operate, the Americans increased their air support and ultimately reinforced the flagging Meo with additional Thai battalions. By 1972 there were 17,000 Thais in action. Beginning in the dry season of 1967–68, the communists annually increased their effort until finally they had two full regular divisions deployed. When new roads had been completed they were able to continue to fight in the rainy season and in 1969 they swept across the Plain of Jars. Briefly, Vang Pao showed his old aggressive capabilities and retook the Plain after heavy bombardment by B-52s – but without permanent result.

Early in 1970, the communists attacked again in force, retook the Plain once more and quickly moved into the hills beyond to lay siege to the central complex of Long Cheng and Sam Thong. By dint of heavy air and artillery bombardment and an influx of Thai troops, the headquarters was successfully defended but the entire civilian population had been launched into a final and truly tragic exodus from which the movement never recovered. In any case, the enemy had achieved its purpose. The USAF beacon at Phou Pha Thi had been captured and all USAF personnel there killed. The USAF also evacuated Long Cheng. Therefore, the threat that had brought on the heavy communist offensive was duly eliminated.

Thus, this once promising irregular effort ended in defeat and public obloquy. The communists are now ensconced in Vientiane, the 'Jolly Green Giants' and the B-52s are long gone and so are perhaps 50,000 Meo refugees. General Vang Pao owns and lives on a mountain ranch in Montana and does his best to help his countrymen who have reached America. Unhappily he can do nothing for those he had to leave behind in Laos.

David Blue

Below: Stacks of US M1 rifles and ammunition boxes are flown in to arm the Laotian forces that the US was using as the war in Southeast Asia spread inexorably from Vietnam to engulf the neighbouring states of Laos and Cambodia. Bottom right: Hill people move down to one of the refugee camps on the plains, carrying their belongings.

Sabre squadrons
The Australian SAS in Vietnam

The first Australian Special Air Service (SAS) troops to enter Vietnam did so as part of a 30-man Australian Army Training Team in mid-1962. These few men were the forerunners of Australian SAS involvement which was to bring great distinction to a relatively new formation in the Australian armed forces.

The Australian SAS originated as 1st SAS Company in July 1957. It was raised and formed at Campbell Barracks, Swanbourne, Western Australia, which remains the regiment's base to this day. The company was originally an Infantry Corps element and became part of the Royal Australian Regiment in 1960. At that time it was redesignated 1st SAS Company Royal Australian Regiment (1st SAS Coy RAR). On 14 September 1964 1st SAS Coy RAR was augmented and redesignated the Australian SAS Regiment. It then consisted of Headquarters and Base Squadron (Training Cadre), 1st and 2nd Sabre Squadrons and 151st Signals Squadron.

In February 1965, the regiment went to war when the 1st Squadron (followed by the 2nd Squadron in 1966) arrived in Borneo as part of the Commonwealth forces involved in the 'Confrontation' between Malaysia and Indonesia. Australian SAS troops initiated operations whose methods and tactics would provide invaluable lessons for their Vietnam service.

Five months before the close of operations in Borneo the Australian SAS began its Vietnam combat service when the newly-formed 3rd Sabre Squadron arrived at Nui Dat in July 1966. After the 3rd Squadron had ended its first tour in February 1967, service was initiated on a rotational basis, with each squadron serving a year from February, until the 2nd Squadron was withdrawn in October 1971 as the Australian commitment was wound down. The squadrons operated out of an area of Australian Task Force Headquarters (ATF HQ) Nui Dat called 'SAS Hill'. Stringently enforced, tight security kept SAS Hill an exclusive inner sanctum for SAS personnel only.

Initial missions were for intelligence-gathering to provide ATF HQ with information on which to base the deployment of regular RAR units against communist forces in the surrounding region, as the Australians consolidated their presence in Phuoc Tay Province. For Vietnam duty the standard SAS patrol formation consisted of five men: lead scout, patrol leader, second-in-command, signaller and medic. Though it was not uncommon for officers to lead patrols, their constituent ranks were usually sergeant, corporal, lance-corporal and two troopers. All were carefully selected for compatability, with teams remaining together for the duration of their tours of duty.

Armament consisted of M16s, CAR15s, SLRs, M79 grenade launchers, and M203s attached to the bottom of M16s, silenced Stirling sub-machine guns (mysteriously procured from the UK), GPMGs, Brens, combat shotguns, varieties of pistols, Claymore mines, M79 40mm grenade launchers and grenades. As ever, it was a matter of personal choice. Many preferred the 7.62mm SLR for its range and hitting power. Testament to this can be found in the SAS Sergeants' Mess at Swanbourne where an SLR (with six inches cut from its barrel) called 'The Bitch' hangs in place of honour.

Generally, SAS troops wore US Special Forces issue uniforms, tiger stripes or olive-drab greens. Depending on the missions, teams would don nondescript, irregular-looking garb not identifiable as belonging to any particular army. Though Bergen packs were worn at times, most essentials were carried as kit items on the belt. These included fishing line, signal mirror, toggle rope, extra British water bottles and the URC-10 beeper/signal transmitter. This compact device was used to summon helicopters when a patrol needed to get out fast. Its loud signal not only homed-in friendly helicopters, however, but also sometimes a sharp-eared enemy. Another favourite piece of kit was the ubiquitous sniper veil/neck-band bandana.

Mission target areas were usually four map grid-squares in size with one designated a 'safety grid' for emergency egress. These areas were located in free-fire zones, where it was assumed anyone moving about was the enemy and thus fair game. Insertion of SAS patrols was usually accomplished at dusk and was executed in such a manner as to provide maximum security for the five-man teams. The patrol would be inserted by chopper, accompanied by helicopter gunships, all moving at full throttle in one direction near the target area. At a signal from the leader, the team chopper and gunships executed a 180 degree turn, flying nap-of-the-earth to the designated insertion point where the patrol would dismount and move out. Gunships remained on station if needed. This method was intended to confuse the enemy and decrease the chance of landing in a 'hot LZ'.

The helicopters of 'Kanga pad'
The lead and insertion helicopters were both ships from the 9th Squadron, Royal Australian Air Force. The 9th Squadron had deployed to Vietnam in mid 1966, and was the primary air support element for SAS operations. Its ships were based at 'Kanga pad', Nui Dat, and were specially fitted out for their missions with twin M60 0.3in machine guns plus a winch for insertion or extraction. Over the course of their respective tours of duty SAS Sabre Squadron soldiers and the personnel of the 9th Squadron developed a very close working relationship. In many instances it was the skill and bravery of the chopper pilots and crews that saved the day for SAS patrols.

On the ground, SAS patrols sought out the worst possible terrain over which to navigate, avoiding ridgelines and never taking lines of least resistance, to ensure cover and concealment while decreasing the likelihood of accidentally running into the enemy. Moving out after breakfast (but not before a recce of immediate surroundings) SAS patrols operated till about 1100 hours. From then until 1500 hours they observed what they called 'pak time', a period when the enemy often increased his movements. SAS patrols would deploy astride a track to listen and observe during pak time, hoping to obtain the intelligence that was so valuable.

Pak time over, patrols moved out till reaching their night laager position. At this point they would cease movement, execute a 'sensory recon', then fan out to form a rough extended perimeter, repeat the recce, then contract to form a tight group. After the evening meal, teams would hide up and spend the night asleep in position. Communication was accomplished by tugging on the fishing line tied to the fingertips of each team member. SAS patrols did not, as a rule, operate at night, opting not to work blindly. Guard was rarely mounted.

Patrols often operated in the enemy's midst, and all communication was via hand signals; there was strict

Left: Two troopers of the Australian SAS, armed with M16 rifles, adopt fire positions immediately after landing their canoe. Note the use of disruptive patterned combat clothing and cam cream (on exposed skin surfaces) which effectively breaks up their outlines and helps them blend into the background.

Left: An SAS field patrol, wearing light webbing and armed with M16 rifles (fitted with grenade launchers) and 7.62mm SLRs, discusses a forthcoming reconnaissance mission. Below: Indigenous troops from a Mobile Strike Force in Vietnam are marched from their barracks by SAS instructor Dave Shields, who won the DSM. All of these troops had recently become airborne qualified. Bottom: A member of the Australian SAS on exercise in rough country uses a convenient and fast method of transport.

noise discipline. On some days patrols moved distances of only about 500m. Stealth and patience were everything. On one mission, an SAS NCO crept so near a Viet Cong camp that he discovered himself in the midst of their jungle firing range, its alley cut through dense undergrowth. There he stayed undetected for three days, before it was safe enough to leave. Another SAS soldier once found himself utilising every bit of his breath control and will-power as he lay in dense cover while a Viet Cong urinated into a bush forming part of that cover.

Such regular proximity to the enemy meant that SAS patrols often found themselves pitted against forces many times their size in close-quarter combat. Training and experience had taught them that short, two- or three-round bursts or single well-aimed shots were far more effective and demoralising than blasting away on full automatic. The Australian SAS had the highest kill ratio of any Vietnam serving unit of its kind since the French Indochina War. They accounted for at least 500 enemy killed in action while losing none to hostile fire themselves. One SAS soldier was killed after falling from a chopper extraction rope.

The Australian SAS repertoire of long range/deep penetration, ambush, harassment and recce patrols had a great influence on the creation of the US Army Long-Range Reconnaissance Patrols (LRRPs), and SAS personnel also taught at the MACV Recondo (reconnaissance commando) School instituted in September 1966 at Nha Trang. Here the art and tactics of long-range patrolling were taught by a professional, experienced cadre. SAS personnel also carried out operations in conjunction with US Special Forces, US Navy SEAL Teams and the LRRPs.

The effectiveness of the Australian SAS in Vietnam was a function of the regiment's 'we can do anything' attitude – supreme will and confidence, based on rigorous training and team inter-reliance. And during their five-and-a-half years service in Vietnam, the Australian SAS Regiment indeed upheld with deeds, distinction and professionalism the regimental motto: 'Who Dares Wins'.

John B. Dwyer

Key Weapons

MODERN SOVIET MBTs

Soviet defence priorities enable the USSR to produce a new-generation main battle tank (MBT) roughly twice as often as its Nato counterparts. In effect this means that a new Soviet MBT will be issued to the various Warsaw Pact armies when its successor is already on the drawing board, and will only last a decade before that successor is brought into service. Nato countries have tended to introduce a new tank design every 20 years or so and to make do by modifying and retrofitting their existing tank forces to keep abreast of up-to-date tank technology. On the surface this situation seems to be weighted in favour of Russian tank designers and Soviet MBTs might be expected to have benefitted from this less-interrupted flow of development and be more than equal to their Western counterparts. In practice, however, this is far from the case. Indeed, Soviet tank technology in many areas seems to be a half step behind.

In 1961 the T62 MBT entered production and eventually became exportable to Soviet allies and clients. In combat conditions during the 1973 Arab-Israeli War it proved markedly inferior to Israeli-crewed Centurions, its rate of fire, main armament, angle of gun-barrel depression and fire control system being particularly inefficient in comparison. Admittedly the Israeli Centurions had been extensively, and often brilliantly, modified in Israel but there was no disguising the fact that they were comparatively antique, having first been produced in 1945. The Soviet Union, however, could afford to view these failings with a certain degree of equanimity since their next generation tanks, the T64 and T72, were already in production, influenced not only by recent Soviet technical advances, but also by the known capabilities of the new generation of Nato MBTs, the German Leopard 1, the British Chieftain and the American

M60. As the T64 and T72 entered service in quantity in the mid 1970s, the Russians could draw some satisfaction from the alarm voiced in Nato military establishments that they had produced two new, threateningly superior weapon systems.

The T64 and T72 are, to some extent, twins; both were developed from the same prototype and are in many ways very similar. The T64 was the first into production in the late 1960s but was soon followed in 1972 by the T72. Since then, production of the T64 has been much more limited – it is built at only one plant while five factories manufacture the T72. Although the T72 seems to be the favoured MBT, having entered service throughout the Warsaw Pact, the US Army considers the T64 to be its combat equal and, as it equips the important group of Soviet forces in East Germany, the Soviet Union obviously shares this belief.

A number of new ideas have gone into the design of the T64 and T72, of which the most striking is that the tanks are crewed by only three men. While the driver, commander and gunner remain, the human loader has been replaced by an automatic loading mechanism, potentially rectifying the T62's poor rate of fire. The introduction of an automatic loading system, however, raises a number of other problems since there is almost certainly a difficulty in making sudden changes in selection of the type of round required, and reports suggest that on occasion one of the gunner's limbs has been selected by the system's mechanical arm and loaded into the breech. In the West, doubts remain as to the reliability of the automatic loader and there has certainly been no move in Nato countries to introduce a three-man crew vehicle. The only non-Soviet MBT to feature this type of configuration is the turretless Swedish S-Tank.

Previous page: A column of Polish T72s rolls across open country. Unlike its sister tank the T64 which is exclusive to Soviet forces, the T72 presently equips all Warsaw Pact armies and has also been supplied to Algeria, Iraq and Libya.

Above: The T62, the backbone of the Soviet armoured forces in the 1960s, on manoeuvres in the Soviet Union. Ten years after it appeared, the T62 was superseded by the T64 and T72 series but remains in service with a great many Soviet foreign clients, and saw considerable action in the Middle East in the 1973 Yom Kippur War.

A further innovation in the T64 and T72 design was the upgunning of the main armament. Prototypes and early production models of the T64 were fitted with the same smooth-bore 115mm gun as the T62, but the decision was soon made to change to the more powerful 125mm armament. As a result, all T64s were refitted with the heavier gun and T72s were similarly equipped from the outset. The 125mm weapon is formidably powerful and completely stabilised. Once the gunner has laid it on target, it will remain aimed at the same spot, theoretically providing a very high degree of first-round accuracy while on the move over rough country. In addition the T64 and T72 are fitted with new-technology fire control systems. The gun-

ner is provided with a laser rangefinder, considerably more accurate than the stadiametric rangefinder on the T62, and an improved panoramic day-night sight. Apart from these initial improvements, the level of sophistication of the fire-control system has been upgraded whenever the pace of technological change dictates; in the 1981 Moscow Parade, T72s lacking the right-side aperture forward of the commander's cupola on the turret roof were spotted, indicating further changes to the system. Syrian experience with the 125mm gun, however, suggests that while this gun, with its very high velocity, is capable of blasting the turret right off an enemy tank, its accuracy is severely impaired by its lack of rifling. A complete

Above: A group of T64s awaits the order to move out while the crews confer over the map on Warsaw Pact manoeuvres.

Below: Crowds welcome a formation of T64s as they move proudly through the streets of an East German town.

picture of the weapon's capability has yet to emerge, but during the first Israeli tank encounter with Syrian T72s in the Lebanon in 1982, 10 Syrian tanks were knocked out by the considerably lighter Israeli 105mm armament.

To complement the increase in firepower, the T64 and T72 are thought by the US Army to have much tougher armour protection than their predecessors. From its first appearance it seemed likely that the armour on the new generation was of the conventional cast and rolled type, rather than the British-developed Chobham type discernible by its characteristic flat-shaped turret front and sides. Since the turrets of the T64 and T72 are obviously of a shape not compatible with Chobham armour, some puzzlement greeted a 1978 US Army report that the new Soviet MBTs were protected by a new advanced type of armour, providing the same degree of protection as Nato's Chobham. The armour on the turrets of the T64 and T72 appeared to be no thicker than that on the T62, so it seemed unlikely that it was spaced, and it was thus concluded that the new armour was a laminate type, incorporating the latest developments in Soviet metallurgy.

Differences between the T64 and T72 have always been small. Essentially the T72 is a slightly larger, wider and heavier tank, fitted with a more powerful engine. Tracks on the T72 are wider, providing a lower ground pressure and a higher power-to-weight ratio, which makes it marginally more agile than the T64. On the T72 the searchlight was moved across the turret to improve the gunner's field of vision, while the 12.7mm turret-roof machine gun was given a pintel mounting to increase its angle of elevation. The roadwheel design is also different, the T64 having six small stamped wheels on either side whereas the T72 is fitted with six larger die-cast rubber-coated road-wheels. Both tanks mount a 7.62mm machine gun co-axial with the main armament, and are provided with snorkels for fording and a full NBC (nuclear, biological, chemical) fit; both can accommodate long-range fuel tanks and front-mounted dozer blades. Both vehicles have a command variant, T64K and T72K, with radio and navigation equipment similar to the T62K command vehicle and a 10m (32ft 9in) mast antenna supported by stays. Neither vehicle can travel with the mast erected.

Far left: Tank crews prepare their T72s for a submerged river crossing. Snorkels are fitted while hatches and gun barrels are sealed. Left: Soviet T72 commanders salute as their vehicles parade majestically through Moscow's Red Square. Below left: A column of T72s, with Hind helicopter gunships in support, simulates a full-scale armoured assault. Below: A Soviet T72 crew makes a routine track inspection during Warsaw Pact manoeuvres. Bottom: With main gun and anti-aircraft machine gun at the ready, the crew of a dug-in Iraqi T72 scans the horizon for any signs of hostile Iranian activity.

By the early 1980s the T72 seemed to have been favoured as the main Soviet and Warsaw Pact army tank to stay in production and be updated when necessary, until it is replaced by the controversial Western-designated 'T80' about which little hard fact is known. In Western military establishments, no agreement has yet been reached as to whether it is a completely new Soviet MBT or merely an update on the T72. In March 1983 the US Department of Defense designated the new tank as T80 although Soviet sources refer to it as the T74. A great deal of fairly wild speculation has gone into the characteristics of the new tank and, while some consider it to be protected by a Chobham-type armour, photographs purporting to be of the T80/74 show it to be very similar to the T64/T72 series, only with modifications to the turret shape. The US Department of Defense, always anxious to improve its tank-design defence-budget allocation, supports the view that the T80/74 is a very real and potent threat to Western security and rumours abound that there may be an even more advanced tank currently under development in the Soviet Union.

Certain features of the T80/74 do, however, seem likely in the light of Soviet tank-development priorities. It is thought to retain the 125mm main armament with automatic loading system, with possible improvement to ammunition, and to introduce a digital fire-control computer and passive night-vision gear. It is also believed that the Soviets have abandoned the torsion-bar suspension fitted to the T64 and T72 in favour of a variable hydro-pneumatic type for improved performance. Such modifications have yet to be seen to be proved, however, and whether the T80/74 will prove a match for the capabilities of its latest Nato counterparts is in itself a matter of total speculation.

T72(T64) MBT

Crew 3
Dimensions Length (gun included) 9.24m (30ft) (**T64**: 9.1m – 29ft 8in); width (including skirts) 4.75m (15ft 5in) (**T64**: 4.64m – 15ft 1in); height 2.37m (7ft 8in) (**T64**: 2.3m – 7ft 6in)
Weight 41,000kg (90,388lb) (**T64**: 38,000kg – 83,775lb)
Engine Diesel developing 750hp (**T64**: Diesel developing 700hp)

Performance Maximum road speed 80km/h (50mph) (**T64**: 70km/h – 43mph); range (internal fuel tanks) 500km (311 miles); range (with long-range fuel tanks) 700km (435 miles); vertical obstacle 0.915m (3ft); trench 3.07m (9ft 9in) (**T64**: 2.72m – 8ft 10in); gradient 60 per cent

Armour Classified
Armament One 125mm gun; one 7.62mm machine gun co-axial with main armament; one 12.7mm anti-aircraft machine gun

Below: Although the T64's 12.7mm anti-aircraft machine gun can be fired remotely while the vehicle is closed down, the T72 featured a pintel-mounted machine gun with better elevation. Although more effective, this system exposes the commander to enemy fire while the machine gun is in use. Below centre: The various types of main-gun ammunition available on the T72 are displayed at the front of a tank's glacis. Ammunition includes HEAT, APFSDS and two types of HE fragmentation round. Bottom: Like all Soviet MBTs, the T72 has the facility to carry long-range fuel tanks at the rear of the vehicle.

Above: One of the early photographs of the Soviet T74 MBT which confirm the view that the T74 is merely an update of the T72 and not the awesome opponent that the US Department of Defense would have the world believe. Right: A US 'artist's impression' of the T74 which shows the tank to have a Chobham type of armour.

Arabian adventures

The campaign in Dhofar 1965–75

Since the oilfields of the Gulf became a vital source of energy supplies for the industrialised West, control of the Strait of Hormuz has been a key strategic objective in the global power struggle. Western strategists feared that if the Strait was dominated by the Soviet Union through a client state, oil supplies could be cut off at any time, with disastrous results. In the 1960s the state on the eastern shore of the Strait, Iran, was considered a reliable ally of the West under the Shah's government, but on the western shore was the Musandam peninsula, part of the potentially unstable Sultanate of Muscat and Oman. British influence predominated in the Sultanate, as it had done for a century past, but the future of the country appeared dangerously uncertain.

The ruler, Sultan Said bin Taimur, was probably the most conservative monarch in the world. Since 1932 he had exercised a doubtful degree of authority over the underpopulated expanses of Muscat, Oman and Dhofar, but such power as he possessed was used to stave off any possibility of change. Every aspect of modern civilisation was banned – from radios to spectacles, from medicines to bicycles – and the inhabitants pursued their subsistence living through agriculture and fishing, cut off from any prospect of

economic development. The Sultan's government and armed forces were in the hands of a number of British administrators and army officers (some seconded from the British Army, others on contract to the Sultan). Britain provided about half the Sultan's revenues, in the form of an annual grant, the rest being raised by taxing the impoverished population. Britain also, in the last resort, guaranteed the Sultan's rule by military force, as was demonstrated in the late 1950s when two SAS squadrons were sent in to put down a revolt by Omanis in the Jebel Akhdar.

In the mid-1960s, however, a more serious threat to the Sultan's power developed in the southern third of his territory, Dhofar. Geographically remote from the rest of the country – 1000km (600 miles) by road from Muscat – the Dhofaris were also completely different in language, history and culture from the Arabs of Muscat and Oman. The Sultan ruled Dhofar as his personal domain, and since the 1950s he had chosen to live in his palace in the capital of Dhofar, Salalah, rather than in Muscat.

Trouble started through emigration. Officially, emigration, like all other forms of contact with the outside world, was banned. But the impoverished Dhofaris were attracted by the possibilities of em-

Below: A patrol of *firqat* move through open country in Dhofar. Although there were question marks about the strict military worth of the *firqat*, they represented an important part of the counter-insurgency strategy followed by the Sultan Qaboos and his advisers, for they symbolised the new policy of trying to win the allegiance of the Dhofaris, rather than merely threatening them with severe punishments, and marked the change of direction that was crucial to the eventual victory.

Above: Men and women alike joined the Popular Liberation movement and readily accepted arms (such as the AK assault rifle held by the woman in the foreground) and training from the Soviet Union and China in their fight against the despotic and reactionary Sultan Said bin Taimur. Not until the young, Sandhurst educated and relatively progressive Sultan Qaboos (right) displaced his father in 1970 was the regime able to show a more attractive face to the Dhofaris.

attempt to throw off the burden of the Sultan's rule.

The first two years of the guerrilla campaign witnessed a series of hit and run raids, chiefly against the road between Salalah and Thamrit – limited clashes which over a year left a few dozen dead on each side. Only a few hundred guerrillas were active. The Sultan's Armed Forces (SAF), comprising the Muscat, Desert and Northern Frontier Regiments, were on the whole lightly equipped, since the Sultan was loath to spend money from his quite limited resources. There were around 1000 SAF troops stationed in Dhofar in the early years of the fighting. Most of the officers were British and many of the troops were also foreigners, Baluchis from Pakistan, with whom Oman had traditional links. The Sultan initially had his own regiment in Dhofar, the Dhofar Force, which was separate from the SAF, but in 1966 he narrowly escaped assassination by members of the Force and henceforth Sultan Said bin Taimur regarded the Dhofaris as unreliable for military use. The Sultan of Oman's Air Force (SOAF) operated out of a British Royal Air Force base at Salalah, but in 1965 its attacking strength consisted of just one Skymaster jet.

Marxist successes

In late 1967 a fundamental change came over the situation when Britain finally withdrew from Aden and the People's Republic of South Yemen was established. The government of the new republic was Marxist, and it quickly exerted a major influence over the conflict in neighbouring Dhofar. Militarily, the guerrillas now enjoyed a secure base across the border and a safe route for weapons' supply and communications with the outside world. Politically, the movement got new backers – the Soviet Union and China. In 1968 the Dhofar Liberation Front became the Popular Front for the Liberation of the Occupied Arabian Gulf (PFLOAG). A Marxist ideology was adopted and the goal of Dhofari independence was replaced by the grandiose project of driving British influence out of all Oman and the neighbouring Gulf states. Selected guerrillas were sent for training to the Soviet Union and China and young Dhofaris were taken across the border into South Yemen for ideological instruction and to learn guerrilla techniques.

The Sultan's forces soon found themselves in difficulties. Salalah was secure behind a barbed wire fence built in 1966 and the coastal plain around it stayed largely in government hands, but in the mountainous interior and west of Dhofar the rebels were dominant. The SAF strove to bring the guerrillas to battle (staging seaborne landings at points along the coast towards the South Yemen border) and some of the SAF officers were very experienced (Colonel Mike Harvey, commander of the Northern Frontier Regiment, was a veteran of Palestine, Korea and Aden), but conditions did not favour the Sultan's men. Another officer, Captain Hepworth, vividly evoked this phase of the war: 'the Sultan's mud forts in the coastal villages were frequently attacked, camps were mortared almost every evening.... Water was very scarce, resupply became tremendously difficult, casualty evacuation was often by donkey and, apart from containing the enemy, we were certainly not winning the war.'

On 23 August 1969 the guerrillas captured the main administrative centre of western Dhofar, Rakhyut, in an assault during a monsoon storm which prevented any air or sea support reaching the defenders. The

ployment in the increasingly wealthy oil states of the Gulf. Inevitably, these Dhofari emigrants came into contact both with some of the luxuries of modern life unknown in their homeland, and with the radical ideas of the Arab nationalism that was sweeping the Middle East. In 1962 a group of emigrants formed a Dhofar Liberation Front, dedicated to achieving independence for Dhofar. Backed by Egypt and Iraq, by 1965 they were ready to launch a small-scale guerrilla war.

Dhofar offers excellent terrain for guerrilla warfare. There is a narrow coastal plain, where the main towns are situated, but the interior is a craggy mountain landscape penetrated only by camel routes. For four months of the year the monsoon descends, bringing drizzle and mist, and scrub and bush vegetation springs up to twice the height of a man, providing excellent cover for guerrilla forces. The mountain tribesmen, semi-nomadic herdsmen who always went armed, resented the Sultan's rule and the taxes he imposed. Many were only too ready to join the politicised Dhofaris returning from abroad in their

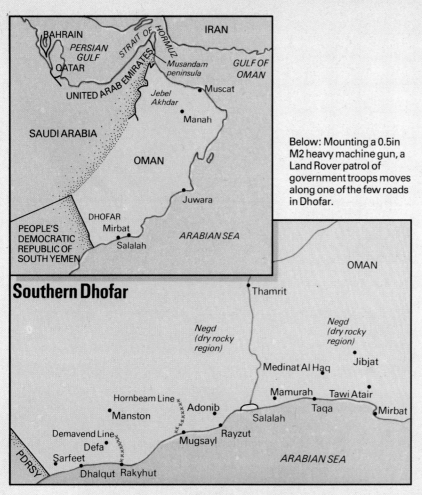

Below: Mounting a 0.5in M2 heavy machine gun, a Land Rover patrol of government troops moves along one of the few roads in Dhofar.

Southern Dhofar

rebels had now established almost complete control of the west and had wide areas of influence to the east of Salalah. In February 1970 the Royal Air Force Regiment had to reinforce the perimeter defences at Salalah airbase after a mortar attack by guerrillas. That August a reporter from *The Times* described Salalah as 'little more than a coastal enclave protected by a wall of barbed wire . . .'

But 1970 was in fact the turning point of the war. The attitudes and policies of Sultan Said had been a major stumbling block to any hope of a government victory: despite rising oil revenues from oilfields in Oman, which had permitted Britain to withdraw the financial subsidy in 1967, he had refused to spend enough on arms to meet the needs of his forces; nor would he spend money on economic development or modernisation, to which he maintained a fixed hostility. There was no prospect of winning the hearts and minds of the Dhofaris without reform – especially as the Sultan offered only the prospect of certain death to any guerrilla defecting to the government side.

The Sultan's son Qaboos bin Said had been educated at Sandhurst and had served in a British infantry regiment. On his return to his country, Qaboos had been made a virtual prisoner in his father's palace, since the Sultan was offended by his 'modern' attitudes. On 23 July 1970, with little violence, a palace coup overthrew Sultan Said and installed his son in his place. Britain has always denied that it had any part in the coup, but there is no question that it perfectly suited British interests. Sultan Qaboos swiftly announced a series of modernising reforms and set about spending the country's mounting oil revenues on development projects and on the armed forces.

It was in 1970 that the first units of the 22nd Special Air Service (SAS) Regiment arrived in Dhofar, officially designated a British Army Training Team (BATT) so that British politicians could claim that no British combat troops were present. A rapid expansion of the SAF began. A fourth regiment was added, the Jebel Regiment, and the existing units were increased in strength, so that SAF numbers rose from around 2500 in 1970 to about 12,000 at the end of 1973. The number of British officers and NCOs in Dhofar increased to some 600, split evenly between those on contract, paid by the Sultan, and those on loan from the British Army, paid by Britain. New Brooke Maine fast patrol boats increased the Sultan's control of sea routes – there were usually two boats patrolling at any one time. Above all, the SOAF was by now in a position to exploit the guerrillas' lack of air cover. With a fleet of helicopters to provide mobility and 12 Strikemasters (armed versions of the Jet Provost trainer) contributing close air support, the Sultan's forces were ready to seize the initiative.

The SAS, with their long experience of counter-insurgency operations, knew that the key to victory

Above: A government Bell Iroquois helicopter touches down in Dhofar's hill country. Right: A *firqat*, one of the local inhabitants who had joined the government forces. Below: An *adoo* (as the guerrillas were called) keeps a lookout for advancing government troops. The Dhofar hill country was ideal for sustaining a guerrilla war.

lay in winning over the Dhofari population. The previous Sultan's hostility to education, health services, road building or any form of economic improvement had left the government with nothing to offer the Dhofaris. Punitive measures against those who supported the guerrillas, such as the burning of villages, had only stiffened resistance. But Sultan Qaboos immediately announced a series of development projects for Dhofar and offered an amnesty to any rebels who wished to change sides. The new policies met with an instant response. The leftward turn of the guerrilla movement in 1968 had alienated many tribal leaders and their followers who found their traditional authority and beliefs under attack and who saw the objectives of the movement growing remote from their own interests. A steady stream of deserters to the government side began.

The SAS took on the task of organising these Dhofaris into *firqat*, companies operating under SAS command. The *firqat* were never fully reliable in their war against the *adoo*, as the guerrillas were called, but their presence on the government side was crucial. Although sometimes ill-disciplined, they offered the possibility of contact with the local population and an example of the beneficial consequences of reconciliation. Intelligence improved dramatically, and aid programmes – the building of wells, veterinary services, help in the marketing of cattle and goats – were well tailored to the interests of the mountain tribes.

But without military success, hearts and minds programmes could have little effect – and the war remained an uphill struggle. The guerrillas numbered some 2000 full-time fighters, backed by a militia of around 3000. They were well armed for their purposes, with Soviet Kalashnikov rifles, RPG-7s for use against the Sultan's Saladin armoured cars,

machine guns, mines, and 122mm Katyusha rocket launchers. For air defence they had only Soviet 14.5mm anti-aircraft machine guns until nearly the end of the war when a few SA-7 SAMs were deployed. For transport, they relied on camels and donkeys.

Unable to make any immediate impression on the guerrilla-held territory in the west of Dhofar, the Sultan's strengthened forces concentrated on the areas in the east and centre of the region. From October to December 1971, in Operation Jaguar, SAS, *firqat* and SAF forces penetrated rebel areas in the east, establishing defensible posts at Jibjat, Medinat Al Haq and other villages, from which offensive operations could be launched and civil aid programmes started. But the freedom of movement enjoyed by the guerrillas from the west meant that even sites near Salalah remained vulnerable. The Salalah-Thamrit road was cut and Salalah airbase came under attack from Katyusha rockets.

In July 1972 the rebels launched an attack on Mirbat which many regard as a crucial point in the war. The guerrillas needed a major propaganda success to reverse the trend of defections and wavering support. They planned to attack under cover of monsoon weather conditions, which they believed would keep the SOAF grounded, and had cleverly decoyed the main defence force away from the town. Their men numbered 250, armed with Kalashnikovs, light and heavy machine guns and recoilless guns. Defending Mirbat were 10 SAS men led by 23-year-old Captain Mike Kealy, and less than 100 *firqat* troops and local policemen. Kealy and his men held Mirbat with actions of great gallantry until help arrived. The guerrillas had underestimated the readiness of SOAF pilots, mostly British, to fly under difficult conditions. When air support arrived, the rebels suffered horrifying losses. To their further misfortune, a fresh SAS squadron had arrived in Dhofar the previous day, and when it joined the counter-attack, the rout was complete.

The Shah backs the Sultan

External support for the Sultan's regime was growing apace. Jordan sent a battalion of special forces and a detachment of engineers, Pakistan contributed about 100 officers and NCOs, but the dominant new involvement came from Iran. The Shah sent men and equipment from late 1972 onwards, increasing to a maximum of 2400 troops, with artillery, helicopter gunships and the support of a naval fleet.

To consolidate the government's hold on east and central Dhofar, the Sultan's forces set about the creation of a defensive line across the country, the Hornbeam Line. Working with British and Jordanian engineers, they constructed a line 53km (33 miles) long, using over 15,000 coils of barbed wire and 4000 anti-personnel mines. It was built in extreme heat, across nearly vertical slopes in territory normally held by the enemy. It proved impossible for the guerrillas to cross the line in strength, and supplies of arms and ammunition to the east almost dried up. Control of the Salalah-Thamrit road was still hotly contested, but from 1973 onwards the situation east of the Hornbeam Line always favoured the government.

Yet all attempts to stop the infiltration of supplies from South Yemen into west Dhofar failed. A strongpoint at Sarfeet, near the border, was seized and held, but it proved impossible to use it as a base from which

to cut the camel routes into Dhofar. From 1972 onwards Sarfeet survived constant artillery bombardment from batteries inside South Yemen employing Soviet 85mm, 122mm and 130mm guns. The position was encircled by guerrilla mortar emplacements and mines. Every drop of water, ammunition and general supplies had to be ferried in by helicopter after a short airstrip fit to take the SOAF's Skyvan transports was put out of action by shelling. In order to avoid mortar fire, the helicopters had to approach at 1800m (6000ft) above ground level, descend in a fast sickening spiral, and load and unload at speed. The military value of holding Sarfeet was doubtful, but its evacuation would have given the rebels an important psychological boost.

Until 1975 the gruelling, seemingly endless warfare continued. The guerrillas could never get near achieving their overall goals. They were dependent on an uprising in Oman if they were to spread their activities beyond Dhofar, but although rebel activity broke out in the Omani interior in June 1970 it remained small-scale and was finally repressed in 1974. Yet repeated efforts failed to dislodge them from their fastnesses in west Dhofar, until in January 1975 the Iranians seized Rakhyut, with the vital support of the British-officered SOAF and shelling from warships offshore. It was the beginning of the end. A new fortified line was quickly created stretching inland from Rakhyut, the Demavend Line. The following October, in a series of swift moves making considerable use of helicopters, the SAF, the Iranians and the SAS-led *firqat* carried the battle forward to a series of positions in line with Sarfeet. Air strikes on the South Yemen border ravaged artillery batteries, and quite suddenly major resistance ceased. In December 1975 the Sultan announced that the war was over.

In fact small bands of guerrillas were still to be found scattered throughout Dhofar, but the back of the rebellion was broken. In late 1976 the last SAS personnel left the country, although Iranian forces remained until the Shah's downfall in 1979.

Graham Brewer

Above: A Strikemaster (an armed version of the Jet Provost trainer) of the Sultan of Oman's airforce. The Strikemasters were used in close support of ground operations. Air power was one of the strongest weapons in the Sultan's arsenal, and Iranian helicopter gunships were especially feared by the insurgents.

Ambush

Ranulph Fiennes was serving in the Royal Scots Greys as a tank troop leader in Westphalia when he applied for secondment to Dhofar in 1967. From 1968 to 1970 he served in the Sultan of Oman's Army and he soon found conditions in South Arabia far from the romantic adventure he had hoped for.

❝Radio Aden announced that the freedom fighters of Dhofar had located a group of British propaganda experts who were attempting to bribe and seduce the plainsfolk of Dhofar. They were following the movements of these specialists with care and would soon eliminate them. Said bin Ghia assured me that we were the specialists and would do well to take care.

The night before returning to the caves of Khalaf upon the agreed date, we sent half the men into the bushes in the foothills above. There were no ambushers to ambush that time but we could not be too careful. In other wadis we fed Bedu families and always told them a future date when we would return. Many of the men began to catch colds and coughs after successive ambushes in the drizzle and the dank cold air, so I stopped the precaution and started to pay our second advertised visit without a protective cordon placed the night before.

Deep within the foothills and hidden by a green sea of camel thorn were many monsoon camps of the cattle herders. The mountains rose abruptly behind them. In August the area took on a ghostly look in the grey *khareef*.

The Wadi Thimreen wound through this region and close to it we found a huddle of mud and thorn rondaavals. The occupants were in a worse state than most, their cattle as emaciated as their children. We doled out food and medicine as usual and promised to return with more the following day.

Only 12 men came with me the next day, including Said bin Ghia; the rest were sick. Corporal Salim and Ali Nasser had three men each. Two Baluchis, Said bin Ghia and Hamid Sultan, with the heavy Browning, stayed with me. We left Murad and the vehicles in the bottom of the Thimreen, our backpacks heavy with food for the village. Once into the bushes Corporal Salim and Ali Nasser disappeared to the flanks. I could see no one but the man on either side.

After an hour moving with great care I smelled the

dung fires of the village. The two Baluchis went off quietly to either side. They returned in a while to confirm the other sections had arrived. Then we moved forward.

I approached the thorn enclosures from the south as on our previous visit. Ahead was sparse foliage and ant hills, then the clearing of the village. There was no one about; not even a cow. I checked through binoculars.

Ali Nasser responded to two finger pressures on my National (radio) and somewhere to the east of the clearing his men crept forward; Corporal Salim to the west. I gave them five minutes then got up. On my left Hamid Sultan arose cradling the ugly machine gun, a camouflage net over its belt of bullets. To the right Said bin Ghia straightened out gleaming with sweat. He was frowning; uneasy. It was too quiet.

We left the last shred of cover and stepped into the clearing. From the west a murderous rattle of Bren gun fire stunned me momentarily. I remember seeing the ripple of earth spurts rising like hailstones landing in a quiet pond. Then the woodpeckers opened up from the other side of the clearing, Soviet RPD automatics, nicknamed due to their rapid rate of fire and the sound of their high velocity bullets.

I felt the shockwaves slap by very close. Said bin Ghia screamed and fell to the ground. I twisted, rolled and lurched back to the nearest ant hill. Hamid was already there struggling with the Browning. Said bin Ghia rolled over and over, very quickly for one so large in the belly. Flour spilled everywhere from his pack, red with his blood, but he reached an ant hill

The wide expanses and rocky nature of the Dhofar border country (bottom) proved an excellent killing zone for the guerrillas and government troops were often induced to pursue the rebels into their mountain strongholds where the soldiers could be easily ambushed. Similarly, the rugged countryside easily obscured rebel encampments from aerial reconnaissance (below).

followed closely by the woodpeckers. For a while it was suicide to move a finger behind the tiny mound. Hamid clasped my back and pulled me towards him with the big gun between us. He grinned and rolled his eyeballs in mock horror.

It seemed as though the *adoo* were intent on digging the ant hill away with their bullets until we were exposed. My shirt tail was loose and a bullet ripped through it. I flinched and felt the fear mount. Earth sprayed on to our faces kicked up from the mound. The vibration of the bullets eating deep into the soil came through clearly as our faces pressed harder against the ant hill. I turned the National on: my signaller was with Murad and the Land Rovers. They had heard the trouble and sent for the jets.

I took stock of things. We had by the skin of our teeth avoided a well laid ambush. Only the skill of Corporal Salim and his three men had saved us. Outflanking the *adoo* position they must have seen our predicament and opened up just in time. Corporal Salim came through on the National; his voice high with excitement. 'This is 52. They are closing on us, Sahb. Twenty or more have moved behind those by the houses, and they know we are but four men.'

Our hope lay in little Ali. He had three good men each with a Bren gun. I told him to close in at once. His acknowledgement was a whispered, '54, Imshaalah'. His men opened fire as one and no more *adoo* bullets came our way, Hamid jammed the Browning tripod onto the mound. One great hand fed the snake of bullets into the chamber, the other panned the gun and squeezed the trigger back. Branches flew from the thorn huts and leaves shredded in the scrub beyond. Then we ran across the clearing. I forgot the pain in my knees. All fear was gone now with the action. The *adoo* had left but bloodstains and heaps of empty cases remained. Corporal Salim's voice came over the National, jubilant. 'They are running Sahb. Shall we follow?' I said no. They would not run for long if we exposed our total number. Bin Ghia's wrist was slashed by a bullet. We dressed it as he swore vengeance on the cowardly dogs, his belly heaving. A bullet splintered the butt of my rifle and ripped on: the *adoo* had reached the slopes overlooking the village and could probably see their error in overestimating our strength. The Baluchis lay out a long fluorescent cloth, T-shaped and pointed at the *adoo* positions above us. A Strikemaster roared in and loosed off four 80mm Sura rockets. There was a malfunction and two exploded close to Ali Nasser's ant hill, showering it with shrapnel. We had been lucky; no one but Said bin Ghia was hurt and the men were pleased with themselves. Two weeks later, intelligence sources confirmed that six guerrillas had died that day. **99**

When on 6 May 1980 a Special Air Service (SAS) counter-terrorist team broke the Iranian Embassy siege in London in the now-famous action lasting 11 minutes, it was probably the first time that the British public at large had heard of the SAS. Yet it was 39 years since Captain David Stirling had founded the formation in Egypt in 1941 for behind-the-lines operations.

Disbanded at the end of World War II, the SAS was re-formed in 1947 as the 21st Special Air Service Regiment, Territorial Army (Artists); the Artists Rifles Association provided '21' with a home in Duke's Road, near Euston Station. But it was not until 1950 that the SAS once more took its place as a part of the Regular Army, specifically as a result of the demands of counter-insurgency.

In 1950 Brigadier J.M. Calvert, who had commanded the SAS Brigade in the closing months of World War II, received an urgent call from General Sir John Harding, Commander-in-Chief of Far East Land Forces, to visit Malaya where a guerrilla movement among the local Chinese population was threatening British rule. Calvert decided to recruit his own special force to search out and destroy the enemy in the depths of the jungle. He called the unit the Malayan Scouts (SAS). Volunteers were recruited from the British Army in the Far East, the Rhodesian Army and the

Territorial Army SAS in Duke's Road. As evidence of the influence of '21' on the formation of the SAS as a unit of the Regular Army, the Malayan Scouts were soon renamed the *22nd* SAS Regiment.

Most of the major SAS operations conducted in Malaya from 1950 to 1959 were in the north near the Thai border. The matted roof of the jungle stretched for hundreds of miles. Aerial survey looking for communist lairs was a thankless task. The communists had to grow their own crops, however, and that meant clearing a patch of the jungle for the purpose. A tell-tale wisp of smoke was enough to reveal their presence. Acceptable dropping zones were non-existent, so after the SAS observer, usually a squadron commander, had spotted a hideaway a team had to parachute on to the tall treetops, descending by rope to the ground.

Shrouded in the Valkyrean gloom with the shrill sounds of the jungle in their ears, the SAS party now faced the prospect of making agonisingly slow progress for perhaps two days. Added to the complexities of jungle navigation and keeping together, they had constantly to be on the alert to kill or be killed. Movement was often impossible without a machete and hacking through the undergrowth made it difficult to conceal one's presence. Patience was essential. Once an enemy camp was under observation, the SAS

Below: Two troopers from the SAS moving at speed across Welsh hill country. From their base in Hereford, much of the SAS training takes place in the Brecon Beacons where survival skills form a large part of the curriculum.

Daring to win
The SAS and counter-insurgency

Training for the SAS

The initial selection of candidates for the SAS is made from among volunteers who have some service in regular army units behind them. Even in the early stages of selection, which include an extensive medical check and a 2.5km (1.5 miles) run which has to be completed within 12 minutes, as many as 10 per cent of volunteers are returned to unit.

For those who pass this basic selection test there then follows a course, some three weeks in length, during which every day is spent under extreme conditions training in the Brecon Beacons. As each day passes the distances to be covered in forced marches is lengthened, the weights to be carried are increased and rest periods, including those for sleep, are quickly decreased. After two weeks a minimum of 15 hours marching per day is required.

In the final week (which is the third for officers and fourth for other ranks) the groups are split up and each individual then works on his own against the clock – this is particularly testing both physically and mentally, though some useful advice has been offered by veterans to help aspiring SAS recruits through this rigorous period: 'Don't sit down half way up a hill but promise yourself a rest at the top, where the wind is so damned unpleasant that you're forced down to the next valley before pausing to get your bearings, which you'll only find by climbing the next hill. If you give up when you're completely shattered, you'll find out too late that the regiment is mainly composed of men who were completely shattered.'

The final and most demanding test at the end of the initial training period is an endurance march; 72km (45 miles) across country carrying a 23kg (50lb) pack, a belt kit weighing 5.5kg (12lb) and an SLR weighing almost 5kg (11lb), all of which must cross the finishing line in 20 hours.

Following this intense physical training course a week is spent making complex military decisions based on too much or too little information, and then comes a battery of intensive specialist courses ranging from demolition to resistance to interrogation. On the successful completion of this period of training the recruit is attached to a troop and is taught a specialised tactical skill such as amphibious warfare or astro-navigation (including a personal vocation such as elementary surgery). In all it takes from two to three years to turn a fully trained soldier into a basically qualified member of the SAS.

Below: SAS men displaying the wide variety of equipment that they are trained to use according to their vocation. Each SAS recruit is taught a specialised tactical skill, from high altitude paradrops to amphibious warfare.

commander had to be certain that all the incumbents were in view before giving the order to fire. From then on it was a matter of survival until retrieval by helicopter could be arranged.

The 22 SAS made a very important contribution to the military campaign in Malaya. They had learned to live and observe in the jungle by practical experience. Iban tribesmen recruited from Sarawak taught them to be superb trackers; and the SAS were better armed than the enemy. But there was another aspect to their work. General Sir Gerald Templer, the Military High Commissioner, was convinced that the campaign would be won not so much by killing the guerrillas as by winning the 'hearts and minds' of the peoples of the Malay peninsula. The SAS had a great success record in befriending and attending to the welfare of the aboriginal tribes that was to provide an example for the more intensified US Special Forces programmes in Vietnam.

As the Malayan campaign drew to a close in the late 1950s, there was an argument advanced in Whitehall and the army that the time had come for the SAS to be disbanded again. However, a role was found for the SAS in 1958–59 supporting the rule of the Sultan of Oman in the south of the Arabian peninsula. The operation against the Omani rebels, culminating in January 1959 with an assault on the Jebel Akhdar (Green Mountain), was not properly speaking a counter-insurgency task, but it gave the SAS another chance to demonstrate their skill in coping with hostile terrain and small-unit warfare.

The SAS's next experience of counter-insurgency proper came in Borneo during the 'Confrontation' with Indonesia from 1962 to 1966. Lieutenant-Colonel John Woodhouse then commanding 22 SAS convinced General Sir Walter Walker that the SAS had a place in the forces defending Brunei, Sarawak and North Borneo (Sabah) against infiltration from Indonesian Borneo (Kalimantan). In January 1963,

Left: A basic SAS field kit including lightweight rations, mess tins and standard tools. Right: Two SAS NCOs plot the progress of a troop's patrol in Oman on an Operations Room map.

Below: An SAS unit replenish their water supplies at a well in the Fadhli State, South Arabian Federation. Bottom: SAS soldiers in a Malaysian village. One of the most successful SAS operations was in Sarawak and Sabah, when infiltration across the border from Indonesia was contained by British forces.

Major Peter de la Billière's A Squadron was dispersed at intervals in two- and four-man teams along the entire 1560km (970 miles) of the Kalimantan border. Once again the SAS were reunited with their Iban tracker friends from the Malayan campaign.

After establishing hides the SAS men set out to win over the 'hearts and minds' of the nearby villagers, living in their longhouses and sharing their food and culture. De la Billière knew that A Squadron alone could not contain cross-border attacks so he devised a 'step up' plan for calling in heliborne infantry and support weapons. The SAS were later reinforced by Major John Watts' D Squadron, HQ Squadron and the Guards Independent Parachute Company; some sharp actions were fought before after three years the Indonesians were repelled from the border areas.

From April 1964 the SAS found themselves back in the Arabian peninsula, this time employing their ability to observe and move across mountainous terrain unseen in the fight against tribesmen in the Radfan. Soon, in Aden, they got their first experience of urban warfare. Here A Squadron (de la Billière) set up a Close Quarter Battle Course for training counter-terrorist squads. These Keeni-Meeni (a Swahili term for a snake's movement in the long grass) teams disguised themselves in Arab attire – the Fijians with the SAS were most proficient in this role. Unlike Malaya and Borneo, there was no attempt to win 'hearts and minds'. By autumn 1967, the fight with Adeni terrorists was over and the British Army pulled out.

In 1970, however, 22 SAS returned to neighbouring Oman to counter an insurgency in the western province of Dhofar. The SAS took on a role similar to the US Special Forces 'A' teams in Vietnam. Welfare and protection from the rebels was bartered with the tribesmen for loyalty to the Sultan. Bands of former guerrillas who rallied to the Sultan were retrained by the SAS and led in effective operations against their former colleagues. The insurgent leaders were both persistent and aggressive, however, and a number of storybook military encounters were fought before a combination of successful counter-insurgency tactics and increasing firepower finally overcame guerrilla resistance in 1975.

During the 1970s increasing consideration was given to the problems of counter-terrorism, rather than counter-insurgency. Small numbers of SAS were secretly deployed in Northern Ireland, where their ability to live rough in the border areas proved an

Right: A mechanised unit of SAS soldiers, on exercise in Wales, try out a specially equipped Land Rover mounting two 7.62mm GPMGs. Below: A South Arabian tribesman and an SAS trooper drink tea together. One of the most important skills of the SAS is their ability to sustain friendly relations with local populations through the provision of food and medical supplies.

important asset. A small Counter Revolutionary Warfare force was set up to deal with hijacks and hostage-taking by terrorists. This involved Close Quarter Battle training with a wide range of weapons. Even before the Iranian Embassy siege, SAS expertise in these matters was internationally recognised. In 1977 the West German anti-terrorist team GSG-9 enlisted SAS advice when a Lufthansa airliner was hijacked and eventually landed at Mogadishu. In the same year there was a minor SAS presence in Holland where a train had been seized by South Moluccans.

In their adaptation to counter-insurgency and counter-terrorist roles the SAS have not lost their original World War II mission of carrying out deep penetration raids behind enemy lines. This is still the regiment's assigned function in case of major war. In the Falklands conflict of 1982 they reverted to the clandestine commando-style role, destroying aircraft on the ground and carrying out reconnaissance missions.

If the SAS have been so successful in counter-insurgency, it is because of their general ability to take on any exceptionally demanding task. The endurance and survival courses for volunteers from the Regular Army at Brecon and on Exmoor are tough but not sadistic. The SAS man must be self-reliant, capable of operating in a small team or on his own. The regiment is highly disciplined but mutual respect is supreme between officers and men.

The SAS is also a regiment of ideas, with a stable body of officers and NCOs accumulating and passing on a body of experience built up in campaign after campaign. They have proved sufficiently flexible to adapt their knowledge and techniques to new situations and varying tasks. Whatever the shape of conflict in the future, the SAS will find a place for their special skills.
Barry Gregory

Colonial crises

Policing the last fragments of empire

Arguably, military intervention by a state in the affairs of its colonies is the most legitimate form of armed action apart from self-defence. Yet even when intervening in colonies, there still needs to be a clear aim in view, the will to act, and the resources to achieve the desired result. The British experience of colonial crises between 1965 and 1969 well illustrates these basic points.

The first and most enduring colonial crisis of the period was in Rhodesia. In a wave of decolonisation in Africa in the first half of the 1960s, Britain had handed over power to a series of black governments representing, as far as could be arranged, the majority of people in the colony concerned. In Rhodesia, however, Ian Smith and his Rhodesian Front insisted on continuing white settler government after independence, terms which Britain would not accept. On 11 November 1965 Smith broke the deadlock by a Unilateral Declaration of Independence (UDI), establishing Rhodesia as an independent white-ruled state.

The British government of the day was a Labour administration with a precarious parliamentary majority, led by Prime Minister Harold Wilson. Insecure in its hold on power, the government was unwilling to escalate the crisis; in any case, Labour was traditionally hostile to the use of military force. Although the British government recognised a legal obligation to the black majority in Rhodesia, and there were immediate demands from Commonwealth

leaders for military intervention, Wilson feared the loss of his parliamentary majority and opted for economic sanctions which he believed would 'bring the rebellion to an end within a matter of weeks rather than months'.

Even if the will had been there, intervention would have proved hazardous. Certainly, Britain still had substantial forces deployed world-wide but it was estimated that as many as 25,000 men might be required to ensure success – although it was also argued that a small unit immediately landed might rally loyalists. Only two battalions were actually available and, through economies in RAF Transport Command, only one could be airlifted at any given time. Assuming an operation mounted from Nairobi, Kenya, transport aircraft with necessary fighter cover would have been at the very limit of their endurance over Rhodesia. How far one battalion would be able to overcome any resistance from the Rhodesian forces was problematical, even if some Rhodesians were unwilling to fire on British troops. The morale of the British troops themselves was also questionable and there was perhaps exaggerated disquiet at the prospect of fighting 'kith and kin'. The alternative was a land invasion from neighbouring Zambia but this would require, in the manner of the Suez operation, a considerable build-up over a prolonged period. Neither course recommended itself to the British Chiefs of Staff, few in the Cabinet appeared willing to act militarily and Wilson himself had repeatedly said

Above: A British soldier patrols an area of Georgetown, British Guiana (now Guyana), while voting takes place during the elections on 7 December 1964. Maintaining order in newly independent or soon-to-be independent colonies was essential if the states were to have a stable beginning to their existence.

that force would not be used.

Some military measures were, however, undertaken. President Kaunda of Zambia had requested British troops because he believed his country's security to be at risk. A battalion and an RAF squadron were offered but, as Kaunda could not agree on the conditions to be attached to their deployment, the idea was dropped. It was decided to establish a transmitter near Francistown in Bechuanaland in order to relay BBC broadcasts to Rhodesia. Since it was feared that the installation might be sabotaged, a company from the 1st Battalion, Gloucestershire Regiment was despatched from Swaziland to guard it in December 1965. A company remained on guard over the transmitter until August 1967.

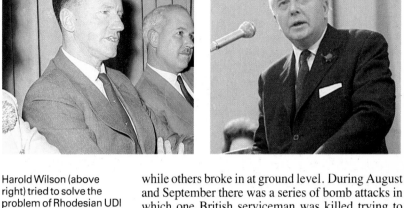

Demonstrations, strikes and riots
On four occasions in the succeeding years British forces were employed rather more successfully in lending aid to the civil power in the colonies. The first was the assistance given to the Hong Kong Police in confronting a series of demonstrations, strikes and riots during the summer and autumn of 1967. Trouble began with a labour dispute at two artificial flower factories in May but it quickly developed into a confrontation between Chinese communists and the colonial authorities. The crowds were urged on by loudspeakers on the top floor of the communist-controlled Bank of China and there were demonstrations against British diplomats in Macao, Peking, Shanghai and Canton. Water supplies from the mainland were cut off by the Chinese between June and October. When a Chinese journalist was arrested in Hong Kong, Anthony Grey of Reuters was arrested in Peking; and shortly after three Chinese newspapers had been closed down in Hong Kong in August, the British mission in Peking was sacked by Red Guards.

Military action in Hong Kong began on 8 July when five policemen were killed and 12 wounded by machine-gun fire from across the Chinese border at Shataukok. Some 550 troops, mostly from the 1st Battalion, 10th Gurkha Rifles were immediately moved close to the frontier. One Gurkha was wounded but British forces did not return the fire. On 12 July troops were used for the first time in direct support of the police in a series of arms raids. In one raid on 4 August troops and police were dropped on the roofs of three buildings by helicopters from HMS *Hermes*

Harold Wilson (above right) tried to solve the problem of Rhodesian UDI without a resort to force, but found that the government of Ian Smith (above) was prepared to risk British military action in order to assert its independence. The question of whether British troops should be committed to Rhodesia was one that occasioned much debate, but in the end the British government resorted to the use of economic sanctions.

Right: A helicopter from the British aircraft carrier HMS *Hermes* landing army troops and police atop an apartment building during arms raids in Hong Kong in August 1967. Below: A mixed group of 20 police and Royal Engineers are held captive by workers from communist China at a frontier post. The British troops occupying the post had been instructed not to open fire and were unable to resist the crowds that captured them.

while others broke in at ground level. During August and September there was a series of bomb attacks in which one British serviceman was killed trying to defuse a bomb and another seriously injured. The four Gurkha battalions in the garrison were also faced with provocative frontier incidents in which Chinese workers, youths or women would rush across the border and surround British posts. On one occasion a mixed group of 20 police and Royal Engineers were held captive for a time and their weapons seized, since British troops were instructed not to open fire. An agreement was eventually concluded over frontier exchanges in November and the situation stabilised by the end of December. In all 47 people, including 10 members of the security forces, had been killed and 781 injured.

A second intervention in aid of the civil power occurred when a state of emergency was declared on the island of Mauritius on 21 January 1968 after gang

warfare between Muslims and Creoles had escalated into racial riots. Previously a company of the 2nd Battalion, Coldstream Guards had been sent to Mauritius on a similar mission from Aden in May 1965, but on this occasion it fell to a company of the 1st Battalion, King's Shropshire Light Infantry (soon to become 3rd Battalion, the Light Infantry) airlifted from Singapore. A second company was also despatched to assist in enforcing the curfew, house-to-house searches and arrests. One company was withdrawn in March, when the island became independent, but the other remained until the end of the year.

Two similar operations were the despatch of men of the Royal Inniskilling Fusiliers (soon to become 1st Battalion, Royal Irish Rangers) to Bermuda in April 1968 during pre-election riots and the landing of Royal Marines on Bermuda in July 1969 to maintain order during a black power conference. The latter year is best remembered, however, for another operation which was inevitably contrasted with the failure to intervene in Rhodesia four years previously – the 'invasion' of Anguilla in the Leeward Islands. Anguilla had been administratively linked with the distant islands of St Kitts and Nevis since 1822 but had frequently requested separation. In February 1967 St Kitts-Nevis-Anguilla were granted internal self-government in association with Britain. Totally neglected by the St Kitts government, the Anguillans declared 'independence' from St Kitts in June 1967. Royal Marines from HMS Salisbury had previously escorted police reinforcements to the island, but the police were expelled by the islanders. Two years of fruitless negotiation followed, including a 12-month period when Anguilla was temporarily administered by a British official. This interim agreement expired in January 1969 at which point Anguilla again declared 'independence'. On 11 March the Parliamentary Under-Secretary at the Foreign and Commonwealth Office, William Whitlock, visited the island to announce a new interim agreement. He succeeded in appearing to snub the Anguillan leader, Ronald Webster, and was besieged by an angry crowd in a local bank manager's house. Amid a fusillade of shots aimed at nobody in particular, Whitlock hastily departed. The British government now seized upon reports that Anguilla was in the hands of the Mafia and that a large number of its 6000 inhabitants were armed. The transparent falsity of such claims became obvious when only 39 assorted weapons and a rusting Napoleonic cannon were discovered on the island.

At 0315 hours on 19 March 1969 a force of 315 men of the 2nd Battalion, the Parachute Regiment and 47 London policemen, all airlifted from Aldershot to Antigua, was landed on Anguilla by the frigates *Minerva* and *Rothesay* to be met only by a barrage of photographers' flashbulbs. International ridicule was heaped upon the operation described by *The Spectator* as the 'War of Whitlock's Ear'. The paratroopers were withdrawn in September while Royal Engineers remained to help modernise Anguilla until September 1971. The Anguilla Act of 1971 restored the island's status as a colony and in February 1976 Anguilla became a 'dependent territory'.

Amid the laughter in the House of Commons over the Anguilla affair, however, came a pungent comment on Britain's stance during these years. After Foreign Secretary Michael Stewart had alluded to the difficulties of military intervention in Rhodesia, his predecessor, George Brown, enquired, 'Are we going to say we can do it where there is only a rusty gun?' **Ian Beckett**

Below: British paratroopers read about their exploits after the military intervention in Anguilla. Bottom: An RAF transport plane from Antigua disgorges British troops and supplies onto a tiny grass airstrip in Anguilla.

Key Weapons

FRIGATES

Designations in the field of warship design tend to be imprecise but the generally accepted meaning of 'frigate' is a vessel concerned primarily with ASW (anti-submarine warfare). Even so, the definition is blurred by the fact that the majority of modern surface warships are between 3500 and 4500 tons displacement and could be termed 'frigates' by virtue of their displacement. At the same time, it should be recognised that because a ship is ASW-orientated she is not necessarily a frigate. It is no coincidence, however, that the frigate and the submarine are the two most common major warships in the inventories of established naval powers, for the role of the submarine is to interdict the seapower of an adversary, while that of the frigate is quite the reverse, to safeguard a nation's seapower.

The frigate was re-introduced by the Royal Navy during World War II as a purpose-built escort vessel, larger than a corvette but smaller than a destroyer. Developments in submarine design necessitated reciprocal improvements in frigate design as well as an overall increase in numbers. In the decade following 1945 the British developed the frigate rapidly, ASW being a matter of great concern. Slow-sinking depth charges, dropped after the ship had lost sonar contact over a submerged target, had given way to spigot mortars such as Hedgehog which fired up to 24 bombs ahead of the ship while sonar contact was still firm. The triple-barrelled Squid and Limbo forward-firing mortars improved firing arcs and range considerably,

Previous page: Armed with a 5in dual-purpose naval gun and an octuple Mk 25 launcher for Sea Sparrow air defence missiles, the Knox-class frigate USS *Roark* gets under way. Above: The Type 21 frigates HMS *Amazon* and HMS *Antelope* (behind). Eight Type 21 frigates were commissioned by the Royal Navy and were notable for the extensive use made of aluminium in the ship's superstructure.

Right: HMS *Antelope* cuts a swathe through the ocean during naval exercises in 1975. The Type 21's lack of an effective point air-defence system was a contributory factor in the loss of HMS *Antelope* (and sister ship *Ardent*) to Argentinian air strikes during the Falklands conflict.

Above: Naval officers inspect a Limbo anti-submarine mortar on board HMS *Tartar* in June 1968. Above right: HMS *Broadsword*, a Royal Navy Type 22 frigate. The Type 22 family were the first Royal Navy frigates to dispense with a primary gun armament in favour of extensive ASW weapons (including two Westland Lynx helicopters and two triple anti-submarine torpedo tubes), Exocet anti-ship missiles and the effective Seawolf point air-defence missile system.

being lethal out to about one kilometre. Their longish time of flight (dead time) was later reduced by rocket-propelled mortar bombs.

To meet the problems posed by faster submarines, interim fast frigates were introduced by the Royal Navy through rebuilding outmoded but recently constructed fleet destroyers. Of these, the Type 15 conversions retained their main machinery, developing about 55,000 ship horse power for about 36 knots. The superstructure was drastically altered to a frigate configuration: forecastle continued well aft, armament reduced to a pair of dual-purpose guns in order to install a full kit of anti-submarine weaponry, including two Limbos, backed by improved sonars. These stop-gap vessels proved that the basic frigate concept was correct and opened the way for the new-generation Type 12 vessels (Whitby class) which differed in essence only in halving the installed power. As a result, much useful hull space was gained for the loss of only six knots in maximum speed.

Technology never stands still, however, and even as these ships were entering service, the submarine took two significant steps forward with the introduction of nuclear propulsion and the tear-drop hull. The combination of the two created the true submarine, capable of remaining submerged almost indefinitely, limited only by the endurance of the crew. Her speed was equal to that of the frigate, yet untrammelled by surface weather conditions. Totally disadvantaged, the frigate required weapons able to reach out rapidly to the limits of target detection.

The early British solution was to add a helicopter; after evaluation, helicopters were incorporated into Type 81 frigates in the early 1960s. Although small in size, they made a great impact on ship layout. Able to carry only anti-submarine torpedoes, the helicopter relied on the ship for targeting data; thus, to enable it to operate effectively at its full potential range, improved sonars were required. Hull-mounted sonars, limited in performance by water noise and ducting,

Right: Armed with two Mk 44 anti-submarine torpedoes a Westland Wasp helicopter banks over towards HMS *Aurora*, a Leander-class frigate. The Leander-class vessels have a top speed of 28.5 knots, and a range of 5500 nautical miles when travelling at a cruising speed of 12 knots.

were increasingly supplemented by variable-depth sonars and sonobuoys, able to work at selected depths below and between the layers of varying salinity and temperature that distort sonar echoes.

The Soviet Navy's first postwar frigates were in the 1900-ton Kola class, which was soon followed by the important Riga class, a conventional type of vessel of 1600 tons with a maximum speed of 28 knots. About 65 Riga-class ships were built in the 1950s and formed the mainstay of the Soviet Navy's escort fleet. Fitted with ASW weapons (two 16-barrel rocket launchers and four depth-charge projectors), one set of triple 21in torpedo tubes and a conventional armament of three 3.9in guns, the Riga class was certainly well armed, but its lack of sophisticated electronics has ensured that these vessels are now relegated to the reserve.

During the 1960s the 950-ton Petya class came into service. These ships were notable in being the first in the world to feature CODOG (combined diesel and gas turbine) propulsion. Electronic equipment was considerably more advanced, with special emphasis on ASW. Towards the end of the 1960s improved Petya-class frigates came into being. Redesignated as a separate Mirka class, they differed from the Petya class in dispensing with a conventional hull. Maximum speed in both classes was in excess of 34 knots.

In contrast to the Royal Navy, the US Navy was fairly slow in developing its modern frigate fleet. The first generation of frigates were conventional escorts, the Dealey, Courtney and Claud Jones classes, which, while highly seaworthy vessels, were insufficient in an ASW role. The second generation of frigates saw the Bronstein class come into service in the early 1960s. Armed with Asroc, two 3in guns and bow-mounted sonar, the Bronstein class was subsequently enlarged to become the Garcia class. Similar to the Garcias are the frigates of the Knox class which were built between 1965 and 1974. With a displacement of just over 3000 tons, the Knox class had a

Opposite page top: Fitted with four Sea Skua air-to-sea missiles, a Royal Navy Lynx helicopter hovers above its parent ship. Opposite centre: The operations room in the Type 21 frigate HMS *Amazon*, reflecting the complexity of modern naval weapons. Opposite below: HMS *Nubian*, a Type 81 frigate. Above: A Soviet Riga-class frigate in the Pacific. Right: A Soviet Petya II-class frigate tails HMS *Eagle* in the Mediterranean. Below: USS *Garcia*, a 3400-ton frigate armed with two 5in dual-purpose guns and an octuple Asroc anti-submarine launcher.

maximum speed of 27 knots and were armed with Sea Sparrow missiles, a 3in gun mounted forward, plus a comprehensive set of ASW weapons including ASROC. The latest American frigate class is the Oliver H. Perry which has a combined AAW/ASW capability which includes Asroc as well as the fast-firing Vulcan-Phalanx gun.

In the West a consensus in frigate design is beginning to emerge, which emphasises ASW tasks. A modern frigate might typically include the following features: for detection she will have hull-mounted sonars, both active and passive. Above this is the flightdeck for one or two helicopters which may have the capacity to deploy 'dunking' sonars and/or sonobuoys, together with MAD (magnetic anomaly detection) gear. For attack she will, ideally, have an anti-submarine stand-off weapon but the helicopter will probably be the primary delivery system.

For defence, the frigate may have a modern fire-and-forget SSM (surface-to-surface missile). If the target is at long range, the helicopter may be required for identification and mid-course correction. A point-defence SAM (surface-to-air missile), backed up by a close-in weapons system of rapid-fire guns working under fully-automatic control should, in theory at least, deal with enemy aircraft. A medium-calibre gun is usually added for greater flexibility in both offence and defence. A full range of electronics is required for surveillance, guidance and communication, with ECM (electronic countermeasures) to confuse hostile systems and ECCM (electronic counter-countermeasures) to confuse their attempts to confuse.

Regrettably, the combined limitations of size and cost allow for few ships to be fitted with the full range of desired equipment and action experience all too rapidly exposes deficiencies. Space has become less of a problem, however, since the gas turbine, sometimes in combination with the diesel, took the place of steam.

Two different elements of ASW: a 12 in quadruple mortar aboard a French Commandant Riviere-class frigate (below left) and a prototype Sikorsky SH-60B Seahawk helicopter undergoes ship trials (below). Bottom: The Knox-class frigate USS *Moinester* on patrol.

War in the Delta

US riverine operations in Vietnam

In 1965 more than eight million people – over half the total population of South Vietnam – lived in the Mekong Delta and over two-thirds of Saigon's essential food supplies came from the region's lush rice paddies. Yet it was here that the South Vietnamese communist movement had its deepest roots, based on a long tradition of peasant hostility to foreign economic exploitation and Saigon bureaucracy. If the South Vietnamese government was to stand any long-term chance of survival, it had to win control of the Delta population.

The Delta stretches south and west of Saigon, an area of 40,000 square km (15,000 square miles) bordered by the South China Sea on the east, the Gulf of Thailand on the west, and Cambodia to the north. As the Mekong flows south into Vietnam it splits into four major rivers, Song My Tho, Song Ham Luong, Song Co Chien and Song Hau Giang. Around and between these rivers, a network of over 2400km (1500 miles) of natural waterways and 4000km (2500 miles) of hand-dug canals provides an extensive system of communications. Most of the Delta is dotted with small hamlets and villages along the waterways, but not all the land is populous and fertile. Along the east and west coasts are dense mangrove swamps such as the Rung Sat, and bordering on Cambodia in the 'Parrot's Beak' region lies the Plain of Reeds, a flat desolate basin with no trees, covered with two or three metres of brackish water during the rainy season and dry as a bone for the rest of the year.

It was in the most fertile of all the Delta provinces, Kien Hoa, that one of the first revolts against French colonial domination took place (in 1940), and it was there that popular hostility to the South Vietnamese regime after 1954 was most widespread. But the level of Viet Cong activity in the Delta was initially low. The insurgents taxed local peasants for rice and received military supplies from the North by sea. Their strategy was essentially a waiting game – to build up credibility through strength. So they remained in base areas outside Saigon, along the Cambodian border, and in the mangrove swamps. In those instances when they chose to go on the offensive, they were extremely effective, brilliantly executing carefully planned and methodically rehearsed set-piece attacks on isolated government outposts and positions. In early 1963, they were able to demonstrate very effectively the success of this tactic by destroying a regular South Vietnamese infantry battalion at Ap Bac.

In 1964 Viet Cong strategy changed as they increased the number of offensive operations. Still working from isolated base areas, their attacks on government posts intensified in both size and scope. At the same time, they began a concentrated terrorist

Below: US troops aboard their patrol gunboat, known as a monitor, take advantage of a break in operations along the Mekong Delta. Note the heavily barred sides of the vessel, designed to deflect grenades and rockets. The creation of such specialised craft was indicative of the unusual demands of this part of the Vietnam War.

campaign against local officials. This strategy of selected offence and calculated intimidation was successful. By early 1965, while the government forces still controlled the large towns and major roads, the countryside and waterways belonged to the insurgents.

By 1965 the Viet Cong forces in the Delta had grown from a handful of revolutionaries in the mangroves of Kien Hoa to 80,000 insurgents, including 50,000 part-time guerrillas, organised into 28 separate battalions with three regimental headquarters. There were no North Vietnamese units in the Delta at this time; in fact, none would be present until after 1968.

Deployment in the Delta

Militarily, the South Vietnamese had established the Delta as IV Corps Tactical Zone, though the critical province of Long An immediately south of Saigon and the Rung Sat Special Zone to the east were in III Corps Tactical Zone. By 1965 three South Vietnamese regular infantry divisions had overall responsibility for the security of the Delta, the 7th in the north at My Tho, the 9th in the centre at Sa Dec, and the 21st in the south at Bac Lieu. There were also five Ranger battalions, one with each division plus two as corps reserve, and three armoured cavalry squadrons (in reality only mechanised infantry companies), one attached to each division. Local security was provided by Regional Forces companies in most districts and Popular Forces and Civilian Irregular Defense Groups (CIDGs) in scattered hamlets. The South Vietnamese Navy tried to police the inland waterways with a makeshift fleet of junks, while also maintaining six river assault groups consisting of ageing World War II landing craft for limited river offensives.

In spite of the increasing success of Viet Cong attacks in 1965, American and South Vietnamese officials agreed that the Delta war would continue to be solely a South Vietnamese responsibility. The critical factor was mutual concern to avoid American ground force operations in heavily populated areas.

Thus American influence was exercised primarily through the presence of 2700 advisers who worked at corps, province, division, battalion and district levels, and a lone US Army combat aviation battalion which provided helicopter support for South Vietnamese combat operations. The US Navy also got involved from 1966, combining with their South Vietnamese counterparts first to cut off resupply of the Viet Cong by sea (using Task Force 115, code-named Market Time) and then to break the Viet Cong stranglehold on the inland waterways (with Task Force 116, code-named Game Warden). In the rice

While US ground forces patrolled overland (above) riverine operations in the Delta required a variety of fast, light craft (right top, a Patrol Air Cushion Vehicle; right centre, a propeller-driven hydrofoil) while the coast also had to be thoroughly policed (right below, South Vietnamese search a peasant fishing vessel for smuggled arms).

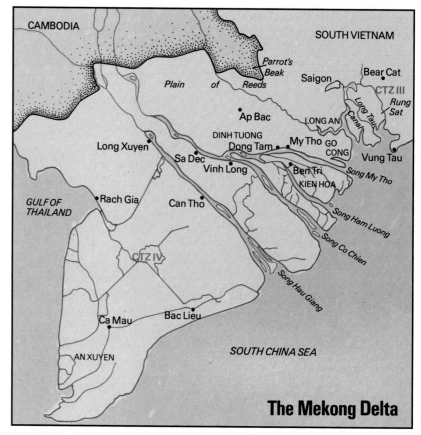

The Mekong Delta

paddies, the South Vietnamese ground forces relied upon one- and two-day multi-battalion sweeps into areas of suspected Viet Cong activity, supported by US helicopters. These operations were only marginally successful as Viet Cong agents gave insurgent units advanced warnings of pending attack, allowing them to slip away. Forays into well defended Viet Cong base areas along the Cambodian border and in the mangrove swamps were consciously avoided for fear of heavy casualties. There were a few South Vietnamese successes, but most patrols resulted in no enemy contact, and US advisers began to refer to them as 'walks in the sun'. Though the Viet Cong avoided contact with regular forces, they concentrated on attacks against Regional and Popular Forces and CIDG units, who were trapped in a static security role that made them extremely vulnerable to Viet Cong raids.

By mid-1966 US and South Vietnamese military chiefs could no longer afford to ignore the deteriorating situation in the Delta, where over one-third of all Viet Cong military actions were taking place. At least 25 per cent of the Delta's population was under the control of the insurgents – in the southern province of An Xuyen, only four per cent of the population lived under government control. But perhaps the most telling fact was that Viet Cong interdiction of the major lines of communication in the Delta had completely disrupted the shipment of rice to Saigon, and, for the first time, the South Vietnamese government had to import rice from abroad to feed the Saigon population. It was now painfully evident that the South Vietnamese military were no longer capable of containing the Viet Cong insurgency in the Delta, and officials in Saigon finally decided to commit American combat troops to the region.

Building 'Base Whiskey'

The initial problem for planners was where to station the American combat units. US officials were anxious to avoid contact with civilians, yet the Delta was densely populated. At the same time, they wanted combat troops to operate (like other American units in Vietnam) from camps close to enemy base areas. They also wished to have ready access to the major waterways. After close study, the Americans selected a sparsely populated area in Dinh Tuong province, immediately next to the Cam Song Secret Zone and on the My Tho River. The site was initially called 'Base Whiskey' but soon became known as Dong Tam, a Vietnamese word that meant 'united hearts and minds'. To provide solid ground on which to construct a base camp, hydraulic dredges were brought in to take sand from the bottom of the river and pump it into a 250 square hectare (600 square acre) rice paddy. Between August 1966 and November 1967, over 17 million cubic tons of fill was shifted from river bottom to rice paddy, creating out of nothing an encampment area capable of taking 12,500 men, with major naval and air facilities.

The unit assigned to the Delta was designated the 9th Infantry Division, the 'Old Reliables', although it was in fact a recently activated unit then undergoing pre-deployment training at Fort Riley, Kansas. The division had been tentatively slated to operate in Long An province, thus completing the American cordon around Saigon, but planners in late 1966 expanded this mission to include riverine operations.

Riverine operations posed a problem for US

Encounter in the Delta

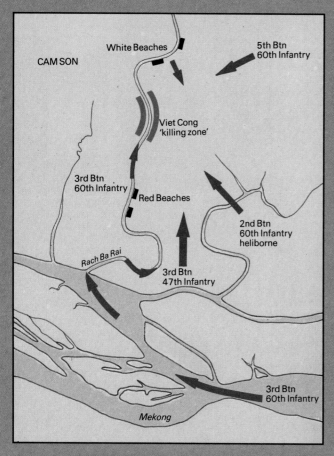

On 14 September 1967, the Mobile Riverine Force headquarters received intelligence reports of a strong Viet Cong presence along the Rach Ba Rai River near to the Cam Son Secret Zone. Despite the fact that the brigade had only just returned from a three-day operation against Viet Cong units, it was immediately mobilised to move against these freshly-located guerrilla concentrations.

The Viet Cong units were reported to be located at a bend in the river some 10km (6 miles) north of its confluence with the Mekong, on a west-facing salient. The US assault plan was to deploy the 3rd Battalion, 60th Infantry to the north of the salient, the 3rd Battalion, 47th Infantry to the south, and naval armoured troop carriers (ATCs) in a blocking position on the river itself; the 5th Battalion, 60th Infantry would advance overland from the east in M113 armoured personnel carriers (APCs), effectively closing the trap. Once the enemy was pinned down, airstrikes and a barrage of shelling from the Force's three artillery batteries would wipe them out. If a few Viet Cong units managed to break out across the river, it was assumed that the South Vietnamese 44th Ranger Battalion, operating independently on the west bank, would intercept their flight. The troops to be deployed north and south of the enemy were to be put ashore from ATCs, although this meant that the force moving into position to the north would actually have to pass along the river in front of the enemy units.

Moving along the Mekong

At 0415 hours on 15 September, the naval convoy carrying 3rd Battalion, 60th Infantry moved into the Mekong and proceeded west towards the junction with the Rach Ba Rai River, led by two empty ATCs acting as minesweepers. As well as ATCs, the convoy included a helicopter landing deck, a medical aid boat, a command boat, and gunboats (known as monitors) which mounted 20mm

guns, 40mm guns and 81mm direct-fire mortars.

At 0700 hours the convoy reached the Rach Ba Rai River and proceeded northwards towards the assault zone at a speed of approximately 13km/h (8mph). At 0730 hours, shortly after passing Red Beach, the landing zone for the southern blocking forces, the convoy came under sporadic smallarms fire. Almost immediately this was followed by an attack with an RPG-2 anti-tank rocket which hit the lead minesweeper. At that same moment the entire convoy came under fire, and responded immediately with all its armaments. The waterway was so narrow that the battle was joined at a range of little more than 30m (33 yards). The ambush was extremely well laid and the Americans found themselves in a Viet Cong 'killing zone' almost 1500m (1640 yards) long. The closeness of the Viet Cong positions made it difficult for the US troops to depress some of their larger calibre weapons far enough to engage the enemy.

Although the situation appeared hopeless, Colonel Doty (the commander of the 3rd Battalion) was convinced that the convoy would eventually break through the ambush and continue according to plan. Artillery fire was called in from two batteries of 105mm guns, but this had only limited success against the Viet Cong bunkers. Suddenly, in the midst of the battle, a boat broke through the ambush zone to the target beach for the northern landing; for a moment, it seemed that the whole convoy might get through. Almost simultaneously, however, at 0745 hours, the order was given to withdraw and reorganise at Red Beach, the southern assault point – the force had suffered heavy casualties and every one of the monitors and minesweepers had been hit.

South of the killing zone

As the shattered convoy reassembled south of the Viet Cong killing zone, events moved very quickly. By 0900 hours the second convoy transporting the 3rd Battalion, 47th Infantry had arrived with reinforcements and supplies. Fresh orders were received to resume the offensive. Two armed helicopters were brought in, and artillery was requested to saturate the area and 'walk' up the bank of the river just ahead of the convoy. Sixteen air strikes were also called in to napalm the Viet Cong positions. At 1000 hours the second attempt began, with the US forces packing considerably more firepower – though lacking the element of surprise.

As the convoy moved northwards towards White Beach (the proposed northern landing zone) it once again came under intense enemy fire. It eventually reached its objective, however, and quickly deployed men onto the beach, despite further heavy casualties. But it was not until 1200 hours that the separate units of the 3rd Battalion, 60th Infantry had linked up, as dense foliage and accurate enemy fire made establishing contact extremely difficult. At this point the plan was changed; all units were to go onto the offensive, instead of remaining in position as blocking groups. Furthermore, the 5th Battalion, 60th Infantry, pushing up from the east, was to be reinforced by the 2nd Battalion which would be deployed by helicopter. Two hundred metres (220 yards) inland from White Beach, the US troops finally broke from the dense cover onto open ground where they immediately fell prey to Viet Cong snipers. Despite the use of accurate artillery barrages to cover the advance, after several hours of battle the 3rd Battalion had only pushed 500m (550 yards) southward.

At 1700 hours Brigade ordered contact to be broken and defensive positions assumed. It was agreed that allowing the Viet Cong to escape was more acceptable than a possible defeat for the US units. In fact the Viet Cong made no attempt to penetrate the US defensive positions, but quietly slipped away under cover of darkness. As far as could be determined the cost of the battle was 79 Viet Cong killed and 130 US casualties, including seven dead.

military planners – the US Army's last experience of river warfare had been more than a century before in the American Civil War. However, the French Army had conducted riverine operations against the North Vietnamese in the Red River Delta during the early 1950s, and the American planners turned to this experience for guidance.

Quite obviously, the major waterways would have to be used and controlled, and this would require the development of specialised naval craft and their correct employment. The fight also had to be taken to the Viet Cong base areas, and this meant that the division would have to be mobile enough to conduct ground-combat operations from a maritime base. All this involved close coordination between the US Army and US Navy. The military planners decided that a brigade of two infantry battalions and one artillery battalion plus normal support units (there were three brigades in the 9th Division) was the proper size for this mobile maritime force.

Roaming the rivers

The Americans envisaged using the major rivers and canals to strike at the Viet Cong base areas, thus simultaneously breaking the insurgents' stranglehold on the waterways. Soldiers of the riverine brigade would live in barracks ships roaming the Delta rivers and canals as part of a maritime task force. Minesweepers would protect the ships from floating explosives. To attack Viet Cong base areas, the infantry would be transported into battle aboard armoured troop carriers, similar to those used in the South Pacific amphibious operations of World War II. Conventional fire support would be provided by armed gunboats, 'monitors', with 20mm and 40mm guns and 81mm mortars, and by 105mm and 155mm artillery fired from barges anchored to the river banks. Using 'hammer and anvil' tactics, multi-battalion sweeps in combination with other assault forces inserted by either helicopter or ground transportation would surround Viet Cong base areas and block possible escape routes. Such a complete seal was a manoeuvre that the South Vietnamese forces had never successfully employed.

A serious problem arose over command and control. While overall direction in Vietnam came from

US Military Assistance Command Vietnam (MACV), the US Army and Navy were separate elements under this headquarters. Functionally, therefore, the riverine force would have to be under the control of either the senior navy or army commander. But neither service would agree to this, so a compromise of 'mutual coordination and cooperation' was improvised.

In December 1966 initial elements of the US 9th Division arrived in Vietnam. With the Dong Tam base not yet ready, the division established a base at camp Bear Cat, east of Saigon. The 2nd Brigade,

Above: US troops adopt an all-round lookout as they cross a river in an Armoured Personnel Carrier. Below: A mixed Viet Cong assault group moves silently downriver in their canoes. Camouflaged and mounting a 7.62mm machine gun, these assault teams were difficult targets to locate. Bottom: Communist forces move onto the offensive.

which was tasked as the riverine brigade, married up with the US Navy and conducted a series of experimental exercises, known as Operation River Raider, in the upper Long Tau shipping channel and in the Rung Sat Special Zone between 16 February and 20 March 1967. After ironing out tactical questions, the brigade then moved to Dong Tam. The two other brigades were tasked to conduct operations in Long An and Hau Nghai provinces.

By 1966 the Viet Cong forces in the Delta were as well armed as those elsewhere in Vietnam. The new breed of 7.62mm Chinese-made weapons were well in evidence and indeed, as early as 1964, South Vietnamese troops had captured a number of AK-47s, SKS carbines, RPD light machine guns and RPG-2 anti-tank grenade launchers. Although their communications equipment was not of the highest quality, it was still adequate and allowed the Viet Cong to intrude onto the voice circuits of US and South Vietnamese transmissions. They were also willing to mount battalion-size attacks and several times demonstrated an ability to slog it out with government forces.

Re-opening the waterways

When the soldiers of the US riverine brigade first struck at enemy base areas, the Viet Cong chose to stand and fight. This proved to be a costly mistake as American firepower and mobility was overwhelming. Viet Cong losses were staggering and American confidence soared. Operation Coronado, a series of forays by the riverine forces into insurgent base areas in the northern portion of the Delta during the last six months of 1967, was spectacularly successful, killing over 1000 Viet Cong, disrupting the insurgency initiative, and re-opening the waterways. During the same period, the brigade of the division in Long An province launched a series of offensives against long-standing Viet Cong base areas in the Plain of Reeds. Again the insurgents chose to stand and fight and suffered heavy losses.

When the US military planners had decided to

commit the 9th Division to the Delta, they had envisaged a steady shift of operations to the south from the Dong Tam area. But events turned out differently. First, the Viet Cong reverted to their old strategy – when engaged by US forces, they would break contact immediately. Next, to counter US riverine mobility, they set deadly ambushes along the waterways deploying their newly-acquired RPGs in strength. As a result, US operations were largely confined to the northern Delta.

The planners and soldiers of the 9th Division also refined their approach to Delta warfare. Instead of brigade-controlled multi-battalion 'hammer and anvil' sweeps by riverine and heliborne troops, operations were now conducted by battalion and company. Soldiers took less equipment on operations to increase their mobility. The exploitation of intelligence was stressed as a means to achieve more contact with the enemy. Emphasis was now placed on airmobile operations. The 9th Division perfected the tactics of 'jitterbugging' – multiple helicopter insertions of small units – and 'seal-and-pile-on', where small

Above: A South Vietnamese soldier keeps the occupants of a small craft covered with his machine gun as a marsh patrol boat approaches suspected Viet Cong smugglers.

Below: A US monitor gunboat, mounting 20mm and 40mm guns as well as an 81mm direct-fire mortar, escorts two armoured troop carriers.

Top: A command and communications boat (CCB) pulls into a riverside village during search and destroy operations. Above: Men of a US infantry patrol from the 2nd Brigade, 9th Infantry, stand guard over a group of Vietnamese peasants suspected of Viet Cong activities, during Operation Concordia Six, a sweep in the Long Tau river.

units developed a situation and then reinforcements were quickly inserted. Ground units conducted platoon and squad patrols known as 'checkerboarding' by day and 'bushmastering' at night. Emphasis was placed on night ambushes and sniper attacks to harass the weary insurgents. A chronic problem for US troops which severely limited sustained operations, however, was 'immersion foot' to which the Americans proved very susceptible. They were not able to operate in the mud of rice paddies and the water of canals for longer than 72 hours without suffering fungus growth on their feet. As a result units had to

stand down every three days to 'dry out' for 24 hours.

The turning point in the Delta war was the Tet offensive, begun in February 1968. The Viet Cong seized the major Delta towns of My Tho, Vinh Long, Can Tho and Ben Tri – a tactic repeated simultaneously throughout South Vietnam. The 9th Division found itself engaged in vicious street fighting before the Viet Cong were finally driven back into the countryside after suffering heavy casualties.

Viet Cong losses appear to have fundamentally affected the military balance in the Delta. In the second half of 1968, with the whole of 9th Division now stationed at the completed Dong Tam base, the Americans were able to shift emphasis to pacification operations, designed to break up Viet Cong political organisation and winkle out guerrillas in densely populated areas. In Operation Speedy Express, the riverine brigade moved to Kien Hoa and Go Cong provinces. The 3rd Brigade continued operations in Long An province, while the 1st Brigade concentrated on securing the portion of Route 4 in Dinh Duong province during Operation People's Road.

When President Richard Nixon announced the beginning of US troop withdrawals in mid-1969, it came as no surprise that the first divisional-sized unit listed for return to the United States was the 9th Division. The Vietnam War was changing from a conflict with guerrilla forces embedded in the local population to a more conventional struggle against the North Vietnamese Army. Distant from North Vietnamese influence, the Delta was becoming one of the easier areas of South Vietnam to defend.

In August 1969 the 9th Division turned over control of Dong Tam base to the 7th Vietnamese Division and possession of the specialised riverine equipment to the Vietnamese Navy and Marines, and began a phased return home, leaving the 3rd Brigade, who had had most experience, gradually to hand over full control to the South Vietnamese. This ended American combat involvement in the Delta war. Viet Cong insurgency had been effectively checked.

Alexander S. Cochran Jr

Road to Victory
The Ho Chi Minh Trail

The Ho Chi Minh Trail, a network of roads and paths running down the spine of the Annamite mountain chain in eastern Laos, was North Vietnam's major military supply route into South Vietnam. Its operation was a miracle of human endurance, courage and organisation, under the direction of General Vo Nguyen Giap, a master of the logistic element of war.

The region through which the Ho Chi Minh Trail passed contained some of the most inhospitable terrain and impenetrable jungle found anywhere in the world. Mountains rose steeply from narrow swampy valleys, reaching a thousand metres or more in height, their sides made permanently slippery by rotting vegetation, to reach needle-sharp peaks and razor-backed ridges or miniature peaks which thrust up like jagged teeth. Everywhere there was double canopy vegetation – dense growth composed of thick stands of bamboo and wild banana laced together by a tangle of vines, the whole covered by the branches of tall tropical trees – offering perfect concealment to users of the Trail. The rainy season, May to October, brought torrential downpours. The strongest memory retained by many who travelled the Trail is of the rainfall; diaries of early infiltrators captured in the South contained page after page of description of the rain in Laos, 'this land cursed by geography' as one writer expressed it.

The journey down the Trail was both arduous and dangerous. Casualty rates throughout the war averaged about 10 per cent. Death came from malaria (at least 50 per cent of all infiltrators in the early days contracted malaria), dysentery, accidents and, from 1964, US air attacks. Yet the Trail never ceased to function.

It was after the May 1959 decision of the North Vietnamese leadership to back armed struggle in the South that it became evident a supply system would be needed. While the insurgents in the South were expected to be generally self-supporting, they would require some personnel and essential equipment not available locally. Hanoi's Central Military Committee consequently established two complementary logistic support groups: the first, Group 559 (its name derived from the date of its formation, May 1959), was to set up and run an overland supply system, the Ho Chi Minh Trail; the second, Group 759 (formed July 1959), was to operate a fleet of coastal vessels smuggling personnel and supplies, mostly into the southernmost tip of South Vietnam. The first Group 759 vessel, the *Phuong Dong 1*, arrived off the Ca Mau peninsula on 14 September 1962 and safely discharged its cargo. In the following years, according to official communist estimates, shipments totalled about 5000 tons per year. However, later in the war, when the US and South Vietnam had established the coastal surveillance system known as Market Time, and particularly after 1970 when Prince Norodom Sihanouk closed Cambodia's port of Sihanoukville (later Kompong Som) to North Vietnamese shipping, this sea infiltration route withered, and the

communists were forced to rely completely on the Ho Chi Minh Trail.

Hanoi's use of Laos as a transit route had its origin in the 1954 Geneva Agreements. While these Agreements were imprecise and vague on many key issues, they were crystal clear in defining as a violation any North Vietnamese military passage across the demilitarized zone (DMZ) that separated North and South Vietnam at the 17th parallel. This meant that, if Hanoi was to observe the conditions of the Geneva Agreements, the only way to get men and supplies into the South by land had to be through Laos, bypassing the DMZ. The 1962 Agreements on Laos, to which North Vietnam was also a party, called for all sides to respect Laotian neutrality, but this Hanoi chose to ignore.

As a transport system, the Ho Chi Minh Trail can be said to have begun at the China border or the Haiphong docks and ended in the communist-dominated areas just outside Saigon, a distance of more than 1600km (1000 miles). The jumping-off points for personnel headed South were at the 'infiltration training camps' of Xuan Mai, outside Hanoi, and Thanh Hoa; the major staging areas for military shipments south were at Vinh and the ports of Dong Hoi and Quang Khe. In a stricter sense, the Trail began at the mountain passes between Vietnam and Laos, Mu Gia and Ban Karai, and ended at one of the four major

entry points in South Vietnam – the three mountain provinces of Kontum, Pleiku and Darlac, and further south (through Cambodia), the border province of Tay Ninh.

The Trail was not a single route, and certainly never the broad straight superhighway conjured up by some writers early in the war. Rather it was a carefully designed network that zig-zagged and criss-crossed within a rectangular mountain corridor that varied from a few hundred metres (at the passes) to about 50km (30 miles) wide, and was 1000-1300km (600-800 miles) long. One helicopter pilot observed: 'The Ho Chi Minh Trail does not look like the Pennsylvania Turnpike. It looks like a plate of spaghetti.'

Above: Communist supply trucks, using platform-mounted camouflage, move slowly down the Ho Chi Minh Trail.

Far left above: The Annamite mountain range in eastern Laos. Despite the inhospitable nature of the terrain, dense jungle, torrential rain and sheer rockfaces, the communist forces used this isolated region for the transport of enormous amounts of war material along the Ho Chi Minh Trail. Far left below: Hundreds of North Vietnamese trucks streaming down the Trail into South Vietnam are photographed by a reconnaissance aircraft.

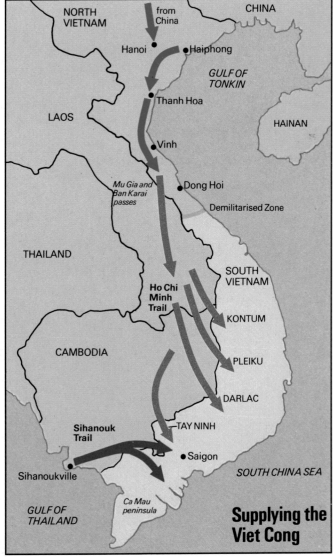

Supplying the Viet Cong

Left: An anti-aircraft battery is wheeled into place to protect construction work on a damaged bridge along the Trail. The engineering battalions of the NVA displayed enormous tenacity in their attempts to maintain the Trail throughout the campaign, despite continual US bombing.

Below: A rare success for the US forces: burnt out North Vietnamese trucks after an air raid against a convoy. Note the erratic spread of bomb craters around the track.

Within this corridor were, at a conservative estimate, some 5500km (3500 miles) of parallel routes that made up the Ho Chi Minh Trail. They ranged from reasonably good roadways to almost impassable tracks, and included some 30 rivers and navigable streams, 10 of which formed an integral part of the Trail.

Construction work on the Trail began in 1959. Initially the route consisted of crude paths, with about 100 way stations a day's march apart. Such marches ranged from 20–30km (12–20 miles) depending on terrain. As the Trail was improved, the 100 initial way stations were consolidated to only 12, each with extensive facilities: underground offices and storage bunkers, infirmaries, repair shops, classrooms and living quarters. At first the way stations serviced small groups of personnel: cadres, couriers bearing documents and guerrilla war textbooks, and southern 'regroupees', persons who had moved North in the mid-1950s and now were being infiltrated back into South Vietnam. Early logistics shipments consisted of modest quantities of weapons, ammunition, medical supplies and communications equipment, often carried by bicycle carts, animals and porters.

The big Trail build-up, in facilities and use, did not come until 1969 with the advent of a high-technology strategy in the South and the abandonment of guerrilla war. The North Vietnamese Army (NVA), which took over the fighting in the South from the decimated Viet Cong, required vastly increased numbers of men and huge amounts of war supplies. Construction work and maintenance, originally in the hands of local Laotians and Montagnards, was transferred to NVA engineering battalions using a full array of modern road-building and construction equipment. Separate units began laying an oil pipeline – completed in about 1973 – parallel to the Trail.

The size of Group 559 grew accordingly – from an initial force of several hundred in 1959 to one numbering about 50,000 late in the war. This was in addition to an estimated 50,000 NVA engineering troops and others permanently assigned to construction and maintenance work. There were also eventually some 12,000 NVA anti-aircraft artillerymen defending the Trail against air attacks.

One method for detecting the presence of personnel or vehicles along the Trail was through the use of seismic detection sensors (above) which were dropped into the foliage from aircraft. Another was the defoliation (inset below, a C-123 sprays jungle with Agent Orange defoliant) of large areas of forest surrounding the Trail (bottom, communist trucks advance through a defoliated area).

Transit time in the early years was about six months, which included periodic 'rest days' to recuperate from the debilitating effects of the arduous journey. By the mid-1960s this travel time had been cut to three months; by the early 1970s to five weeks, if high priority was assigned. By the end of the war in 1975, the Trail could be covered in a mere 10 days.

The 12 major way stations became storage facilities in addition to stopover points. Few shipments went the entire route in a single through-trip; more commonly, material was shuttled from station to station over a period of months. Each move involved painstaking efforts to sort and arrange the goods in anticipation of use in future offensives. This practice was in part dictated by the weather, transport being easier during the dry season (November to the end of April). The storage-shuttle-storage system also meant there was little connection between the level of Trail traffic and the possibility of launching military offensives. US intelligence experts in the early days attempted to predict offensives on the basis of supply build-ups, but soon realised that an offensive was often launched without prior build-up, or that heavy traffic on the Trail was not necessarily followed by a major campaign.

Trail of destruction

Duty on the Trail, for Group 559 personnel as well as for those moving down it, grew increasingly perilous with the start of US air attacks in May 1965. Most feared were the B-52 bombers flying out of Guam; their devastating bomb loads were delivered from so high that the people on the ground had no warning of their approach. Then again, helicopter gunships would suddenly appear above the treetops, unloading their miniguns and rocket pods, and large areas of the Trail were defoliated by chemical sprays, leaving a spectral forest stripped of leaves. About two million tons of bombs were dropped on the Trail during the war, a quarter of the total of bombs dropped in the whole Vietnam conflict, and it is probably safe to estimate that US air strikes destroyed from 15 to 20 per cent of the cargo that started down the Trail.

The Trail's air defences were considerable, employing about 1000 anti-aircraft weapons in some 150 gun battery complexes. These included 23mm, 37mm, and 100mm guns as well as surface-to-air missiles. About 15 per cent of total US air losses during the war occurred over the Trail. The NVA also employed various clever passive defence measures – camouflage, decoy truck convoys (using false headlights), fake supply dumps to draw enemy fire, and repair work rigged to appear incomplete (for instance, a bridge over a stream which had been bombed would be rebuilt just beneath the water surface, thus appearing from the air to be still out of commission).

The US also made extensive use of sophisticated technology in an attempt to shut down or at least sharply reduce Trail traffic. Conventional surveillance techniques were still used – long-range infiltration teams composed of Montagnards were sent in from Vietnam to camp on the mountain peaks overlooking the Trail and count passing trucks, radioing the data back to headquarters each morning – but they were augmented by an astonishing range of surveillance devices. Air-dropped sensors that burrowed into the ground or hung in the trees were able to pick up voices dozens of metres away and truck motors hundreds of metres distant. Small inconspicuous

sensors called 'buttons' were dropped into the ankle-deep ground vegetation and emitted a short burst of radio signal when stepped on or kicked. Overhead, planes circled as their computers sorted out and analysed this flow of radio signals. Starlight, a super television camera that could pick up and intensify a millionfold the smallest light source on the ground, even a lit cigarette, was fitted on C-123 cargo planes circling the Trail area. Extensive use was also made of infra-red photography which, because of heat differential, could detect tunnels, camouflage, even a hot truck engine through foliage. This sort of surveillance clearly did have some effect in bringing in bomber attacks on target, but it never accomplished any major reduction in traffic along the Trail.

US Army commanders were convinced that only by sending in large-scale ground forces could the flow of men and equipment down the Trail be stopped, but until 1971 this was ruled out for fear of escalating the conflict. The South Vietnamese Army did occupy portions of the Trail for several months in early 1971, but the operation could not be sustained. US Special Forces carried out ambush patrols against the Trail throughout the years of US involvement in Vietnam, but these efforts were later judged to have been generally unsuccessful.

To sustain the guerrilla war of the early 1960s, communist military forces in the South needed only about 60 tons of war material a day – about 20 truckloads. Changed strategy altered these requirements. By the late 1960s Soviet freighters at Haiphong were discharging about 160,000 tons of cargo a day – weapons, vehicles, petroleum, food – much of it destined for the South. Tonnage transported on the Trail rose accordingly, from about 100 tons a week in 1963 to about 400 a week in 1965 and to over 10,000 tons a week by 1970. In the 1969-73 period, the Americans estimated an average of 2000 to 3000 trucks were on the Trail at any one time, although there were great variations. For instance, in December 1970 a one-day aerial surveillance of the whole length of the corridor revealed nearly 15,000 trucks and vehicles on the Trail. North Vietnamese General Van Tien Dung said after the war that 10,000 trucks were used in the 1974–75 logistics effort prior to the final battle.

Of course, much of the cargo was consumed by those who operated the Trail. Even late in the war it was estimated that to sustain the Trail operation, Group 559 required 10 tons of supplies to deliver one ton.

Movement of personnel also rose sharply from 1969. An estimated 1800 persons used the Trail in 1959, most of them assigned to Group 559. In the early 1960s the infiltration rate was around 5000 per year. Then it rose steadily and sharply in the early 1970s when, as General Dung put it later, 'a river of revolutionary forces' moved down the Trail. In all probability a million people travelled down the Ho Chi Minh Trail, over a third of them to their deaths.

Clearly, throughout the war the Trail played a central role in Hanoi's strategy; without it, the war could not have been won. The Group 559 staff, engineers and drivers who kept the supplies flowing are celebrated as heroes in today's communist Vietnam, and with good reason, for the Trail represented an outstanding organisational accomplishment in the face of overwhelming natural obstacles and intensive enemy attack. **Douglas Pike**

Junction City
On the offensive in War Zone C

Between March and December 1966 the number of US military personnel committed to South Vietnam escalated from some 215,000 to 385,000, allowing for the first time in the war a major sustained offensive against the Viet Cong strongholds north of Saigon in III Corps Tactical Zone. In May 1966 General William C. Westmoreland directed Lieutenant-General Seaman, commanding II Field Force Vietnam, to initiate plans for an extensive operation in War Zone C where the 9th Viet Cong Division was active. From the outset the planners realised the crucial role that intelligence would play and in November 'pattern-activity analysis' of the area began. This involved the minute plotting on maps of information gathered from a wide range of sources including aerial reconnaissance, ground-patrol reports, details of arms and supply caches uncovered and captured documents. As the data poured in a general picture of Viet Cong locations and movements emerged, providing the basis for both overall and day-to-day operational planning.

Operation Junction City had been planned to begin on 8 January 1967 but it was decided to hold back the operation until the imminent commitment of the 9th Infantry Division to South Vietnam had been effected. Also, the results of pattern-activity analysis in War Zone C suggested the need for a preliminary operation against the Iron Triangle and the Thanh Dinh Forest area immediately to the south. General Westmoreland thus postponed Junction City until late February and scheduled the Iron Triangle operation, Cedar Falls, for 8 January. Operation Cedar Falls was the first multi-divisional operation of the war and some 15,000 US and South Vietnamese troops were involved. Despite the capture of substantial quantities of weapons and food supplies and the killing of 750 Viet Cong during the extensive search and destroy operations, the Viet Cong were again active in the Iron Triangle within a week of the operation's completion at the end of January. Junction City, however, was to be a far more ambitious operation, involving more than 25,000 US and South Vietnamese troops over a much larger area and time-scale.

One of the problems facing the planners of such an operation was keeping the main objective a secret during the positioning of forces and the massive logistic build-up. To this

Above: Trussed and bound, Viet Cong prisoners await interrogation after Operation Junction City. Despite the magnitude of the operation, which involved some 25,000 US and South Vietnamese troops, only 34 communist prisoners were captured.

Left: With parachutes blossoming as far as the eye can see, 845 members of the 173rd Airborne Division drop into War Zone C, making the largest US combat jump since the Korean War and opening the airborne offensive of Operation Junction City.

end, two smaller and seemingly unrelated operations, code-named Gadsden and Tucson, were devised to look like routine search and destroy missions, so as not to arouse enemy suspicions and trigger off large-scale Viet Cong force redeployments. Operation Gadsden involved the US 3rd Brigade, 4th Infantry Division and the 196th Light Infantry Brigade in the area around Lo Go and Xom Giua, close to the Cambodian border. Intelligence reports suggested that Lo Go was a major supply-distribution centre for Viet Cong units operating out of Cambodia and that the area would reveal large supply and ammunition caches, base camps and hospital and training facilities. The 19-day operation, launched on 3 February, went as planned, involving a combination of airmobile and mechanised battalion attacks against the Viet Cong who consistently employed small-unit guerrilla tactics. By 21 February the two brigades had counted 161 Viet Cong dead and captured large quantities of supplies and war material, but more importantly, they had taken up blocking positions in the area along Route 22 to the extreme west of War Zone C. Similarly, Operation Tucson, launched on 14 February, allowed the 1st and 3rd Brigades of the 1st Infantry Division (The Big Red One) to position their forces in the eastern sector of the Zone under the disguise of search and destroy missions against the Viet Cong storage areas and base camps 16km (10 miles) to the south of Minh Tanh. On 18 February search and destroy activity ceased, and the two brigades prepared for the opening phase of Junction City proper.

Phase One focused on the area between Route 4 which ran north from Tay Ninh, and the Cambodian border which bounded the area 16km (10 miles) to the west and in the north. At 0813 hours on 22 February the 1st Brigade, 1st Division began with a three-

battalion assault along Route 246, initiating what was to be a nine-battalion airmobile attack to cordon off the whole northern side of the area. At 0900 hours, 845 paras of the 173rd Airborne made the largest US combat jump since the Korean War 3km (two miles) north of Katum, while a further three battalions of the 25th Infantry and two battalions of the 173rd Airborne landed in the northwest and northeast of the area respectively. Meanwhile, since 0630 hours, ground units of the 3rd Brigade, 1st Division had been pushing north up Route 4, eventually linking up with the 173rd Airborne at 1500 hours just south of Katum. With the forces deployed during Operation Gadsden blocking the west, the 1st Brigade, 1st Division in the north, and the 173rd Airborne and 3rd Brigade on Route 4 in the east, 18 battalions and 13 mutually supporting firebases were poised in a horseshoe formation around the area.

The next few days of Phase One called for the combined 2nd Brigade, 25th Infantry Division and the 11th Armored Cavalry Regiment to drive north into the open end of the horseshoe, trapping Viet Cong forces inside, while searching out the Central Office of South Vietnam (COSVN) headquarters. Around the horseshoe the various forces improved their defensive positions and conducted search and destroy operations, during which a unit of the 1st Brigade, 1st Division uncovered a series of camps belonging to the military affairs section of the COSVN. Generally, contact with the Viet Cong was limited to small unit (under 10 men) firefights until the morning of 28 February when Company B, 1st Battalion, 16th Infantry left their night defensive position on Route 4 to carry out a search and destroy sweep eastwards. At 1030 hours, lead elements of the unit, which were slowly making their way through thick

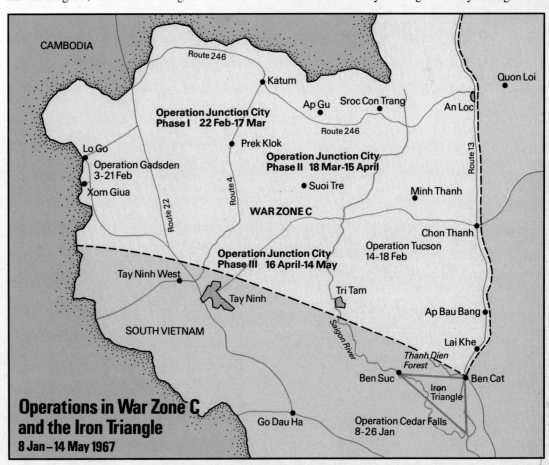

Operations in War Zone C and the Iron Triangle
8 Jan – 14 May 1967

CAMBODIA

Route 246

Katum

Ap Gu   Sroc Con Trang   An Loc

Quon Loi

Operation Junction City Phase I   22 Feb-17 Mar

Route 246

Lo Go

Prek Klok

Operation Junction City Phase II   18 Mar-15 April

Operation Gadsden 3-21 Feb

Xom Giua

Suoi Tre

Minh Thanh

Route 22

Route 4

WAR ZONE C

Chon Thanh

Route 13

Operation Junction City Phase III   16 April-14 May

Operation Tucson 14-18 Feb

Tay Ninh West

Tri Tam

Tay Ninh

Ap Bau Bang

SOUTH VIETNAM

Saigon River

Lai Khe

Thanh Dien Forest

Ben Suc   Ben Cat

Iron Triangle

Go Dau Ha

Operation Cedar Falls 8-26 Jan

jungle in two columns, ran into a large Viet Cong force on its way to ambush US convoys on Route 4. An intense battle ensued with the Viet Cong firing from well-camouflaged positions on the ground and in the trees. The air force was called in, dropping cluster bombs at treetop level, while supporting artillery pounded the immediate area. Although at one point the company was almost completely surrounded, the Americans' superior firepower wore down the Viet Cong until they retreated in mid-afternoon.

End of Phase One

A further large battle was fought at Prek Klok by the 2nd Battalion (Mechanised), 2nd Infantry at a fire support base (FSB) where engineers were building a Special Forces Camp and an airstrip. The Viet Cong attacked the battalion's positions at night with heavy mortars, recoilless rifles and RPG-2 anti-tank weapons. After an opening half-hour barrage, two battalions of the 272nd Regiment, 9th Viet Cong Division launched a ground assault against the base which by now had called for a massive sweeping artillery attack from three nearby FSBs, the services of a C-47 minigun-armed gunship, and some 100 airstrikes with bombs, rockets and 20mm cannon fire. After an hour of heavy fighting the Viet Cong assault began to falter and by morning they had lost some 160 men. Phase One of the operation continued until 17 March, by which time a COSVN psychological propaganda office and large quantities of supplies had been uncovered during the numerous search and destroy operations carried out in the area.

Although Phase Two was not due to begin until 18 March, numerous redeployments had been effected earlier in the month in the eastern sector of the Zone. A bridge had been built over the Saigon River at its junction with Route 246, and the 1st Brigade, 1st Division had opened and improved the road between Sroc Con Trang and An Loc. To the south the 1st Brigade, 9th Division had opened Route 13 between Lai Khe and An Loc. During Phase Two, which lasted 29 days, intensive search and destroy operations were mounted in the area north of Minh Thanh between Routes 13 and 4. Most of the action was confined to platoon-size engagements with the exception of three major battles fought on 19 and 21 March and 1 April.

On 19 March a troop of the 3rd Squadron, 5th Cavalry Regiment, deployed at an FSB just outside Ap Bau Bang, came under attack from the 2nd and 3rd Battalions, 273rd Regiment, 9th Viet Cong Division. As at Prek Klok the combination of cluster munitions, canister rounds and napalm decimated the Viet Cong. Further north on 21 March, at Suoi Tre, two battalions which had air-landed to establish an FSB came under a massive assault from the 272nd Regiment, 9th Viet Cong Division. Heavy fighting broke out, with the Viet Cong getting within hand-grenade range of a battalion command post. Two and a half hours after the battle had begun, relief armoured units arrived and the Viet Cong withdrew leaving over 640 dead.

The final major battle of Phase Two was fought at Ap Gu, north of Route 246, on 1 April. Again, the Viet Cong attacked in force following a heavy softening-up bombardment with mortars and the fighting was ferocious to the point of hand-to-hand combat. Cluster bombs were dropped within 30m (33 yards) of the Americans' own positions and the surrounding woods were strafed with minigun and rocket fire from helicopter gunships. Two B-52 bomber strikes were made on enemy withdrawal routes as the Viet Cong broke contact and withdrew with heavy casualties.

Towards the end of Phase Two, contact with the Viet Cong had become steadily sparser but in view of success in some areas of the operation a third phase was initiated by the 3rd Brigade, 4th Division in the lower western sector of the Zone around Tay Ninh. On 21 April, five days after the start of Phase Three, 1st Brigade, 9th Division with a company of tanks and the South Vietnamese 36th Ranger Battalion assumed the 3rd Brigade's mission and continued operations. Viet Cong units were now almost impossible to locate and three weeks later, on 14 May, Operation Junction City was wound up.

Since 22 February over 2700 Viet Cong had been killed, but although some one and a half million pages of documents were captured, the operation had been far from a complete success. The COSVN had been subjected to severe disruption, its forces being made to withdraw into Cambodia, but, as in the case of Cedar Falls, the US and South Vietnamese forces did not have the strength to maintain their hold on the area as the units involved were required for redeployment elsewhere. General Westmoreland had hoped to retain a brigade for further operations in the western sector of War Zone C but it was soon needed in the north of the country, and as the units withdrew reconnaissance revealed that the Viet Cong were again moving into the areas so recently swept.

Jonathan Reed

Above: A US infantry unit, including sniffer dogs, moves in tactical 'file' formation along a recently cut trail as they pursue enemy units during Operation Junction City.

Key Weapons

SOVIET BOMBERS

In 1945, prompted by American development of the atomic bomb, Stalin ordered the development of a Russian equivalent. Aided by information from a number of 'atom spies', the Soviet Union exploded its first nuclear weapon in September 1949. But the development of a suitable delivery system was a much greater problem, for although the story of Russian strategic bombers had stretched back to 1914, Soviet air doctrine up to World War II had been primarily concerned with the support of ground operations.

In the years immediately after World War II, the Soviet aircraft industry proved incapable of producing a bomber with truly intercontinental range which could attack America, lacking as it did any experience in the key technologies necessary for the production of such an aircraft. Soviet access to the advanced aeronautical research being carried out in Germany at the time of her defeat helped greatly and not for the first time Russian designers proved to be quick learners. Just how quick was shown by the appearance of the Tupolev Tu-4 (Nato code-name Bull) strategic bomber at the Tushino air display of August 1947. Even more surprising was the fact that the Tu-4 was not a Russian design but an American one, for it was quite simply a copy of the Boeing B-29.

The story of the Tu-4 is one of the most ironic in aviation history and began in July 1944 with the arrival on Soviet soil of a US 20th Air Force B-29, damaged while bombing Japan. Between this date and the end of the war with Japan, two more Superfortresses were acquired in the same manner, none of which was returned to the American authorities. On Stalin's direct order, the Tupolev design group dismantled the aircraft and then began the arduous task of producing a production airframe. In its day, the B-29 was one of the most complex warplanes in existence and it says much for the Soviet engineers that they got a prototype into the air in only three years.

The first operational Tu-4s were delivered to the strategic arm of the air force, the DA (Dal'naya Aviatsiya – the Long Range Aviation), in mid-1949 and by the end of the year 300 such aircraft were in service. The Tu-4 represented the first real nuclear threat to the American heartland, for it could reach Chicago, Los Angeles and New York with a worthwhile weapons load. Although such raids would have been suicidal for the crews, who would never make it back to friendly territory, such sacrifices were not unknown in the Soviet military and the threat posed by the Bull was taken very seriously.

The quest for greater range led the design groups Tupolev and Myasishchev to begin work on potential replacements for the Tu-4. Two prototypes appeared during 1949: the Tupolev Tu-80 and the Myasishchev DVB-202, both of which were based on the Tu-4.

In the event, both types were overtaken by international developments. The appearance of the American B-36, with its ability to reach targets over the whole of the developed area of the Soviet Union, and the deterioration of East-West relations made it imperative that the USSR should have a similarly wide-ranging delivery system as quickly as possible. Neither the Tu-80 nor the DVB-202 offered the necessary performance and both were dropped. Tupolev returned to the drawing-board and produced the Tu-85, the USSR's last piston-engined warplane, which appeared in 1951. Essentially a scaled-up Tu-80, the Tu-85 offered a range of 8850km (5500 miles) with a 5000kg (11,023lb) bomb load. Impress-

ive as these figures were, the Tu-85 fell short of requirements. Its shortcomings were emphasised when it became obvious that such a bomber could not survive the new breed of American interceptors and the arrival of the Boeing B-47 turbojet bomber rendered the concept of a piston-engined aircraft obsolete at a stroke.

The application of jet engines to the bomber brought about a massive leap forward in performance, a point not lost on Soviet designers. Ever since the end of World War II they had been working on the development of both jet and turboprop engines, helped in no small part by a large number of captive German engineers and the supply by Britain of a number of Nene turbojets in 1947.

In view of these factors it is not surprising that the Tu-85 was abandoned in favour of the development of the jet-powered Tu-88 and turboprop Tu-95 bombers. The Tu-88 first flew in 1952 and entered service with the DA in 1954 as the Tu-16 (Nato code-name Badger). The Tu-16 retained numerous elements of the Tu-85 mated to a new swept wing carrying two massive 9500kg (20,950lb) thrust Mikulin AM-3M turbojets at the roots. These engines gave the Badger a performance similar to that of the B-47 and the type remained in production until the mid-1960s. The usefulness of the Tu-16 can be gauged from the fact that some 700 such aircraft are estimated still to be in service, 300 of them operated by the DA.

Some 12 variants of the basic Tu-16 design have been identified, three of which appear to be specific to the DA. The first of these, known in the West as Badger-A, was the initial production model configured for the delivery of free-fall conventional and nuclear bombs. This basic airframe later surfaced as the Badger-G and GMod which are equipped to carry two large stand-off missiles below the wings. The G is armed with either AS-5 Kelt land attack/anti-shipping missiles or the later AS-6 Kingfish weapon, while the GMod carries the AS-6 only. The DA's current Badgers can operate against both land and sea targets and, according to the US Department of Defense, represent a 'significant theatre strike capability'.

While Tupolev worked on the Tu-16, Myasishchev was busy with the USSR's first jet-powered strategic bomber, the M-4 (Nato code-name Bison). This new bomber was an impressive shoulder-wing design powered by four 8700kg (19,180lb) thrust Mikulin AM-3 turbojets. In the event, it proved short on range and was little used after its entry into service

Previous page: A Soviet Tu-20 Bear photographed over the North Sea while shadowing Nato forces during the September 1974 exercise Northern Merger. Above: The Tu-4 Bull, the Soviet copy of the US B-29, provided the DA with its first long-range nuclear delivery system.

Opposte Page. Top: A Tu-16 Badger keeps a watchful eye on Nato naval forces engaged in exercise Ocean Safari in 1975. Centre above left: A belly view of the Tu-16 which clearly shows the two massive wing-root-mounted AM-3M turbojets. Centre above right: A nose view of the Tu-16 showing the two AS-5 Kelt missiles mounted below the wings. Centre below: A Soviet-built Egyptian Tu-16 photographed by a reconnaissance aircraft from the American attack carrier USS Shangri-La on Nato exercise Dawn Patrol in the Mediterranean in 1969. Bottom: An AVMF (Soviet Naval Aviation) Tu-16 on long-range maritime reconnaissance. Admiral Gorshkov's naval-expansion programme of the 1960s included a steady transference of Tu-16s from the DA to the AVMF where they became the AVMF's first missile-carrying aircraft.

Tu-16 (Badger-A)

Type Seven-man heavy bomber
Dimensions Span 32.93m (108ft ½in); length
34.8m (114ft 2in); height 10.8m (35ft 5in)
Weight Empty 37,000kg (81,570lb); maximum
take-off 72,000kg (158,730lb)
Powerplant Two 9500kg (20,950lb) thrust Mikulin
AM-3M turbojets

Performance Maximum speed 945km/h (587mph)
at 9000m (30,000ft)
Range Approx 4800km (2980 miles)

Ceiling 13,000m (42,650ft)
Armament Seven 23mm NR-23 cannon; up to
9000kg (19,180lb) of free-fall conventional or
nuclear weapons

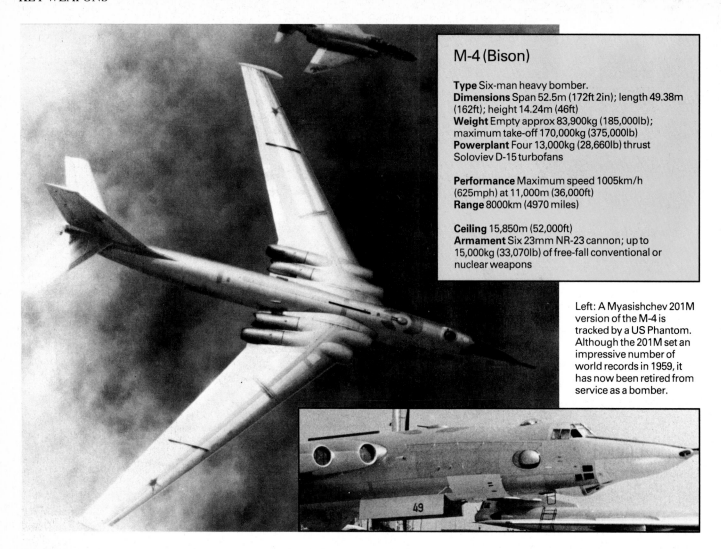

M-4 (Bison)

Type Six-man heavy bomber.
Dimensions Span 52.5m (172ft 2in); length 49.38m (162ft); height 14.24m (46ft)
Weight Empty approx 83,900kg (185,000lb); maximum take-off 170,000kg (375,000lb)
Powerplant Four 13,000kg (28,660lb) thrust Soloviev D-15 turbofans

Performance Maximum speed 1005km/h (625mph) at 11,000m (36,000ft)
Range 8000km (4970 miles)

Ceiling 15,850m (52,000ft)
Armament Six 23mm NR-23 cannon; up to 15,000kg (33,070lb) of free-fall conventional or nuclear weapons

Left: A Myasishchev 201M version of the M-4 is tracked by a US Phantom. Although the 201M set an impressive number of world records in 1959, it has now been retired from service as a bomber.

Above: The M-4 Bison C maritime reconnaissance aircraft was a further development of the Bison B fitted with an extended nose to house a large search radar unit.

during 1956. Those that did become operational were modified, from 1957 onwards, to overcome these limitations; they have provision for in-flight refuelling and are re-engined with Soloviev D-15 turbofans. Current estimates put the number of M-4s in service with the DA at 73, 30 of which are believed to have been converted into tankers.

Even more impressive and eminently more successful than the M-4 was Tupolev's Tu-95 which first took to the air during 1954. Unique as the world's only operational turboprop bomber, the Tu-95 again drew heavily on earlier designs, being essentially the fuselage of the Tu-85 married to swept-back tail and wing surfaces. Power was provided by four Kuznetsov turboprops, each driving eight-bladed, counter-rotating propellers. Indeed, the development of these engines gave the West its first real clues to the aircraft's performance for they were designed by a team which included many Germans who were eventually repatriated. Their subsequent interrogation revealed the capabilities of the NK-12 turboprop and allowed realistic estimates of the Tu-95 to be made.

Given the service designation Tu-20 (Nato code-name Bear) the Tu-95 entered service during 1956 and finally gave the Soviet Union a completely viable intercontinental delivery system for its nuclear weapons. It is perhaps ironic that having achieved this goal, the Soviet Union turned towards ballistic missiles as its prime nuclear strike force.

Nevertheless, the Tu-20 was too good an aeroplane to be discarded and the six variants produced from the basic design all remain in service today. Current estimates put the number of Bears in service with the DA at 113, divided unequally between Bear-A and Bear-B models. The two types differ in that the A is configured to carry free-fall weapons while the B was originally modified to carry the AS-3 Kangaroo stand-off missile. This fearsome weapon is still the largest air-to-surface missile ever built but is probably no longer in service. Those Bear-Bs still in use now carry the smaller AS-4 Kitchen missile.

Successful as the Tu-20 was and is, the Tupolev bureau was not content to rest on its laurels and in 1959 produced the Tu-105 as a successor to the Tu-16. Powered by two Koliesov afterburning turbojets, the Tu-105 was Russia's first supersonic heavy bomber. Entering service during 1963 under the service designation Tu-22 (Nato code-name Blinder), it is capable of dash speeds in the order of Mach 1.5, but has proved to be somewhat short on range. Some 150 Tu-22s are believed to be in service with the DA, the number being made up by two models, the Blinder-A and the Blinder-B. The A is configured for free-fall weapons whilst the B carries the AS-4 air-to-surface missile. It is this latter model which is believed to make up the bulk of the DA's Tu-22 strength.

The shortcomings of the Tu-22 were overcome in the next Tupolev bomber design to see service, the Tu-22M (Nato code-name Backfire). Retaining some elements of the Tu-22, this extremely potent warplane employs a variable-geometry wing and is capable of speeds twice that of sound. Believed to have

first flown during 1969-70, current estimates put the number of Backfires in service with the DA at about 100 with a production rate of 30 a year. The Tu-22M, or Tu-26 as some sources describe it, came into prominence during the SALT II negotiations when the US delegation declared it to be a strategic system which would have to be included in the talks. The Soviet negotiators vehemently denied this and the whole subject nearly wrecked the talks. Although the Soviet Union may well employ the Tu-22M as a theatre weapon, there can be little doubt that with in-flight refuelling, the type is quite capable of delivering attacks on targets in a large section of North America.

Currently, the Soviet Union is developing a new supersonic strategic bomber for service up to the end of the century. Attempts to create such an aircraft began in 1957 when the Myasishchev M-50 (Nato code-named Bounder) appeared. Although capable of dash speeds in the order of Mach 1.4, the type appears to have been bedevilled by aerodynamic problems and was abandoned. The same fate befell the next Soviet attempt in this field, a Sukhoi design which appeared during the mid-1970s. Powered by four turbojets mounted together beneath the fuselage, the type employed a double-delta wing and has been credited with a maximum speed three times that of sound. Why the type was not continued beyond the prototype stage remains a mystery.

The latest aircraft being developed in this category is again a Tupolev design which had been given the Nato code-name Blackjack. Very similar in configuration to the American B-1 (although some 20 per cent bigger overall), Blackjack employs variable-geometry wings and is credited with a Mach 2 performance. The type is expected to enter squadron service with the DA during 1986 and to have a production run of about 100 examples.

There can be little doubt that with the emergence of the ICBM (intercontinental ballistic missile), the DA has become the 'Cinderella' arm of the Soviet Air Force. Nonetheless, its current equipment still poses a major problem to the Nato countries, especially with the widespread use of the Backfire and the introduction of the Blackjack. More subtly, the Soviet strategic bomber programme represent an aeronautical achievement which can stand alongside any in the West and one which does much to destroy the myth of the Soviet Union being technologically backward.

Tu-20 (Bear-A)

Type Heavy bomber
Dimensions Span 51.1m (167ft 8in); length 47.5m (155ft 10in); height 12.12m (39ft 9in)
Weight Empty 75,000kg (165,400lb); maximum take-off 170,000kg (375,000lb)
Powerplant Four 14,795hp Kuznetsov NK-12MV turboprops

Performance Maximum speed 845km/h (525mph) at 8000m (26,000ft)
Range 11,300km (7020 miles)

Ceiling 13,500m (44,300ft)
Armament Six 23mm NR-23 cannon; up to 20,000kg (44,100lb) of free-fall conventional or nuclear weapons

Top: An AVMF Tu-142 (AVMF designation for the Tu-20) Bear D is accompanied by a British Phantom from HMS *Ark Royal*. The Bear D features a large ventral radome and while this example, photographed in 1977, retains the tail cannon turret, more recent Bear Ds show the turret replaced by an extended tail housing which is thought to contain a long low-frequency antenna. Above: The tail turret of a Tu-20 which is armed with the NR-23 23mm cannon.

Tu-22 (Blinder-A)

Type Heavy bomber
Dimensions Span 28m (91ft 10in); length 41.5m (136ft 2in); height 10.4m (34ft)
Weight Empty 40,000kg (90,700lb)
Powerplant Believed to be two Koliesov VD-7 afterburning turbojets

Performance Maximum speed 1600km/h (1000mph) at 11,000m (36,000ft)
Range 3100km (1926 miles)

Ceiling Between 13,700m (45,000ft) and 18,000m (60,000ft)
Armament One 23mm cannon; approx 8000kg (17,600lb) of free-fall conventional or nuclear weapons

Above right: Powered by its two rear-mounted afterburning turbojets, a Soviet Tu-22 Blinder takes off. Right: Tu-22s also equip the Libyan Air Force and at least one aircraft saw action in support of Uganda against Tanzania in 1978. Below right and bottom: The Mach 2 Tu-26 Backfire cruises at high altitude over the Baltic.

Tu-22M (Backfire-A)

Type Heavy bomber
Dimensions Span 34.5m (113ft) at 20 degrees of sweep, 26.2m (86ft) at 55 degrees of sweep; length 40.23m (132ft); height 10.1m (33ft)
Weight Empty 54,500kg (120,000lb); maximum take-off 122,000kg (269,000lb)
Powerplant Believed to be two 20,000kg (44,090lb) thrust Kutnetsov NK-144 afterburning turbofans

Performance Maximum speed 2125km/h (1320mph) at 11,000m (36,000ft)
Range 5500km (3420 miles)

Ceiling Between 9000m (62,300ft) and 17,000m (55,000ft)
Armament Two 23mm cannon; up to 12,000kg (26,455lb) of free-fall conventional or nuclear weapons